D1766122

VARRO

ON THE LATIN LANGUAGE

I

LCL 333

VARRO

ON THE LATIN LANGUAGE

BOOKS V–VII

WITH AN ENGLISH TRANSLATION BY

ROLAND G. KENT

HARVARD UNIVERSITY PRESS

CAMBRIDGE, MASSACHUSETTS

LONDON, ENGLAND

First published 1938
Revised and reprinted 1951

LOEB CLASSICAL LIBRARY® is a registered trademark
of the President and Fellows of Harvard College

ISBN 978-0-674-99367-9

Printed on acid-free paper and bound by
The Maple-Vail Book Manufacturing Group

CONTENTS

INTRODUCTION

VARRO'S LIFE AND WORKS

Marcus Terentius Varro was born in 116 B.C., probably at Reate in the Sabine country, where his family, which was of equestrian rank, possessed large estates. He was a student under L. Aelius Stilo Praeconinus, a scholar of the equestrian order, widely versed in Greek and Latin literature and especially interested in the history and antiquities of the Roman people. He studied philosophy at Athens, with Antiochus of Ascalon. With his tastes thus formed for scholarship, he none the less took part in public life, and was in the campaign against the rebel Sertorius in Spain, in 76. He was an officer with Pompey in the war with the Cilician pirates in 67, and presumably also in Pompey's campaign against Mithradates. In the Civil War he was on Pompey's side, first in Spain and then in Epirus and Thessaly.

He was pardoned by Caesar, and lived quietly at Rome, being appointed librarian of the great collection of Greek and Latin books which Caesar planned to make. After Caesar's assassination, he was proscribed by Antony, and his villa at Casinum, with his personal library, was destroyed. But he himself escaped death by the devotion of friends, who concealed him, and he secured the protection of Octavian.

He lived the remainder of his life in peace and quiet, devoted to his writings, and died in 27 B.C., in his eighty-ninth year.

Throughout his life he wrote assiduously. His works number seventy-four, amounting to about six hundred and twenty books ; they cover virtually all fields of human thought : agriculture, grammar, the history and antiquities of Rome, geography, law, rhetoric, philosophy, mathematics and astronomy, education, the history of literature and the drama, satires, poems, orations, letters.

Of all these only one, his *De Re Rustica* or *Treatise on Agriculture*, in three books, has reached us complete. His *De Lingua Latina* or *On the Latin Language*, in twenty-five books, has come down to us as a torso ; only Books V. to X. are extant, and there are serious gaps in these. The other works are represented by scattered fragments only.

VARRO'S GRAMMATICAL WORKS

The grammatical works of Varro, so far as we know them, were the following :

De Lingua Latina, in twenty-five books, a fuller account of which is given below.

De Antiquitate Litterarum, in two books, addressed to the tragic poet L. Accius, who died about 86 B.C. ; it was therefore one of Varro's earliest writings.

De Origine Linguae Latinae, in three books, addressed to Pompey.

Περὶ Χαρακτήρων, in at least three books, on the formation of words.

Quaestiones Plautinae, in five books, containing

viii

interpretations of rare words found in the comedies of Plautus.

De Similitudine Verborum, in three books, on regularity in forms and words.

De Utilitate Sermonis, in at least four books, in which he dealt with the principle of anomaly or irregularity.

De Sermone Latino, in five books or more, addressed to Marcellus, which treats of orthography and the metres of poetry.

Disciplinae, an encyclopaedia on the liberal arts, in nine books, of which the first dealt with *Grammatica*.

The extant fragments of these works, apart from those of the *De Lingua Latina*, may be found in the Goetz and Schoell edition of the *De Lingua Latina*, pages 199-242 ; in the collection of Wilmanns, pages 170-223 ; and in that of Funaioli, pages 179-371 (see the Bibliography).

VARRO'S *DE LINGUA LATINA*

Varro's treatise *On the Latin Language* was a work in twenty-five books, composed in 47 to 45 B.C., and published before the death of Cicero in 43.

The first book was an introduction, containing at the outset a dedication of the entire work to Cicero. The remainder seems to have been divided into four sections of six books each, each section being by its subject matter further divisible into two halves of three books each.

Books II.-VII. dealt with the *impositio vocabulorum*, or how words were originated and applied to things

INTRODUCTION

and ideas. Of this portion, Books II.-IV. were probably an earlier smaller work entitled *De Etymologia*
or the like ; it was separately dedicated to one
Septumius or Septimius, who had at some time,
which we cannot now identify, served Varro as
quaestor. Book II. presented the arguments which
were advanced against Etymology as a branch of
learning ; Book III. presented those in its favour as a
branch of learning, and useful ; Book IV. discussed
its nature.

Books V.-VII. start with a new dedication to Cicero.
They treat of the origin of words, the sources from
which they come, and the manner in which new words
develop. Book V. is devoted to words which are the
names of places, and to the objects which are in the
places under discussion ; VI. treats words denoting
time-ideas, and those which contain some time-idea,
notably verbs ; VII. explains rare and difficult words
which are met in the writings of the poets.

Books VIII.-XIII. dealt with derivation of words
from other words, including stem-derivation, declension of nouns, and conjugation of verbs. The first
three treated especially the conflict between the
principle of Anomaly, or Irregularity, based on *consuetudo* ' popular usage,' and that of Analogy, or
Regularity of a proportional character, based on *ratio*
' relation ' of form to form. VIII. gives the arguments
against the existence of Analogy, IX. those in favour
of its existence, X. Varro's own solution of the con-
flicting views, with his decision in favour of its existence. XI.-XIII. discussed Analogy in derivation, in
the wide sense given above : probably XI. dealt with
nouns of place and associated terms, XII. with time-
ideas, notably verbs, XIII. with poetic words.

INTRODUCTION

Books XIV.-XIX. treated of syntax. Books XX.-XXV. seem to have continued the same theme, but probably with special attention to stylistic and rhetorical embellishments.

Of these twenty-five books, we have to-day, apart from a few brief fragments, only Books V. to X., and in these there are several extensive gaps where the manuscript tradition fails.

The fragments of the *De Lingua Latina*, that is, those quotations or paraphrases in other authors which do not correspond to the extant text of Books V.-X., are not numerous nor long. The most considerable of them are passages in the *Noctes Atticae* of Aulus Gellius ii. 25 and xvi. 8. They may be found in the edition of Goetz and Schoell, pages 3, 146, 192-198, and in the collections of Wilmanns and Funaioli (see the Bibliography).

It is hardly possible to discuss here even summarily Varro's linguistic theories, the sources upon which he drew, and his degree of independence of thought and procedure. He owed much to his teacher Aelius Stilo, to whom he refers frequently, and he draws heavily upon Greek predecessors, of course, but his practice has much to commend it : he followed neither the Anomalists nor the Analogists to the extreme of their theories, and he preferred to derive Latin words from Latin sources, rather than to refer practically all to Greek origins. On such topics reference may be made to the works of Barwick, Kowalski, Dam, Dahlmann, Kriegshammer, and Frederik Muller, and to the articles of Wölfflin in the eighth volume of the *Archiv für lateinische Lexikographie*, all listed in our Bibliography.

INTRODUCTION

THE MANUSCRIPTS OF THE
DE LINGUA LATINA

The text of the extant books of the *De Lingua Latina* is believed by most scholars to rest on the manuscript here first listed, from which (except for our No. 4) all other known manuscripts have been copied, directly or indirectly.

1. *Codex Laurentianus* li. 10, folios 2 to 34, parchment, written in Langobardic characters in the eleventh century, and now in the Laurentian Library at Florence. It is known as *F*.

F was examined by Petrus Victorius and Iacobus Diacetius in 1521 (see the next paragraph); by Hieronymus Lagomarsini in 1740; by Heinrich Keil in 1851; by Adolf Groth in 1877; by Georg Schoell in 1906. Little doubt can remain as to its actual readings.

2. In 1521, Petrus Victorius and Iacobus Diacetius collated *F* with a copy of the *editio princeps* of the *De Lingua Latina*, in which they entered the differences which they observed. Their copy is preserved in Munich, and despite demonstrable errors in other portions, it has the value of a manuscript for v. 119 to vi. 61, where a quaternion has since their time been lost in *F*. For this portion, their recorded readings are known as *Fv*; and the readings of the *editio princeps*, where they have recorded no variation, are known as (*Fv*).

3. The *Fragmentum Cassinense* (called also *Excerptum* and *Epitome*), one folio of *Codex Cassinensis* 361, parchment, containing v. 41 *Capitolium dictum* to the end of v. 56; of the eleventh century. It was

probably copied direct from *F* soon after *F* was written, but may possibly have been copied from the archetype of *F*. It is still at Monte Cassino, and was transcribed by Keil in 1848. It was published in facsimile as an appendix to *Sexti Iulii Frontini de aquaeductu Urbis Romae*, a phototyped reproduction of the entire manuscript, Monte Cassino, 1930.

4. The grammarian Priscian, who flourished about A.D. 500, transcribed into his *De Figuris Numerorum* Varro's passage on coined money, beginning with *multa*, last word of v. 168, and ending with *Nummi denarii decuma libella*, at the beginning of v. 174. The passage is given in H. Keil's *Grammatici Latini* iii. 410-411. There are many manuscripts, the oldest and most important being *Codex Parisinus* 7496, of the ninth century.

5. *Codex Laurentianus* li. 5, written at Florence in 1427, where it still remains ; it was examined by Keil. It is known as *f*.

6. *Codex Havniensis*, of the fifteenth century ; on paper, small quarto, 108 folia ; now at Copenhagen. It was examined by B. G. Niebuhr for Koeler, and his records came into the hands of L. Spengel. It is known as *H*.

7. *Codex Gothanus*, parchment, of the sixteenth century, now at Gotha ; it was examined by Regel for K. O. Mueller, who published its important variants in his edition, pages 270-298. It is known as *G*.

8. *Codex Parisinus* 7489, paper, of the fifteenth century, now at Paris ; this and the next two were examined by Donndorf for L. Spengel, who gives their different readings in his edition, pages 661-718. It is known as *a*.

9. *Codex Parisinus* 6142, paper, of the fifteenth

century; it goes only to viii. 7 *declinarentur*. It is known as *b*.

10. *Codex Parisinus* 7535, paper, of the sixteenth century; it contains only v. 1-122, ending with *dictae*. It is known as *c*.

11. *Codex Vindobonensis* lxiii., of the fifteenth century, at Vienna; it was examined by L. Spengel in 1835, and its important variants are recorded in the apparatus of A. Spengel's edition. It is known as *V*.

12. *Codex Basiliensis* F iv. 13, at Basel; examined by L. Spengel in 1838. It is known as *p*.

13. *Codex Guelferbytanus* 896, of the sixteenth century, at Wolfenbüttel; examined by Schneidewin for K. O. Mueller, and afterwards by L. Spengel. It is known as *M*.

14. *Codex B*, probably of the fifteenth century, now not identifiable; its variants were noted by Petrus Victorius in a copy of the *Editio Gryphiana*, and either it or a very similar manuscript was used by Antonius Augustinus in preparing the so-called *Editio Vulgata*.

These are the manuscripts to which reference is made in our critical notes; there are many others, some of greater authority than those placed at the end of our list, but their readings are mostly not available. In any case, as *F* alone has prime value, the variants of other than the first four in our list can be only the attempted improvements made by their copyists, and have accordingly the same value as that which attaches to the emendations of editors of printed editions.

Fuller information with regard to the manuscripts may be found in the following:

INTRODUCTION

Leonhard Spengel, edition of the *De Lingua Latina* (1826), pages v-xviii.

K. O. Mueller, edition (1833), pages xii-xxxi.

Andreas Spengel, edition (1885), pages ii-xxviii.

Giulio Antonibon, *Supplemento di Lezioni Varianti ai libri de lingua Latina* (1899), pages 10-23.

G. Goetz et F. Schoell, edition (1910), pages xi-xxxv.

THE LAURENTIAN MANUSCRIPT *F*

Manuscript *F* contains all the extant continuous text of the *De Lingua Latina,* except v. 119 *trua quod* to vi. 61 *dicendo finit* ; this was contained in the second quaternion, now lost, but still in place when the other manuscripts were copied from it, and when Victorius and Diacetius collated it in 1521. There are a number of important lacunae, apart from omitted lines or single words ; these are due to losses in its archetype.

Leonhard Spengel,[a] from the notations in the manuscript and the amount of text between the gaps, calculated that the archetype of *F* consisted of 16 quaternions, with these losses :

Quaternion 4 lacked folios 4 and 5, the gap after v. 162.

Quaternion 7 lacked folio 2, the end of vi. and the beginning of vii., and folio 7, the gap after vii. 23.

Quaternion 11 was missing entire, the end of viii. and the beginning of ix.

Quaternion 15 lacked folios 1 to 3, the gap after x. 23, and folios 6 to 8, the gap after x. 34.

The amount of text lost at each point can be cal-

[a] *Über die Kritik der Varronischen Bücher de Lingua Latina*, pp. 5-12.

culated from the fact that one folio of the archetype held about 50 lines of our text.

There is a serious transposition in *F*, in the text of Book V. In § 23, near the end, after *qui ad humum*, there follows *ut Sabini*, now in § 32, and so on to *Septimontium*, now in § 41 ; then comes *demissior*, now in § 23 after *humum*, and so on to *ab hominibus*, now in § 32, after which comes *nominatum* of § 41. Mueller,[a] who identified the transposition and restored the text to its true order in his edition, showed that the alteration was due to the wrong folding of folios 4 and 5 in the first quaternion of an archetype of *F* ; though this was not the immediate archetype of *F*, since the amount of text on each page was different.

This transposition is now always rectified in our printed texts ; but there is probably another in the later part of Book V., which has not been remedied because the breaks do not fall inside the sentences, thus making the text unintelligible. The sequence of topics indicates that v. 115-128 should stand between v. 140 and v. 141 [b] ; there is then the division by topics :

General Heading	v. 105
De Victu	v. 105-112
De Vestitu	v. 113-114, 129-133
De Instrumento	v. 134-140, 115-128, 141-183

[a] In the preface to his edition, pp. xvii-xviii. The disorder in the text had previously been noticed by G. Buchanan, Turnebus, and Scaliger, and discussed by L. Spengel, *Emendationum Varronianarum Specimen I*, pp. 17-19.

[b] L. Spengel, *Emendationum Varronianarum Specimen I*, pp. 13-19, identified this transposition, but considered the transpositions to be much more complicated, with the following order: §§ 105-114, §§ 129-140, § 128, §§ 166-168, §§ 118-127, §§ 115-117, §§ 141-165, § 169 on.

Then also vi. 49 and vi. 45 may have changed places, but I have not introduced this into the present text; I have however adopted the transfer of x. 18 from its manuscript position after x. 20, to the position before x. 19, which the continuity of the thought clearly demands.

The text of *F* is unfortunately very corrupt, and while there are corrections both by the first hand and by a second hand, it is not always certain that the corrections are to be justified.

THE ORTHOGRAPHY OF THE
DE LINGUA LATINA

The orthography of *F* contains not merely many corrupted spellings which must be corrected, but also many variant spellings which are within the range of recognized Latin orthography, and these must mostly be retained in any edition. For there are many points on which we are uncertain of Varro's own practice, and he even speaks of certain permissible variations : if we were to standardize his orthography, we should do constant violence to the best manuscript tradition, without any assurance that we were in all respects restoring Varro's own spelling. Moreover, as this work is on language, Varro has intentionally varied some spellings to suit his etymological argument ; any extensive normalization might, and probably would, do him injustice in some passages. Further, Varro quotes from earlier authors who used an older orthography ; we do not know whether Varro, in quoting from them, tried to use their original orthography, or merely used the orthography which was his own habitual practice.

I have therefore retained for the most part the spellings of *F*, or of the best authorities when *F* fails, replacing only a few of the more misleading spellings by the familiar ones, and allowing other variations to remain. These variations mostly fall within the following categories :

1. EI : Varro wrote EI for the long vowel I in the nom. pl. of Decl. II (ix. 80) ; but he was probably not consistent in writing EI everywhere. The manuscript testifies to its use in the following : *plebei* (gen. ; *cf. plebis* vi. 91, in a quotation) v. 40, 81, 158, vi. 87 ; *eidem* (nom. sing.) vii. 17 (*eadem F*), x. 10 ; *scirpeis* vii. 44 ; *Terentiei* (nom.), *vireis Terentieis* (masc.), *Terentieis* (fem.) viii. 36 ; *infeineiteis* viii. 50 (changed to *infiniteis* in our text, *cf.* ⟨*in*⟩*finitam* viii. 52) ; *i*⟨*e*⟩*is* viii. 51 (*his F*), ix. 5 ; *iei* (nom.) ix. 2, 35 ; *hei re*⟨*e*⟩*i fer*⟨*re*⟩*ei de*⟨*e*⟩*i* viii. 70 ; *hinnulei* ix. 28 ; *utrei* (nom. pl.) ix. 65 (*utre.I. F* ; *cf. utri* ix. 65) ; ⟨*B*⟩*a*⟨*e*⟩*biei*, *B*⟨*a*⟩*ebieis* x. 50 (alongside *Caelii, Celiis*).

2. AE and E : Varro, as a countryman, may in some words have used E where residents of the city of Rome used AE (*cf.* v. 97) ; but the standard orthography has been introduced in our text, except that E has been retained in *seculum* and *sepio* (and its compounds : v. 141, 150, 157, 162, vii. 7, 13), which always appear in this form.

3. OE and U : The writing OE is kept where it appears in the manuscript or is supported by the context : *moerus* and derivatives v. 50, 141 *bis*, 143, vi. 87 ; *moenere, moenitius* v. 141 ; *Poenicum* v. 113, viii. 65 *bis* ; *poeniendo* v. 177. OE in other words is the standard orthography.

INTRODUCTION

4. VO UO and VU UU : Varro certainly wrote
only VO or UO, but the manuscript rarely shows
VO or UO in inflectional syllables. The examples
are *novom* ix. 20 (corrected from *nouum* in *F*) ; *nominatuom* ix. 95, x. 30 (both *-tiuom F*) ; *obliquom* x. 50 ;
loquontur vi. 1, ix. 85 ; *sequontur* x. 71 ; *clivos* v. 158 ;
perhaps *amburvom* v. 127 (*impurro Fv*). In initial
syllables VO is almost regular : *volt* vi. 47, etc. ;
volpes v. 101 ; *volgus* v. 58, etc., but *vulgo* viii. 66 ;
Volcanus v. 70, etc. ; *volsillis* ix. 33. Examples of the
opposite practice are *aequum* vi. 71 ; *duum* x. 11 ;
antiquus vi. 68 ; *sequuntur* viii. 25 ; *confluunt* x. 50.
Our text preserves the manuscript readings.

5. UV before a vowel : Varro probably wrote U and
not UV before a vowel, except initially, where his
practice may have been the other way. The examples
are : *Pacuius* v. 60, vi. 6 (*catulus* (*Fv*)), 94, vii. 18, 76,
and *Pacuvius* v. 17, 24, vii. 59 ; gen. *Pacui* v. 7, vi. 6,
vii. 22 ; *Pacuium* vii. 87, 88, 91, 102 ; *compluium*,
impluium v. 161, and *pluvia* v. 161, *compluvium* v. 125 ;
simpuium v. 124 bis (*simpulum* codd.) ; cf. *panuvellium*
v. 114. Initially : *uvidus* v. 24 ; *uvae, uvore* v. 104 ·
uvidum v. 109.

6. U and I : Varro shows in medial syllables a
variation between U and I, before P or B or F or M
plus a vowel. The orthography of the manuscript
has been retàined in our text, though it is likely
that Varro regularly used U in these types :

The superlative and similar words : *albissumum*
viii. 75 ; *frugalissumus* viii. 77 ; *c⟨a⟩esi⟨s⟩sumus* viii.
76 ; *intumus* v. 154 ; *maritumae* v. 113 ; *melissumum*
viii. 76 ; *optumum* vii. 51 ; *pauperrumus* viii. 77 ;
proxuma etc. v. 36, 93, ix. 115, x. 4, 26 ; *septuma* etc.
ix. 30, x. 46 *ter* ; *Septumio* v. 1, vii. 109 ; *superrumo*

INTRODUCTION

vii. 51 ; *decuma* vi. 54. *Cf. proxima optima maxima*
v. 102, *minimum* vii. 101, and many in viii. 75-78.

Compounds of *-fex* and derivatives : *pontufex* v. 83,
pontufices v. 83 (*F²* for *pontifices*) ; *artufices* ix. 12 ;
sacruficiis v. 98, 124. *Cf. pontifices* v. 23, vi. 54, etc. ;
artifex v. 93, ix. 111, etc. ; *sacrificium* vii. 88, etc.

Miscellaneous words : *monumentum* v. 148, but
monimentum etc. v. 41, vi. 49 *bis* ; *mancupis* v. 40, but
mancipium etc. v. 163, vi. 74, 85 ; *quadrupes* v. 34,
but *quadripedem* etc. vii. 39 *bis*, *quadriplex* etc. x. 46
etc., *quadripertita* etc. v. 12 etc.

7. LUBET and LIBET : Varro probably wrote
lubet, lubido, etc., but the orthography varies, and the
manuscript tradition is kept in our text : *lubere
lubendo* vi. 47, *lubenter* vii. 89, *lubitum* ix. 34, *lubidine*
x. 56 ; and *libido* vi. 47, x. 60, *libidinosus Libentina
Libitina* vi. 47, *libidine* x. 61.

8. H : Whether Varro used the initial H according
to the standard practice at Rome, is uncertain. In
the country it was likely to be dropped in pronunciation ; and the manuscript shows variation in its use.
We have restored the H in our text according to the
usual orthography, except that *irpices*, v. 136 *bis*, has
been left because of the attendant text. Examples
of its omission are *Arpocrates* v. 57 ; *Ypsicrates* v. 88 ;
aedus ircus v. 97 ; *olus olera* v. 108, x. 50 ; *olitorium*
v. 146 ; *olitores* vi. 20 ; *ortis* v. 103, *ortórum* v. 146 *bis*,
orti vi. 20 ; *aruspex* vii. 88. These are normalized in
our text, along with certain other related spellings :
sepulchrum vii. 24 is made to conform to the usual
sepulcrum, and the almost invariable *nichil* and
nichili have been changed to *nihil* and *nihili*.

9. X and CS : There are traces of a writing CS for
X, which has in these instances been kept in the text :

arcs vii. 44 (*ares F*) ; *acsitiosae* (*ac sitiose F*), **acsitiosa**
(*ac sitio a- F*) vi. 66 ; *ducs* (*duces F*) x. 57.

10. DOUBLED CONSONANTS : Varro's practice in this
matter is uncertain, in some words. *F* regularly
has *littera* (only *literis* v. 3 has one T), but *obliterata*
(ix. 16, *-atae* ix. 21, *-avit* v. 52), and these spellings
are kept in our text. *Communis* has been made
regular, though *F* usually has one M ; *casus* is invariable, except for *de cassu in cassum* viii. 39, which
has been retained as probably coming from Varro
himself. *Iupiter*, with one P, is retained, because
invariable in *F* ; the only exception is *Iuppitri* viii. 33
(*iuppiti F*), which has also been kept. *Numo* vi. 61,
for *nummo*, has been kept as perhaps an archaic
spelling. *Decusis* ix. 81 has for the same reason been
kept in the citation from Lucilius. In a few words
the normal orthography has been introduced in the
text : *grallator* vii. 69 *bis* for *gralator*, *grabatis* viii. 32
for *grabattis*. For combinations resulting from prefixes see the next paragraph.

11. CONSONANTS OF PREFIXES : Varro's usage here
is quite uncertain, whether he kept the unassimilated
consonants in the compounds. Apparently in some
groups he made the assimilations, in others he did not.
The evidence is as follows, the variant orthography
being retained in our text :

Ad-c- : always *acc-*, except possibly *adcensos* vii.
58 (*F²*, for *acensos F¹*).

Ad-f- : always *aff-*, except *adfuerit* vi. 40.

Ad-l- : always *all-*, except *adlocutum* vi. 57, *adlucet*
vi. 79, *adlatis* (*ablatis F*) ix. 21.

Ad-m- : always *adm-*, except *ammonendum* v. 6,
amministrat vi. 78, *amminicula* vii. 2, *amminister* vii. 34
(*F²*, for *adm- F¹*).

INTRODUCTION

Ad-s- : regularly *ass-*, but also *adserere* vi. 64, *adsiet* vi. 92, *adsimus* vii. 99, *adsequi* viii. 8, x. 9, *adsignificare* often (always except *assignificant* vii. 80), *adsumi* viii. 69, *adsumat* ix. 42, *adsumere* x. 58.

Ad-sc-, ad-sp-, ad-st- : always with loss of the D, as in *ascendere, ascribere, ascriptos* (vii. 57), *ascriptivi* (vii. 56), *aspicere, aspectus, astans*.

Ad-t- : always *att-*, except *adtributa* v. 48, and possibly *adtinuit* (F^1, but *att-* F^2) ix. 59.

Con-l-, con-b-, con-m-, con-r-: always *coll-, comb-, comm-, corr-*.

Con-p- : always *comp-*, except *conpernis* ix. 10.

Ex-f- : always *eff-*, except *exfluit* v. 29.

Ex-s- : *exsolveret* v. 176, *exsuperet* vi. 50, but *exuperantum* vii. 18 (normalized in our text to *exsuperantum*).

Ex-sc- : *exculpserant* v. 143.

Ex-sp- : always *expecto* etc. vi. 82, x. 40, etc.

Ex-sq- : regularly *Esquiliis* ; but *Exquilias* v. 25, *Exquiliis* v. 159 (*Fv*), normalized to *Esq-* in our text.

Ex-st : *extat* v. 3, vi. 78 ; but *exstat* v. 3, normalized to *extat* in our text.

In-l- : usually *ill-*, but *inlicium* vi. 88 *bis*, 93 (*illicitum F*), 94, 95, *inliceret* vi. 90, *inliciatur* vi. 94 ; the variation is kept in our text.

In-m- : always *imm-*, except in ⟨*in*⟩*mutatis* vi. 38, where the restored addition is unassimilated to indicate the negative prefix and not the local *in*.

In-p- : always *imp-*, except *inpos* v. 4 *bis* (once *ineos F*), *inpotem* v. 4 (*inpotentem F*), *inplorat* vi. 68.

Ob-c-, ob-f-, ob-p- : always *occ-, off-, opp-*.

Ob-t- : always *opt-*, as in *optineo* etc. vii. 17, 91, x. 19, *optemperare* ix. 6.

Per-l- : *pellexit* vi. 94, but *perlucent* v. 140.

INTRODUCTION

Sub-c-, sub-f-, sub-p- : always *succ-, suff-, supp-,* except *subcidit* v. 116.

Sub-s- and *subs-* + consonant : regularly *sus-* + consonant, except *subscribunt* vii. 107.

Sub-t- : only in *suptilius* x. 40.

Trans-l- : in *tralatum* vi. 77, vii. 23, 103, x. 71 ; *tralaticio* vi. 55 (*tranlatio Fv*) and *translaticio* v. 32, vi. 64 (*tranślatio F, tranlatio Fv*), *translaticiis* vi. 78.

Trans-v- : in *travolat* v. 118, and *transversus* vii. 81, x. 22, 23, 43.

Trans-d- : in *traducere.*

12. DE and DI : The manuscript has been followed in the orthography of the following : *directo* vii. 15, *dirigi* viii. 26, *derecti* x. 22 bis, *deriguntur derectorum* x. 22, *derecta directis* x. 43, *directas* x. 44, *derigitur* x. 74 ; *deiunctum* x. 45, *deiunctae* x. 47.

13. SECOND DECLENSION : Nom. sing. and acc. sing. in *-uom* and *-uum*, see 5.

Gen. sing. of nouns in *-ius* : Varro used the form ending in a single I (*cf.* viii. 36), and a few such forms stand in the manuscript : *Muci* v. 5 (*muti F*) ; *Pacui* v. 7, vi. 6, vii. 22 ; *Mani* vi. 90 ; *Quinti* vi. 92, *Ephesi* viii. 22 (*ephesis F*), *Plauti et Marci* viii. 36, *dispendi* ix. 54 (quoted, metrical ; alongside *dispendii* ix. 54). The gen. in II is much commoner ; both forms are kept in our text.

Nom. pl., written by Varro with EI (*cf.* ix. 80) ; examples are given in 1, above.

Gen. pl. : The older form in *-um* for certain words (*denarium, centumvirum*, etc.) is upheld viii. 71, ix. 82, 85, and occurs occasionally elsewhere : *Velabrum* v. 44, *Querquetulanum* v. 49, *Sabinum* v. 74, etc.

Dat.-abl. pl., written by Varro with EIS (*cf.* ix. 80) ;

examples are given in 1, above, but the manuscript regularly has IS.

Dat.-abl. pl. of nouns ending in *-ius*, *-ia*, *-ium*, are almost always written IIS ; there are a few for which the manuscript has IS, which we have normalized to IIS : *Gabis* v. 33, ⟨*Es*⟩*quilis* v. 50, *hostis* v. 98, *Publicis* v. 158, *Faleris* v. 162, *praeverbis* vi. 82 (cf. *praeverbiis* vi. 38 *bis*), *mysteris* vii. 34 (cf. *mysteriis* vii. 19), *miliaris* ix. 85 (*militaris F*).

Deus shows the following variations : Nom. pl. *de*⟨*e*⟩*i* viii. 70, *dei* v. 57, 58 *bis*, 66, 71, vii. 36, ix. 59, *dii* v. 58, 144, vii. 16 ; dat.-abl. pl. *deis* v. 122, vii. 45, *diis* v. 69, 71, 182, vi. 24, 34, vii. 34.

14. THIRD DECLENSION : The abl. sing. varies between E and I : *supellectile* viii. 30, 32, ix. 46, and *supellectili* ix. 20 (*-lis F*) ; cf. also *vesperi* (*uespert- F*) and *vespere* ix. 73.

Nom. pl., where ending in IS in the manuscript, is altered to ES; the examples are *mediocris* v. 5; *partis* v. 21, 56; *ambonis* v. 115; *urbis* v. 143; *aedis* v. 160; *compluris* vi. 15; *Novendialis* vi. 26 ; *auris* vi. 83 ; *disparilis* viii. 67 ; *lentis* ix. 34; *omnis* ix. 81; *dissimilis* ix. 92.

Gen. pl. in UM and IUM, see viii. 67. In view of *dentum* viii. 67, expressly championed by Varro, *Veientum* v. 30 (*uenientum F*), *caelestum* vi. 53, *Quiritum* vi. 68 have been kept in our text.

Acc. pl. in ES and IS, see viii. 67. Varro's distribution of the two endings seems to have been purely empirical and arbitrary, and the manuscript readings have been retained in our text.

15. FOURTH DECLENSION : Gen. sing. : Gellius, *Noctes Atticae* iv. 16. 1, tells us that Varro always used UIS in this form. Nonius Marcellus 483-494 M. cites

eleven such forms from Varro, but also *sumpti*. The *De Lingua Latina* gives the following partial examples of this ending : *usuis* ix. 4 (*suis F*), x. 73 (*usui F*), *casuis* x. 50 (*casuum F*), x. 62 (*casus his F*). Examples of this form ending in US are kept in our text : *fructus* v. 34, 134, *senatus* v. 87, *exercitus* v. 88, *panus* v. 105, *domus* v. 162, *census* v. 181, *motus* vi. 3, *sonitus* vi. 67 *bis*, *sensus* vi. 80, *usus* viii. 28, 30 *bis*, *casus* ix. 76, *manus* ix. 80.

Gen. pl.: For the variation between UUM and UOM see 4, above. The form with one U is found in *tribum* v. 56, *ortum* v. 66, *manum* vi. 64 (*manu F*), *magistratum* viii. 83 (*-tus F*), *declinatum* x. 54 ; these have been normalized in our text to UUM (except *manum*, in an archaic formula). Note the following forms in the manuscript : *cornuum* v. 117, *declinatuum* vi. 36 (*-tiuum Fv*), x. 31, 32, 54, *sensuum* vi. 80 ; *tribuum* vi. 86; *fructuum* ix. 27 ; *casuum* ix. 77, x. 14, 23, *manuum* ix. 80, *nominatuom* (*-tiuom F*) ix. 95, x. 30, *nominatuum* x. 19.

16. HETEROCLITES : There are the following : gen. sing. *plebei* v. 40, 81, 158, vi. 87, and *plebis* vi. 91 ; nom. sing. *elephans* and acc. pl. *elephantos* vii. 39 ; abl. sing. *Titano* vii. 16 ; abl. pl. *vasis* v. 121, *poematis* vii. 2, 36, viii. 14, and *poematibus* vii. 34.

17. GREEK FORMS : There are the following : acc. sing. *analogian* ix. 1, 26, 33, 34, 45, 49, 76, 79, 105, 113, 114, but also *analogiam* ix. 90, 100, 110, x. 2, and *analogia⟨m⟩* ix. 95, 111. Acc. sing. *Aethiopa* viii. 38 (*ethiopam F*). Nom. pl. *Aeolis* v. 25, 101, 102, 175, *Athenaiis* viii. 35.

18. FORMS OF IS AND IDEM : The forms in the manuscript are kept in our text ; there are the following to be noted :

Nom. sing. masc.: *idem* often; also *eidem* vii. 17 (*eadem F*), x. 10.

Nom. pl.: *ii* v. 26, ix. 2; *iei* ix. 2, 35; *idem* ix. 19.

Dat.-abl. pl.: *eis* vi. 18, vii. 102, ix. 4, x. 8; *ieis* viii. 51 (*his F*, but assured by context), ix. 5; *is* vii. 5 (*dis F*); *iisdem* vi. 38; *isdem* vii. 8 (*hisdem F*), viii. 35 *bis* (*hisdem F*).

19. QUOM and CUM etc.: Varro wrote *quom*, *quor*, *quoius*, *quoi*, and not *cum*, *cur*, *cuius*, *cui*, though the latter spellings are much commoner in the manuscripts, the readings of which are kept in our text. *Quom* is not infrequent, being found vi. 42, 56, vii. 4, 105, viii. 1, x. 6, and in other passages where slight emendation is necessary. *Quor* is found only corrected to *cur*, viii. 68, 71, and hidden under *quorum* corrected to *quod*, viii. 78. *Quoius* is written viii. 44, ix. 43, x. 3, and in other passages where emendation is necessary. *Quoi* nowhere appears, unless it should be read for *qui* vi. 72, and *quoique* for *quoque* ix. 34, adopted in our text.

Both *qui* and *quo* are used for the abl. sing. of the relative, and *quis* and *quibus* for the dat.-abl. pl., and similar forms for *quidam*. *In quo* is used with a plural antecedent of any gender: v. 108, vi. 2, 55, 82, vii. 26, viii. 83, ix. 1, x. 8, 41.

20. ALTER and NEUTER: Gen. *alii* ix. 67 is found as well as *alterius* ix. 91; *neutri* ix. 62, *neutra⟨e⟩* x. 73, as well as *neutrius* ix. 1; dat. fem. *aliae* x. 15.

21. CONTRACTED PERFECTS: Only the contracted perfects are found, such as *appellarunt* v. 22 etc., *declinarit* v. 7, *aberraro* v. 13, *appellassent* ix. 69, *curasse* vii. 38, *consuerunt consuessent* ix. 68, *consuerit* ix. 14 *bis*; exceptions, *novissent* vi. 60, *auspicaverit* vi. 86 (quoted), *nuncupavero* vii. 8 (quoted), *vitaverunt* x. 9.

Similarly, the V is omitted after I, as in *praeterii* ix. 7, *prodierunt* v. 13, *expediero* viii. 24, etc. ; exception, *quivero* v. 5 (F^2, for *quiero* F^1).

22. PONO in Perfect : The text always has *posui* and its forms, except twice, which we have standardized : *imposiverunt* viii. 8, *imposierint* ix. 34.

23. GERUNDIVES : Varro used the old form of the gerundive and gerund with UND in the third and fourth conjugations, but the forms have mostly been replaced by those with END. The remaining examples of the older form are *ferundo* v. 104, *ferundum* vi. 29, *faciundo* vii. 9, *quaerundae* vii. 35, *reprehendundi* ix. 12, *reprehendundus* ix. 93.

24. VERSUS : The older forms *vorto, vorti, vorsus* are not found in the manuscript. The adverbial compounds of *versus* have (with one exception) been retained in our text as they appear in the manuscript : *susus versus* v. 158, *susum versus* ix. 65; *deorsum, susum* v. 161 ; *rursus* vi. 46, 49, ix. 86 ; *deosum versus* ix. 86 ; *prosus* and *rusus* (*rosus F*) x. 52.

THE EDITIONS OF THE
DE LINGUA LATINA

There are the following printed editions of the *De Lingua Latina,* some of which appeared in numerous reprintings :

1. *Editio princeps,* edited by Pomponius Laetus ; without statement of place and date, but probably printed at Rome by Georgius Lauer, 1471. It rests upon a manuscript similar to *M.*

A second printing, also without place and date, but probably printed at Venice by Franc. Renner de

Hailbrun, 1472, was used by Victorius and Diacetius in recording the readings of *F*, and this copy was used by L. Spengel for his readings of *F* and of Laetus ; as compared with the 1471 printing, it shows a number of misprints.

2. *Editio vetustissima*, edited by Angelus Tifernas with but slight variation from the edition of Laetus ; probably printed at Rome by Georgius Sachsel de Reichenhal, 1474.

3. *Editio Rholandelli*, edited by Franciscus Rholandellus Trivisanus ; printed at Venice, 1475. It shows improvement over the edition of Laetus, by the introduction of readings from relatively good manuscripts.

4. *Editio Veneta*, similar to the preceding, but in the same volume with *Nonius Marcellus* and *Festus* ; first printed in 1483, and reprinted in 1492 by Nicolaus de Ferraris de Pralormo (L. Spengel's *Editio Veneta I*), and in 1498 by Magister Antonius de Gusago (Spengel's *Veneta II*).

A Venice edition of 1474, printed by Ioh. de Colonia and Ioh. Manthem de Gherretzen, was used by Goetz and Schoell and cited as *Ed. Ven.* in their edition.

5. *Editio Baptistae Pii*, edited by Baptista Pius, an eclectic text based on previous editions, but with some independent emendations ; printed at Milan by Leonardus Pachel, 1510.

6. *Editio Aldina*, edited by Aldus Manutius after the edition of Pius, but with some changes through his own emendations and in accordance with manuscript testimony, possibly including that of *F* ; printed at Venice by Aldus, 1513. The volume includes the *Cornucopia Perotti*, the *De Lingua Latina*, *Festus*, and *Nonius Marcellus* ; it was reprinted at Venice by

INTRODUCTION

Aldus in 1517 and 1527, and at Basel and Paris several times, up to 1536. The 1527 printing shows some improvements (see 7).

7. *Editio Parisiensis*, edited by Michael Bentinus, and essentially following the Aldine of 1527, for which Bentinus collated a number of manuscripts and used their readings ; it includes also the *Castigationes* or *Corrections* of Bentinus, a series of critical and explanatory comments. It was printed at Paris by Colinaeus, 1529.

8. *Editio Gryphiana*, similar to the preceding, including the *Castigationes* of Bentinus, and the fragments of the *Origines* of M. Porcius Cato ; for its preparation, Petrus Victorius had transcribed the readings of *B* as far as ix. 74. It was published at Lyons by Sebastian Gryphius, 1535.

9. *Editio Vulgata*, edited by Antonius Augustinus, with the readings of *B* (received from Petrus Victorius) and the help of Angelus Colotius, Octavius Pantagathus, and Gabriel Faernus ; it was printed at Rome by Vinc. Luchinus in 1554 and again by Antonius Bladus in 1557.

The text of the *De Lingua Latina* has been regarded as greatly corrupted in this edition, since Augustinus based it on a poor manuscript, introduced a great number of his own emendations, and attempted a standardization of the orthography, notably in writing *quom* and the like, and in using EI for long I in endings (*e.g.*, dat.-abl. pl. *heis libreis*, acc. pl. *simileis*, gen. sing. *vocandei*). Despite his errors, he has made a number of valuable emendations, as will be seen from the citations in our apparatus criticus.

The text of this edition was rather closely followed by all editors except Vertranius and Scioppius, and

Scaliger in his emendations, until the edition of Leonhard Spengel in 1826.

10. *Editio Vertranii*, edited by M. Vertranius Maurus, following the edition of Augustinus, but discarding the spellings of the type *quom* and the use of EI for long I, and making a large number of his own conjectural emendations ; printed at Lyons by Gryphii Heredes, 1563.

11. *Coniectanea in M. Terentium Varronem de Lingua Latina*, by Josephus Scaliger ; not an edition, but deserving a place here, as it contains numerous textual criticisms as well as other commentary ; written in 1564, and published at Paris in 1565. Both these *Coniectanea* and an *Appendix ad Coniectanea* (the original date of which I cannot determine) are printed with many later editions of the *De Lingua Latina*.

12. *Editio Turnebi*, edited by Adrianus Turnebus, who used a manuscript very similar to *p* and made numerous emendations ; printed at Paris by A. Wechelus, 1566 (Turnebus died 1565).

13. *Opera quae supersunt*, with Scaliger's *Coniectanea*, printed at Paris by Henr. Stephanus, 1569.

14. Edition of Dionysius Gothofredus, containing only an occasional independent alteration ; in *Auctores Linguae Latinae in unum corpus redacti*, printed at Geneva by Guilelmus Leimarius, 1585.

15. Edition, with the notes of Ausonius Popma ; printed at Leiden ex officina Plantiniana, 1601.

16. *Editio Gaspari Scioppii*, edited by Gaspar Scioppius, who relied on data of Gabriel Faernus and on collations of Vatican manuscripts by Fulvius Ursinus ; it contains many valuable textual suggestions, though perhaps most of them belong to Ursinus rather than to Scioppius (who expressly gives credit to Faernus,

Turnebus, and Ursinus).   It was printed at Ingolstad in 1602 ; reprinted in 1605.

17. *Editio Bipontina*, in two volumes, the second containing a selection of the notes of Augustinus, Turnebus, Scaliger, and Popma ; issued at Bipontium (Zweibrücken in Bavaria), 1788.

18. *M. Terenti Varronis de Lingua Latina libri qui supersunt*, edited by Leonhard Spengel of Munich ; the first scientific edition, resting on readings of F (but only as represented by Fv), H, B, a, b, c, and a comparison of all, or almost all, the previous editions. It was printed in Berlin by Duncker und Humbloth, 1826.

19. *M. Terenti Varronis de Lingua Latina librorum quae supersunt*, edited by Karl Ottfried Mueller, who added the readings of G to his critical apparatus. Mueller has the merit of setting the paragraphs of v. 23-41 in their proper order, and of placing brief but valuable explanatory material in his notes, in addition to textual criticism.   This edition was printed at Leipzig by Weidmann, 1833.

20. *M. T. Varronis librorum de Lingua Latina quae supersunt*, reprinted after Mueller's edition with a very few textual changes by A. Egger ; issued at Paris by Bourgeois-Maze, 1837.

21. *Varron de la Langue Latine*, a translation into French by Huot, accompanied by Mueller's text ; in the *Collection des Auteurs Latins avec la traduction en français*, directed by Nisard, printed at Paris by Firmin Didot Frères and issued by Dubochet et Cie., 1845.

22. *Libri di M. Terenzio Varrone intorno alla lingua latina*, edited and translated with notes by Pietro Canal ; in the *Biblioteca degli Scrittori Latini* with

translation and notes; printed at Venice by Gius. Antonelli, 1846–1854. It was reprinted in 1874, with addition of the fragments, to which notes were attached by Fed. Brunetti.

This edition is little known, and deserves more attention than it has received, although Canal was very free with his emendation of the text; but he used a number of additional manuscripts which are in the libraries of Italy.

23. *M. Terenti Varronis de Lingua Latina libri*, edited by Andreas Spengel after the death of his father Leonhard, who had been working on a second edition for nearly fifty years when he died; printed at Berlin by Weidmann, 1885.

This edition is notable because of the abundant critical apparatus.

24. *M. Terenti Varronis de Lingua Latina quae supersunt*, edited by Georg Goetz and Friedrich Schoell; printed at Leipzig by Teubner, 1910.

This edition is very conservative, many corrupt passages being marked with a dagger and left in the text, while excellent emendations for the same are relegated to the apparatus criticus or to the *Annotationes* at the end of the volume; but it has great value for its citation of abundant testimonia and its elaborate indexes.

Two errors of earlier editors may be mentioned at this point. Since Varro in v. 1 speaks of having sent three previous books to Septumius, our Book V. was thought to be Book IV.; and it was not until Spengel's edition of 1826 that the proper numbering came into use. Further, Varro's remark in viii. 1 on the subject matter caused the early editors to think that they had

INTRODUCTION

De Lingua Latina Libri Tres (our v.-vii.), and *De Analogia Libri Tres* (our viii.-x.) ; Augustinus in the Vulgate was the first to realize that the six books were parts of one and the same work, the *De Lingua Latina.*

It is convenient to list here, together, the special treatments of the passage on the city of Rome, **v.** 41-56, which is given by the *Fragmentum Cassinense* :

H. Keil, *Rheinisches Museum* vi. 142-145 (1848).

L. Spengel, *Über die Kritik der varronischen Bücher de Lingua Latina* ; in *Abhandl. d. k. bayer. Ak. d. Wiss.* 7, 47-54 (1854).

B. ten Brink, *M. Terentii Varronis Locus de Urbe Roma* ; Traiecti ad Rhenum, apud C. Van der Post Juniorem, 1855.

H. Jordan, *Topographie der Stadt Rom im Alterthum* ii. 599-603 (Berlin, 1871).

BIBLIOGRAPHY

A bibliography of editions, books, and articles, for the period 1471–1897, is given by Antonibon, *Supplemento di Lezioni Varianti*, pages 179-187 ; but there are many misprints, and many omissions of items. Bibliographical lists will be found in the following :

Bibliotheca Philologica Classica, supplement to *Bursian's Jahresberichte.*

Dix années de philologie classique 1914–1924, i. 428-429, edited by J. Marouzeau (1927).

L'Année philologique i. for 1924–1926 ; ii. for 1927, etc., edited by J. Marouzeau (1928 ff.).

INTRODUCTION

Critical summaries of the literature will be found as follows :

1826–1858 : *Philologus* xiii. 684-751 (1858), by L. Mercklin.

1858–1868 : *Philologus* xxvii. 286-331 (1868), by A. Riese.

1867–1876 : *Philologus* xl. 649-651 (1881), merely listed.

1877–1890 : *Bursian's Jahresberichte über den Fortschritt der klassischen Philologie* lxviii. 121-122 (1892), by G. Goetz.

1891–1901 : *Bursian's Jrb.* cxiii. 116-128 (1901), by P. Wessner.

1901–1907 : *Bursian's Jrb.* cxxxix. 85-89 (1908), by R. Kriegshammer.

1901–1920 : *Bursian's Jrb.* clxxxviii. 52-69 (1921), by P. Wessner.

1921–1925 : *Bursian's Jrb.* ccxxxi. 35-38 (1931), by F. Lammert.

For the period before the edition of L. Spengel in 1826, it is unnecessary to do other than refer to the list of editions ; for other writings on Varro were few, and they are mostly lacking in importance, apart from being inaccessible to-day. The following selected list includes most of the literature since 1826, which has importance for the *De Lingua Latina*, either for the text and its interpretation, or for Varro's style, sources, and method ; but treatises dealing with his influence on later authors have mostly been omitted from the list :

Antonibon, Giulio : *Contributo agli studi sui libri de Lingua Latina ; Rivista di Filologia* xvii. 177-221 (1888).

INTRODUCTION

Antonibon, G.: *De Codice Varroniano Mutinensi;* *Philologus* xlviii. 185 (1889).

Antonibon, G.: *Supplemento di Lezioni Varianti ai libri De Lingua Latina de M. Ter. Varrone;* Bassano, 1899.

Barwick, K.: *Remmius Palämon und die römische Ars grammatica;* Leipzig, 1922 (*Philologus*, Suppl. xv. 2).

Bednara, Ernst: *Archiv für lateinische Lexikographie* xiv. 593 (1906).

Bergk, Th.: *Quaestiones Lucretianae;* Index Lectionum in Acad. Marburg. 1846-1847.

Bergk, Th.: *De Carminum Saliarium Reliquiis;* Index Lectionum in Acad. Marburg. 1847–1848.

Bergk, Th.: *Quaestiones Ennianae;* Index Scholarum in Univ. Hal. 1860.

Bergk, Th.: *Varroniana;* Index Scholarum in Univ. Hal. 1863.

Bergk, Th.: *De Paelignorum Sermone;* Index Scholarum in Univ. Hal. 1864.

Bergk, Th.: *Zeitschrift für die Altertumswissenschaft* ix. 231 (1851), xiv. 138-140 (1856).

Bergk, Th.: *Philologus* xiv. 186, 389-390 (1859), xxx. 682 (1870), xxxii. 567 (1873), xxxiii. 281, 301-302, 311 (1874).

Bergk, Th.: *Jahrbücher für classische Philologie* lxxxiii. 317, 320-321, 333-334, 633-637 (1861); ci. 829-832, 841 (1870).

Bergk, Th.: *Rheinisches Museum* xx. 291 (1865).

Bergk, Th.: *Kleine Philologische Schriften* (Halle, 1884); passim, reprinting most of the articles listed above.

Birt, Th.: *Rheinisches Museum* liv. 50 (1899).

INTRODUCTION

Birt, Th. : *Philologus* lxxxiii. 40-41 (1928).

Boissier, Gaston : *Étude sur la vie et les ouvrages de M. T. Varron* ; Paris, 1861, 2nd ed. 1875.

Boot, J. C. G. : *Mnemosyne* xxii. 409-412 (1894).

Brakmann, C. : *Mnemosyne* lx. 1-19 (1932).

ten Brink, B. : *M. Terentii Varronis Locus de Urbe Roma* ; Traiecti ad Rhenum, 1855.

Brinkmann, A. : *Simpuvium—simpulum ; Archiv für lateinische Lexikographie* xv. 139-143 (1908).

Buecheler, F. : *Rheinisches Museum* xxvii. 475 (1872).

Buecheler, F. : *Archiv für lateinische Lexikographie* ii. 119, 619-624 (1885).

Christ, Wilhelm : *Philologus* xvi. 450-464 (1860), xvii. 59-63 (1861).

Christ, Wilhelm : *Archiv für lateinische Lexikographie* ii. 619-624 (1885).

Dahlmann, Hellfried : *Varro und die hellenistische Sprachtheorie* ; Berlin, 1932 (*Forschungen zur klass. Phil.* v.).

Dahlmann, Hellfried : *M. Terentius Varro*, article in Pauly-Wissowa's *Real-Encyc. d. class. Altertumswiss.* Suppl. vol. vi. 1172-1277 (1935).

Dam, R. J. : *De Analogia, observationes in Varronem grammaticamque Romanorum* ; Campis, 1930.

Ellis, Robinson : *Journal of Philology* xix. 38, 178-179 (1891).

Ellis, Robinson : *Hermathena* xi. 353-363 (1901).

Fay, Edwin W. : *Varroniana ; American Journal of Philology* xxxv. 149-162, 245-267 (1914).

Foat, W. G. : *Classical Review* xxix. 79 (1915).

Fraccaro, Plinio : *Studi Varroniani* ; Padova, 1907.

xxxvi

INTRODUCTION

Funaioli, Hyginus : *Grammaticae Romanae Fragmenta* ;
 Leipzig, 1907.

Galdi, M. : *Rivista Indo-Greco-Italica* xi. 3-4, 21-22
 (1927).

Georges, K. E. : *Philologus* xxxiii. 226 (1874).

Goetz, Georg : *Berliner Philologische Wochenschrift*,
 1886, 779-783.

Goetz, Georg : *Quaestiones Varronianae* ; Index
 Scholarum in Univ. Ienensi, 1886–1887.

Goetz, Georg : *Aelius Stilo*, article in Pauly-Wissowa's
 Real-Enc. d. cl. Altw. i. 532-533 (1894), Suppl.
 vol. i. 15 (1903).

Goetz, Georg : *Göttingische Gelehrte Anzeigen*, 1908,
 815-827.

Goetz, Georg : *Zur Würdigung der grammatischen
 Arbeiten Varros ; Abhandl. der kön. sächs. Gesell-
 schaft d. Wiss.* xxvii. 3, 67-89 (1909).

Goetz, Georg : *Berliner Philologische Wochenschrift*,
 1910, 1367-1368.

Groth, Adolfus : *De M. Terenti Varronis de Lingua
 Latina librorum codice Florentino* ; Argentorati,
 1880.

Haupt, Moritz : *Hermes* i. 401-403 (1866), iii. 147-
 148 (1869), iv. 332-334 (1870).

Haupt, Moritz : *Opuscula* (3 vols., 1875, 1876, 1876),
 ii. 192-195, iii. 355-357, 477.

Heidrich, Georg : *Der Gebrauch des Gerundiums und
 Gerundivums bei Varro* ; Jahresbericht, Gymn.
 Melk, 1890.

Heidrich, Georg : *Bemerkungen über den Stil des Varro* ;
 Jahresbericht, Gymn. Melk, 1891.

Henry, Victor : *De sermonis humani origine et natura
 M. Terentius Varro quid senserit* ; Insulis, 1883.

INTRODUCTION

Hertz, M. : *Jahrbücher für classische Philologie* cix. 249-255 (1874).

Hirschfeld, O. : *Hermes* viii. 469 (1874).

Hultsch, Fr. : *Philologus* xxii. 346 (1865).

Hultsch, Fr. : *Metrologicorum Scriptorum reliquiae* ii. 49-51 ; Leipzig, 1866.

Jacobs : *Varietas lectionum in Varronis libris de Lingua Latina ; Beiträge zur älteren Litteratur* ii. 217-222 (1836).

Jahn, Otto : *Hermes* ii. 246-247 (1867).

Jeep, J. W. L. : *Zur Geschichte der Lehre von den Redeteilen bei den lateinischen Grammatikern* ; Leipzig, 1893.

Jonas, Richard : *Zum Gebrauch der Verba frequentativa und intensiva in der älteren lateinischen Prosa* ; Gymn. Posen, 1879.

Jordan, Heinrich : *Hermes* ii. 83, 89 (1867), xv. 118-121 (1880).

Jordan, Heinrich : *Topographie der Stadt Rom im Alterthum*, vol. i. 1, 1878 ; i. 2, 1885 ; i. 3, revised by Ch. Huelsen, 1907 ; vol. ii. 1871, especially pages 237-290, 599-603 ; Berlin.

Jordan, Heinrich : *Kritische Beiträge zur Geschichte der lateinischen Sprache*, Berlin, 1879 ; passim, esp. pages 90-91, 96-103, 131, 138, 224, 321.

Keil, Heinrich : *Das Fragmentum Casinense des Varro de Lingua Latina ; Rheinisches Museum* vi. 142-145 (1847).

Kent, R. G. : *On the Text of Varro, de Lingua Latina ; Trans. Am. Philol. Assn.* lxvii. 64-82 (1936).

Kowalski, G. : *Studia Rhetorica ; Eos* xxxi. 141-168 (1928).

Kriegshammer, Robert : *De Varronis et Verrii Fontibus quaestiones selectae* ; Leipzig, 1903.
Krumbiegel, Richard : *De Varroniano Scribendi Genere quaestiones* ; Leipzig, 1892.

Lachmann, Karl : *Rheinisches Museum* vi. 106-125 (1839) ; new series, ii. 356-365 (1842), iii. 610-611 (1845) ; reprinted in *Kleinere Schriften* ii. 162-187 (1876).
Lachmann, Karl : *In T. Lucretii Cari de Rerum Natura libros Commentarius* (1850), passim ; 4th ed., 1882, with index.
Lahmeyer, Gustav : *Philologus* xxii. 100-105 (1865).
Lersch, Laurenz : *Die Sprachphilosophie der Alten* i. 117-127 (1838), ii. 143-153 (1840), iii. 169-172 (1841) ; Bonn.
Lobeck, Chr. Aug. : *Aglaophamus* ii. 1002-1004 ; Königsberg, 1829.
Luebbert, Ed. : *Commentationes Pontificales* ; Berlin, 1859.

Madvig, J. N. : *Adversaria Critica* i. 178, ii. 166-178 ; Copenhagen, 1871 and 1873.
Mercklin, Ludwig : *De Junio Gracchano commentatio* ; particulae duae, Dorpat, 1840, 1841.
Mercklin, Ludwig : *Quaestiones Varronianae* ; Index Scholarum in Univ. Dorpat. 1852.
Mercklin, Ludwig : *De Varronis tralaticio scribendi genere quaestiones* ; Index Scholarum in Univ. Dorpat. 1858.
Mette, H. J. : *De Cratete Mallota seu Pergameno* ; Berlin, 1931.
Mette, H. J. : *Varroniana* (supplement to preceding); Berlin, 1931.

Mueller, August : *De Priscis Verborum Formis Var-ronianis* ; Halle, 1877.

Mueller, C. F. W. : *Zeitschrift für das Gymnasial-wesen* xix. 421-424, 792-800, 867-874 (1865).

Mueller, K. O. : *Zur Topographie Roms : Über die Fragmente der Sacra Argeorum bei Varro, de Lingua Latina V (IV)*, 8 ; in Böttiger, *Archäologie und Kunst* i. 69-94 ; Breslau, 1828.

Mueller, K. O. : *Sextus Pompeius Festus*, edition, page xliv ; Leipzig, 1839.

Mueller, Lucian : *Jahrbücher für classische Philologie* xcvii. 427 (1868).

Mueller, Lucian : *Rheinisches Museum* xxiv. 553-557 (1869).

Muller Jzn, Fridericus : *De veterum imprimis Ro-manorum studiis etymologicis*, pages 115-248 ; Utrecht, 1910.

Nettleship, H. : *Latin Grammar in the First Century ; Journal of Philology* xv. 189-214 (1886).

Neukirch, J. H. : *De Fabula Togata Romanorum*, pages 71, 83, 89, 96, 99, 122, 188, 278 ; Leipzig, 1833.

Norden, Eduard : *Rheinisches Museum* xlviii. 348-354 (1893).

Norden, Eduard : *De Stilone Cosconio Varrone gram-maticis commentatio* ; Index Scholarum in Univ. Greifswald. 1895.

Norden, Eduard : *Die antike Kunstprosa vom VI. Jahrhundert vor Christus bis in die Zeit der Renais-sance* i. 194-200 ; Leipzig, 1898.

Oxé, C. E. L. : *De M. Ter. Varronis etymis quibusdam commentatio* ; Gymn. Programm, Kreuznach, 1859.

INTRODUCTION

Oxé, C. E. L. : *M. Terenti Varronis librorum de lingua Latina argumentum* ; Gymn. Programm, Kreuznach, 1871.

Pape, Wilhelm : *Lectiones Varronianae* ; Berlin, 1829.
Plasberg, O. : *Rheinisches Museum* liii. 70, 75-76 (1898).

Reiter, Hugo : *Quaestiones Varronianae grammaticae* ; Königsberg, 1882.
Reiter, Hugo : *Observationes criticae in M. Terenti Varronis de lingua Latina libros* ; Jahresbericht, Gymn. Braunsberg, 1884.
Reitzenstein, R. : *M. Terentius Varro und Johannes Mauropus von Euchaita* ; Leipzig, 1901.
Ribbeck, Otto : *Die Composition der Varronischen Bücher V-VII de lingua Latina ; Rheinisches Museum* xli. 618-626 (1886).
Riese, Alexander : *Philologus* xxvii. 305-306 (1868).
Ritschl, Fr. W. : *Jahrbücher für classische Philologie* xcvii. 341-343 (1868).
Roehrscheidt, K. : review of Reitzenstein ; *Göttingische Gelehrte Anzeigen*, 1908, 791-814.
Roessner, Otto : *De praepositionum ab de ex usu Varroniano* ; Halle, 1888.
Roth, K. L. : *Über das Leben des M. Terentius Varro* ; Gymn. Programm, Basel, 1857 (also separately issued).
Roth, K. L. : *Philologus* xvii. 175-176 (1861).

Samter, Ernest : *Quaestiones Varronianae* ; Berlin, 1891.
Schwabe, L. : *Jahrbücher für Philologie* ci. 350-352 (1870).

INTRODUCTION

Sitzler, Johann : *Über den Kasusgebrauch bei Varro* ; Beilage zum Gymn. Programm, Tauberbischofsheim, 1889.

Skutsch, F. : *Hermes* xxxii. 96-97 (1897).

Skutsch, F. : *Rheinisches Museum* lxi. 603-609 (1906).

Spengel, Andreas : *Bemerkungen zu Varro de lingua Latina* ; Sitzungsber. d. kön. bayer. Akad. d. Wiss., phil.-hist. Cl. 1885, 243-272.

Spengel, Leonhard : *Emendationum Varronianarum Specimen I* ; Munich, 1830.

Spengel, L. : review of Mueller's edition ; *Jahrbücher für Philologie* xi. 1-20 (1834).

Spengel, L. : *Zeitschrift für die Altertumswissenschaft* iv. 142-144 (1846).

Spengel, L. : *Über die Kritik der Varronischen Bücher de Lingua Latina* ; Abhandl. d. kön. bayer. Akad. d. Wiss. vii. 2. 1-54 (1854).

Spengel, L. : *Commentatio de emendanda ratione librorum M. Terentii Varronis de lingua Latina* ; Munich, 1858 (to F. Thiersch, on semicentennial of the doctorate).

Spengel, L. : *Philologus* xvii. 288-306 (1861).

Spengel, L. : *Die sacra Argeorum bei Varro ;* *Philologus* xxxii. 92-105 (1873).

Stieber, G. M. : *Varroniana : Die griechischen Fremdwörter bei Varro de Lingua Latina, Orthographie, Lautlehre, Index der bei Varro befindlichen Fremdwörter* ; typed dissertation, Würzburg, 1921.

Stowasser, J. M. : *Wiener Studien*, vii. 38-39 (1885).

Stroux, Johannes : *Antidoron, Festschrift Jacob Wackernagel* 309-325 ; Göttingen, 1924.

Stuenkel, Ludwig : *De Varroniana verborum formatione* ; Strassburg, 1875.

Usener, H. : *Ein altes Lehrgebäude der Philologie ; Sitzungsber. d. kön. bayr. Akad. d. Wiss. zu München, phil.-hist. Cl.* 1892, 582-648.

van der Vliet, J. : *Mnemosyne* xx. 416 (1892).

Voigt, Moritz : *Rheinisches Museum* xxiv. 332-335 (1869), xxxiii. 150 (1878).

W—, H. : *Jahrbücher für classische Philologie* lxxxvii. 740 (1863).

Wackernagel, J. : *Hermes* lviii. 460 (1923).

Walter, Fritz : *Philologus* lxxv. 484-485 (1919).

Walter, F. : *Philologische Wochenschrift* l. 827 (1930).

Weber, Julius : *Quaestionum Grammaticarum Specimen* ; Jena, 1914.

Wilmanns, August : *De M. Terenti Varronis libris grammaticis particula* ; Bonn, 1863.

Wilmanns, August : *De M. Terenti Varronis libris grammaticis* ; Berlin, 1864 (the preceding, with addition of the fragments).

Wölfflin, Eduard : *Archiv für lateinische Lexikographie* ii. 5, 89, 324 (1885), viii. 411-440, 563-585 (1898).

Zander, K. M. : *Versus italici antiqui*, page 24 ; Lund, 1890.

Zippmann, A. : *De loco Varroniano qui est de Lingua Latina* viii. 44 ; Gymn. Programm, Scheidemühl, 1869.

Zumpt : review of L. Spengel's edition ; *Jahrbücher für wissenschaftliche Kritik*, 1827, 1513-1527.

OUR TEXT OF THE *DE LINGUA LATINA*

When a text is to be confronted by a translation, that text must be presented in an intelligible wording, with emendations of corrupt passages and the filling up of the gaps. It happens that while some of the corrupt passages in this work are quite desperate, many can be restored, and many gaps can be filled, with some degree of confidence, since Festus, Nonius Marcellus, and others have quoted practically verbatim from Varro; with the aid of their testimonia, many obscure passages can be restored to clarity. This has been the procedure in the present volumes; if any departures from the manuscript authority seem violent, they are required as a basis for a translation. Yet the present text is throughout as conservative as is consistent with the situation.

The text has in fact been so arranged as to show, with least machinery, its relation to the best tradition. With the use of italics and of pointed brackets, and the aid of the critical apparatus, any reader may see for himself exactly what stands in the manuscript. The use of symbols and the like is explained on pages xlix-l.

THE CRITICAL APPARATUS

The critical apparatus is intended to show how the text is derived from the best manuscript tradition, namely *F*, or where *F* fails, then *Fv* or other good codices.

In each item, there is given first the name of the scholar making the emendation which is in the text, after which the reading of *F* is given. It is therefore not necessary to name *F* except in a few places where there might be confusion; if the reading is not that of *F*, then the manuscript is specified. Where the emendation of a scholar has been anticipated by a copyist of some manuscript, the reference to this manuscript is commonly given.   If several successive emendations have been necessary to reach the best reading, the intermediate stages are given in reverse order, working back to the manuscript.   For ease of typography, manuscript abbreviations are mostly presented in expanded form.

The reader may therefore evaluate the text which is here presented ; but the present editor has made no attempt to present the almost countless emendations which have been made by scholars and which have not been adopted here.

THE TRANSLATION OF THE *DE LINGUA LATINA*

The translation of the *De Lingua Latina* presents problems which are hardly to be found in any other of the works translated for the Loeb Classical Library. For the constant (and inevitable) interpretations of one Latin word by another, which Varro had to present in order to expound its origin, requires the translator to keep the Latin words in the translation, glossed with an English equivalent.   In this way only can the translation be made intelligible.

Because of the technical nature of the subject it has been necessary to follow the Latin with some degree of closeness, or the points made by Varro will be lost.   If the translation is at times difficult to understand, it is because most of us are not accustomed to dealing with matters of technical linguistics; and even though Varro lacks the method of modern scholars in the subject, he has his own technique and must be followed in his own way.

The numerous metrical citations which Varro gives from Latin authors are translated in the same metre, though sometimes the translation is slightly shorter or longer than the Latin.

There are only two translations of the *De Lingua Latina* into a modern language : that of Huot into French, a mere paraphrase which often omits whole sentences, and that of Canal into Italian (Nos. 21 and 22 in our list of Editions). There is no translation into German, nor any into English before the present volumes.

THE NOTES TO THE TRANSLATION

The notes are planned to give all needed help to the understanding of a difficult subject matter ; they cover matters of technical linguistics, historical and geographical references, points of public and private life. They explain briefly any unusual word-forms and syntactical uses, and label as incorrect all false etymologies (of which there are many), either explicitly or by indicating the correct etymology. They state the sources of quotations from other authors and works, giving references to a standard collection of fragments if the entire work is not extant. They name the metres of metrical quotations, if the metre is other than dactylic, or iambic, or trochaic.

The fragments of Greek and Latin authors are cited in the notes according to the following scheme : Festus (and the excerpts of Paulus Diaconus), by page and line, edition of K. O. Mueller, Leipzig, 1839.

Grammatici Latini, by volume, page, and line, edition of H. Keil, Leipzig, 1855–1880.

Nonius Marcellus, by page and line, edition of J. Mercier, 1589; 2nd ed., 1614; reprinted 1825.

For the following authors :

Accius : see Ribbeck and Warmington, below.

Ennius : see Vahlen and Warmington, below.

Lucilius : *C. Lucilii Carminum Reliquiae*, ed. F. Marx, 2 vols., Leipzig, 1904–1905.

Naevius : see Ribbeck, Warmington, Baehrens, Morel, below.

Pacuvius : see Ribbeck and Warmington, below.

Plautus, fragments : edition of F. Ritschl, Leipzig, 1894; the same numbering in G. Goetz and F. Schoell, Leipzig, 1901.

von Arnim, J. : *Stoicorum Veterum Reliquiae* ; Leipzig, 1903.

Baehrens, Emil : *Fragmenta Poetarum Romanorum* ; Leipzig, 1886.

Bremer, F. P. : *Iurisprudentiae Antehadrianae quae supersunt* ; Leipzig, 1896–1901.

Bruns, Georg : *Fontes Iuris Romani Antiqui* ; revised by Th. Mommsen ; 7th ed., revised by O. Gradenwitz, Tübingen, 1909.

Buettner, Richard : *Porcius Licinus und der litterarische Kreis des Q. Lutatius Catulus* ; Leipzig, 1893.

Funaioli, Hyginus : *Grammaticae Romanae Fragmenta* ; Leipzig, 1907.

Hultsch, Friedrich : *Polybii Historiae* ; Berlin, 1867–1872.

INTRODUCTION

Huschke, P. E. : *Iurisprudentiae Anteiustinianae Reliquiae* ; 6th ed., revised by E. Seckel and B. Kuebler, Leipzig, 1908.

Jordan, Heinrich : *M. Catonis praeter librum de re rustica quae extant* ; Leipzig, 1860.

Kaibel, G. : *Comicorum Graecorum Fragmenta*, vol. i. Part I ; Berlin, 1899.

Maurenbrecher, Bertold : *Carminum Saliarium reliquiae ; Jahrbücher für classische Philologie*, Suppl., vol. xxi. 313-352 (1894).

Morel, Willy : *Fragmenta Poetarum Latinorum* ; Leipzig, 1927.

Mueller, Karl, and Theodor Mueller : *Fragmenta Historicorum Graecorum* ; Paris, 1841–1870.

Nauck, August : *Aristophanis Byzantii Grammatici Alexandrini Fragmenta* ; Halle, 1848.

Peter, Hermann : *Historicorum Romanorum Fragmenta* ; Leipzig, 1883.

Preibisch, Paul : *Fragmenta Librorum Pontificiorum* ; Tilsit, 1878.

Regell, Paul : *Fragmenta Auguralia* ; Gymn. Hirschberg, 1882.

Ribbeck, Otto : *Scaenicae Romanorum Poesis Fragmenta* : vol. i., *Tragicorum Romanorum Fragmenta*, 3rd ed., Leipzig, 1897 ; vol. ii., *Comicorum Romanorum Fragmenta*, 3rd ed., Leipzig, 1898 (occasional references to the 2nd ed.).

Rose, Valentin : *Aristotelis qui ferebantur librorum fragmenta* ; Leipzig, 1886.

Rowoldt, Walther : *Librorum Pontificiorum Romanorum de Caerimoniis Sacrificiorum Reliquiae* ; Halle, 1906.

Schneider, Otto : *Callimachea* ; Leipzig, 1870.

Schoell, Rudolph : *Legis Duodecim Tabularum Reliquiae* ; Leipzig, 1866.

xlviii

INTRODUCTION

Usener, Hermann : *Epicurea* ; Leipzig, 1887.

Vahlen, J. : *Ennianae Poesis Reliquiae*, 2nd ed., Leipzig, 1903 (the 3rd ed., 1928, is an unchanged reprint).

Warmington, E. H. : *Remains of Old Latin*, in the Loeb Classical Library ; vol. i. (Ennius, Caecilius), 1935 ; vol. ii. (Livius Andronicus, Naevius, Pacuvius, Accius), 1936 ; Cambridge (Mass.) and London.

SYMBOLS AND ABBREVIATIONS

Letters and words not in the manuscript, but added in the text, are set in ⟨ ⟩, except as noted below.

Letters changed from the manuscript reading are printed in italics.

Some obvious additions, and the following changes, are sometimes not further explained by critical notes :

> *a*e with italic *a*, for manuscript *e*.
> *o*e, with italic *o*, for manuscript *ae* or *ę*.
> italic *b* and *v*, for manuscript *u* and *b*.
> italic *f* and *ph*, for manuscript *ph* and *f*.
> italic *i* and *y*, for manuscript *y* and *i*.
> italic *h*, for an *h* omitted in the manuscript.

The manuscripts are referred to as follows ; readings without specification of the manuscript are from *F* :

> *F* = Laurentianus li. 10 ; No. 1 in our list.
> F^1 or m^1, the original writer of *F*, or the first hand.
> F^2 or m^2, the corrector of *F*, or the second hand.
> *Fv* = readings from the lost quaternion of *F*, as recorded by Victorius ; our No. 2.

Frag. Cass. = Cassinensis 361 ; our No. 3.
 f = Laurentianus li. 5 ; our No. 5.
 H = Havniensis ; our No. 6.
 G = Gothanus ; our No. 7.
 a = Parisinus 7489 ; our No. 8.
 b = Parisinus 6142 ; our No. 9.
 c = Parisinus 7535 ; our No. 10.
 V = Vindobonensis lxiii. ; our No. 11.
 p = Basiliensis *F* iv. 13 ; our No. 12.
 M = Guelferbytanus 896 ; our No. 13.
 B = that used by Augustinus ; our No. 14.

The following abbreviations are used for editors and editions (others are referred to by their full names) :

Laetus = editio princeps of Pomponius Laetus.
 Rhol. = Rholandellus, whose first edition was in 1475.
 Pius = Baptista Pius, edition of 1510.
 Aug. = Antonius Augustinus, editor of the Vulgate edition 1554, reprinted 1557.
 Sciop. = Gaspar Scioppius, edition of 1602, reprinted 1605.
 L. Sp. = Leonhard Spengel, edition of 1826 (and articles).
 Mue. = Karl Ottfried Mueller, edition of 1833.
 A. Sp. = Andreas Spengel, edition of 1885 (and articles).
 GS. = G. Goetz and F. Schoell, edition of 1910.

1

INTRODUCTION

SUPPLEMENT TO BIBLIOGRAPHY

The following items should be added to the bibliography given on pages xxxiii-xliii :

von Blumenthal, A. : *Indogermanische Forschungen* liii. 120 (1935).

Dahlmann, H. : *Varronis De Lingua Latina Buch viii* ; Berlin, 1940.

Giffard, A. E. : *Revue de Philologie* lxi. 82-83 (1935).

Hoenigswald, H. M. : *American Journal of Philology* lxviii. 198-199 (1947).

Kent, R. G. : *Transactions of the American Philological Association* lxxviii. 123-130 (1947).

Klotz, A. : *Philologus* xcvi. 18-27 (1943).

Leumann, Ernst : *Glotta* xii. 148 (1923).

Leumann, Manu : *Glotta* xi. 185-188 (1922).

Oko, J. : *Eos* xxxviii. 157-168 (1937).

Rose, H. J. : *Folk-Lore* xlvii. 396-398 (1936).

Also the following critical reviews of the first printing of this translation :

Bolling, G. M. : *Language* xiv. 292-300 (1938), xv. 129 (1939).

Collart, Jean : *Revue de Philologie* lxv. 261-263 (1939), lxvi. 65 (1940).

DeWitt, N. W. : *Classical Weekly* xxxii. 52 (1938).

Ernout, A. : *Bulletin de la Société de Linguistique* xl. 3. 65-67 (1939).

Fordyce, C. J. : *The Classical Review* liii. 131 (1939).

Klotz, A. : *Philologische Wochenschrift* lx. 246-248 (1940).

Marouzeau, J. : *Revue des Études latines* xvii. 200-202 (1939).

P[ostgate], J. W. : *Oxford Magazine*, 23 Feb. 1939.

Sturtevant, E. H. : *American Journal of Philology*
lxiii. 361-363 (1942).

Whatmough, J. : *Classical Philology* xxxiv. 379-383
(1939), xxxv. 82-86 (1940).

VARRO

M. TERENTI VARRONIS
DE LINGUA LATINA

De Disciplina Originum Verborum ad Ciceronem

LIBER IIII EXPLICIT ; INCIPIT

LIBER V

I. 1. Quemadmodum vocabula essent imposita rebus in lingua Latina, sex libris exponere institui. De his tris ante hunc feci quos Septumio misi : in quibus est de disciplina, quam vocant ἐτυμολογικήν[1] : quae contra ea⟨m⟩[2] dicerentur, volumine primo, quae pro ea, secundo, quae de ea, tertio. In his ad te scribam, a quibus rebus vocabula imposita sint in lingua Latina, et ea quae sunt in consuetudine apud ⟨populum et ea quae inveniuntur apud⟩[3] poetas.

2. Cum[1] unius cuiusque verbi naturae sint duae, a qua re et in qua re vocabulum sit impositum (itaque

§ 1. [1] *For* ethimologicen. [2] *Rhol., for* ea. [3] *Added by A. Sp.*
§ 2. [1] *Rhol., for* cui.

---

§ 1. [a] Books II.-VII.; Book I. was introductory.
[b] Books II.-IV. [c] Quaestor to Varro, *cf.* vii. 109 ; but when or where is not known. Possibly he was the writer on architecture mentioned by Vitruvius, *de Arch.* vii. praef. 14, and even the composer of the *Libri Observationum* men-

2

MARCUS TERENTIUS VARRO'S
ON THE LATIN LANGUAGE

On the Science of the Origin of Words,
addressed to Cicero

BOOK IV ENDS HERE, AND HERE BEGINS

BOOK V

I. 1. In what way names were applied to things
in Latin, I have undertaken to expound, in six books.[a]
Of these, I have already composed three [b] before this
one, and have addressed them to Septumius [c]; in
them I treat of the branch of learning which is called
Etymology. The considerations which might be raised
against it, I have put in the first book ; those adduced
in its favour, in the second; those merely describing
it, in the third. In the following books, addressed
to you,[d] I shall discuss the problem from what things
names were applied in Latin, both those which are
habitual with the ordinary folk, and those which are
found in the poets.

2. Inasmuch as each and every word has two
innate features, from what thing and to what thing

tioned by Quintilian, *Inst. Orat.* iv. 1. 19.   [d] Cicero, to
whom Varro addresses the balance of the work, Books
V.-XXV., written apparently in 47–45 B.C.

3

a qua re sit pertinacia cum requi⟨ri⟩tur,[2] ostenditur[3] esse a perten⟨den⟩do[4]; in qua re sit impositum dicitur cum demonstratur, in quo non debet pertendi et pertendit, pertinaciam esse, quod in quo oporteat manere, si in eo perstet, perseverantia sit), priorem illam partem, ubi cur et unde sint verba scrutantur, Graeci vocant ἐτυμολογίαν,[5] illam alteram περ⟨ὶ⟩ σημαινομένων. De quibus duabus rebus in his libris promiscue dicam, sed exilius de posteriore.

3. Quae ideo sunt obscuriora, quod neque omnis impositio verborum extat,[1] quod vetustas quasdam delevit, nec quae extat sine mendo omnis imposita, nec quae recte est imposita, cuncta manet (multa enim verba li⟨t⟩teris commutatis sunt interpolata), neque omnis origo est nostrae linguae e vernaculis verbis, et multa verba aliud nunc ostendunt, aliud ante significabant, ut hostis : nam tum eo verbo dicebant peregrinum qui suis legibus uteretur, nunc dicunt eum quem tum dicebant perduellem.

4. In quo genere verborum aut casu erit illustrius unde videri possit origo, inde repetam. Ita fieri oportere apparet, quod recto casu quom[1] dicimus inpos,[2] obscurius est esse a potentia qua⟨m⟩[3] cum

[2] *GS.*, *for* sequitur. [3] *For* hostenditur. [4] *Rhol.*, *for* pertendo. [5] *For* ethimologiam.

§ 3. [1] *For* exstat.

§ 4. [1] *Aug.*, *with B*, *for* quem. [2] *p*, *Laetus*, *for* ineos. [3] *For* qua.

---

§ 2. [a] Properly an abstract formed from *pertinax*, itself a compound of *tenax* ' tenacious,' derived from *tenere* ' to hold.'

§ 3. [a] *Cf.* vii. 49.

§ 4. [a] Not from *potentia* ; but both from radical *pot-*.

the name is applied (therefore, when the question is raised from what thing *pertinacia* ' obstinacy ' is,[a] it is shown to be from *pertendere* ' to persist ' : to what thing it is applied, is told when it is explained that it is *pertinacia* ' obstinacy ' in a matter in which there ought not to be persistence but there is, because it is *perseverantia* ' steadfastness ' if a person persists in that in which he ought to hold firm), that former part, where they examine why and whence words are, the Greeks call Etymology, that other part they call Semantics. Of these two matters I shall speak in the following books, not keeping them apart, but giving less attention to the second.

3. These relations are often rather obscure for the following reasons : Not every word that has been applied, still exists, because lapse of time has blotted out some. Not every word that is in use, has been applied without inaccuracy of some kind, nor does every word which has been applied correctly remain as it originally was ; for many words are disguised by change of the letters. There are some whose origin is not from native words of our own language. Many words indicate one thing now, but formerly meant something else, as is the case with *hostis* ' enemy ' : for in olden times by this word they meant a foreigner from a country independent of Roman laws, but now they give the name to him whom they then called *perduellis* ' enemy.' [a]

4. I shall take as starting-point of my discussion that derivative or case-form of the words in which the origin can be more clearly seen. It is evident that we ought to operate in this way, because when we say *inpos* ' lacking power ' in the nominative, it is less clear that it is from *potentia* [a] ' power ' than when we

5

dicimus inpotem[4]; et eo obscurius fit, si dicas pos
quam[5] inpos : videtur enim pos significare potius
pontem quam potentem.

5. Vetustas pauca non depravat, multa tollit.
Quem puerum vidisti formosum, hunc vides defor-
mem in senecta. Tertium seculum non videt eum
hominem quem vidit primum. Quare illa quae iam
maioribus nostris ademit oblivio, fugitiva secuta
sedulitas Muci[1] et Bruti retrahere nequit. Non, si
non potuero indagare, eo ero tardior, sed velocior
ideo, si quivero. Non mediocres[2] enim tenebrae in
silva ubi haec captanda neque eo quo pervenire
volumus semitae tritae, neque non in tramitibus
quaedam obiecta[3] quae euntem retinere possent.

6. Quorum verborum novorum ac veterum discordia omnis in consuetudine com⟨m⟩uni, quot modis[1]
commutatio sit facta qui animadverterit, facilius
scrutari origines patietur verborum : reperiet enim
esse commutata, ut in superioribus libris ostendi,
maxime propter bis quaternas causas. Litterarum
enim fit demptione aut additione et propter earum
tra⟨ie⟩ctionem[2] aut commutationem, item syllabarum
productione ⟨aut correptione, denique adiectione aut

---

[4] *Aug., for* inpotentem.   [5] *Aug., with B, for* postquam.
    § 5.   [1] *For* muti.   [2] *For* mediocris.   [3] *For* oblecta.
    § 6.   [1] *After* modis, *Fr. Fritzsche deleted* litterarum.
[2] *Scaliger and Popma, for* tractationem.

---

[b] Avoided in practice, in favour of dissyllabic *potis*.   [c] Because the nasal was almost or quite lost before *s* ; *cf.* the
regular inscriptional spelling *cosol = consul*.
    § 5.   [a] P. Mucius Scaevola and M. Junius Brutus, distin-
guished jurists and writers on law in the period 150–130 B.C.
Mucius, as pontifex maximus, seems to have collected and

by examples, in the preceding books, of what sort these phenomena are, I have thought that here I need only set a reminder of that previous discussion.

7. Now I shall set forth the origins of the individual words, of which there are four levels of explanation. The lowest is that to which even the common folk has come ; who does not see the sources of *argentifodinae* [a] ' silver-mines ' and of *viocurus* ' road-overseer ' ? The second is that to which old-time grammar has mounted, which shows how the poet has made each word which he has fashioned and derived. Here belongs Pacuvius's [b]

> The whistling of the ropes,

here his [c]

> Incurvate-neckèd flock,

here his [d]

> With his mantle he beshields his arm.

8. The third level is that to which philosophy ascended, and on arrival began to reveal the nature of those words which are in common use, as, for example, from what *oppidum* ' town ' was named, and *vicus* ' row of houses,' [a] and *via* ' street.' The fourth is that where the sanctuary is, and the mysteries of the high-priest : if I shall not arrive at full knowledge there, at any rate I shall cast about for a conjecture, which even in matters of our health the physician sometimes does when we are ill.

verse in Quintilian, *Inst. Orat.* i. 5. 67, *Nerei repandirostrum incurvicervicum pecus.*   [d] *Hermiona, Trag. Rom. Frag.* 186 Ribbeck[3], *R.O.L.* ii. 232-233 Warmington ; the entire verse in Nonius Marcellus, 87. 23 M. : *currum liquit, clamide contorta astu clipeat braccium.*

§ 8.   [a] From this meaning, either an entire small ' village ' or a ' street ' in a large city.

VARRO

9. Quodsi summum gradum non attigero, tamen secundum praeteribo, quod non solum ad Aristophanis lucernam, sed etiam ad Clean*th*is lucubravi. Volui praeterire eos, qui poetarum modo verba ut sint ficta expediunt. Non enim videbatur consentaneum qua⟨e⟩re⟨re⟩[1] me in eo verbo quod finxisset Ennius causam, neglegere quod ante rex Latinus finxisset, cum poeticis multis verbis magis delecter quam utar, antiquis magis utar quam delecter. An non potius mea verba illa quae hereditate a Romulo rege venerunt quam quae a poeta Livio relicta ?

10. Igitur quoniam in haec sunt tripertita verba, quae sunt aut nostra aut aliena aut oblivia, de nostris dicam cur sint, de alienis unde sint, de obliviis relinquam : quorum partim qu*id* ta⟨men⟩ invenerim *au*t opiner[1] scribam. In hoc libro dicam de vocabulis locorum et quae in his sunt, in secundo de temporum et quae in his fiunt, in tertio de utraque re a poetis comprehensa.

11. Pythagoras Samius ait omnium rerum initia esse bina ut finitum et infinitum, bonum et malum,

§ 9.   [1] *Aug., for* quare.
§ 10.   [1] *After A. Sp., with* tamen *from Fay's* quo loco tamen ; *for* quo ita inuenerim ita opiner.

---

§ 9.   [a] Aristophanes of Byzantium, 262–185 B.C., pupil of Zenodotus and Callimachus at Alexandria, and himself one of the greatest of the Alexandrian grammarians, who busied himself especially with the textual correction and editing of the Greek authors, notably Homer, Hesiod, and the lyric poets.   [b] *Frag.* 485 von Arnim ; Cleanthes of Assos, 331–232 B.C., pupil and successor of Zeno, founder of the Stoic school of philosophy (died 264), as head of the school, at Athens, and author of many works on all phases of the Stoic teaching.   [c] L. Livius Andronicus, *c.* 284–202 B.C., born at Tarentum ; first epic and dramatic poet of the Romans.
§ 11.   [a] Pythagoras, born probably in Samos about 567 B.C.,

9. But if I have not reached the highest level, I shall none the less go farther up than the second, because I have studied not only by the lamp of Aristophanes,[a] but also by that of Cleanthes.[b] I have desired to go farther than those who expound only how the words of the poets are made up. For it did not seem meet that I seek the source in the case of the word which Ennius had made, and neglect that which long before King Latinus had made, in view of the fact that I get pleasure rather than utility from many words of the poets, and more utility than pleasure from the ancient words. And in fact are not those words mine which have come to me by inheritance from King Romulus, rather than those which were left behind by the poet Livius ?[c]

10. Therefore since words are divided into these three groups, those which are our own, those which are of foreign origin, and those which are obsolete and of forgotten sources, I shall set forth about our own why they are, about those of foreign origin whence they are, and as to the obsolete I shall let them alone : except that concerning some of them I shall none the less write what I have found or myself conjecture. In this book I shall tell about the words denoting places and those things which are in them ; in the following book I shall tell of the words denoting times and those things which take place in them ; in the third I shall tell of both these as expressed by the poets.

11. Pythagoras the Samian [a] says that the primal elements of all things are in pairs, as finite and infinite,

removed to Croton in South Italy about 529 and was there the founder of the philosophic-political school of belief which attaches to his name. His teachings were oral only, and were reduced to writing by his followers.

11

vitam et mortem, diem et noctem. Quare item duo status et motus, ⟨utrumque quadripertitum⟩[1] : quod stat aut agitatur, corpus, ubi agitatur, locus, dum agitatur, tempus, quod est in agitatu, actio. Quadripertitio magis sic apparebit : corpus est ut cursor, locus stadium qua currit, tempus hora qua currit, actio cursio.

12. Quare fit, ut ideo fere omnia sint quadripertita et ea aeterna, quod neque unquam tempus, quin fuerit[1] motus : eius *enim*[2] intervallum tempus ; neque motus, ubi non locus et corpus, quod alterum est quod movetur, alterum ubi ; neque ubi is agitatus, non actio ibi. Igitur initiorum quadrigae locus et corpus, tempus et actio.

13. Quare quod quattuor genera prima rerum, totidem verborum : e quis ⟨de⟩ locis et *i*is[1] rebus qu*a*e in his videntur in hoc libro summatim ponam. Sed qua cognatio eius erit verbi quae radices egerit extra fines suas, persequemur. S*a*epe enim ad limitem arboris radices sub vicini prodierunt segetem. Quare non, cum de locis dicam, si ab agro ad agr*a*rium[2] hominem, ad agricolam pervenero, aberraro. Multa

§ 11. [1] *Added by L. Sp.*
§ 12. [1] *For* fuerint.   [2] *Aug., for* animi.
§ 13. [1] *L. Sp., for* uerborum enim horum dequis locis et
his.   [2] *L. Sp., for* agrosium.

§ 13. [a] Celebrated on April 23 and August 19, when an offering of new wine was made to Jupiter ; *cf.* vi. 16 and vi. 20.

good and bad, life and death, day and night. Therefore likewise there are the two fundamentals, station and motion, each divided into four kinds : what is stationary or is in motion, is body ; where it is in motion, is place ; while it is in motion, is time ; what is inherent in the motion, is action. The fourfold division will be clearer in this way : body is, so to speak, the runner, place is the race-course where he runs, time is the period during which he runs, action is the running.

12. Therefore it comes about that for this reason all things, in general, are divided into four phases, and these universal ; because there is never time without there being motion—for even an intermission of motion is time— ; nor is there motion where there is not place and body, because the latter is that which is moved, and the former is where ; nor where this motion is, does there fail to be action. Therefore place and body, time and action are the four-horse team of the elements.

13. Therefore because the primal classes of things are four in number, so many are the primal classes of words. From among these, concerning places and those things which are seen in them, I shall put a summary account in this book ; but we shall follow them up wherever the kin of the word under discussion is, even if it has driven its roots beyond its own territory. For often the roots of a tree which is close to the line of the property have gone out under the neighbour's cornfield. Wherefore, when I speak of places, I shall not have gone astray, if from *ager* ' field ' I pass to an *agrarius* ' agrarian ' man, and to an *agricola* ' farmer.' The partnership of words is one of many members : the Wine Festival *a* cannot be set

societas verborum, nec Vinalia sine vino expediri nec
Curia Calabra sine calatione potest aperiri.

II. 14.   Incipiam de locis *ab*[1] ipsius loci origine.
Locus est, ubi locatum quid esse potest, ut nunc
dicunt, collocatum.   Veteres id dicere solitos apparet
apud Plautum :

> Filiam habeo grandem dote cassa⟨m⟩ atque
>   inlocabil*e*⟨m⟩[2]
> Neque eam queo locare cuiquam.

Apud Ennium :

> O Terra T*h*raeca, ubi Liberi fanum inc*lu*tum[3]
> Maro[4] locavi⟨t⟩.[5]

15.   Ubi quidque consistit, locus.   Ab eo praeco
dicitur locare, quod usque idem it,[1] quoad in aliquo
constitit pretium.   In⟨de⟩[2] locarium quod datur in
stabulo et taberna, ubi consistant.   Sic loci muliebres,
ubi nascendi initia consistunt.

III. 16.   Loca natura⟨e⟩[1] secundum antiquam
divisionem prima duo, terra et caelum, deinde particulatim utriusque multa.   Caeli dicuntur loca su-

---

§ 14.   [1] *Sciop., for* sub.   [2] *So Plautus, for* cassa dote
atque inlocabili *F ; Plautus also has* virginem *for* filiam.
[3] *Wilhelm, for* inciuium.   [4] *For* miro *F*[2], maro *F*[1].
[5] *Ribbeck, for* locaui.
§ 15.   [1] *Turnebus, for* id emit.   [2] *Laetus, for* in.
§ 16.   [1] *Aug., for* natura.

---

[b] A place on the Capitoline Hill, near the cottage of
Romulus, and also the meeting held there on the Kalends,
when the priests announced the number of days until the
Nones ; *cf.* vi. 27, and Macrobius, *Saturnalia,* i. 15. 7.
§ 14.   [a] The uncompounded word ; which, like its compound,
meant both ' established in a fixed position ' and ' established
in a marriage.'   [b] *Aulularia,* 191-192.   [c] That is, in
marriage.   [d] *Trag. Rom. Frag.* 347-348 Ribbeck[3] ; *R.O.L.*

on its way without wine, nor can the *Curia Calabra* 'Announcement Hall'[b] be opened without the *calatio* 'proclamation.'

II. 14. Among places, I shall begin with the origin of the word *locus* 'place' itself. *Locus* is where something can be *locatum*[a] 'placed,' or as they say nowadays, *collocatum* 'established.' That the ancients were wont to use the word in this meaning, is clear in Plautus[b]:

> I have a grown-up daughter, lacking dower,
>   unplaceable,[c]
> Nor can I place her now with anyone.

In Ennius we find[d]:

> O Thracian Land, where Bacchus' fane renowned
> Did Maro place.

15. Where anything comes to a standstill, is a *locus* 'place.' From this the auctioneer is said *locare* 'to place' because he is all the time likewise going on until the price comes to a standstill on someone. Thence also is *locarium* 'place-rent,' which is given for a lodging or a shop, where the payers take their stand. So also *loci muliebres* 'woman's places,' where the beginnings of birth are situated.

III. 16. The primal places of the universe, according to the ancient division, are two, *terra* 'earth' and *caelum* 'sky,' and then, according to the division into items, there are many places in each. The places of the sky are called *loca supera* 'upper places,' and

i. 376-377 Warmington. Maro, son of Euanthes and priest of Apollo in the Thracian Ismaros, in thanks for protection for himself and his followers, gave Ulysses a present of excellent wine (*Odyssey*, ix. 197 ff.). Because of this, later legend drew him into the Dionysiac circle, as son or grandson of Bacchus, or otherwise. There were even cults of Maro himself in Maroneia, Samothrace, and elsewhere.

pera et ea deorum, terrae loca infera et ea hominum. Ut Asia sic caelum dicitur modis duobus. Nam et Asia, quae non Europa, in quo etiam Syria, et Asia dicitur prioris pars Asiae, in qua est Ionia ac provincia nostra.

17. Sic caelum et pars eius, summum ubi stellae, et id quod Pacuvius cum demonstrat dicit :

> Hoc vide circum supraque quod complexu continet Terram.

Cui subiungit :

> Id quod nostri caelum memorant.

A qua bipertita divisione Luci*lius*[1] suorum un⟨i⟩us[2] et viginti librorum initium fecit hoc :

> Aetheris et terrae genitabile quaerere tempus.

18. Caelum dictum scribit Aelius, quod est caelatum, aut contrario nomine, celatum quod apertum est ; non male, quod ⟨im⟩positor[1] multo potius ⟨caelare⟩[2] a caelo quam caelum a caelando. Sed non

---

§ 17. [1] *Scaliger, for* lucretius.   [2] *Laetus, for* unum.
§ 18. [1] *GS., for* posterior.   [2] *Added by Scaliger.*

---

§ 16. [a] Asia originally designated probably only a town or small district in Lydia, and then came to be what we now call Asia Minor, and finally the entire continent.   [b] Ionia was a coastal region of Asia Minor, including Smyrna, Ephesus, Miletus, etc., and was included within *provincia nostra.* But ' our province ' ran much farther inland, comprising Phrygia, Mysia, Lydia, Caria (Cicero, *Pro Flacco*, 27. 65), which explains the ' and.'

§ 17. [a] *Chryses, Trag. Rom. Frag.* 87-88 and 90 Ribbeck[3]; *R.O.L.* 2. 202-203, lines 107-108, 111 Warmington.   [b] *Satirae,* verse 1 Marx. As there were thirty books of Lucilius's *Satires,* the limitation to twenty-one by Varro must be based on another division (for which there is evidence), thus : Books XXVI.-XXX. were written first, in various metres; I.-XXI.,

these belong to the gods ; the places of the earth are *loca infera* ' lower places,' and these belong to mankind. *Caelum* ' sky ' is used in two ways, just as is Asia. For Asia means the Asia, which is not Europe, wherein is even Syria ; and Asia means also that part [a] of the aforementioned Asia, in which is Ionia [b] and our province.

17. So *caelum* ' sky ' is both a part of itself, the top where the stars are, and that which Pacuvius means when he points it out [a] :

> See this around and above, which holds in its embrace
> The earth.

To which he adds :

> That which the men of our days call the sky.

From this division into two, Lucilius set this as the start of his twenty-one books [b] :

> Seeking the time when the ether above and the
> earth were created.

18. *Caelum*, Aelius writes,[a] was so called because it is *caelatum* ' raised above the surface,' or from the opposite of its idea,[b] *celatum* ' hidden ' because it is exposed ; not ill the remark, that the one who applied the term took *caelare* ' to raise ' much rather from *caelum* than *caelum* from *caelare*. But that second

to which Varro here alludes, were a second volume, in dactylic hexameters, which Lucilius had found to be the best vehicle for his work; XXII.-XXV. were a third part, in elegiacs, probably not published until after their author's death.

§ 18.   [a] Page 59 Funaioli.   *Caelum* is probably connected with a root seen in German *heiter* ' bright,' and not with the words mentioned by Varro.   [b] Derivation by the contrary of the meaning, as in *ludus, in quo minime luditur* ' school, in which there is very little playing ' (Festus, 122. 16 M.).

minus illud alterum de celando ab eo potuit dici, quod
interdiu celatur, quam quod noctu non celatur.

19. Omnino e⟨g⟩o¹ magis puto a chao cho⟨um
ca⟩vum² et hinc caelum, quoniam, ut dixi, "hoc circum
supraque quod complexu continet terram," cavum
caelum. Itaque dicit Androm⟨ed⟩a³ Nocti :

> Qu*ae*⁴ cava caeli
> Signitenentibus conficis bigis ;

et Agamemno :

> In altisono caeli clipeo :

cavum enim clipeum ; et Ennius item ad cavationem :

> Caeli ingentes fornices.

20. Quare ut a cavo cavea et cau*l*lae¹ et convallis,
cavata vallis, et cave⟨rn⟩ae² ⟨a⟩³ cavatione⁴ ut cavum,⁵
sic ortum, unde omnia apud *H*esiodum, a chao cavo
caelum.

IV. 21. Terra dicta ab eo, ut Aelius scribit, quod

§ 19. ¹ *Aldus, for* eo. ² *GS. ;* choum hinc cavum
Mue. ; for chouum. ³ *Scaliger, for* androma. ⁴ *Aug.,*
for noctique.
§ 20. ¹ *Scaliger, for* cauile. ² *GS., for* cauea e.
³ *Added by Mue.* ⁴ *Mue., for* cauitione. ⁵ *Vertranius,*
for cauium.

---

§ 19. ª Latin *cavum* is not related to Greek *chaos*, but it is
the source of all the Latin words in § 19 and § 20, except
caelum and *convallis*. ᵇ Ennius, *Trag. Rom. Frag.* 95-96
Ribbeck³ ; *R.O.L.* i. 256-257 Warmington ; anapaestic.
ᶜ Ennius, *Trag. Rom. Frag.* 177-178 Ribbeck³ ; *R.O.L.* i.
300-301 Warmington ; anapaestic. ᵈ Ennius, *Trag. Rom.*
Frag. 374 Ribbeck³ ; *R.O.L.* i. 364-365 Warmington.
§ 20. ª Commonly meaning the spectators' part of the
theatre ; but also ' stall, bird-cage, bee-hive.' ᵇ Also

origin, from *celare* ' to hide,' could be said from this fact, that by day it *celatur* ' is hidden,' no less than that by night it is not hidden.

19. On the whole I rather think that from *chaos* came *choum* and then *cavum* [a] ' hollow,' and from this *caelum* ' sky,' since, as I have said, " this around and above, which holds in its embrace the earth," is the *cavum caelum* ' hollow sky.' And so Andromeda says to Night,[b]

> You who traverse the hollows of sky
> With your chariot marked by the stars.

And Agamemnon says,[c]

> In the shield of the sky, that soundeth on high,

for a shield is a hollow thing. And Ennius likewise, with reference to a cavern,[d]

> Enormous arches of the sky.

20. Wherefore as from *cavum* ' hollow ' come *cavea* [a] ' cavity,' and *caullae* [b] ' hole or passage,' and *convallis* [c] ' enclosed valley ' as being a *cavata vallis* ' hollowed valley,' and *cavernae* ' caverns ' from the *cavatio* ' hollowing,' as a *cavum* ' hollow thing,' [d] so developed *caelum* ' sky ' from *cavum*, which itself was from *chaos*, from which, in Hesiod,[e] come all things.

IV. 21. *Terra* [a] ' earth ' is — as Aelius [b] writes — named from this fact, that it *teritur* ' is trodden ';

' sheepfold.'   [c] Apparently out of place ; but perhaps Varro had in mind a pronunciation with only a slight nasal sound, virtually *covallis*, *cf. contio* from *coventio* (*coventionid* occurs in an old inscription).   [d] This text is a desperate attempt to bring sense into the passage.   [e] *Theogony*, 123 ff.

§ 21. [a] From *tersā* ' dry '; *tritura* and *tribulum* are the only words in the section connected with *tero.*   [b] Page 67 Funaioli.

VARRO

teritur. Itaque tera in augurum libris scripta cum
R uno. Ab eo colonis locus com⟨m⟩unis qui prope
oppidum relinquitur teritorium, quod maxime teritur.
Hinc linteum quod teritur corpore extermentarium.
Hinc in messi tritura, quod tum frumentum teritur,
et tri*bul*um,[1] qui teritur. Hinc fines agrorum termini,
quod eae part*es*[2] propter limitare iter maxime teruntur; itaque hoc cum I[3] in Latio aliquot locis dicitur, ut apud Accium, non terminus, sed ter⟨i⟩men[4];
hoc Graeci quod τέρμονα. Pote vel illinc; Euander
enim, qui venit in Palatium, e Graecia Arcas.

22. Via[1] quidem iter, quod ea vehendo teritur, iter
item[2] actus, quod agendo teritur; etiam ambitus
⟨i⟩ter,[3] quod circumeundo teritur: nam ambitus
circuitus; ab eoque Duodecim Tabularum interpretes
' ambitus parietis ' circuitum esse describunt. Igitur
tera terra et ab eo poetae appellarunt summa terrae
quae sola teri possunt, ' sola terrae.'

§ 21. [1] *For* triuolum. [2] *For* partis. [3] *L. Sp., for* is.
[4] *L. Sp., for* termen.
§ 22. [1] *Lachmann, for* uias. [2] *A. Sp., for* iterum.
[3] *Groth, for* ter.

---

[c] No consonants were doubled in the writing of Latin until
about 200 B.C., and then not regularly for some decades;
before 200 B.C., *terra* was necessarily written *tera*. [d] Page
16 Regell. [e] Derivative of *terra*. [f] From *extergere* ' to
wipe off.' [g] From a different root *ter-* ' to cross over.'
[h] *Trag. Rom. Frag.,* page 262 Ribbeck[3]; *R.O.L.* ii. 599
Warmington. [i] See Livy, i. 5.
§ 22. [a] Of uncertain etymology, but not from *vehere*.
[b] *Amb-itus=circu-itus* in meaning; *-itus* and *iter* both from
the root in *ire* ' to go.' [c] The fundamental Roman laws,
traditionally drawn up by the Decemvirs of 451-450 B.C.
[d] Page 136 Schoell; page 113 Funaioli. [e] *Cf.* Ennius,
Ann. 455 Vahlen[2]; *R.O.L.* ii. 208-209 Warmington; page

therefore it is written *tera*[c] in the Books of the Augurs,[d] with one R. From this, the place which is left near a town as common property for the farmers, is the *territorium*[e] 'territory,' because it *teritur* 'is trodden' most. From this, the linen garment which *teritur* 'is rubbed' by the body, is an *extermentarium*.[f] From this, in the harvest, is the *tritura* 'threshing,' because then the grain *teritur* 'is rubbed out,' and the *tribulum* 'threshing-sledge,' with which it *teritur* 'is rubbed out.' From this the boundaries of the fields are called *termini*,[g] because those parts *teruntur* 'are trodden' most, on account of the boundary-lane. Therefore this word is pronounced with I in some places in Latium, not *terminus*, but *terimen*, and this form is found in Accius[h] : it is the same word which the Greeks call τέρμων. Perhaps the Latin word comes from the Greek ; for Evander, who came to the Palatine, was an Arcadian from Greece.[i]

22. A *via*[a] 'road' is indeed an *iter* 'way,' because it *teritur* 'is worn down' by *vehendo* 'carrying in wagons' ; an *actus* 'driving-passage' is likewise an *iter*, because it is worn down by *agendo* 'driving of cattle.' Moreover an *ambitus*[b] 'edge-road' is an *iter* 'way,' because it *teritur* 'is worn' by the going around : for an edge-road is a circuit ; from this the interpreters of the *Twelve Tables*[c] define the *ambitus* of the wall[d] as its circuit. Therefore *tera*, *terra* ; and from this the poets[e] have called the surface of the earth, which *sola* 'alone' can be trod, the *sola*[f] 'soil' of the earth.

---

75 Funaioli ; Lucretius, ii. 592 ; Catullus, 63. 7.   [f] Though *solus* 'lone' has a long vowel, and *solum* 'soil' has a short vowel ; but Varro normally disregards the differences of quantity.

VARRO

23. Terra, ut putant, eadem et humus ; ideo Ennium in terram cadentis dicere :

> Cubitis pinsibant humum ;

et quod terra sit humus, ideo is humatus mortuus, qui terra obrutus ; ab eo qui Romanus combustus est, ⟨si⟩[1] in sepulcrum[2] eius abiecta gleba non est aut si os exceptum est mortui ad familiam purgandam, donec in purgando humo[3] est opertum (ut pontifices dicunt, quod inhumatus sit), familia funesta manet. Et dicitur humilior, qui[4] ad humum[5] demissior, infimus humillimus, quod in mundo infima humus.

24. Humor hinc. Itaque ideo Lucilius :

> Terra abiit in nimbos humoremque.[1]

Pacuvius :

> Terra exhalat[2] auram atque auroram humidam ;

⟨humidam⟩[3] humectam ; hinc ager uliginosus humidissimus ; hinc udus uvidus ; hinc sudor et udor.

§ 23. [1] *Added by Turnebus.* [2] *For* sepulchrum. [3] *Aldus, for* homo. [4] *Mue., for* quae. [5] *After* humum *in F, is found the passage* ut Sabini § 32 *to* Septimontium § 41 *; Mue., following G. Buchanan and Turnebus, recognized the interchange of two leaves of the archetype of F and restored the text to its proper order.*

§ 24. [1] *Kent, for* imbremque, *for without* humor *or a derivative the citation is irrelevant.* [2] *Laetus, for* exalat. [3] *Added by Fay.*

---

§23. [a] *Trag. Rom. Frag.* 396 Ribbeck[3] ; *R.O.L.* i. 376-377 Warmington. [b] *Gleba* in a collective sense. [c] *Cf.* frag. 170 Rowoldt. [d] *Quod,* contracted for *quoad.*

§ 24. [a] *Humor,* properly *umor,* got its *h* by popular association with *humus,* with which it is not etymologically connected. [b] 1308 Marx ; five feet of a spondaic dactylic

23. *Humus* ' soil ' is, as they think, the same as *terra* ' earth '; therefore, they say, Ennius meant men falling to the earth when he said,[a]

> With their elbows the soil they were smiting.

And because *humus* ' soil ' is *terra* ' earth,' therefore he who is dead and covered with *terra* is *humatus* ' inhumed.' From this fact, if on the burial-mound of a Roman who has been burned on the pyre clods [b] are not thrown, or if a bone of the dead man has been kept out for the ceremony of purifying the household, the household remains in mourning; in the latter case, until in the purification the bone is covered with *humus* —as the pontifices say,[c] as long as [d] he is *in-humatus* ' not inhumed.' Also he is called *humilior* ' more humble,' who is more downcast toward the *humus*; the lowest is said to be *humillimus* ' most humble,' because the *humus* is the lowest thing in the world.

24. From this comes also *humor* [a] ' moisture.' So therefore Lucilius says [b]:

> Gone is the earth, disappeared into clouds and moisture.

Pacuvius says [c]:

> The land exhales a breeze and dawning damp;

humida,[d] the same as *humecta* ' damp.' From this, a marshy field is *humidissimus* ' most damp '; from this, *udus* [e] and *uvidus* ' damp '; from this, *sudor* [f] ' sweat ' and *udor* ' dampness.'

---

hexameter.   [c] *Trag. Rom. Frag.* 363 Ribbeck[3]; *R.O.L.* ii. 322-323 Warmington.   [d] From same base as *humor*; so also *humectus*.   [e] Syncopated form of *uvidus*, which, with its abstract substantive *udor*, contains the base of *humor* in a simpler form (without the *m*).   [f] Akin to English *sweat*, and not connected with the other Latin words here discussed.

VARRO

25. Is si quamvis deorsum in terra, unde sumi[1]
pote, puteus ; nisi potius quod *Aeolis* dicebant ut
πύταμον sic πύτεον a potu,[2] non ut nunc φρέ⟨αρ⟩.[3] A
puteis oppidum ut Puteoli, quod incircum eum locum
aquae frigidae et caldae multae, nisi a putore potius,
quod putidus odoribus saepe ex sulphure et alumine.
Extra oppida a puteis puticuli, quod ibi in puteis
obruebantur homines, nisi potius, ut Aelius scribit,
puticuli[4] quod putescebant ibi cadavera proiecta, qui
locus publicus ultra Esquilias.[5] Itaque eum Afranius
puti*l*ucos[6] in Togata appellat, quod inde suspiciunt
per p*u*teos[7] lumen.
26. Lacus lacuna magna, ubi aqua contineri potest.
Palus paululum aquae in altitudinem et palam latius
diffusae. Stagnum a Graeco, quod *ü*[1] στεγνόν quod
non habet rimam.[2] Hinc ad villas rutunda[3] stagna,
quod rutundum facillime continet, anguli maxime
laborant.

§ 25. [1] *For* summi. [2] *Buttmann, for* potamon sic po
tura potu. [3] *Victorius, for* φρε. [4] *Mue., for* puticulae.
[5] *For* exquilias. [6] *Scaliger, for* cuticulos. [7] *Canal, for*
perpetuos.
§ 26. [1] *For* ll. [2] *Scaliger, for* nomen habet primam.
[3] *B, for* rutundas.

---

§ 25. [a] Or ' pit ' ; derivative of root in *putare* ' to cut,
think,' *cf. amputare* ' to cut off.' [b] *Aeolis*, nom. pl. = Greek
Αἰολεῖς. [c] This and πύτεος are unknown in the extant
remains of Aeolic Greek, but a number of Aeolic words show
the change : ἄπυ for ἀπό, ὑμοίως for ὁμοίως. [d] The modern
Pozzuoli, on the Bay of Naples, in a locality characterized
by volcanic springs and exhalations ; Varro's derivation is
correct. [e] Page 65 Funaioli. [f] The Roman ' potters'
field,' for the poor and the slaves. [g] *Com. Rom. Frag.*
430 Ribbeck[3] ; with a jesting transposition of the consonants.
Cf. for a similar effect ' pit-lets ' and ' pit-lights.' The
description suggests that they were constructed like the
Catacombs.

25. If this moisture is in the ground no matter how far down, in a place from which it *pote* ' can ' be taken, it is a *puteus* ' well ' [a]; unless rather because the Aeolians [b] used to say, like πύταμος [c] for ποταμός ' river,' so also πύτεος ' well ' for ποτέος ' drinkable,' from *potus* ' act of drinking,' and not φρέαρ ' well ' as they do now.   From *putei* ' wells ' comes the town-name, such as *Puteoli*,[d] because around this place there are many hot and cold spring-waters ; unless rather from *putor* ' stench,' because the place is often *putidus* ' stinking ' with smells of sulphur and alum.   Outside the towns there are *puticuli* ' little pits,' named from *putei* ' pits,' because there the people used to be buried in *putei* ' pits ' ; unless rather, as Aelius [e] writes, the *puticuli* are so called because the corpses which had been thrown out *putescebant* ' used to rot ' there, in the public burial-place [f] which is beyond the Esquiline.   This place Afranius [g] in a comedy of Roman life calls the *Putiluci* ' pit-lights,' for the reason that from it they look up through *putei* ' pits ' to the *lumen* ' light.'

26. A *lacus* ' lake ' is a large *lacuna* [a] ' hollow,' where water can be confined.   A *palus* [b] ' swamp ' is a *paululum* ' small amount ' of water as to depth, but spread quite widely *palam* ' in plain sight.'   A *stagnum* [c] ' pool ' is from Greek, because they gave the name στεγνός [d] ' waterproof ' to that which has no fissure.   From this, at farmhouses the *stagna* ' pools ' are round, because a round shape most easily holds water in, but corners are extremely troublesome.

---

§ 26.   [a] *Lacuna* is a derivative of *lacus*.   [b] *Palus, paululum, palam* are all etymologically distinct.   [c] Properly, a pool without an outlet ; perhaps akin to Greek σταγών ' drop (of liquid).'   [d] Original meaning, ' covered.'

VARRO

27. Fluvius, quod fluit, item flumen : a quo lege praediorum urbanorum scribitur[1] :

> Stillicidia fluminaque[2] ut⟨i nunc, ut⟩ ita[3] cadant
> fluantque ;

inter haec hoc inter⟨est⟩, quod stillicidium eo quod stillatim cad*it*,[4] flumen quod fluit continue.

28. Amnis id flumen quod circuit aliquod : nam ab ambitu amnis. Ab hoc qui circum Aternum[1] habitant, Amiternini appellati. Ab eo qui populum candidatus circum i*t*,[2] ambit, et qui aliter facit, indagabili ex ambitu causam dicit. Itaque Tiberis amnis, quod ambit Martium Campum et urbem ; oppidum Interamna dictum, quod inter amnis est constitutum ; item Antemnae, quod ante amnis, qu⟨a⟩ An*io*[3] influit in Tiberim, quod bello male acceptum consenuit.

29. Tiberis quod caput extra Latium, si inde nomen quoque exfluit in linguam nostram, nihil ⟨ad⟩[1] ἐτυμολόγον Latinum, ut, quod oritur ex Samnio,

§ 27. [1] *For* scribitur scribitur. [2] *For* flumina quae. [3] *L. Sp., after Gothofredus, for* ut ita. [4] *a, Pape, for* cadet.

§ 28. [1] *Aug., with B, for* alterunum. [2] *For* id. [3] *Canal, for* quanto.

§ 29. [1] *Added by Thiersch.*

---

§ 27. [a] *Cf. Digest.* viii. 2. 17. [b] That is, rain-waters dripping from roofs and streams resulting from rain shall in city properties not be diverted from their present courses. Such supplies of water were in early days a real asset.

§ 28. [a] Probably to be associated with English *Avon* (from Celtic word for ' river '), and not with *ambire* ' to go around.' [b] Good etymology ; Amiternum was an old city in the Sabine country, on the Aternus River ; with *ambi-* ' around ' in the form *am-*, as in *amicire* ' to place (a garment) around.'

27. *Fluvius* ' river ' is so named because it *fluit* ' flows,' and likewise *flumen* ' river ' : from which is written, according to the law of city estates,[a]

Stillicidia ' rain-waters' and *flumina* ' rivers' shall be allowed to fall and to flow without interference.[b]

Between these there is this difference, that *stillicidium* ' rain-water ' is so named because it *cadit* ' falls ' *stillatim* ' drop by drop,' and *flumen* ' river ' because it *fluit* ' flows ' uninterruptedly.

28. An *amnis* [a] is that river which goes around something ; for *amnis* is named from *ambitus* ' circuit.' From this, those who dwell around the Aternus are called *Amiternini* ' men of Amiternum.' [b] From this, he who *circum it* ' goes around ' the people as a candidate, *ambit* ' canvasses,' and he who does otherwise than he should, pleads his case in court as a result of his investigable *ambitus* ' canvassing.' [c] Therefore the Tiber is called an *amnis*, because it *ambit* ' goes around ' the Campus Martius and the City [d] ; the town Interamna [e] gets its name from its position *inter amnis* ' between rivers ' ; likewise Antemnae, because it lies *ante amnis* ' in front of the rivers,' where the Anio flows into the Tiber—a town which suffered in war and wasted away until it perished.

29. The Tiber, because its source is outside Latium, if the name as well flows forth from there into our language, does not concern the Latin etymologist ; just as the Volturnus,[a] because it starts from

[c] That is, for corrupt electioneering methods.　　[d] The Tiber swings to the west at Rome, forming a virtual semicircle.
[e] A city in Umbria, almost encircled by the river Nar.
　§ 29.　[a] Adjective from *voltur* ' vulture '; there was a Mt. Voltur farther south, on the boundary between Samnium and Apulia.

Volturnus nihil ad Latinam linguam : at² quod proximum oppidum ab eo secundum mare Volturnum, ad nos, iam³ Latinum vocabulum, ut Tiberinus no⟨me⟩n.⁴ Et colonia enim nostra Volturnum⁵ et deus Tiberinus.

30. Sed de Tiberis nomine anceps historia. Nam et suum Etruria et Latium suum esse credit, quod fuerunt qui ab Thebri vicino regulo Veientum¹ dixerint appellatum,² primo Thebrim. Sunt qui Tiberim priscum nomen Latinum Albulam vocitatum litteris tradiderint, posterius propter Tiberinum regem Latinorum mutatum, quod ibi interierit : nam hoc eius ut tradunt sepulcrum.³

V. 31. Ut omnis natura in caelum et terram divisa est, sic caeli regionibus terra in Asiam et Europam. Asia enim iacet ad meridiem et austrum, Europa ad septemtriones et aquilonem. Asia dicta ab nympha, a qua et Iapeto traditur Prometheus. Europa ab Europa Agenoris, quam ex *Ph*⟨o⟩enice¹ Manlius

² *For* ad.   ³ *After* iam, *A. Sp. deleted* ad.   ⁴ *A. Sp., for* non.   ⁵ *Aug., with* B, *for* uolturnus.
   § 30.   ¹ *Aug., for* uenientum.   ² *For* appellatam.   ³ *For* sepulchrum.
   § 31.   ¹ *For* fenice.

ᵇ The god of the river Tiber.
   § 30.   ᵃ No probable etymology has been proposed.   ᵇ Veii was one of the twelve cities of Etruria, about twelve miles north of Rome ; it was taken and destroyed by the Romans under Camillus in 396 B.C.   ᶜ Page 117 Funaioli.   ᵈ 'Whitish,' from *albus* ' white ' ; or perhaps more probably ' the mountain stream,' containing a pre-Italic word seen in *Alpes* ' Alps.'   ᵉ King of Alba Longa, ninth in descent from Aeneas, and great-grandfather of Numitor and Amulius; he lost his life in crossing the river (**Livy**, i. 3).

Samnium, has nothing to do with the Latin language; but because the nearest town to it along the sea is Volturnum, it has come to us and is now a Latin name, as also the name Tiberinus. For we have both a colony named Volturnum and a god named Tiberinus.[b]

30. But about the name of the Tiber [a] there are two accounts. For Etruria believes it is hers, and so does Latium, because there have been those who said that at first, from Thebris, the near-by chieftain of the Veians,[b] it was called the Thebris. There are also those who in their writings [c] have handed down the story that the Tiber was called Albula [d] as its early Latin name, and that later it was changed on account of Tiberinus [e] king of the Latins, because he died there ; for, as they relate, it was his burial-place.

V. 31. As all *natura* is divided into sky and earth, so with reference to the regions of the sky the earth is divided into Asia and Europe. For Asia is that part which lies toward the noonday sun and the south wind, Europe that which lies toward the Wain [a] and the north wind.[b] Asia was named from the nymph [c] who, according to tradition, bore Prometheus to Iapetus. Europe was named from Europa [d] the daughter of Agenor, who, Manlius [e] writes, was carried off from Phoenicia by the Bull ; a remarkable

§ 31. [a] In America usually called the Dipper. [b] The points of the compass are here, as often with the ancients, somewhat distorted. [c] Concerning Asia, see Hesiod, *Theogony*, 359 ; and *cf.* Herodotus, iv. 45. [d] Concerning Europa, see Herodotus, iv. 45 ; Horace, *Odes*, iii. 27. 25-76 ; Ovid, *Metamorphoses*, ii. 833-875. [e] Or Mallius, or Manilius ; the names are often confused in the manuscripts. He cannot be identified. See *Frag. Poet. Rom.*, page 284 Baehrens, and *Gram. Rom. Frag.* 85 Funaioli.

scribit taurum exportasse, quorum egregiam imaginem ex aere Pyt*h*agoras Tarenti.

32. Europae loca multae incolunt nationes. Ea fere nominata aut translaticio nomine ab hominibus[1] ut Sabini et Lucani, aut declinato ab hominibus, ut Apulia et Latium, ⟨aut⟩[2] utrumque, ut Etruria et Tusci.[3] Qua regnum fuit Latini, universus ager dictus Latius, particulatim oppidis cognominatus, ut a Pr*a*eneste Praenestinus, ab Aricia Aricinus.

33. Ut nostri augures publici disserunt, agrorum sunt genera quinque : Romanus, Gabinus, peregrinus, hosticus, incertus. Romanus dictus unde Roma ab Rom⟨ul⟩o[1] ; Gabinus ab oppido Gabi⟨i⟩s ; peregrinus ager pacatus, qui extra Romanum et Gabinum, quod uno modo in his serv⟨a⟩ntur[2] auspicia ; dictus peregrinus a pergendo, id est a progrediendo : eo enim[3] ex agro Romano primum progrediebantur : quocirca Gabinus quo*que*[4] peregrinus, sed quo*d*[5] auspicia habet[6] singularia, ab reliquo discretus ;

---

§ 32.   [1] *Cf.* § 23, *crit. note* 5.   [2] *Added by Aug.*
[3] *Scaliger, for* Tuscia.

§ 33.   [1] *Rhol., for* Romo ; *cf.* viii. 80.   [2] *Laetus, for* seruntur.   [3] *For* eo quod enim.   [4] *Scaliger, for* quo siue.   [5] *Turnebus, for* quos.   [6] *Turnebus, for* habent.

---

[f] Pythagoras of Rhegium, distinguished for his statues of athletes, flourished in the middle of the fifth century B.C.

§ 32.   [a] Such names as *Sabini, Lucani, Tusci* meant originally the people and not the countries.

§ 33.   [a] Page 19 Regell.   [b] Or possibly Romus (*Romo* F); for Festus, 266 b 23-27 M., states that according to Antigonus, an Alexandrian writer, Rome received its name from Rhomus, a son of Jupiter, who founded a city on the Palatine.

bronze group of the two was made by Pythagoras [f] at Tarentum.

32. The various localities of Europe are inhabited by many different nations. They are in general denominated by names transferred from the men, like *Sabini* ' the Sabine country,' and *Lucani* ' the country of the Lucanians,' or derived from the names of the men, like Apulia and Latium, or both, like Etruria and *Tusci.*[a] Where Latinus once had his kingdom, the field-lands as a whole are called Latian ; but when taken piecemeal, they are named after the towns, as Praenestine from Praeneste, and Arician from Aricia.

33. As our State Augurs set forth,[a] there are five kinds of fields : Roman, Gabine, peregrine, hostic, uncertain. ' Roman ' field-land is so called from Romulus,[b] from whom Rome got its name. ' Gabine ' is named from the town Gabii.[c] The ' peregrine ' is field-land won in war and reduced to peace, which is apart from the Roman and the Gabine, because in these latter the auspices are observed in one uniform manner : ' peregrine '[d] is named from *pergere* ' to go ahead,' that is, from *progredi* ' to advance '; for into it their first advance was made out of the Roman field-land. By the same reasoning, the Gabine also is peregrine, but because it has auspices of its own special sort it is held separate from the rest.

[c] An ancient Latin city midway between Rome and Praeneste, where Sextus Tarquinius took refuge after his expulsion from Rome. It fought against Rome at Lake Regillus, and thereafter declined into poverty and was almost deserted, though it was revived by the emperors of the first two Christian centuries. [d] Derivative of *peregri* ' abroad, away from home ; to, from, or in a foreign land,' which is either prep. *per* ' through ' + loc. *agri*, or a loc. of a compound *pero-agro-* ' distant field-land.'

VARRO

hosticus dictus ab hostibus ; incertus is, qui de his
quattuor qui sit ignoratur.

VI. *34.* Ager dictus in quam terram quid agebant,
et unde quid agebant fructus causa ; ali⟨i⟩, quod[1] id
Graeci dicunt ἀγρό⟨ν⟩. Ut ager quo[2] agi poterat,
sic qua agi actus. Eius finis minimus constitutus in
latitudinem pedes quattuor (fortasse an ab eo quattuor, quod ea quadrupes agitur) ; in longitudinem
pedes centum viginti ; in quadratum actum et latum
et longum esset centum viginti. Multa antiqui duo-
denario numero finierunt ut duodecim decuriis actum.

35. Iugerum dictum iunctis duobus actibus quad-
ratis. Centuria prim⟨um⟩ a[1] centum iugeribus dicta,
post duplicata retinuit nomen, ut tribus a p⟨ar⟩tibus[2]
⟨populi tripartito divisi dictae nunc⟩[3] multiplicatae
idem tenent nomen. Ut qua[4] agebant actus, sic qua
vehebant, viae[5] dictae ; quo[6] fructus convehebant,
villae. Qua ibant, ab itu[7] iter appellarunt ; qua id
anguste, semita, ut semiter dictum.

§ 34. [1] *L. Sp., for* aliquod. [2] *Turnebus, for* quod.
§ 35. [1] *L. Sp., for* prima. [2] *GS., for* actibus. [3] *Added
by GS., cf. Columella,* v. 1. 7. [4] *Aug., for* quo. [5] *Laetus,
for* actus viae. [6] *Aldus, for* quod. [7] *Laetus, for* habitu.

§ 34. [a] Connexion of *ager* with *agere* doubtful, for the
original meaning was wild land, not subjected to human use ;
but this had been replaced even in early Latin by the meaning
of tilled land or land used for grazing animals. The equation
with the Greek word is correct. [b] Page 114 Funaioli.
§ 35. [a] About two-thirds of an acre. [b] Abstract noun
from *centum* ' hundred ' ; applied chiefly to a company of
soldiers. [c] From *tri-bhu-s* ' being three ' ; the final number of tribes was thirty-five. [d] Not from *vehere.* [e] From
32

' Hostic ' is named from the *hostes* ' enemies.' ' Uncertain ' field-land is that of which it is not known to which of these four classes it belongs.

VI. 34. *Ager* ' field ' is the name given to land into which they used *agere* ' to drive ' something, or from which they used to drive something,[a] for the sake of the produce ; but others say [b] that it is because the Greeks call it ἀγρός. As an *ager* ' field ' is that to which driving can be done, so that whereby driving can be done is an *actus* ' driveway.' Its least limit is set at four feet in width—four perhaps from the fact that by it a four-footed animal is driven—and one hundred and twenty feet in length. For a square actus, both in breadth and in length, the limit would be one hundred and twenty feet. There are many things which the ancients delimited with a multiple of twelve, like the *actus* of twelve ten-foot measures.

35. A *iugerum* [a] is the name given to two square *actus*, *iuncti* ' joined ' together. A *centuria* [b] ' century ' was named originally from *centum* ' one hundred ' *iugera*, and later, when doubled, kept its name, just as the *tribus* [c] ' tribes,' which got their name from the three parts into which the people were divided, still keep the same name though their number has been multiplied. As where they *agebant* ' drove ' were *actus* ' driveways,' so where they *vehebant* ' transported ' were *viae* [d] ' highways ' ; whither they *convehebant* ' transported ' their produce were *villae* [e] ' farmhouses.' Whereby they went, they called an *iter* ' road ' from *itus* ' going ' ; where the going was narrow, was a *semita* [f] ' by-path,' as though it were called a *semiter* ' half-road.'

vicus ' dwelling-place.'   [f] From *sed* ' apart ' + *mita*, from *meare* ' to go.'

VARRO

36. Ager cultus ab eo quod ibi cum terra semina
coalescebant, et *u*bi n⟨on⟩ consitus[1] incultus. Quod
primum ex agro plano fructus capiebant, campus
dictus ; posteaquam proxuma superiora loca colere
c⟨o⟩eperunt, a colendo colles appellarunt; quos
agros non colebant propter silvas aut id genus, ubi
pecus possit pasci, et possidebant, ab usu s⟨al⟩vo[2]
saltus nominarunt. Haec etiam Graeci νέμη,[3] nostri
nemora.

37. Ager quod videbatur pec*u*dum[1] ac pecuniae
esse fundamentum, fundus dictus, aut quod fundit
quotquot annis multa. Vineta ac vineae a vite multa.
Vitis a vino, id a vi ; hinc vindemia, quod est vinidemia aut vitidemia. Seges ab satu, id est semine.
Semen, quod non plane id quod inde ; hinc seminaria,
sementes,[2] item alia. Quod segetes ferunt, fruges,

---

§ 36.   [1] *Wissowa, for* ab inconsitus.   [2] *Lachmann, for*
suo.   [3] *Lachmann, for* NhMh.
§ 37.   [1] *For* pecodum.   [2] *Laetus, for* sementem.

---

§ 36.   [a] Participle of *colere* ' to till, cultivate.'   [b] Not from
capere.   [c] Not from *colere*.   [d] A ' leap,' from *salire* ' to
leap ' ; then a ' narrow passage (which can be leapt across),'
' defile ' ; then a ' valley of mixed woods and pasture-land.'
[e] Like *saltus,* a mixture of woods and pasture-land, but not
necessarily in a valley between hills or mountains.
§ 37.   [a] Derivative of *fundus* ; *fundere* is unrelated.
[b] *Vinum, vinetum, vinea, vin-demia* (*demere* ' to take off ') go
together ; *vitis* and *vis* are unrelated.   [c] *Satus, semen,*

36. *Ager cultus* [a] 'cultivated field-land' is so named from the fact that there the seeds *coalescebant* 'united' with the land, and where it is not *consitus* 'sown' it is called *incultus* 'uncultivated.' Because they first used *capere* 'to take' the products from the level field-land, it was called *campus* [b] 'plain'; after they began to till the adjacent higher places, they called them *colles* [c] 'hills' from *colere* 'to till.' The fields which they did not till on account of woods or that kind where flocks can be grazed, but still they took them for private use, they called *saltus* [d] 'woodland-pastures' from the fact that their use was *salvus* 'saved.' These moreover the Greeks call νέμη 'glades' and we call *nemora* [e] 'groves.'

37. Field-land, because it seemed to be the *fundamentum* [a] 'foundation' of animal flocks and of money, was called *fundus* 'estate,' or else because it *fundit* 'pours out' many things every year. *Vineta* and *vineae* 'vineyards,' from the many *vites* 'grape-vines.' *Vitis* [b] 'grapevine' from *vinum* 'wine,' this from *vis* 'strength'; from this, *vindemia* 'vintage,' because it is *vinidemia* 'wine-removal' or *vitidemia* 'vine-removal.' *Seges* [c] 'standing grain' from *satus* 'sowing,' that is, *semen* 'seed.' *Semen* [d] 'seed,' because it is not completely that which comes from it; from this, *seminaria* 'nursery-gardens,' *sementes* 'sowings,' and likewise other words. What the *segetes* 'fields of grain' *ferunt* 'bear,' are *fruges* [e] 'field-produce';

---

seminaria, sementes go together, but *seges* probably is not related to them.   [d] Varro takes *semen* as from *semis* 'half,' because the *semen* is less in quantity than that which grows from it; an incorrect etymology.   [e] *Fruges, frui, fructus* belong together, but *ferre* is unrelated; Varro takes *fruges* from *ferre*, *frui* from *fruges*, *fructus* from *frui*.

a fruendo fructus, a spe spicae, ubi et culmi, quod in summo campo nascuntur et sum⟨m⟩um culmen.

38. Ubi frumenta secta, ut terantur, arescunt,[1] area. Propter horum similitudinem in urbe loca pura areae ; a quo potest etiam ara deum, quod pura, nisi potius ab ardore, ad quem ut sit fit ara ; a quo ipsa area non abest, quod qui arefacit ardor est solis.

39. Ager restibilis, qui restituitur ac reseritur quotquot annis ; contra qui intermittitur, a novando novalis ager. Arvus et arationes ab arando ; ab eo quod aratri vomer sustulit, sulcus[1]; quo ea terra iacta, id est proiecta, porca.

40. Prata dicta ab eo, quod sine opere parata. Quod in agris quotquot annis rursum[1] facienda eadem, ut rursum capias fructus, appellata rura. Dividi t⟨am⟩en esse ius[2] scribit Sulpicius plebei rura largiter ad ⟨ad⟩oream.[3] Praedia dicta, item ut praedes, a

§ 38.   [1] *L. Sp.*, *for* et arescant.
§ 39.   [1] *Laetus*, *for* sulcos.
§ 40.   [1] *For* rursum rursum.   [2] *Lachmann*, *for* dividit in eos eius.   [3] *Fay*, *for* ad aream.

---

[1] *Spes* and *spica* are unrelated ; Varro was misled by the rustic pronunciation *speca*, mentioned by him in *De Re Rustica*, i. 48. 2.   [9] *Culmus* and *culmen* are unrelated.

§ 38.   [a] *Arescunt, area, ara, ardor, arefacit* belong together.   [b] Unoccupied by buildings or the like ; in the country, free also of bushes and trees.   [c] Applied in the city to building lots, courtyards, and free spaces before a temple or other building, and around an altar.

§ 39.   [a] That is, *re + stabilis* ' again standing firm ' ; while *restituere* is *re + statuere*, ultimately to same root as *stabilis*.   [b] Properly from a root meaning ' draw, pull.'   [c] Not connected with *proiecta*, but with English *furrow*.

§ 40.   [a] Incorrect etymologies.   [b] i. 241 Bremer; perhaps Servius Sulpicius Rufus, a legal authority, contemporary with Cicero.   [c] *Praedium* is a derivative of *praes* (pl.

from *frui* ' to enjoy ' comes *fructus* ' fruits ' ; from *spes* [f] ' hope ' comes *spicae* ' ears of grain,' where are also the *culmi* [g] ' grain-stalks,' because they grow on the top of the plain, and a top is a *culmen.*

38. Where the cut grain-sheaves *arescunt* [a] ' dry out ' for threshing, is an *area* ' threshing-floor.' On account of the likeness to these, clean places [b] in the city are called *areae* ; from which may be also the Gods' *ara* ' altar,' because it is clean [c]—unless rather from *ardor* ' fire ' ; for the intention of using it for an *ardor* makes it an *ara* ; and from this the *area* itself is not far away, because it is the *ardor* of the sun which *arefacit* ' does the drying.'

39. *Ager restibilis* [a] ' land that withstands use ' is that which *restituitur* ' is restored ' and replanted yearly ; on the other hand, that which receives an intermission is called *novalis ager* ' renewable field-land,' from *novare* ' to renew.' *Arvus* ' ploughable ' and *arationes* ' ploughings,' from *arare* ' to plough '; from this, what the ploughshare *sustulit* ' has removed ' is a *sulcus* [b] ' furrow '; whither that earth is thrown, that is, *proiecta* ' thrown forth,' is the *porca* [c] ' ridge.'

40. *Prata* [a] ' meadows ' are named from this, that they are *parata* ' prepared ' without labour. *Rura* [a] ' country-lands ' are so called because in the fields the same operations must be done every year *rursum* ' again,' that you may again get their fruits. Sulpicius [b] writes, however, that it is a just right for the country-lands of the populace to be divided for lavish distribution as bonus to discharged soldiers. *Praedia* [c] ' estates ' are named, as also *praedes* ' bondsmen,' *praedes*), a compound of *prae* + *vas* ' guarantor '; *praestare* has the same prefix, but a different root.

praestando, quod ea pignore data publice mancup*is*[4] fidem praestent.

VII. 41. Ubi nunc est Roma, Septimontium[1] nominatum ab tot montibus quos postea urbs muris comprehendit ; e quis Capitolinum dictum, quod hic, cum fundamenta foderentur aedis Iovis, caput huma-num dicitur inventum. Hic[2] mons ante Tarpeius dictus a virgine Vestale Tarpcia, quae ibi ab Sa*b*inis necata armis et sepulta : cuius nominis monimentum relictum, quod etiam nunc eius rupes Tarpeium appellatur saxum.

42. Hunc antea montem Saturnium appellatum prodiderunt et ab eo Lat*i*⟨um⟩[1] Saturniam terram, ut etiam Ennius appellat. Antiquum oppidum in hoc fuisse Saturnia⟨m⟩[2] scribitur. Eius vestigia etiam nunc manent tria, quod Saturni fanum in faucibus, quod Saturnia Porta quam Iunius scribit ibi, quam nunc vocant Pandanam, quod post aedem Saturni in aedificiorum legibus privatis parietes postici " muri ⟨Saturnii⟩ "[3] sunt scripti.

43. Aventinum aliquot de causis dicunt. Naevius

---

[4] *Gesner, for* mancupes.

§ 41. [1] *Turnebus, for* septem montium ; *cf. also* § 23, *crit. note* 5. [2] *For* hinc.

§ 42. [1] *Ten Brink, for* late. [2] *Aug., with B, for* hac fuisse saturnia. [3] *Added by ten Brink ; Frag. Cass. has* murisssunt.

---

§ 41. [a] Somehow a derivative of *caput* ; but the story of finding a head was invented to explain the name.

§ 42. [a] Ennius, *Ann.* 25 Vahlen[2] ; *R.O.L.* i. 12-13 Warmington ; the metre demands the nominative case. GS. think that Ennius may have written *Saturnia tellus,* as Vergil does in *Aen.* viii. 329 ; but Ovid, *Fasti,* v. 625,

from *praestare* ' to offer as security,' because these, when given as pledge to the official authorities, *praestent* ' guarantee ' the good faith of the party in the case.

VII. 41. Where Rome now is, was called the Septimontium from the same number of hills which the City afterwards embraced within its walls ; of which the Capitoline *a* got its name because here, it is said, when the foundations of the temple of Jupiter were being dug, a human *caput* ' head ' was found. This hill was previously called the Tarpeian, from the Vestal Virgin Tarpeia, who was there killed by the Sabines with their shields and buried ; of her name a reminder is left, that even now its cliff is called the Tarpeian Rock.

42. This hill was previously called the Saturnian Hill, we are informed by the writers, and from this Latium has been called the Saturnian Land, as in fact Ennius *a* calls it. It is recorded that on this hill was an old town, named Saturnia. Even now there remain three evidences of it : that there is a temple of Saturn by the passage leading to the hill ; that there is a Saturnian gate which Junius writes *b* of as there, which they now call Pandana *c* ; that behind the temple of Saturn, in the laws for the buildings of private persons, the back walls of the houses are mentioned as " Saturnian walls." *d*

43. The name of the Aventine is referred to

has *Saturnia terra.*   *b* i. 38 Bremer.   *c* So called *quod semper pateret* (Festus, 220. 17 M.), ' because it was always open ' (*cf. pandere* ' to throw open ').   *d* The third point becomes clear only by ten Brink's insertion of *Saturnii* ; the use of *muri* ' city-walls ' for *parietes* ' building-walls ' shows that the walls at this place had once formed part of a set of city-walls.

ab avibus, quod eo se ab Tiberi ferrent aves, alii ab
rege Aventino Albano, quod ⟨ibi⟩[1] sit sepultus,
alii A⟨d⟩ventinum[2] ab adventu hominum, quod
co⟨m⟩mune Latinorum ibi Dianae templum sit constitutum. Ego maxime puto, quod ab advectu :
nam olim paludibus mons erat ab reliquis disclusus.
Itaque eo ex urbe advehebantur ratibus, cuius vestigia, quod ea qua tum ⟨advectum⟩[3] dicitur Velabrum, et unde escendebant ad ⟨in⟩fimam[4] Novam
Viam locus sacellum ⟨Ve⟩labrum.[5]

44. Velabrum a vehendo. Velaturam facere
etiam nunc dicuntur qui id mercede faciunt. Merces
(dicitur a merendo et *a*ere) huic vecturae qui ratibus
transibant quadrans. Ab eo Lucilius scripsit :

Quadrantis ratiti.

VIII. 45. Reliqua urbis loca olim discreta, cum
Argeorum sacraria septem et viginti in ⟨quattuor⟩

§ 43.   [1] *Added by Laetus.*   [2] *Mue., with* M, *for* auen-
tinum.   [3] *Added by* L. Sp.   [4] *Turnebus, for* fimam.
[5] *Mue., for* labrum.

---

§ 43.   [a] *Page* 115 Funaioli. Etymologies of place-names
are particularly treacherous ; none of those given here explains *Aventinus.* Varro elsewhere (*de gente populi Romani,*
quoted by Servius *in Aen.* vii. 657) says that some Sabines
established here by Romulus called it *Aventinus* from the
Avens, a river of the district from which they had come.
[b] *Frag. Poet. Rom.* 27 Baehrens ; *R.O.L.* ii. 56-57 Warmington.   [c] The spelling with *d* is required by the sense.
[d] Varro says that a ferry-raft was called a *velabrum,* and
that this name was transferred to the passage on which the
rafts had plied, when it was filled in and had become a street;
but that there survived a chapel in honour of the ferry-rafts.
§ 44.   [a] Correct etymology.   [b] Incorrect etymology.

several origins.[a] Naevius [b] says that it is from the
aves ' birds,' because the birds went thither from
the Tiber ; others, that it is from King Aventinus
the Alban, because he is buried there ; others that it
is the Adventine [c] Hill, from the *adventus* ' coming ' of
people, because there a temple of Diana was established in which all the Latins had rights in common.
I am decidedly of the opinion, that it is from *advectus*
' transport by water ' ; for of old the hill was cut off
from everything else by swampy pools and streams.
Therefore they *advehebantur* ' were conveyed ' thither
by rafts ; and traces of this survive, in that the way
by which they were then transported is now called
Velabrum ' ferry,' and the place from which they
landed at the bottom of New Street is a chapel of the
Velabra.[d]

44. Velabrum [a] is from *vehere* ' to convey.'   Even
now, those persons are said to do *velatura* ' ferrying,'
who do this for pay.   The *merces* [b] ' pay ' (so called
from *merere* ' to earn ' and *aes* ' copper money ') for
this ferrying of those who crossed by rafts was a
farthing.   From this Lucilius wrote [c] :

Of a raft-markèd farthing.[d]

VIII. 45.   The remaining localities of the City
were long ago divided off, when the twenty-seven [a]

[c] 1272 Marx.   [d] The *quadrans* or fourth of an *as* was
marked with the figure of a raft.

§ 45.   [a] It would seem simpler if the shrines numbered
twenty-four, six in each of the four sections of Rome.   But
both here and in vii. 44 the number is given as twenty-seven.
It is hardly likely that in both places XXUII (=XXVII) has
been miswritten for XXIIII ; yet this supposition must be
made by those who think that the correct number is twenty-
four.

partis[1] urbi⟨s⟩[2] sunt disposita. Argeos dictos putant a principibus, qui cum *Hercule* Argivo venerunt Romam et in Saturnia subsederunt. E quis prima scripta est regio Suburana,[3] secunda Esquilina, tertia Collina, quarta Palatina.

46. In Suburanae[1] regionis parte princeps est *C*aelius mons a *C*aele Vibenna,[2] Tusco, duce nobili, qui cum sua manu dicitur Romulo venisse auxilio contra *T*atium[3] regem. Hinc post *C*aelis[4] obitum, quod nimis munita loca tenerent neque sine suspicione essent, deducti dicuntur in planum. Ab eis dictus Vicus Tuscus, et ideo ibi Vortumnum stare, quod is deus Etruriae princeps ; de Caelianis qui a suspicione liberi essent, traductos in eum locum qui vocatur Caeliolum.

47. Cum Caelio[1] coniunctum Carinae et inter eas quem locum Caer⟨i⟩olensem[2] appellatum apparet,

§ 45. [1] *L. Sp.*, *for* sacraria in septem et uiginti partis. [2] *Laetus, for* urbi. [3] *Aug., for* suburbana F^1, subura F^2.

§ 46. [1] *Aug., with B, for* suburbanae. [2] *Frag. Cass., for* uibenno ; *cf. Tacitus, Ann.* iv. 65. [3] *Puccius, with Servius in Aen.* v. 560, *for* latinum. [4] Coelis *Aug., for* celii.

§ 47. [1] *Laetus, for* celion. [2] *Kent ;* Caeliolensem *ten Brink (and similarly through the section) ; for* ceroniensem.

---

[b] Puppets or dolls made of rushes, thrown into the Tiber from the *Pons Sublicius* every year on May 14, as a sacrifice of purification ; the distribution of the shrines from which they were brought was to enable them to take up the pollution of the entire city. Possibly the dolls were a substitute for human victims. The name *Argei* perhaps indicates that the ceremony was brought from Greece.

§ 46. [a] Comparison with § 47, § 50, § 52, § 54, shows that shrines of the Argei *b* were distributed among the four sections of the City. The Argei, they think, were named from the chieftains who came to Rome with Hercules the Argive, and settled down in Saturnia. Of these sections, the first is recorded as the Suburan region, the second the Esquiline, the third the Colline, the fourth the Palatine.

46. In the section of the Suburan region, the first shrine *a* is located on the Caelian Hill, named from Caeles Vibenna, a Tuscan leader of distinction, who is said to have come with his followers to help Romulus against King Tatius. From this hill the followers of Caeles are said, after his death, to have been brought down into the level ground, because they were in possession of a location which was too strongly fortified and their loyalty was somewhat under suspicion. From them was named the *Vicus Tuscus* ' Tuscan Row,' and therefore, they say, the statue of Vertumnus stands there, because he is the chief god of Etruria ; but those of the Caelians who were free from suspicion were removed to that place which is called *Caeliolum* ' the little Caelian.' *b*

47. Joined to the Caelian is *Carinae* ' the Keels ' ; and between them is the place which is called *Caerio-*

the *sacra Argeorum* (§ 50) used *princeps*, *terticeps*, etc., to designate numerically the shrines in each *pars* ; and that the place-name was set in the nominative alongside the neuter numeral : therefore " the first is the Caelian Hill " means that the first shrine is located on that hill. *Cf.* K. O. Mueller, *Zur Topographie Roms : über die Fragmenta der Sacra Argeorum bei Varro*, *de Lingua Latina*, v. 8 (pp. 69-94 in C. A. Böttiger, *Archäologie und Kunst*, vol. i., Breslau, 1828). *b* The *Caeliolum*, spoken of also as the *Caeliculus* (or -*um*) by Cicero, *De Har. Resp.* 15. 32, and as the *Caelius Minor* by Martial, xii. 18. 6, seems to have been a smaller and less important section of the Caelian Hill.

quod primae regionis quartum sacrarium scriptum sic
est :

Caer⟨i⟩olens*is*[3] : quarticeps[4] circa Minervium qua in
Caeliu⟨m⟩ monte⟨m⟩[5] itur : in tabernola est.

Caer⟨i⟩olensis[6] a Carinarum[7] iunctu dictus ; Carinae
pote a[8] caeri⟨m⟩onia,[9] quod hinc oritur caput Sacrae
Viae ab Streniae sacello quae pertinet in arce⟨m⟩,[10]
qua sacra quotquot mensibus feruntur in arcem et
per quam augures ex arce profecti solent inaugurare.
Huius Sacrae Viae pars haec sola volgo nota, quae
est a Foro eunti primore[11] clivo.

48.   Eidem regioni adtributa Subura, quod sub
muro terreo Carinarum ; in eo est Argeorum sacellum sextum.   Subura⟨m⟩[1] Iunius scribit ab eo, quod
fuerit sub antiqua urbe ; cui testimonium potest esse,
quod subest ei[2] loco qui terreus murus vocatur.   Sed
⟨ego a⟩[3] pago potius Succusano dictam puto Suc-
cusam : ⟨quod in nota etiam⟩[4] nunc scribitur ⟨SVC⟩[5]

[3] *Kent, for* cerolienses.   [4] *Aug., for* quae triceps.
[5] *Aug., for* celio monte.   [6] *Kent, for* cerulensis.   [7] *For*
carinaerum.   [8] *Jordan, for* postea.   [9] cerimonia *Bek-
ker, for* cerionia.   [10] *Aug., and Frag. Cass., for* arce.
[11] *Aldus, for* primoro.

§ 48.   [1] *Wissowa, for* subura.   [2] *Victorius, for* et.
[3] *Added by Laetus* (a *Frag. Cass.*).   [4] *Added by Mue.,
after Quintilian, Inst. Orat.* i. 7. 29.   [5] *Added by Mercklin, to fill a gap capable of holding three letters, in* F *; cf.
Quintilian, loc. cit.*

§ 47.   [a] That is, *Caeliolensis* ' pertaining to the *Caeliolus*.'
Through separation in meaning from the primitive, the *r* has
been subject to regular dissimilation as in *caerulus* for **caelu-*

lensis,[a] obviously because the fourth shrine of the first region is thus written in the records :

> *Caeriolensis* : fourth [b] shrine, near the temple of Minerva, in the street by which you go up the Caelian Hill ; it is in a booth.[c]

Caeriolensis is so called from the joining of the *Carinae* with the Caelian. *Carinae* is perhaps from *caerimonia* ' ceremony,' because from here starts the beginning of the Sacred Way, which extends from the Chapel of Strenia [d] to the citadel, by which the offerings are brought every year to the citadel, and by which the augurs regularly set out from the citadel for the observation of the birds. Of this Sacred Way, this is the only part commonly known, namely the part which is at the beginning of the Ascent as you go from the Forum.

48. To the same region is assigned the Subura,[a] which is beneath the earth-wall of the *Carinae* ; in it is the sixth chapel of the Argei. Junius [b] writes that Subura is so named because it was at the foot of the old city (*sub urbe*) ; proof of which may be in the fact that it is under that place which is called the earth-wall. But I rather think that from the Succusan district it was called *Succusa*; for even now when abbreviated it is written SVC, with C and not B as third

lus, Parilia for *Palilia* ; possibly association with *Carinae* furthered the change. [b] *Cf.* § 46, note *a*. [c] The words *sinistra via* or *dexteriore via* may have been lost before *in tabernola* ; *cf.* ten Brink's note. [d] A goddess of health and physical well-being.

§ 48. [a] Etymology entirely uncertain. The neuters *quod* and *in eo*, referring to *Subura*, mutually support each other. [b] M. Junius Gracchanus, contemporary and partisan of the Gracchi ; page 11 Huschke. He wrote an antiquarian work *De Potestatibus.*

tertia littera C, non B. Pagus Succusanus, quod succurrit Carinis.

49. Secundae regionis Esquiliae.[1] Alii has scripserunt ab excubiis regis dictas, alii ab eo quod ⟨aesculis⟩[2] excultae a rege Tullio essent. Huic origini magis concinunt loca vicina,[3] quod ibi lucus dicitur Facutalis et Larum Querquetulanum sacellum et lucus[4] Mefitis et Iunonis Lucinae, quorum angusti fines. Non mirum : iam diu enim late avaritia una ⟨domina⟩[5] est.

50. Esquiliae duo montes habiti, quod pars ⟨Oppius pars⟩[1] Cespius[2] mons suo antiquo nomine etiam nunc in sacris appellatur. In Sacris Argeorum scriptum sic est :

Oppius Mons : princeps ⟨Es⟩quili⟨i⟩s[3] uls[4] lucum Facutalem[5] ; sinistra via[6] secundum m⟨o⟩erum est.

Oppius Mons : terticeps cis[7] lucum[8] Esquilinum ; dexterior⟨e⟩[9] via in tabernola est.

Oppius Mons : quarticeps c⟨i⟩s[10] lucum[11] Esquilinum ; via dexteriore[12] in figlinis est.

§ 49. [1] *Turnebus, for* esquilinae.   [2] *Added by ten Brink.*   [3] *GS., for* uicini.   [4] *Laetus, for* lacus.   [5] *GS., for* unae.

§ 50. [1] *Added by Mue.*   [2] *For* cespeus.   [3] *Kent ;* Exquilis *Mue., for* quilis.   [4] *Lindsay ;* ouls *Mue. ; for* ouis.   [5] *Laetus, for* lacum facultalem.   [6] *Scaliger, for* quae.   [7] *Mue., for* terticepsois.   [8] *Aldus, for* lacum.   [9] *Kent, for* dexterior.   [10] *Mue., for* quatricepsos.   [11] *Laetus, for* lacum.   [12] *Kent, for* uiam dexteriorem.

[c] As stated by Quintilian, *Inst. Orat.* i. 7. 29.   [d] This association was made easy by the fact that r was normally lost in Latin before *ss* : *cf. rursum* and *rusum, dorsum* and *Dossennus.* Hence one might take *Succusa* to be *succur(s)sā* ; but such an *s*, representing *ss*, could not become *r* as in *Subura.*

letter.[c] The Succusan district is so named because it *succurrit* [d] ' runs up to ' the *Carinae*.

49.   To the second region belongs the Esquiline.[a] Some [b] say that this was named from the king's *excubiae* ' watch-posts,' others that it was from the fact that it was planted with *aesculi* ' oaks ' by King Tullius.   With this second origin the near-by places agree better, because in that locality there is the so-called Beech Grove,[c] and the chapel of the Oak-Grove Lares,[d] and the Grove of Mefitis [e] and of Juno Lucina [f]—whose territories are narrow.   And it is not astonishing ; for now this long while, far and wide, Greed has been the one and only mistress.

50.   The Esquiline includes two hills, inasmuch as the Oppian part and the Cespian [a] part of the hill are called by their own old names even now, in the sacrifices.   In the *Sacrifices of the Argei* there is the following record [b] :

Oppian Hill : first shrine, on the Esquiline, beyond the Beech Grove ; it is on the left side of the street along the wall.
Oppian Hill : third shrine, this side of the Esquiline Grove ; it is in a booth on the right-hand side of the street.
Oppian Hill : fourth shrine, this side of the Esquiline Grove ; it is on the right-hand side of the street among the potteries.

§ 49.   [a] By origin, *ex-queliai* ' dwelling-places outside,' in contrast to the *inquilini* ' dwellers inside ' the walls of the city.   [b] Page 115 Funaioli.   [c] *Facutalis* has the C in its old use with the value of *g*.   [d] Not otherwise known, but the emendations proposed seem violent; *Querquetulanum* is gen. pl.   [e] Goddess of malodorous exhalations, with the function of averting their pestilential effect.   [f] Juno as goddess of child-birth.
§ 50.   [a] Usually spelled *Cispius*, but Varro has *Cesp-*.   [b] Page 6 Preibisch.

Cespius[13] Mons: quinticeps *cis*[14] lucum[15] Poetelium; Esquiliis[16] est.

Cespius Mons: sexticeps apud *a*edem Iunonis Lucinae, ubi *a*editumus habere solet.

51. Tertiae regionis colles quinque ab deorum fanis appellati, e quis nobiles duo. Coll*is*[1] Viminal*is*[2] a Iove Vimin⟨i⟩o,[3] quod ibi ara e⟨ius⟩.[4] Sunt qui, quod ibi vimin*eta*[5] fuerint. Coll*is*[6] Quirinalis, ⟨quod ibi⟩[7] Quirini fanum. Sunt qui a Quiritibus, qui cum Tatio Curibus venerunt a*d* Roma⟨m⟩,[8] quod ibi habuerint castra.

52. Quod vocabulum coniunctarum regionum nomina obliteravit. Dictos enim collis pluris apparet ex Argeorum Sacrificiis, in quibus scriptum sic est:

Collis Quirinalis: terticeps *cis*[1] *a*edem Quirini.
Collis Salutaris: quarticeps adversum est ⟨A⟩pol⟨l⟩*i*nar cis[2] *a*edem Salutis.

---

[13] *Mue.*, *for* sceptius. [14] *Mue.*, *for* quinticepsois. [15] *Laetus*, *for* lacum. [16] *Scaliger*, *for* esquilinis.
§ 51. [1] *L. Sp.*, *for* colles. [2] *Laetus*, *for* uiminales. [3] *Aug.*, *with B*, *for* uimino ; *cf. Festus*, 376 a 10 *M*. [4] *L. Sp.*, *after ten Brink* (arae eius), *for* arae. [5] *G*, *Aug.*, *for* uiminata. [6] *Laetus*, *for* colles. [7] *Added by L. Sp.* [8] *Ten Brink ;* Romam *Laetus ; for* ab Roma.
§ 52. [1] *Mue.*, *for* terticepsois. [2] Apollinar cis *Mue.*, *for* pilonarois.

---

[c] Apparently to be associated with *putidus* 'stinking,' because of the mention of *Mefitis* a few lines before; but if so, the *oe* is a false archaic spelling, out of place in *putidus* and its kin. Another possibility is that it is to be connected with the plebeian gens *Poetelia* ; one of this name was a member of the Second Decemvirate, 450 B.C. [d] That is, adjacent to the sacristan's dwelling.

Cespian Hill : fifth shrine, this side of the Poetelian ᶜ
Grove ; it is on the Esquiline.

Cespian Hill : sixth shrine, at the temple of Juno Lucina,
where the sacristan customarily dwells.ᵈ

51. To the third region belong five hills, named
from sanctuaries of gods ; among these hills are two
that are well-known. The Viminal Hill got its name
from Jupiter *Viminius* ' of the Osiers,' because there
was his altar ; but there are some ᵃ who assign its
name to the fact that there were *vimineta* ' willow-
copses ' there. The Quirinal Hill was so named
because there was the sanctuary of Quirinus ᵇ ;
others ᶜ say that it is derived from the Quirites, who
came with Tatius from Cures ᵈ to the vicinity of
Rome, because there they established their camp.

52. This name has caused the names of the
adjacent localities to be forgotten. For that there
were other hills with their own names, is clear from
the *Sacrifices of the Argei*, in which there is a record
to this effect ᵃ :

Quirinal Hill : third shrine, this side of the temple of
Quirinus.

Salutary Hill ᵇ : fourth shrine, opposite the temple of
Apollo, this side of the temple of Salus.

§ 51.   ᵃ Page 118 Funaioli.   ᵇ *Quirinalis, Quirinus,
Quirites* belong together ; but *Cures* is probably to be kept
apart.   ᶜ Page 116 Funaioli.   ᵈ An ancient city of the
Sabines, about twenty-four miles from Rome, the city of
Tatius and the birthplace of Numa Pompilius, successor of
Romulus ; *cf.* Livy, i. 13, 18.

§ 52.   ᵃ Page 6 Preibisch.   ᵇ *Salutaris*, from *salus*
' preservation ' ; the temple perhaps marked the place of a
victory in a critical battle, or commemorated the end of a
pestilence. We do not know whether this *Salus* was the
same as *Iuppiter Salutaris*, mentioned by Cicero, *De Finibus*,
iii. 20. 66 ; *cf.* the Greek Ζεὺς σωτήρ ' Zeus the Saviour.'

VARRO

Collis Mucialis: quinticeps apud *a*edem Dei Fidi[3]; in delubro, ubi *a*editumus habere solet.

Collis[4] Latiaris[5]: sexticeps in Vico Inste*i*ano[6] summo, apud au⟨gu⟩raculum[7]; aedificium solum est.

Horum deorum arae, a quibus cognomina habent, in eius regionis partibus sunt.

53. Quartae regionis Palatium, quod Pallantes cum Euandro venerunt, qui et Palatini; ⟨alii quod Palatini⟩,[1] aborigines ex agro Reatino, qui appellatur Palatium, ibi conse⟨de⟩runt[2]; sed hoc alii a Palanto[3] uxore Latini putarunt. Eundem hunc locum a pecore dictum putant quidam; itaque N*a*evius Balatium appellat.

54. Huic Cermalum et Velias[1] coniunxerunt, quod in hac regione[2] scriptum est:

Germalense: quinticeps apud *a*edem Romuli.

Et

Veliense[3]: sexticeps in Velia apud *a*edem deum Penatium.

[3] *For* de i de fidi.   [4] *For* colles.   [5] *M, Laetus, for* latioris.   [6] *Jordan, for* instelano ; *cf. Livy,* xxiv. 10. 8, in vico Insteio.   [7] *Turnebus, for* auraculum.

§ 53.   [1] *Added by A. Sp.*   [2] *Frag. Cass., M, Laetus, for* conserunt.   [3] *Mue.,* (Palantho *L. Sp.*), *for* palantio ; *cf. Fest.* 220. 6 *M.*

§ 54.   [1] *For* uellias.   [2] *M, Laetus, for* religione.   [3] *Bentinus, for* uelienses.

---

[c] *Mucialis,* apparently from the gens *Mucia*; the first known Mucius was the one who on failing to assassinate Porsenna, the Etruscan king who was besieging Rome, burned his right hand over the altar-fire and thus gained the cognomen *Scaevola* ' Lefty.' Several Mucii with the cognomen *Scaevola* were prominent in the political and legal life of Rome from 215 to 82 B.C.   [d] *Deus Fidius* was an aspect of Jupiter ; *cf.* Greek Ζεὺς πίστιος.   [e] *Latiaris* 'pertaining to Latium'; *Iuppiter Latiaris* was the guardian deity of the Latin Confederation, *cf.* Cicero, *Pro Milone,* 31. 85.

Mucial Hill [c]: fifth shrine, at the temple of the God of Faith,[d] in the chapel where the sacristan customarily dwells.

Latiary Hill [e]: sixth shrine, at the top of Insteian Row, at the augurs' place of observation ; it is the only building.

The altars of these gods, from which they have their surnames, are in the various parts of this region.

53. To the fourth region belongs the Palatine,[a] so called because the Pallantes came there with Evander, and they were called also Palatines ; others think that it was because Palatines, aboriginal inhabitants of a Reatine district called Palatium,[b] settled there ; but others [c] thought that it was from Palanto,[d] wife of Latinus. This same place certain authorities think was named from the *pecus* ' flocks ' ; therefore Naevius [e] calls it the *Balatium* [f] ' Bleat-ine.'

54. To this they joined the Cermalus [a] and the Veliae,[b] because in the account of this region it is thus recorded [c] :

Germalian : fifth shrine, at the temple of Romulus,

and

Velian : sixth shrine, on the Velia, at the temple of the deified Penates.

§ 53. [a] For *Palatium*, there is no convincing etymology. [b] An ancient city of the Sabines, on the Via Salaria, forty-eight miles from Rome, on the banks of the river Velinus. [c] Page 116 Funaioli. [d] According to Festus, 220. 5 M., Palanto was the mother of Latinus ; she is called Pallantia by Servius *in Aen.* viii. 51. [e] *Frag. Poet. Rom.* 28 Baehrens ; *R.O.L.* ii. 56-57 Warmington. [f] As though from *balare* ' to bleat.'

§ 54. [a] There is no etymology for *Cermalus* ; the word began with C, but for etymological purposes Varro begins it with G, relying on the fact that in older Latin C represented two sounds, *c* and *g*. [b] Apparently used both in the singular, *Velia*, and in the plural, *Veliae* ; there is no etymology. [c] Page 7 Preibisch.

VARRO

Germalum a germanis Romulo et Remo, quod ad
ficum ruminalem, et ii ibi inventi, quo aqua hiberna
Tiberis eos detulerat in alveolo expositos. Veliae
unde essent plures accepi causas, in quis quod ibi
pastores Palatini ex ovibus[4] ante tonsuram inventam
vellere lanam sint soliti, a quo vellera[5] dicuntur.

IX. 55. Ager Romanus primum divisus in partis
tris, a quo tribus appellata Titiensium,[1] Ramnium,
Lucerum. Nominatae, ut ait Ennius, Titienses ab
Tatio, Ramnenses ab Romulo, Luceres, ut Iunius,
ab Lucumone ; sed omnia haec vocabula Tusca, ut
Volnius, qui tragoedias[2] Tuscas scripsit, dicebat.

56. Ab hoc partes[1] quoque quattuor urbis tribus
dictae, ab locis Suburana, Palatina, Esquilina, Collina ;
quinta, quod sub Roma, Romilia ; sic reliquae[2]
tri⟨gin⟩ta[3] ab his rebus quibus in Tribu⟨u⟩m Libro[4]
scripsi.

X. 57. Quod ad loca quaeque his coniuncta fuerunt,

---

[4] *Victorius, for* quibus.   [5] *Laetus, for* uelleinera (uellaera
Frag. Cass.).

§ 55.   [1] *Groth, for* tatiensium.   [2] *For* tragaedias.

§ 56.   [1] *For* partis.   [2] *For* reliqua, *altered from* reliquae.   [3] *Turnebus, for* trita.   [4] *Frag. Cass., L. Sp.,
for* libros.

---

[d] Page 118 Funaioli.

§ 55.   [a] Roman possessions in land, both state property
and private estates ; as opposed to *ager peregrinus* ' foreign
land.'   [b] None of the etymologies is probable, which is
not surprising, as they were of non-Latin origin, whether or
not they were Etruscan.   [c] *Ann.* i. frag. lix. Vahlen[2];
R.O.L. i. 38-39 Warmington.   [d] Page 121 Funaioli ;
page 11 Huschke.   [e] Page 126 Funaioli ; Volnius is not
mentioned elsewhere.

§ 56.   [a] The four *urbanae tribus* ' city tribes.'   [b] The

Germalus, they say, is from the *germani* ' brothers '
Romulus and Remus, because it is beside the Fig-tree
of the Suckling, and they were found there, where the
Tiber's winter flood had brought them when they had
been put out in a basket.   For the source of the name
Veliae I have found several reasons,[d] among them,
that there the shepherds of the Palatine, before the
invention of shearing, used to *vellere* ' pluck ' the wool
from the sheep, from which the *vellera* ' fleeces ' were
named.

IX. 55.   The Roman field-land [a] was at first
divided into *tris* ' three ' parts, from which they called
the Titienses, the Ramnes, and the Luceres each a
tribus ' tribe.'   These tribes were named,[b] as Ennius
says,[c] the Titienses from Tatius, the Ramnenses from
Romulus, the Luceres, according to Junius,[d] from
Lucumo ;   but all these words are Etruscan, as Volnius,[e] who wrote tragedies in Etruscan, stated.

56.   From this, four parts of the City also were
used as names of tribes, the Suburan, the Palatine,
the Esquiline, the Colline,[a] from the places ;   a fifth,
because it was *sub Roma* ' beneath the walls of Rome,'
was called Romilian [b] ;   so also the remaining thirty [c]
from those causes which [d] I wrote in the *Book of the
Tribes*.

X. 57.   I have told what pertains to places and
those things which are connected with them ;   now of

first of the *rusticae tribus* ' country tribes,' called also *Ro-
mulia* ;   Festus, 271. 1 M., attributes the name to their being
inhabitants of a district which Romulus had taken from Veii.
[c] Thirty-five tribes in all, some named from their places of
origin, others from Roman gentes.   The three original names,
given in § 55, went out of use as tribe names long before the
time of Varro.   [d] *Quibus* for *quas*, attracted to the case of
its antecedent.

dixi ; nunc de his quae in locis esse solent immortalia et mortalia expediam, ita ut prius quod ad deos pertinet dicam. Principes dei Caelum et Terra. Hi dei idem qui Aegypti[1] Serapis et Isis, etsi *H*arpocrates digito significat, ut taceam.[2] Idem principes in Latio Saturnus et O*p*s.[3]

58. Terra enim et Caelum, ut ⟨Sa⟩mothracum[1] initia docent, sunt dei magni, et hi quos dixi multis nominibus, non quas ⟨S⟩amo⟨th⟩racia[2] ante portas statuit duas virilis species aeneas dei magni,[3] neque ut volgus putat, hi Samot*h*races dii, qui Castor et Pollux, sed hi mas et femina et hi quos Augurum Libri scriptos habent sic " divi potes,"[4] pro illo quod Samot*h*races θεοὶ δυνατοί.[5]

59. Haec duo Caelum et Terra, quod anima et corpus. Humidum et frigidum terra, sive

> Ova par*ire*[1] solet genus pennis condecoratum,
> Non animam,

§ 57. [1] *For* quia egipti.   [2] *Turnebus, for* tata seam.
[3] *For* obs.
   § 58. [1] *Laetus, for* mothracum.   [2] *Laetus, for* ambracia.   [3] *Laetus, for* imagini.   [4] *Laetus, for* diui qui potes.   [5] *Aug., for* ΤΗϵΟϵδΥΝΑΤΟϵ.
   § 59. [1] *Laetus, for* parere.

§ 57. [a] The chief gods of the Egyptians ; their last child was Harpocrates, the youthful aspect of the Sun-God Horus. Harpocrates was commonly represented with his finger on his lips, imposing silence (*cf.* Catullus, 74. 4) ; the passage seems

these things which are wont to be in places, I shall explain those which deal with immortals and with mortals, in such a way that first I shall tell what pertains to the gods. The first gods were *Caelum* ' Sky ' and *Terra* ' Earth.' These gods are the same as those who in Egypt are called Serapis and Isis,[a] though Harpocrates with his finger make a sign to me to be silent. The same first gods were in Latium called Saturn and Ops.

58. For Earth and Sky, as the mysteries of the Samothracians [a] teach, are Great Gods, and these whom I have mentioned under many names, are not those Great Gods whom Samothrace [b] represents by two male statues of bronze which she has set up before the city-gates, nor are they, as the populace thinks, the Samothracian gods,[c] who are really Castor and Pollux ; but these are a male and a female, these are those whom the *Books of the Augurs* [d] mention in writing as " potent deities," for what the Samothracians call " powerful gods."

59. These two, Sky and Earth, are a pair like life [a] and body. Earth is a damp cold thing, whether

Eggs the flock that is feather-adorned is wont to give birth to,
Not to a life,

to indicate that some orthodox Romans scorned the Egyptian deities and objected to their identification with the Roman gods, a prejudice which the scholar Varro did not share.

§ 58. [a] Mystic rites in honour of the Cabiri. [b] An island in the northern Aegean, off the coast of Thrace. [c] The Cabiri, popularly identified with Castor and Pollux, since they were all youthful male deities to whom protective powers were attributed. [d] Page 16 Regell.

§ 59. [a] Not quite ' soul,' though it is that which distinguishes the living body from the dead body.

ut ait Ennius, et

> Post inde venit divinitus pullis
> Ipsa anima,

sive, ut Zenon Cit⟨ie⟩us,[2]

> Animalium semen ignis is qui anima[3] ac mens.

Qui caldor e caelo, quod h*u*ic[4] innumerabiles et immortales ignes. Itaque Epicharmus ⟨cum⟩[5] dicit de mente humana ait

> Istic est de sole sumptus ignis ;

idem ⟨de⟩ sole[6] :

> Isque totus mentis est,

ut humores frigidae sunt humi, ut supra ostendi.

60. Quibus iuncti Caelum et Terra omnia ex ⟨se⟩ genuerunt,[1] quod per hos natura

> Frigori miscet calorem atque h*u*mori[2] aritudinem.

Recte igitur Pacuius quod ait

> Animam *a*ether adiugat,

et Ennius

> terram corpus quae de*d*erit,[3] ipsam
> capere, neque dispendi facere hilum.

---

[2] *Aug., for* citus.   [3] *Laetus, for* animam.   [4] *Lachmann, for* hinc.   [5] *Added by L. Sp.*   [6] *L. Sp., for* idem solem.   § 60. [1] *Laetus, for* exgenuerunt.   [2] *For* homori.   [3] *Scaliger, for* deperit.

---

[b] *Ann.* 10-12 Vahlen[2]; *R.O.L.* i. 6-7 Warmington. [c] *Frag.* 126 von Arnim. Zeno, of Citium in Cyprus, removed to Athens, where he became the founder of the Stoic school of philosophy ; he lived about 331-264 B.C.

as Ennius says,[b] and

> Thereafter by providence comes to the fledglings
> Life itself,

or, as Zeno of Citium says,[c]

> The seed of animals is that fire which is life and mind.

This warmth is from the Sky, because it has count-less undying fires. Therefore Epicharmus, when he is speaking of the human mind, says [d]

> That is fire taken from the Sun,

and likewise of the sun,

> And it is all composed of mind,

just as moistures are composed of cold earth, as I have shown above.[e]

60. United with these,[a] Sky and Earth produced everything from themselves, because by means of them nature

> Mixes heat with cold, and dryness with the wet.[b]

Pacuvius is right then in saying [c]

> And heaven adds the life,

and Ennius in saying that [d]

> The body she's given
> Earth does herself take back, and of loss not a whit
> does she suffer.

---

[d] Ennius, *Varia*, 52-53 Vahlen[2]; *R.O.L.* i. 412-413 Warming-ton.   [e] *Cf.* v. 24.

§ 60.   [a] That is, heat and moisture.   [b] Ennius, *Varia*, 46 Vahlen[2]; *R.O.L.* i. 410-411 Warmington.   [c] *Trag. Rom. Frag.* 94 Ribbeck[3]; *R.O.L.* ii. 204-205 Warmington. [d] *Ann.* 13-14 Vahlen[2]; *R.O.L.* i. 6-7 Warmington; indirectly quoted, and therefore not metrical; *cf.* ix. 54.

Animae et corporis discessus quod natis is exi⟨t⟩us,[4] inde exitium, ut cum in unum ineunt, initia.

61. Inde omne corpus, ubi nimius ardor aut humor, aut interit aut, si manet, sterile. Cui testis aestas et hiems, quod in altera[1] aer ardet et spica aret, in altera natura ad nascenda cum imbre et frigore luctare non volt et potius ver[2] expectat. Igitur causa nascendi duplex : ignis et aqua. Ideo ea nuptiis in limine adhibentur, quod coniungit⟨ur⟩[3] hic, et mas[4] ignis, quod ibi semen, aqua femina, quod fetus[5] ab eius humore, et horum vinctionis vis[6] Venus.

62. Hinc comicus[1] :

> Huic victrix Venus, videsne haec ?

Non quod vincere velit Venus, sed vincire. Ipsa Victoria ab eo quod superati vinciuntur. Utrique testis[2] poesis, quod et Victoria et Venus dicitur caeligena : Tellus enim quod prima vincta Caelo, Victoria ex eo. Ideo haec cum corona et palma, quod corona vinclum

---

[4] *Sciop.*, *for* nati sis exius.

§ 61. [1] *Mue.*, *for* altero. [2] *Aldus*, *for* totius uere. [3] *A. Sp.*, *for* coniungit. [4] *G, H, a for* mars. [5] *For* faetus. [6] *Pape ;* iunctionis vis *Turnebus ; for* uinctione suis.

§ 62. [1] *Laetus*, *for* comicos. [2] *For* testes.

---

§ 61. [a] On arrival at her husband's house, the Roman bride was required to touch fire and water (or perhaps was sprinkled with water), as initiation into the family worship. [b] Apparently *Venus* is said to be the basis of the word *vinctio*; wrong.

§ 62. [a] *Com. Rom. Frag.*, page 133 Ribbeck[3]. [b] It is morphologically possible, but not likely, that *victrix* stands for the agent noun to *vincire* ; *vincere* ' to conquer ' and *vincire* ' to bind ' seem to be distinct etymologically.

Inasmuch as the separation of life and body is the *exitus* ' way out ' for all creatures born, from that comes *exitium* ' destruction,' just as when they *ineunt* ' go into ' unity, it is their *initia* ' beginnings.'

61. From this fact, every body, when there is excessive heat or excessive moisture, perishes, or if it survives, is barren. Summer and winter are witnesses to this : in the one the air is blazing hot and the wheat-ears dry up ; in the other, nature has no wish to struggle with rain and cold for purposes of birth, and rather waits for spring. Therefore the conditions of procreation are two : fire and water. Thus these are used at the threshold in weddings,[a] because there is union here, and fire is male, which the semen is in the other case, and the water is the female, because the embryo develops from her moisture, and the force that brings their *vinctio* ' binding ' is *Venus* [b] ' Love.'

62. Hence the comic poet says,[a]

> Venus is his victress, do you see it ?

not because Venus wishes *vincere* ' to conquer,' but *vincire* ' to bind.' [b] Victory herself is named from the fact that the overpowered *vinciuntur* ' are bound.' [c] Poetry bears testimony to both, because both Victory and Venus are called heaven-born ; for *Tellus* ' Earth,' because she was the first one bound to the Sky, is from that called Victory.[d] Therefore she is connected with the *corona* ' garland ' and the *palma* ' palm,' [e] because the garland is a binder of the head and is

---

[c] *Victoria* belongs to *vincere* ' to conquer.'   [d] Earth as a productive, nourishing divinity ; identification with *Victoria* is not found elsewhere.   [e] The customary symbols of victory.

capitis et ipsa a vinctura dicitur vier*i*, ⟨id⟩ est vinciri[3] ;
a quo est in Sota Enni :

> Ibant malaci viere Veneriam corollam.

Palma,[4] quod ex utraque parte natura vincta habet
paria folia.

63.   Poetae de Caelo quod semen igneum cecidisse
dicunt in mare ac natam " e spumis " Venerem,
coniunctione ignis et humoris, quam habent vim
significant esse Ve⟨ne⟩ris.[1]   A qua vi natis dicta vita
et illud a Lucilio :

> Vis est vita, vides, vis nos facere omnia cogit.

64.   Quare quod caelum principium, ab satu est
dictus Saturnus, et quod ignis, Saturnalibus cerei
superioribus mittuntur.   Terra Ops, quod hic omne
opus et hac opus ad vivendum, et ideo dicitur Ops
mater, quod terra mater.   Haec enim

> Terris gentis omnis peperit et resumit denuo,

quae

> Dat cibaria,

---

[3] *Sciop.*, *for* uiere est uincere.   [4] *Scaliger*, *for* palmam.
    § 63.   [1] *L. Sp. ;* significantes Veneris *Laetus ; for* significantes se ueris.

---

[f] *Vincire* is in fact derived from an extension of the root
seen in *viere*.   [g] 25 Vahlen[2]; *R.O.L.* i. 404-405 Warmington.   [h] *Palma* and *paria* are etymologically separate.
    § 63.   [a] A Greek legend, invented to connect the name of
Aphrodite with ἀφρός ' foam ' ; *cf.* Hesiod, *Theogony*, 188-
198.   The name *Aphrodite* is probably of Semitic origin.

itself, from *vinctura* ' binding,' said *vieri* ' to be plaited,'
that is, *vinciri* ' to be bound ' *f* ; whence there is the
line in Ennius's *Sota g* :

> The lustful pair were going, to plait the Love-god's
> garland.

Palma ' palm ' is so named because, being naturally
bound on both sides, it has *paria* ' equal ' leaves.*h*

63. The poets, in that they say that the fiery seed
fell from the Sky into the sea and Venus was born
" from the foam-masses," *a* through the conjunction
of fire and moisture, are indicating that the *vis* ' force'
which they have is that of Venus. Those born of this
vis have what is called *vita b* ' life,' and that was meant
by Lucilius *c* :

> Life is force, you see ; to do everything force doth
> compel us.

64. Wherefore because the Sky is the beginning,
Saturn was named from *satus a* ' sowing '; and
because fire is a beginning, waxlights are presented to
patrons at the Saturnalia.*b* *Ops c* is the Earth, because in it is every *opus* ' work ' and there is *opus*
' need ' of it for living, and therefore Ops is called
mother, because the Earth is the mother. For she *d*

> All men hath produced in all the lands, and takes
> them back again,

she who

> Gives the rations,

b Vis and *vita* are not connected etymologically.   *c* 1340
Marx.
§ 64. *a* This etymology is unlikely.   *b* Confirmed by
Festus, 54. 16 M.   *c Ops* and *opus* are connected etymologically.   *d* Ennius, *Varia*, 48 Vahlen²; *R.O.L.* i. 412-
413 Warmington.

ut ait Ennius, quae

> Quod gerit fruges, Ceres;

antiquis enim quod nunc G C.[1]

65. Idem hi dei Caelum et Terra Iupiter et Iuno, quod ut ait Ennius :

> Istic est is Iupiter quem dico, quem Graeci vocant
> Aerem, qui ventus est et nubes, imber postea,
> Atque ex imbre frigus, vent*us*[1] post fit, aer denuo.
> Haec⟨e⟩[2] propter Iupiter sunt ista quae dico tibi,
> Qu*i*[3] mortalis, ⟨arva⟩[4] atque urbes beluasque omnis
> iuvat.

Quod hi⟨n⟩c[5] omnes et sub hoc, eundem appellans dicit :

> Divumque hominumque pater rex.

Pater, quod patefacit semen : nam tum es*se*[6] conceptum ⟨pat⟩et,[7] inde cum exit quod oritur.

66. Hoc idem magis ostendit antiquius Iovis nomen : nam olim Diovis et Di⟨e⟩spiter[1] dictus, id est dies pater ; a quo dei dicti qui inde, et di*us*[2] et

---

§ 64. [1] *Lachmann ;* C quod nunc G *Mue. ; for* quod nunc et.

§ 65. [1] *Laetus, for* uentis. [2] *Mor. Haupt ;* hacece *Mue. ; for* haec. [3] *Aug., with B, for* qua. [4] *Added by Schoell.* [5] L. Sp., *for* hic. [6] *Mue., for* est. [7] *Mue., for* et.

§ 66. [1] *Laetus, for* dispiter. [2] *Bentinus, for* dies.

---

[a] *Varia*, 49-50 Vahlen[2]; *R.O.L.* i. 412-413 Warmington; gerit and *Ceres* are not connected. [f] There was a time when C had its original value *g* (as in Greek, where the third letter is gamma) and had taken over also the value of K. The use of the symbol G for the sound *g* was later. C in the value *g* survived in C.=*Gaius*, Cn.=*Gnaeus*.

§ 65. [a] *Varia*, 54-58 Vahlen[2] ; *R.O.L.* i. 414-415 Warmington. [b] *Iupiter* and *iuvare* are not related. [c] *An-*

as Ennius says,[e] who

> Is Ceres, since she brings (*gerit*) the fruits.

For with the ancients, what is now G, was written C.[f]

65. These same gods Sky and Earth are Jupiter and Juno, because, as Ennius says,[a]

> That one is the Jupiter of whom I speak, whom Grecians call
> Air ; who is the windy blast and cloud, and afterwards the rain ;
> After rain, the cold ; he then becomes again the wind and air.
> This is why those things of which I speak to you are Jupiter :
> Help he gives [b] to men, to fields and cities, and to beasties all.

Because all come from him and are under him, he addresses him with the words [c] :

> O father and king of the gods and the mortals.

Pater ' father ' because he *patefacit* [d] ' makes evident ' the seed ; for then it *patet* ' is evident ' that conception has taken place, when that which is born comes out from it.

66. This same thing the more ancient name of Jupiter [a] shows even better : for of old he was called *Diovis* and *Diespiter*, that is, *dies pater* ' Father Day ' [b] ; from which they who come from him are called *dei* ' deities,' and *dius* ' god ' and *divum* ' sky,' whence *sub divo* ' under the sky,' and *Dius Fidius* ' god of

nales, 580 Vahlen[2]; *R.O.L.* i. 168-169 Warmington. [d] *Pater* and *patere* are not related.

§ 66. [a] *Iu-* in *Iupiter, Diovis, Dies, deus, Dius, divum* belong together by etymology. [b] K. O. Mueller thought that Varro meant *dies* as the old genitive, ' father of the day,' instead of as a nominative in apposition ; but this is hardly likely.

VARRO

divum, unde sub divo, Dius Fidius. Itaque inde eius perforatum tectum, ut ea videatur divum, id est caelum. Quidam negant sub tecto per hunc deierare oportere. Aelius Dium Fid⟨i⟩um dicebat Diovis filium, ut Graeci Διόσκορον Castorem, et putabat[3] hunc esse Sancum[4] ab Sabina lingua et Herculem a Graeca. Idem hic Dis[5] pater dicitur infimus, qui est coniunctus terrae, ubi omnia ⟨ut⟩[6] oriuntur ita[7] aboriuntur ; quorum quod finis ortu⟨u⟩m, Orcus[8] dictus.

67. Quod Iovis Iuno coniunx et is Caelum, haec Terra, quae eadem Tellus, et ea dicta, quod una iuvat cum Iove, Iuno, et Regina, quod huius omnia terrestria.

68. Sol[1] vel quod ita Sabini, vel ⟨quod⟩[2] solus[3] ita lucet, ut ex eo deo dies sit. Luna, vel quod sola lucet noctu. Itaque ea dicta Noctiluca in Palatio : nam ibi noctu lucet templum. Hanc ut Solem Apollinem quidam Dianam vocant (Apollinis vocabulum Graecum alterum, alterum Latinum), et hinc quod luna in altitudinem et latitudinem simul it,[4] Diviana appellata. Hinc Epicharmus Ennii Proserpinam quoque

---

[3] *Puccius, for* putabant.   [4] *Scaliger, for* sanctum.
[5] *Mue., for* dies.   [6] *Added by Mue.*   [7] *Mue., for* ui.
[8] *Turnebus, for* ortus.
   § 68.   [1] *Laetus, with M, for* sola.   [2] *Added by Aug.,*
with B.   [3] *Sciop., for* solum.   [4] *L. Sp., for* et.

---

[c] Page 60 Funaioli.   [d] Sabine *Sancus* and the Umbrian divine epithet *Sançio-* are connected with Latin *sancire* 'to make sacred,' *sacer* 'sacred.'   [e] *Dis* is the short form of *dives* 'rich,' *cf.* the genitive *divitis* or *ditis,* and is not connected with *dies* ; it is a translation of the Greek Πλούτων 'Pluto,' as 'the rich one,' from πλοῦτος 'wealth.'   [f] The Italic god of death, not connected with *ortus,* but perhaps with *arcere* 'to hem in,' as 'the one who restrains the dead.'
   § 67.   [a] Not connected either with *Iupiter* or with *iuvare.*

faith.' Thus from this reason the roof of his temple is pierced with holes, that in this way the *divum*, which is the *caelum* ' sky,' may be seen. Some say that it is improper to take an oath by his name, when you are under a roof. Aelius *c* said that *Dius Fidius* was a son of *Diovis*, just as the Greeks call Castor the son of Zeus, and he thought that he was *Sancus* in the Sabine tongue,*d* and *Hercules* in Greek. He is likewise called *Dispater* *e* in his lowest capacity, when he is joined to the earth, where all things vanish away even as they originate ; and because he is the end of these *ortus* ' creations,' he is called *Orcus*.*f*

67. Because Juno is Jupiter's wife, and he is Sky, she *Terra* ' Earth,' the same as *Tellus* ' Earth,' she also, because she *iuvat* ' helps ' *una* ' along ' with Jupiter, is called Juno,*a* and *Regina* ' Queen,' because all earthly things are hers.

68. *Sol* *a* ' Sun ' is so named either because the Sabines called him thus, or because he *solus* ' alone ' shines in such a way that from this god there is the daylight. *Luna* ' Moon ' is so named certainly because she alone ' *lucet* ' shines at night. Therefore she is called *Noctiluca* ' Night-Shiner ' on the Palatine ; for there her temple *noctu lucet* ' shines by night.' *b* Certain persons call her Diana, just as they call the Sun Apollo (the one name, that of Apollo, is Greek, the other Latin) ; and from the fact that the Moon goes both high and widely, she is called *Diviana*.*c* From the fact that the Moon is wont to be under the

---

§ 68. *a* Not connected with *solus*. *b* Either because the white marble gleams in the moonlight, or because a light was kept burning there all night. *c* An artificially prolonged form of *Diana* ; Varro seems to have had in mind *deviare* ' to go aside ' as its basis.

VARRO

appellat, quod solet esse sub terris. Dicta Proserpina, quod haec ut serpens modo in dexteram modo in sinisteram partem late movetur. Serpere et proserpere idem dicebant, ut Plautus quod scribit :

Quasi proserpens bestia.

69. Quae ideo quoque videtur ab Latinis Iuno Lucina dicta vel quod est e⟨t⟩[1] Terra, ut physici dicunt, et lucet ; vel quod[2] ab luce eius qua quis conceptus est usque ad eam, qua partus quis in lucem, ⟨l⟩una[3] iuvat, donec mensibus actis produxit in lucem, ficta ab iuvando et luce Iuno Lucina. A quo parientes eam invocant : luna enim nascentium dux quod menses huius. Hoc vidisse antiquas apparet, quod mulieres potissimum supercilia sua attribuerunt ei deae. Hic enim debuit maxime collocari Iuno Lucina, ubi ab diis lux datur oculis.

70. Ignis a ⟨g⟩nascendo,[1] quod hinc nascitur et omne quod nascitur ignis s⟨uc⟩cendit[2] ; ideo calet, ut qui denascitur eum amittit ac frigescit. Ab ignis iam maiore vi ac violentia Volcanus dictus. Ab eo quod

§ 69. [1] *L. Sp.*, *for* e. [2] *For* quod uel. [3] *Sciop.*, *for* una.
§ 70. [1] *Mue.*, *for* nascendo. [2] *GS.*, *for* scindit.

[d] Ennius, *Varia*, 59 Vahlen[2]. *Proserpina* is really borrowed from Greek Περσεφόνη, but transformed in popular speech into a word seemingly of Latin antecedents. [e] *Poenulus* 1034, *Stichus* 724 ; in both passages meaning a snake.
§ 69. [a] *Lucina*, from *lux* 'light,' indicates Juno as goddess of child-birth. [b] Equal to 'full moon,' or 'month.'
66

lands as well as over them, Ennius's *Epicharmus* calls her *Proserpina.*[d] Proserpina received her name because she, like a *serpens* ' creeper,' moves widely now to the right, now to the left. *Serpere* ' to creep ' and *proserpere* ' to creep forward ' meant the same thing, as Plautus means in what he writes [e] :

> Like a forward-creeping beast.

69. She appears therefore to be called by the Latins also Juno Lucina,[a] either because she is also the Earth, as the natural scientists say, and *lucet* ' shines ' ; or because from that light of hers [b] in which a conception takes place until that one in which there is a birth into the light, the Moon continues to help, until she has brought it forth into the light when the months are past, the name Juno Lucina was made from *iuvare* ' to help ' and *lux* ' light.' From this fact women in child-birth invoke her ; for the Moon is the guide of those that are born, since the months belong to her. It is clear that the women of olden times observed this, because women have given this goddess credit notably for their eyebrows.[c] For Juno Lucina ought especially to be established in places where the gods give light to our eyes.

70. *Ignis* ' fire ' is named from *gnasci* [a] ' to be born,' because from it there is birth, and everything which is born the fire enkindles ; therefore it is hot, just as he who dies loses the fire and becomes cold. From the fire's *vis ac violentia* ' force and violence,' now in greater measure, Vulcan was named.[a] From the fact that fire on account of its brightness *fulget*

---

[e] Because the eyebrows protect the eyes by which we enjoy the light (Festus, 305 b 10 M.) ; *cf.* H. J. Rose, *Folk-Lore*, xlvii. 396-398.

§ 70.   [a] False etymologies.

ignis propter splendorem fulget, fulg*ur*[3] et fulmen, et fulgur⟨itum⟩[4] quod fulmine ictum.

71. ⟨In⟩[1] contrariis diis, ab aquae lapsu lubrico lympha. Lympha Iuturna quae iuvaret : itaque multi *a*egroti propter id nomen hinc aquam petere solent. A fontibus et fluminibus ac ceter*i*s aqu*i*s[2] dei, ut Tiberinus ab Tiberi, et ab lacu Velini Velinia, et Lymphae Com⟨m⟩*o*til⟨e⟩s[3] ad lacum Cutiliensem a commotu, quod ibi insula in aqua commovetur.

72. Neptunus, quod mare terras obnubit ut nubes caelum, ab nuptu, id est opertione, ut antiqui, a quo nuptiae, nuptus dictus. Salacia Neptuni ab salo. Ven*i*lia[1] a veniendo ac vento illo, quem Plautus dicit :

> Quod *ille*[2] dixit qui secundo vento vectus est
> Tranquillo mari,[3] ventum gaudeo.

73. Bellona ab bello nunc, quae Duellona a duello.

---

[3] *Canal, for* fulgor.   [4] *Turnebus, for* fulgur.

§ 71.   [1] Added by Madvig, who began the sentence here instead of after *diis*.   [2] *V, p, for* ceteras aquas.   [3] *GS., for* comitiis.

§ 72.   [1] *Aug., for* uen*c*lia.   [2] *MSS. of Plautus, for* ibi *F*.   [3] *MSS. of Plautus have* mare.

---

[b] The three words are from *fulgere* ' to flash '; but the *-itum* of *fulguritum* is suffixal only, and is not connected with *ictum*.

§ 71.   [a] Properly from the Greek νύμφη, with dissimilative change of the first consonant.   [b] The first part may be the same element seen in *Iupiter*, but is certainly not connected with *iuvare*.   [c] A lake in the Sabine country, formed by the spreading out of the Avens River a few miles southeast of Interamna.   [d] A lake in the Sabine country, a few miles east of Reate, in which there was a floating island which drifted with the wind.

§ 72.   [a] *Neptunus* is not connected with the other words, though *nubes* may perhaps be related to *nubere* and its

' flashes,' come *fulgur* ' lightning-flash ' and *fulmen* ' thunderbolt,' and what has been *fulmine ictum* ' hit by a thunderbolt ' is called *fulguritum.*[b]

71. Among deities of an opposite kind, *Lympha*[a] ' water-nymph ' is derived from the water's *lapsus lubricus* ' slippery gliding.' Juturna[b] was a nymph whose function was *iuvare* ' to give help ' ; therefore many sick persons, on account of this name, are wont to seek water from her spring. From springs and rivers and the other waters gods are named, as Tiberinus from the river Tiber, and Velinia from the lake of the Velinus,[c] and the *Commotiles* ' Restless ' Nymphs at the Cutilian Lake,[d] from the *commotus* ' motion,' because there an island *commovetur* ' moves about ' in the water.

72. Neptune,[a] because the sea veils the lands as the clouds veil the sky, gets his name from *nuptus* ' veiling,' that is, *opertio* ' covering,' as the ancients said ; from which *nuptiae* ' wedding,' *nuptus* ' wedlock ' are derived. Salacia,[b] wife of Neptune, got her name from *salum* ' the surging sea.' Venilia[c] was named from *venire* ' to come ' and that *ventus* ' wind ' which Plautus mentions[d] :

> As that one said who with a favouring wind was borne
> Over a placid sea : I'm glad I went.[e]

73. *Bellona* ' Goddess of War ' is said now, from *bellum*[a] ' war,' which formerly was *Duellona*, from

derivatives. [b] Almost certainly an abstract substantive to *salax* ' fond of leaping, lustful, provoking lust '; though popularly associated with *salum*. [c] There is a *Venilia* in the *Aeneid*, x. 76, a sea-nymph who is the mother of Turnus. [d] *Cistellaria*, 14-15. [e] Punning on *ventum* : the last phrase may mean also " I'm glad there was a wind."

§ 73. [a] Correct.

Mars ab eo quod maribus in bello praeest, aut quod Sabinis acceptus ibi est Mamers. Quirinus a Quiritibus. Virtus ut viri*tus*[1] a virilitate. Honos ab[2] onere : itaque honestum dicitur quod oneratum, et dictum :

> Onus est honos qui sustinet rem publicam.

Castoris nomen Graecum, Pollucis a Graecis ; in Latinis litteris veteribus nomen quod est, inscribitur ut Πολυδεύκης[3] Polluces, non ut nunc[4] Pollux. Concordia a corde congruente.

74. Feronia, Minerva, Novensides a Sabinis. Paulo aliter ab eisdem dicimus haec : *P*alem,[1] Vestam, Salutem, Fortunam, Fontem, Fidem. E⟨t⟩ ar*ae*[2] Sabinum linguam olent, quae Tati regis voto sunt Romae dedicatae : nam, ut annales dicunt, vovit Opi, Flor*ae*, Vediovi[3] Saturnoque, Soli, Lunae, Volcano et Summano, itemque Larundae, Termino, Quirino, Vortumno, Laribus, Dianae Lucinaeque ; e quis nonnulla nomina in utraque lingua habent radices, ut arbores quae in confinio natae in utroque agro ser-

---

§ 73. [1] *Scaliger, for* uiri ius.   [2] *After* ab, *Woelfflin deleted* honesto.   [3] *For* pollideuces.   [4] *For* nuns.

§ 74. [1] *Scaliger, for* hecralem.   [2] *Mue., for* ea re. [3] *Mue., for* floreue dioioui.

---

[b] *Mars* and *Mamers* go together, but *mares* ' males ' is quite distinct.   [c] *Virtus* is in fact from *vir*.   [d] *Honos* and *onus* are quite distinct.   [e] *Com. Rom. Frag.*, page 147 Ribbeck[3].   [f] As in inscriptions, where such spellings are found.   [g] Essentially correct.

§ 74. [a] An old Italian goddess, later identified with Juno. [b] Apparently ' new settlers,' from *novus* and *insidere*, used of the gods brought from elsewhere as distinct from the *indigetes* or native gods.   [c] It is unlikely that all the deities of the

duellum. *Mars* is named from the fact that he commands the *mares* ' males ' in war, or that he is called *Mamers* [b] among the Sabines, with whom he is a favourite. *Quirinus* is from *Quirites.* *Virtus* 'valour,' as *viritus,* is from *virilitas* 'manhood.' [c] *Honos* 'honour, office ' is said from *onus* [d] ' burden ' ; therefore *honestum* ' honourable ' is said of that which is *oneratum* ' loaded with burdens,' and it has been said :

Full onerous is the honour which maintains the state.[e]

The name of *Castor* is Greek, that of *Pollux* likewise from the Greeks ; the form of the name which is found in old Latin literature [f] is *Polluces,* like Greek Πολυδεύκης, not *Pollux* as it is now. *Concordia* ' Concord ' is from the *cor congruens* ' harmonious heart.' [g]

74. *Feronia,*[a] *Minerva,* the *Novensides* [b] are from the Sabines. With slight changes, we say the following, also from the same people [c] : *Pales,*[d] *Vesta, Salus,* Fortune, *Fons,*[e] *Fides* ' Faith.' There is scent of the speech of the Sabines about the altars also, which by the vow of King Tatius were dedicated at Rome : for, as the *Annals* tell, he vowed altars to *Ops, Flora, Vediovis* and Saturn, Sun, Moon, Vulcan and *Summanus,*[f] and likewise to *Larunda,*[g] *Terminus, Quirinus, Vertumnus,* the *Lares, Diana* and *Lucina* ; some of these names have roots in both languages,[h] like trees which have sprung up on the boundary line and creep about

next two lists were brought in from elsewhere ; many of the names are perfectly Roman.   [d] Goddess of the shepherds, who protected them and their flocks.   [e] God of Springs ; *cf.* vi. 22.   [f] A mysterious deity who was considered responsible for lightning at night.   [g] Called also *Lara,* a tale-bearing nymph whom Jupiter deprived of the power of speech.   [h] Quite possible, but very unlikely in the cases of Saturn and Diana.

71

VARRO

punt[4] : potest enim Saturnus hic de alia causa esse dictus atque in Sabinis, et sic Diana,[5] de quibus supra dictum est.

XI. 75. Quod ad immortalis attinet, haec ; deinceps quod ad mortalis attinet videamus. De his animalia in tribus locis quod sunt, in aere, in aqua, in terra, a summa parte ⟨ad⟩[1] infimam descendam. Primum nomin⟨a⟩ omni*um*[2] : alites ⟨ab⟩ alis,[3] volucres a volatu. Deinde generatim : de his pleraeque ab suis vocibus ut haec : upupa, cuculus, corvus, *h*irundo, ulula, bubo ; item haec : pavo, anser, gallina, columba.

76. Sunt quae aliis de causis appellatae, ut noctua, quod noctu canit et vigilat, lusci⟨ni⟩ola,[1] quod luctuose canere existimatur atque esse ex Attica Progne in luctu facta avis. Sic galeri*t*us[2] et motacilla, altera quod in capite habet plumam elatam, altera quod semper movet caudam. Merula, quod mera, id est sola, volitat ; contra ab eo graguli, quod gregatim,

[4] *For* serpent.   [5] *Aldus, for* dianae.
§ 75. [1] *Added by* G, H.   [2] *Fay ;* nomen omnium *Mue. ; for* nomen nominem.   [3] *Aug., for* alii.
§ 76. [1] *Victorius, for* lusciola.   [2] *Aug., with* B, *for* galericus.

---

[f] Saturn in § 64, Diana in § 68.
§ 75. [a] The first six, except *hirundo* (of unknown etymology), are onomatopoeic. Of the last four, *pavo* is borrowed from an Oriental language ; *anser* is an old Indo-European word ; *gallina* is ' the Gallic bird ' ; *columba* is named from its colour.
§ 76. [a] Perhaps correct, if from *luges-cania* ' sorrow-singer.'   [b] Procne, daughter of Pandion king of Athens and wife of Tereus king of Thrace, killed her son Itys and served him to his father for food, in revenge for his ill-treatment and infidelity ; see Ovid, *Metamorphoses*, vi. 424-674. [c] Literally ' hooded,' wearing a *galerum* or hood-like helmet. [d] If not correct, then a very reasonable popular etymology.

72

in both fields : for Saturn might be used as the god's name from one source here, and from another among the Sabines, and so also Diana ; these names I have discussed above.[i]

XI. 75. This is what has to do with the immortals; next let us look at that which has to do with mortal creatures. Amongst these are the animals, and because they abide in three places—in the air, in the water, and on the land—I shall start from the highest place and come down to the lowest. First the names of them all, collectively : *alites* ' winged birds ' from their *alae* ' wings,' *volucres* ' fliers ' from *volatus* ' flight.' Next by kinds : of these, very many are named from their cries, as are these : *upupa* ' hoopoe,' *cuculus* ' cuckoo,' *corvus* ' raven,' *hirundo* ' swallow,' *ulula* ' screech-owl,' *bubo* ' horned owl ' ; likewise these : *pavo* ' peacock,' *anser* ' goose,' *gallina* ' hen,' *columba* ' dove.' [a]

76. Some got their names from other reasons, such as the *noctua* ' night-owl,' because it stays awake and hoots *noctu* ' by night,' and the *lusciniola* ' nightingale,' because it is thought to *canere* ' sing ' *luctuose* ' sorrowfully ' [a] and to have been transformed from the Athenian Procne [b] in her *luctus* ' sorrow,' into a bird. Likewise the *galeritus* [c] ' crested lark ' and the *motacilla* ' wagtail,' the one because it has a feather standing up on its head, the other because it is always moving its tail.[d] The *merula* ' blackbird ' is so named because it flies *mera* ' unmixed,' that is, alone [e] ; on the other hand, the *graguli* [f] ' jackdaws ' got their names because they fly *gregatim* ' in flocks,' as certain

[e] That is, without other birds, like wine without water : an absurd etymology.   [f] Properly *graculi* ; not connected with *greges*.

ut quidam Graeci greges γέργερα. Ficedula⟨e⟩[3] et miliariae a cibo, quod altera*e* fico, alterae milio fiunt pingues.

XII. 77. Aquatilium vocabula animalium partim sunt vernacula, partim peregrina. Foris mur*a*ena, quod μύραινα Graece, cybium[1] et thynnus, cuius item partes Graecis vocabulis omnes, ut melander atque uraeon. Vocabula piscium pleraque translata a terrestribus ex aliqua parte similibus rebus, ut anguilla, lingulaca, sudis[2]; alia a coloribus, ut haec : asellus, umbra, turdus ; alia a vi quadam, ut haec : lupus, canicula, torpedo. Item in conchyliis aliqua ex Graecis, ut peloris, ostrea, echinus. Vernacula ad similitudinem, ut surenae,[3] pectunculi, ungues.

XIII. 78. Sunt etiam animalia in aqua, quae in terram interdum exeant : alia Graecis vocabulis, ut polypus, h*i*ppo⟨s⟩ potamios,[1] crocodilos,[2] alia Latinis,

---

[3] *Ed. Veneta, for* ficedula.
§ 77.   [1] *Aldus, for* cytybium.   [2] *Aldus, for* lingula casudis.   [3] *For* syrenae.
§ 78.   [1] *L. Sp., for* yppo potamios.   [2] *For* crocodillos.

---

[g] Correct; Varro, *De Re Rustica*, iii. 5. 2, speaks of *miliariae* as prized delicacies, raised and fattened for the table.
§ 77.   [a] The identification of many animals and fishes is quite uncertain, and the translation is therefore tentative. But the etymological views in § 77 and § 78 are approximately correct.   [b] More precisely, the flesh of the young tunny salted in cubes.   [c] Seemingly a variant form for *melandryon*, Greek μελάνδρυον 'slice of the large tunny called μελάνδρυς or black-oak.'   [d] From Greek οὐραῖος 'pertaining to the tail (οὐρά).'   [e] Diminutive of *anguis* 'snake.'   [f] Because flat like a *lingua* 'tongue' ; *lingulaca* means also

Greeks call *greges* ' flocks ' γέργερα. *Ficedulae* ' fig-peckers ' and *miliariae* ' ortolans ' are named from their food,[g] because it is the ones become fat on the *ficus* ' fig,' the others on *milium* ' millet.'

XII. 77. The names of water animals are some native, some foreign.[a] From abroad come *muraena* ' moray,' because it is μύραινα in Greek, *cybium* ' young tunny '[b] and *thunnus* ' tunny,' all whose parts likewise go by Greek names, as *melander*[c] ' black-oak-piece ' and *uraeon*[d] ' tail-piece.' Very many names of fishes are transferred from land objects which are like them in some respect, as *anguilla*[e] ' eel,' *lingulaca*[f] ' sole,' *sudis*[g] ' pike.' Others come from their colours, like these : *asellus* ' hake,' *umbra* ' umbra,' *turdus* ' wrasse.'[h] Others come from some physical power, like these : *lupus* ' sea-bass,' *canicula* ' dogfish,' *torpedo* ' electric ray.'[i] Likewise among the shellfish there are some from Greek, as *peloris* ' sunset shell,' *ostrea* ' oyster,' *echinus* ' sea-urchin ' ; and also native words that point out a likeness, as *surenae*,[j] *pectunculi*[k] ' scallops,' *ungues*[l] ' razor-clams.'

XIII. 78. There are also animals in the water, which at times come out on the land : some with Greek names, like the octopus, the hippopotamus, the crocodile ; others with Latin names, like *rana* ' frog,'

' chatter-box, talkative woman.' [g] On land, a ' stake.'
[h] On land, respectively ' little ass,' ' shadow,' ' thrush.'
[i] On land, respectively ' wolf,' ' little dog,' ' numbness.'
[j] Of unknown meaning, and perhaps a corrupt reading ; Groth, *De Codice Florentino*, 27 (105), suggests *pernae* from Pliny, *Nat. Hist.* xxxii. 11. 54. 154, who mentions the *perna* as a sea-mussel standing on a high foot or stalk, like a haunch of ham with the leg. [k] On land, ' little combs,' diminutive of *pecten*. [l] ' Finger-nails ' ; perhaps not the razor-clam, but a small clam shaped like the finger-nail.

ut rana, ⟨anas⟩,[3] mergus ; a quo Graeci ea quae in
aqua et terra possunt vivere vocant ἀμφίβια. E quis
rana ab sua dicta voce, anas a nando, mergus quod
mergendo in aquam captat escam.

79. Item alia[1] in hoc genere a Graecis, ut querquedula, ⟨quod⟩[2] κερκήδης,[3] alcedo,[4] quod ea ἀλκυών;
Latina, ut testudo, quod testa tectum hoc animal,
lolligo, quod subvolat, littera commutata, primo volligo. Ut Aegypti in flumine quadrupes sic in Latio,
nominati lu⟨t⟩ra[5] et fiber. Lu⟨t⟩ra,[5] quod succidere
dicitur arborum radices in ripa atque eas dissolvere :
ab ⟨luere⟩ lutra.[6] Fiber, ab extrema ora fluminis
dextra et sinistra maxime quod solet videri, et antiqui
februm dicebant extremum, a quo in sagis fimbr⟨i⟩ae
et in iecore extremum fibra, fiber dictus.

XIV. 80. De animalibus in locis terrestribus quae
sunt hominum propria primum, deinde de pecore,
tertio de feris scribam. Incipiam ab honore publico.

[3] *Added by Aug.*
§ 79. [1] *L. Sp., with B, for* aliae. [2] *Added by Kent.*
[3] *GS., for* cerceris. [4] *Groth ;* halcedo *Laetus ; for*
algedo. [5] *GS. ;* lytra *Turnebus ; for* lira. [6] *Stroux ;*
ab luere *Scaliger ; for* ab litra.

§ 78. [a] *Cf.* § 77, note *a.*
§ 79. [a] Conjectural purely. [b] An absurd etymology.
[c] Originally *udra* ' water-animal,' with *l* from association with
lutum ' mud ' or *lutor* ' washer.' Varro attributes to the
otter the tree-felling habit of the beaver. [d] Properly ' the
brown animal.' [e] *Fiber, fimbriae, fibra* have no etymological connexion.

anas ' duck,' *mergus* ' diver.' Whence the Greeks give the name *amphibia* to those which can live both in the water and on the land. Of these, the *rana* is named from its voice, the *anas* from *nare* ' to swim,' the *mergus* because it catches its food by *mergendo* ' diving ' into the water.[a]

79. Likewise there are other names in this class, that are from the Greeks, as *querquedula* ' teal,' because it is κερκίδης,[a] and *alcedo* ' kingfisher,' because this is ἀλκυών ; and Latin names, such as *testudo* ' tortoise,' because this animal is covered with a *testa* ' shell,' and *lolligo* ' squid,' because it *volat* ' flies ' up from under,[b] originally *volligo*, but now with one letter changed. Just as in Egypt there is a quadruped living in the river, so there are river quadrupeds in Latium, named *lutra* ' otter ' and *fiber* ' beaver.' The *lutra* [c] is so named because it is said to cut off the roots of trees on the bank and set the trees loose : from *luere* ' to loose,' *lutra*. The beaver [d] was called *fiber* because it is usually seen very far off on the bank of the river to right or to left, and the ancients called a thing that was very far off a *februm* ; from which in blankets the last part is called *fimbriae* ' fringe ' and the last part in the liver is the *fibra* ' fibre.' [e]

XIV. 80. Among the living beings on the land, I shall speak first of terms which apply to human beings, then of domestic animals, third of wild beasts. I shall start from the offices of the state. The Consul [a] was

§ 80. [a] Properly, *consulere* is derived from *consul*. Of *consul*, at least four reasonable etymologies are proposed, the simplest being that it is from *com+sed* ' those who sit together,' as there were two consuls from the beginning ; the *l* for *d* being a peculiarity taken from the dialect of the Sabines (*cf. lingua* for older *dingua*).

VARRO

Consu nominatus qui consuleret populum et senatum,
nisi illinc potius unde Accius[1] ait in Bruto :

> Qui recte consulat, consul cluat.[1]

Praetor dictus qui praeiret iure et exercitu ; a quo id
Lucilius :

> Ergo praetorum est ante et praeire.

81.   Censor ad cuius censionem, id est arbitrium,
censeretur populus.   Aedilis qui aedis sacras et
privatas procuraret.   Quaestores a quaerendo, qui
conquirerent publicas pecunias et maleficia, quae
triumviri capitales nunc conquirunt ; ab his postea
qui quaestionum iudicia exercent quaes⟨i⟩tores[1]
dicti.   Tribuni militum, quod terni tribus tribubus
Ramnium, Lucerum, Titium olim ad exercitum mittebantur.   Tribuni plebei, quod ex tribunis militum
primum tribuni plebei facti, qui plebem defenderent,
in secessione Crustumerina.

82.   Dictator, quod a consule dicebatur, cui dicto
audientes omnes essent.   Magister equitum, quod

§ 80.   [1] Later codices, for tatius F^1, II, p^2, taccius F^2, V, a.
[2] GS., after an unnamed friend of Scaliger, for consulciat.
    § 81.   [1] Mommsen, for quaestores.

[b] Trag. Rom. Frag. 39 Ribbeck[3] ; R.O.L. ii. 564-565 Warmington.   [c] Iure is dative.   [d] 1160 Marx.
    § 81.   [a] The tribunus was by etymology merely the ' man
of the tribus or tribe,' and therefore did not derive his name
from the word for ' three,' except indirectly ; cf. § 55.
[b] That is, elected by the plebeians from among their military
tribunes whom they had chosen to lead them in their Secession to the Sacred Mount (which may have lain in the territory of Crustumerium), in 494 B.C.   Their persons were

so named as the one who should *consulere* ' ask the advice of ' people and senate, unless rather from this fact whence Accius takes it when he says in the *Brutus* [b] :

> Let him who counsels right, be called the Consul.

The Praetor was so named as the one who should *praeire* ' go before ' the law [c] and the army ; whence Lucilius said this [d] :

> Then to go out in front and before is the duty of praetors.

81. The *Censor* was so named as the one at whose *censio* ' rating,' that is, *arbitrium* ' judgement,' the people should be rated. The *Aedile*, as the one who was to look after *aedes* ' buildings ' sacred and private. The *Quaestors,* from *quaerere* ' to seek,' who *conquirerent* ' should seek into ' the public moneys and illegal doings, which the *triumviri capitales* ' the prison board ' now investigate ; from these, afterwards, those who pronounce judgement on the matters of investigation were named *quaesitores* ' inquisitors.' The *Tribuni* [a] *Militum* ' tribunes of the soldiers,' because of old there were sent to the army three each on behalf of the three tribes of Ramnes, Luceres, and Tities. The *Tribuni Plebei* ' tribunes of the *plebs*,' because from among the tribunes of the soldiers tribunes of the *plebs* were first created,[b] in the Secession to Crustumerium, for the purpose of defending the *plebs* ' populace.'

82. The *Dictator*, because he was named by the consul as the one to whose *dictum* ' order ' all should be obedient.[a] The *Magister Equitum* ' master of the

---

sacrosanct, enabling them to carry out their duty of protecting the plebeians against the injustice of the patrician officials.

§ 82. [a] Rather, because he *dictat* ' gives orders.'

summa potestas huius in equites et accensos, ut est summa populi dictator, a quo is quoque *magister populi* appellatus. Reliqui, quod minores quam hi magistri, dicti magistratus, ut ab albo albatus.

XV. 83.   Sacerdotes universi a sacris dicti. Pontufices, ut[1] Scaevola Quintus pontufex maximus dicebat, a posse et facere, ut po⟨te⟩ntifices.[2] Ego a ponte arbitror : nam ab his Sublicius est factus primum ut restitutus saepe, cum ideo sacra et u*l*s[3] et cis Tiberim non mediocri ritu fiant.   Curiones dicti a curiis, qui fiunt ut in his sacra faciant.

84.   Flamines, quod in Latio capite velato erant semper ac caput cinctum habebant filo, f⟨i⟩lamines[1] dicti.   Horum singuli cognomina habent ab eo deo cui sacra faciunt ; sed partim sunt aperta, partim obscura : aperta ut Martialis, Volcanalis ; obscura Dialis et Furinalis, cum Dialis ab Iove sit (Diovis enim), Furi⟨n⟩alis a Furri*na*,[2] cuius etiam in fastis

§ 83.   [1] *After* ut, *Ed. Veneta deleted* a.   [2] *GS., for* pontifices, *cf.* v. 4.   [3] *For* uis.
§ 84.   [1] *Canal, for* flamines, *cf. Festus,* 87. 15 *M.*   [2] *L. Sp. ;* Furina *Aldus ; for* furrida.

---

[b] Not quite ; for *magistratus* is a fourth declension substantive, ' office of magister,' then ' holder of such an office,' while *albatus* is a second declension adjective.
§ 83.   [a] Q. Mucius Scaevola, consul 95 B.C., and subsequently Pontifex Maximus ; proscribed and killed by the Marian party in 82.   He was a man of the highest character and abilities, and made the first systematic compilation of the *ius civile* ; see i. 19 Huschke.   [b] Varro may be right, though perhaps it was the ' bridges ' between this world and the next which originally the pontifices were to keep in repair ;   *cf. Class. Philol.* viii. 317-326 (1913).   [c] The wooden bridge on piles, traditionally built by Ancus Marcius.   [d] The *curia*

cavalry,' because he has supreme power over the cavalry and the replacement troops, just as the dictator is the highest authority over the people, from which he also is called *magister*, but of the people and not of the cavalry. The remaining officials, because they are inferior to these *magistri* ' masters,' are called *magistratus* ' magistrates,' derived just as *albatus* ' whitened, white-clad ' is derived from *albus* ' white.' [b]

XV. 83. The *sacerdotes* ' priests ' collectively were named from the *sacra* ' sacred rites.' The *pontifices* ' high-priests,' Quintus Scaevola [a] the Pontifex Maximus said, were named from *posse* ' to be able ' and *facere* ' to do,' as though *potentifices*. For my part I think that the name comes from *pons* ' bridge ' [b] ; for by them the Bridge-on-Piles [c] was made in the first place, and it was likewise repeatedly repaired by them, since in that connexion rites are performed on both sides of the Tiber with no small ceremony. The *curiones* were named from the *curiae* ; they are created for conducting sacred rites in the *curiae*. [d]

84. The *flamines* [a] ' flamens,' because in Latium they always kept their heads covered and had their hair girt with a woollen *filum* ' band,' were originally called *filamines*. Individually they have distinguishing epithets from that god whose rites they perform ; but some are obvious, others obscure : obvious, like *Martialis* and *Volcanalis* ; obscure are *Dialis* and *Furinalis*, since *Dialis* is from Jove, for he is called also Diovis, and *Furinalis* from Furrina,[b] who even has a

was the fundamental political unit in the early Roman state ; it was an organization of *gentes*, originally ten to the *curia*, and ten *curiae* to each of the three tribes.

§ 84.   [a] Of uncertain etymology, but not from *filamen*.
[b] A goddess, practically unknown ; *cf.* vi. 19.

VARRO

feriae Furinales sunt. Sic flamen Falacer a divo patre Falacre.

85. Salii ab salitando, quod facere in comitiis in sacris quotannis et solent et debent. Luperci, quod Lupercalibus in Lupercali sacra faciunt. Fratres Arvales dicti qui sacra publica faciunt propterea ut fruges ferant arva : a ferendo et arvis Fratres Arvales dicti. Sunt qui a fratria dixerunt : fratria est Graecum vocabulum partis[1] hominum, ut ⟨Ne⟩apoli[2] etiam nunc. Sodales Titii ⟨ab avibus titiantibus⟩[3] dicti, quas in auguriis certis observare solent.

86. Fetiales, quod fidei publicae inter populos praeerant : nam per hos fiebat ut iustum conciperetur bellum, et inde desitum, ut f⟨o⟩edere fides pacis constitueretur. Ex his mittebantur, ante quam conciperetur, qui res repeterent, et per hos etiam nunc fit foedus,[1] quod fidus Ennius scribit dictum.

§ 85. [1] *Aug.*, *for* patris. [2] *Turnebus*, *for* apoli. [3] *Added by A. Sp.*, *after Laetus* (a titiis avibus).
§ 86. [1] *For* faedus.

---

[e] An old Italic mythical hero ; quite obscure.
§ 85. [a] From *salire* ' to leap,' of which *salitare* is a derivative. [b] Priests of the God Lupercus, who *arcet* ' keeps away ' the *lupi* ' wolves ' from the flocks. [c] *Arvales* from *arva* ; but *fratres* has nothing to do with *ferre*. [d] Page 116 Funaioli. [e] ' Political brotherhood,' from φράτηρ ' clan brother ' ; any reference to it is here out of place. [f] According to Tacitus, *Ann.* i. 54, they were established by Titus Tatius for the preservation of certain Sabine religious practices.
§ 86. [a] Perhaps from an old word meaning ' law,' from the root seen in *feci* ' I made, established ' ; but without connexion with the words in the text. *Foedus, fides, fidus* are closely connected with one another. [b] In the early

82

Furinal Festival in the calendar. So also the Flamen *Falacer* from the divine father Falacer.[c]

85. The *Salii* were named [a] from *salitare* ' to dance,' because they had the custom and the duty of dancing yearly in the assembly-places, in their ceremonies. The *Luperci* [b] were so named because they make offerings in the *Lupercal* at the festival of the Lupercalia. *Fratres Arvales* ' Arval Brothers ' was the name given to those who perform public rites to the end that the ploughlands may bear fruits : from *ferre* ' to bear ' and *arva* ' ploughlands ' they are called *Fratres Arvales*.[c] But some have said [d] that they were named from *fratria* ' brotherhood ' : *fratria* is the Greek name of a part of the people,[e] as at Naples even now. The *Sodales Titii* ' Titian Comrades ' are so named from the *titiantes* ' twittering ' birds which they are accustomed to watch in some of their augural observations.[f]

86. The *Fetiales* [a] ' herald-priests,' because they were in charge of the state's word of honour in matters between peoples ; for by them it was brought about that a war that was declared should be a just war, and by them the war was stopped, that by a *foedus* ' treaty ' the *fides* ' honesty ' of the peace might be established. Some of them were sent before war should be declared, to demand restitution of the stolen property,[b] and by them even now is made the *foedus* ' treaty,' which Ennius writes [c] was pronounced *fidus*.

days wars started chiefly as the result of raids in which property, cattle, and persons had been carried off. [c] Page 238 Vahlen[2] ; *R.O.L.* i. 564 Warmington ; Ennius probably wished by a pun to indicate a relation between *foedus* and the adjective *fidus* which, in his opinion, did not really exist (though it did).

XVI. 87.   In re militari praetor dictus qui praeiret
exercitui.   Imperator, ab imperio populi qui eos, qui
id attemptasse⟨n⟩t, oppressi⟨t⟩[1] hostis.   Legati qui
lecti publice, quorum opera consilioque uteretur
peregre magistratus, quive nuntii senatus aut populi
essent.   Exercitus, quod exercitando fit melior.
Legio, quod leguntur milites in delectu.

88.   Cohors, quod ut in villa ex pluribus tectis
coniungitur ac quiddam fit unum, sic hic[1] ex manipulis
pluribus copulatur[2]: cohors quae in villa, quod circa
eum locum pecus cooreretur, tametsi cohortem in
villa *Hyp*sicrates[3] dicit esse Graece χόρτον[4] apud
poetas dictam.   Manipul*u*s[5] exercitus minima[6] manus
quae unum sequitur signum.   Centuria qu*i*[7] sub uno
centurione sunt, quorum centenarius iustus numerus.

89.   Milites, quod trium milium primo legio fiebat
ac singulae tribus Titiensium, Ramnium, Lucerum
milia militum mittebant.   Hastati dicti qui primi

---

§ 87.   [1] *Aug., with B, for* oppressi.
§ 88.   [1] *Mue., for* his.   [2] *G, H, Laetus, for* populatur.
[3] *Aldus,   for* ipsicrates.   [4] *Turnebus,   for*   cohorton.
[5] *L. Sp., for* manipulos.   [6] *L. Sp., for* minimas.   [7] *Mue.,*
for quae.

---

§ 87.   [a] So named because he *imperat* ' gives orders ' ; in
practice, it was a title conferred upon a general after a victory,
by spontaneous acclamation of his soldiers.   [b] Meaning
' delegated,' participle of *legare* (akin to *legere*).
§ 88.   [a] Prefix *co-*+*hort-s*, the second part being the same
as *hortus* ' enclosed place as garden,' and Greek χόρτος.
[b] A grammarian, mentioned also by Gellius, xvi. 12. 6 ; see
Funaioli,   page   107.   [c] A   ' handful,'   from   *manus* + a
derivative of the root in *plere* ' to fill.'   [d] This and the
following words are from *centum* ' hundred.'

XVI. 87. In military affairs, the praetor was so called as the one who should *praeire* ' go at the head ' of the army. The *imperator* ^a ' commander,' from the *imperium* ' dominion ' of the people, as the one who crushed those enemies who had attacked it. The *legati* ^b ' attachés,' those who were *lecti* ' chosen ' officially, whose aid or counsel the magistrates should use when away from Rome, or who should be messengers of the senate or of the people. The *exercitus* ' army,' because by *exercitando* ' training ' it is improved. The *legio* ' legion,' because the soldiers *leguntur* ' are gathered ' in the levy.

88. The *cohors* ^a ' cohort,' because, just as on the farm the *cohors* ' yard ' *coniungitur* ' is joined together ' of several buildings and becomes a certain kind of unity, so in the army it *copulatur* ' is coupled together ' of several maniples : the *cohors* which is on the farm, is so called because around that place the flock *cooritur* ' assembles,' although Hypsicrates ^b says that the *cohors* on the farm, as said by the poets, is the word which in Greek is χόρτος ' farmyard.' The *manipulus* ^c ' maniple ' is the smallest *manus* ' troop ' which has a standard of its own to follow. The *centuria* ^d ' century ' consists of those who are under one *centurio* ' centurion,' whose proper number is *centenarius* ' one hundred each.'

89. *Milites* ^a ' soldiers,' because at first the legion was made of three *milia* ' thousands,' and the individual tribes of Titienses, Ramnes, and Luceres sent their *milia* ' thousands ' of *milites* ' soldiers.' The *hastati* ' spearmen ' were so called as those who in the first line fought with *hastae* ' spears,' the *pilani* ' jave-

§ 89. ^a *Milites* and *milia* are not connected etymologically.

hastis pugnabant, pilani qui pilis, principes qui a principio gladiis ; ea post commutata re militari minus illustria sunt. Pilani triar*ii*[1] quoque dicti, quod in acie tertio ordine extremi[2] subsidio deponebantur ; quod hi subsidebant ab eo subsidium dictum, a quo Plautus :

> Agite nunc, subsid*i*te[3] omnes quasi solent triarii.

90. Auxilium appellatum ab auctu, cum accesserant ei qui adiumento essent alienigenae. Praesidium dictum qui extra castra praesidebant in loco aliquo, quo tutior regio esset. Obsidium dictum ab obsidendo, quo minus hostis egredi posset. In⟨si⟩di*ae*[1] item ab *in*sidendo,[2] cum id ideo facerent quo facilius deminuerent hostis. Duplicarii dicti quibus ob virtutem duplicia cibaria ut darentur institutum.

91. Turma terima (E in U abiit), quod ter deni equites ex tribus tribubus Titiensium, Ramnium, Lucerum fiebant. Itaque primi singularum decuriarum decuriones dicti, qui ab eo in singulis turmis sunt etiam nunc terni. Quos hi primo administros

§ 89. [1] *For* triani.   [2] *Aug. (quoting a friend), for* extremis.   [3] *Laetus*, *for* subsidete.
§ 90. [1] *L. Sp., for* indie.   [2] *Studemund (quoted by Groth), for* ab absidendo.

---

[b] By origin, the 'foremost' in the fight, the men of the first line, later shifted in position.   [c] By origin, 'that which sits or remains close by, under the outer edge of something'; Varro's etymology is correct, except for his interpretation of the verb.   [d] *Frivolaria*, frag. V Ritschl.
§ 91.   [a] Etymology uncertain, but not as in the text.

lin-men ' as being those who fought with *pila* ' jave-
lins,' the *principes* [b] ' first-men ' as those who from the
principium ' beginning ' fought with swords ; these
words were less perspicuous later, when tactics had
been changed. The *pilani* are called also *triarii*
' third-line-men,' because in the battle arrangement
they were set in the rear, in the third line, as reserves ;
because these men habitually *subsidebant* ' sat ' while
waiting, from this fact the *subsidium* [c] ' reserve force '
got its name, whence Plautus says [d] :

> Come now, all of you sit by as troopers in reserve
> are wont.

90. *Auxilium* ' auxiliaries ' was so called from
auctus ' increase,' when those foreigners who were
intended to give help had added themselves to the
fighters. *Praesidium* ' garrison ' was said of those
who *praesidebant* ' sat in front ' outside the main camp
somewhere, that the district might be safer. *Obsidium* ' siege ' was said from *obsidere* ' to sit in the
way,' that the enemy might not be able to sally forth.
Insidiae ' ambush ' likewise from *insidere* ' to sit in a
place,' since they did this that they might more easily
diminish the enemy's forces. *Duplicarii* ' doublers '
were those to whom by order *duplicia* ' double ' rations
were given on account of their notable valour.

91. *Turma* [a] ' squadron ' is from *terima* (the E has
changed to U), because they were composed of *ter*
' three times ' ten horsemen, from the three tribes
of Titienses, Ramnes, and Luceres. Therefore the
leaders of the individual *decuriae* ' groups of ten '
were called decurions, who from this fact are even
now three in each squadron. Those whom at first the
decurions themselves *adoptabant* ' chose ' as their

87

ipsi sibi adoptabant, optiones vocari coepti,[1] quos nunc propter ambitionem tribuni faciunt. Tubicines a tuba et canendo, similiter liticines.[2] Classicus[3] a classe, qui item cornu ⟨aut lit⟩uo[4] canit, ut tum cum classes comitiis ad comit⟨i⟩atum[5] vocant.

XVII. 92. Quae a fortuna vocabula, in his quaedam minus aperta ut pauper, dives, miser, beatus, sic alia. Pauper a paulo lare. Mendicus a minus, cui cum opus est minus nullo est. Dives a divo qui ut deus nihil[1] indigere videtur. Opulentus ab ope, cui eae opimae ; ab eadem inops qui eius indiget, et ab eodem fonte copis[2] ac copiosus. Pecuniosus a pecunia magna, pecunia a pecu : a pastoribus enim horum vocabulorum origo.

XVIII. 93. Artificibus maxima causa ars, id est, ab arte medicina ut sit medicus dictus, a sutrina sutor, non a medendo ac suendo, quae omnino ultima huic rei : ⟨hae enim⟩[1] earum rerum radices, ut in proxumo

---

§ 91. [1] *For* caepti.   [2] *Rhol., for* litigines.   [3] *A. Sp., for* classicos.   [4] *A. Sp., for* cornu uo.   [5] *Vertranius, for* comitatum.
§ 92. [1] *For* nichil.   [2] *Turnebus, for* copiis.
§ 93. [1] *Added by Reitzenstein.*

---

[b] That is, from *lituus* ' cornet ' and *canere*.
§ 92. [a] *Pau-per* has the same first element as *pau-lus*. [b] Derivative of *mendum* ' error, defect.' [c] Quite possibly, since the gods were thought of as conferring wealth ; *dives* is derived from *divus* as *caeles* is from *caelum*. [d] From *co-opis*. [e] The earliest unit of value was a domestic animal; *cf.* English *fee* and German *Vieh* ' cattle,' both cognate to Latin *pecu*.
§ 93. [a] Properly *medicina* from *medicus*, which is from *mederi*, etc.

88

assistants, were at the start called *optiones* ' choices ' ; but now the tribunes, to increase their influence, do the appointing of them. *Tubicines* ' trumpeters,' from *tuba* ' trumpet ' and *canere* ' to sing or play ' ; in like fashion *liticines* [b] ' cornetists.' The *classicus* ' class-musician ' is named from the *classis* ' class of citizens ' ; he likewise plays on the horn or the cornet, for example when they call the classes to gather for an assembly.

XVII. 92. Among the words which have to do with personal fortune, some are not very clear, such as *pauper* ' poor,' *dives* ' rich,' *miser* ' wretched,' *beatus* ' blest,' and others as well. *Pauper* [a] is from *paulus lar* ' scantily equipped home.' *Mendicus* [b] ' beggar ' is from *minus* ' less,' said of one who, when there is a need, has *minus* ' less ' than nothing. *Dives* ' rich ' is from *divus* [c] ' godlike person,' who, as being a *deus* ' god,' seems to lack nothing. *Opulentus* ' wealthy ' is from *ops* ' property,' said of one who has it in abundance ; from the same, *inops* ' destitute ' is said of him who lacks *ops*, and from the same source *copis* [d] ' well supplied ' and *copiosus* ' abundantly furnished.' *Pecuniosus* ' moneyed ' is from a large amount of *pecunia* ' money ' ; *pecunia* is from *pecu* ' flock ' : for it was among keepers of flocks that these words originated. [e]

XVIII. 93. For artisans the chief cause of the names is the art itself, that is, that from the *ars medicina* ' medical art ' the *medicus* ' physician ' should be named, and from the *ars sutrina* ' shoemaker's art ' the *sutor* ' shoemaker,' and not directly from *mederi* ' to cure ' and *suere* ' to sew,' though these are the absolutely final sources for such names. [a] For these are the roots of these things, as will be shown in the

89

libro aperietur. Quare quod ab arte artifex dicitur nec multa in eo obscura, relinquam.

94. Similis causa quae ab scientia voca⟨n⟩tur[1] aliqua ut praestigiator, monitor, nomenclator ; sic etiam quae a studio[2] quodam dicuntur, cursor, natator, pugil. Etiam in hoc genere quae sunt vocabula pleraque aperta, ut legulus, alter ab oleis, alter ab uvis. Haec si minus aperta vindemiator, vestigator et venator, tamen idem, quod vindemiator vel quod vinum legit[3] dicitur vel quod de viti id demunt ; vestigator a vestigiis ferarum quas indagatur ; venator a vento,[4] quod sequitur cervum[5] ad ventum et in ventum.[6]

XIX. 95. Haec de hominibus : hic quod sequitur de pecore, haec. Pecus ab eo quod perpascebant, a quo pecora universa. Quod in pecore pecunia tum pastoribus consistebat et standi fundamentum pes (a quo dicitur in aedificiis area pes magnus et qui negotium instituit pedem posuisse), a pede pecudem appellarunt, ut ab eodem pedicam et pedisequum et pecul⟨i⟩ariae[1] oves aliudve quid : id enim peculium primum. Hinc peculatum publicum primo ⟨di-

---

§ 94. [1] *B, M, Aug.*, *for* uocatur.   [2] *Sciop.*, *for* spatio. [3] *L. Sp.*, *for* legere.   [4] *Aug.* (*quoting a friend*), *for* uentu.   [5] *Scaliger*, *for* uerbum.   [6] *Aug.* (*quoting a friend*), *for* aduentum et inuentum.

§ 95. [1] *Lachmann*, *for* peculatoriae.

---

[b] This promise seems not to be kept.

§ 94. [a] For this meaning, *cf.* Festus, 138 b 29 and 139. 8 M.   [b] *Cf.* v. 37, where *vindemia* is discussed.

§ 95. [a] *Pecus* is an inherited word which cannot be further analysed ; to it belong all the words here given, which begin with *pec-*. It has no connexion with *pes* 'foot.'   [b] To *pes* 'foot' belong all the words here given which begin with *ped-*.

90

next book.[b] Therefore, because an artisan is called from his art and not many names in this class are obscure, I shall leave them and go on.

94.   There is a like origin for those names which are given from some special skill, such as *praestigiator* 'juggler,' *monitor* 'prompter,'[a] *nomenclator* 'namer'; so also those which are derived from a special interest, such as *cursor* 'runner,' *natator* 'swimmer,' *pugil* 'boxer.'   The words which are in this class too, are generally obvious, like *legulus* 'picker,' one of olives and the other of grapes.   If these are less obvious in the cases of *vindemiator*, *vestigator*, and *venator*, still the same principle holds, that *vindemiator* 'vintager' is said either because he gathers the *vinum* 'wine' or because they *demunt* 'take' this from the *vitis* 'grape-vine'[b]; *vestigator* 'tracker,' from the *vestigia* 'tracks' of the beasts which he trails; *venator* 'hunter' from *ventus* 'wind,' because he follows the stag towards the wind and into the wind.

XIX. 95.   So much about men: what comes next here is about cattle, as follows.   *Pecus*[a] 'cattle,' from the fact that they *perpascebant* 'grazed,' whence as a whole they were called *pecora* 'flocks and herds.' Because the herdsmen's *pecunia* 'wealth' then lay in their *pecus* 'flocks' and the base for standing is a *pes* 'foot' (from which in buildings the ground is called a great *pes*[b] 'foot' and a man who has founded a business is said to have established his *pes* 'footing'), from *pes* 'foot' they gave the name *pecus, pecudis* 'one head of cattle,' just as from the same they said *pedica* 'fetter' and *pedisequus* 'footman' and *peculiariae* 'privately owned' sheep or anything else: for this was the first private property.   Hence they called it a *peculatus* 'peculation' from the state in the beginning, when

xer⟩u⟨n⟩t[2] cum pecore diceretur multa et id esse⟨t⟩[3] coactum in publicum, si erat aversum.

96. Ex quo[1] fructus maior, hic[2] est qui Graecis usus : ⟨sus⟩, quod ὖς, bos, quod βοῦς, taurus, quod ⟨ταῦρος⟩, item ovis, quod ὄις : ita enim antiqui dicebant, non ut nunc πρόβατον. Possunt in Latio quoque ut in Graecia ab suis vocibus haec eadem ficta. Armenta, quod boves ideo maxime parabant, ut inde eligerent ad arandum ; inde arimenta dicta, postea I tertia littera extrita. Vitulus, quod Graece antiquitus ἰταλός, aut quod plerique vegeti, vegitulus.[3] Iuvencus, iuvare qui iam ad agrum colendum posset.

97. Capra carpa, a quo scriptum

Omnicarpae caprae.

Hircus,[1] quod Sabini fircus ; quod illic fedus,[2] in Latio rure hedus, qui in urbe ut in multis A addito haedus.[3] Porcus, quod Sabini dicunt[4] aprunu⟨m⟩ porcu⟨m⟩[5] ; proi⟨n⟩de[6] porcus, nisi si a Graecis, quod Athenis in libris sacrorum scripta est πόρκη e⟨t⟩ πόρκο⟨s⟩.[7]

---

[2] *Fay, for* ut.   [3] *Aug., for* esse.

§ 96.   [1] *Mue., for* qua.   [2] *Mue., for* hinc.   [3] *Laetus, for* uigitulus.

§ 97.   [1] *Aug., for* ircus.   [2] *For* faedus.   [3] *Aug., for* aedus.   [4] *Laetus, for* dicto.   [5] *Kent ;* aprinum porcum L. *Sp. ;* aprum porcum *Scaliger ; for* apruno porco.   [6] *Turnebus, for* poride.   [7] *Kent, for* porcae porco.

---

§ 96.   [a] Correct equations ; but the Latin words are not derived from the Greek : the four pairs are from the ancestral language, and only *sus* is likely to be onomatopoeic. [b] The Greek word is not the source of the Latin word, but is borrowed from it ; there is no satisfactory etymology of *vitulus*.   [c] Really ' youthful,' a derivative of *iuvenis* ' young man,' and not from *iuvare.*

§ 97.   [a] Wrong.   [b] An old inherited word.   [c] Idena fine was imposed in *pecus* ' cattle ' and there was a collection into the state treasury, of what had been diverted.

96. Regarding cattle from which there is larger profit, there is the same use of names here as among the Greeks : *sus* ' swine,' the same as ὖς ; *bos* ' cow,' the same as βοῦς ; *taurus* ' bull,' the same as ταῦρος ; likewise *ovis* ' sheep,' the same as ὄις [a] : for thus the ancients used to say, not πρόβατον as they do now. This identity of the names in Latium and in Greece may be the result of invention after the natural utterances of the animals. *Armenta* ' plough-oxen,' because they raised oxen especially that they might select some of them for *arandum* ' ploughing ' ; thence they were called *arimenta*, from which the third letter I was afterwards squeezed out. *Vitulus* calf,' because in Greek it was anciently ἰταλός [b] ; or from *vegitulus*, a name given because most calves are *vegeti* ' frisky.' A *iuvencus* [c] ' bullock ' was one which could now *iuvare* ' help ' in tilling the fields.

97. *Capra* ' she-goat ' was originally *carpa* ' cropper,' [a] from which is written

All-cropping she-goats.

Hircus ' buck,' which the Sabines call *fircus* ; and what there is *fedus*, in Latium is *hedus* ' kid ' in the country, and in the City it is *haedus*, with an added A, as is the case with many words. *Porcus* [b] ' pig,' because the Sabines say *aprunus* [c] *porcus* ' boar pig ' ; therefore *porcus* ' pig,' unless it comes from the Greeks, because at Athens in the *Books of the Sacrifices* πόρκη ' female pig ' is written, and πόρκος ' male pig.'

tical with the Plautine *aprugnus*, from *apro-gnos* ' born of the boar.'

93

VARRO

98. Aries, ⟨ut⟩[1] quidam[2] dicebant, ⟨ab⟩[3] aris[4];
veteres nostri ariuga, hinc ariugus.[5] Haec sunt
qu*a*rum[6] in sacruficiis exta in oll*a*,[7] non in veru co-
quuntur, quas et Accius scribit et in pontificiis libris
videmus. In hosti⟨i⟩s eam dicunt ariug*a*m[8] quae
cornua habeat; quoniam si[9] cui ovi mari testiculi
dempti et ideo vi[10] natura versa, verbex declinatum.

99. Pecori ovillo quod agnatus, agnus. Catulus a
sagaci sensu et acuto, ⟨ut Cato⟩[1] Catulus; hinc canis:
nisi quod ut tuba ac cornu, a⟨li⟩quod[2] signum cum
dent,[3] canere dicuntur, quod hic item et noctulucus in
custodia et in venando signum voce dat, canis dictus.

XX. 100. Ferarum vocabula item partim peregrina, ut panthera, leo: utraque Graeca, a quo etiam
et rete quoddam panther et le*a*ena et muliercula
Pantheris et Le*a*ena. Tigris qui est ut leo varius, qui

---

§ 98. [1] *Added by Kent.* [2] *GS., for* qui eam.
[3] *Added by Kent.* [4] *Kent;* areis *Fay; for* ares.
[5] *Kent, for* ariugas. [6] *Aug., for* quorum. [7] *For* ollo.
[8] *Kent;* arvigam *Mue.; for* ariugem. [9] *Lindemann,*
for is. [10] *Sciop., for* ut.
  § 99. [1] *Added by GS.* [2] *Mue., for* cornua quod.
[3] *Victorius, for* dente.

---

§ 98. [a] An old word. [b] An obscure word, found in
various forms: *harviga* (Festus), *hariga* (Donatus *in Phorm.*).
ἄριχα (Hesychius). Varro takes *ariuga* as a derivative of
ara+*iug*-; but it may perhaps better be taken as *hariuga*,
from *hara* ' sty ' (formation like *agri-cola* and *nocti-luca*),
losing the *h* by association with *aries*. Others suggest connexion with *haru-* as in *haruspex*, which would give a form
harviga. At any rate, *ariuga* is feminine because of an
implied *hostia*, and the agreements are feminine in the next
two sentences; *ariugus* is merely a masculine form invented
to correspond to the masculine *aries*. [c] *Rom. Trag.*
Frag., page 227 Ribbeck.[2] [d] Frag. 82 Rowoldt. [e] Also
spelled *vervex* and *berbex*; not connected with *versa*.

94

98. *Aries* [a] ' ram,' as some used to say, from *arae* ' altars ' ; our ancients said *ariuga* [b] ' altar-mate,' and from this formed a masculine *ariugus*. These are those whose vital organs are in the sacrifices boiled in a pot and not roasted on a spit, of which Accius writes [c] and which we see in the *Pontifical Books.*[d] Among sacrificial victims, that victim which by the specifications is to have horns, they call an *ariuga* ; but if the testicles are removed from a male sheep and its nature is thereby forcibly *versa* ' altered,' the name *verbex*[e] ' wether ' is derived as its designation.

99. An *agnus* ' lamb ' is so named because it is *agnatus* ' born as an addition ' [a] to the flock of sheep. A *catulus* ' puppy ' is named from its quick and keen scent, like the names *Cato* and *Catulus* [b] ; and from this, *canis* [c] ' dog ' : unless, just as the trumpet and the horn are said to *canere* ' sing ' when they give some signal, so the *canis* is named because it likewise, both when guarding the house day or night, and when engaged in hunting, gives the signal with its voice.

XX. 100. The names of wild beasts are likewise some of them foreign, such as *panthera*[a] ' panther,' *leo*[b] ' lion ' : both Greek, whence also certain nets called panther and lioness, and there are courtesans named Pantheris and Leaena. The *tigris* ' tiger,' which is as it were a striped lion, which as yet they have not been

§ 99. [a] Wrong. [b] It is very doubtful if *catulus* ' puppy ' is a diminutive of *catus* ' sharp, shrewd,' as is implied by Varro ; but *Cato* and *Catulus* as proper names go with *catus*. [c] Wrong.

§ 100. [a] Ultimately of Indian origin, transformed into a seemingly Greek word (the ' all-beast ') by the Greeks, and thence given to the Romans. [b] *Leo* and *leaena*, from Greek, but borrowed by the Greeks from some unknown source.

VARRO

vivus capi adhuc non potuit, vocabulum e lingua
Armenia : nam ibi et sagitta et quod vehementis-
simum flumen dicitur Tigris. Ursi Lucana origo vel,
unde illi, nostri ab ipsius voce. Camelus suo nomine
Syriaco in Latium venit, ut Alexandrea camelopardalis nuper adducta, quod erat figura ut camelus,
maculis ut panthera.

101. Apri ab eo quod in locis asperis, nisi a Graecis
quod hi ⟨κ⟩άπροι.[1] Caprea a similitudine quadam
caprae. Cervi, quod magna cornua gerunt, *g*ervi,[2]
G in C mutavit ut in multis. Lepus, quod Sicu⟨li, ut
Aeo⟩lis[3] quidam Gr*a*eci, dicunt λέπoριν : a Roma
quod orti Siculi, ut annales veteres nostri dicunt,
fortasse hinc illuc tulerunt et hic reliquerunt id
nomen. Volpes, ut Aelius dicebat, quod volat
pedibus.

XXI. 102. Proxima animalia sunt ea quae vivere
dicuntur neque habere animam, ut virgulta. Virgultum dicitur a viridi, id a vi quadam humoris ; quae
si exaruit, moritur. Vitis, quod ea vini origo. Malum,
quod Graeci *A*eolis dicunt μᾶλον. Pinus, . . .
Iuglans, quod cum haec nux antequam purgatur

§ 101. [1] *Bentinus, for* aproe. [2] *M, Laetus, for* corui.
[3] *GS., for* siculis, *cf. Varro, De Re Rust.* iii. 12. 6.

---

[c] Not from Armenian, but from Persian, through Greek.
Varro forgot that a tiger was presented to the city of Athens
by Seleucus Nicator (c. 358-280 B.C.); see Athenaeus, xiii.
6. 57 = 590 *a*. [d] An old inherited word. [e] Correct; of
Semitic origin. [f] Through the Greek ; the second part
is *pardalis*, from an Indian word which also denoted the
panther.
   § 101. [a] Wrong ; the Greek word corresponds to Latin
caper. [b] Wrong. [c] Page 69 Funaioli. [d] Wrong.
   § 102. [a] All etymologies in this paragraph are wrong,
except those of *malum* and *iuglans*.

96

able to take alive, has its name from the Armenian language,[c] for in Armenia both an arrow and a very swift river are named *Tigris*. The name of the *ursus*[d] ' bear ' is of Lucanian origin, or our ancestors called it from its voice, and so did the Lucanians. The *camelus* ' camel ' has come to Latium bringing its own Syrian name with it,[e] and so has the *camelopardalis*[f] ' giraffe ' which was recently brought from Alexandria, so called because it was in form like a camel and in spots like a panther.

101. *Apri*[a] ' boars,' from the fact that they frequent *aspera* ' rough ' places, unless from the Greeks, because in Greek these are ⟨κ⟩άπροι. *Caprea* ' roe-deer,' from a certain likeness to the *capra* ' she-goat.' *Cervi* ' stags,' because they *gerunt* ' carry ' big horns, and so they are *gervi*[b]; the word has changed G to C, as has happened in many words. *Lepus* ' hare,' because the Sicilians, like certain Aeolian Greeks, say λέπορις. Inasmuch as the Sicilians originated from Rome, as our old *Annals* say, perhaps they carried the word from here to Sicily, but also left it here behind them. *Volpes* ' fox,' as Aelius[c] used to say, because it *volat* ' flies ' with its *pedes* ' feet.'[d]

XXI. 102.[a] The next living beings to be discussed are those which are said to live, and yet do not breathe, such as bushes. *Virgultum* ' bush ' is said from *viridis* ' green,' and *viridis* from a certain *vis* ' power ' of moisture : if this moisture has thoroughly dried out, the bush dies. *Vitis* ' grape-vine,' because it is the source of *vinum* ' wine.' *Malum* ' apple,' because the Aeolian Greeks call it μᾶλον. The *pinus* ' pine,' . . . The *iuglans* ' walnut,' because while this nut is like an acorn before it is cleansed of its hull, the inner nut,

97

similis glandis, haec glans optima et maxima a Iove
et glande iuglans est appellata. Eadem nux, quod
ut nox aerem huius sucus corpus facit atrum.

103. Quae in *h*ortis nascuntur, alia peregrinis
vocabulis, ut Gr*a*ecis ocimum, menta, ruta quam nunc
πήγανον appellant ; item caulis, lapat*h*ium, radix :
sic enim antiqui Graeci, quam nunc ῥάφανον[1] ; item
haec Graecis vocabulis : serpyllum, rosa, una littera
commutata ; item ex his Graecis Latina κολίανδρον,
μαλάχη,[2] κύμινον ; item lilium ab λειρίῳ[3] et malva ab
μαλαχῃ[4] et sis*y*mbrium a σισυμβρίῳ.[5]

104. Vernacula : lact⟨u⟩c⟨a⟩[1] a lacte, quod *h*olus
id habet lact ; brassica[2] ut p⟨r⟩aesica,[3] quod ex eius
scapo minutatim praesicatur ; asparagi, quod ex
asperis virgultis leguntur et ipsi scapi asperi sunt, non
leves ; nisi Graecum : illic quoque enim dicitur
ἀσπάραγος.[4] Cucumeres dicuntur a curvore, ut curvimeres dicti. Fructus a ferundo, res eae quas[5] fundus
et eae ⟨quas⟩ qu*a*e[6] in fundo ferunt ut fruamur.

---

§ 103. [1] *For* raphanum.   [2] *For* malachen.   [3] *For*
lirio.   [4] *For* malache.   [5] *A. Sp., for* sysimbrio.
    § 104. [1] *M, Laetus, for* lacte.   [2] *Laetus, for* blassica.
[3] *Turnebus ;* praeseca *Aldus ; for* passica.   [4] *For* asparagus.   [5] *A. Sp., for* ea equas.   [6] *Mue., for* ea eque.

---

[b] *Optima et maxima* suggests Jupiter *Optimus Maximus.*
[c] The juice of the walnut-hull does make a very dark stain.
    § 103. [a] All the examples in this section have come into
Latin from Greek, except *radix, rosa, malva. Radix* is
native Latin, and its Greek equivalent had a different meaning. *Rosa* and *malva,* and their Greek equivalents, were
separately derived from an earlier language native in the

being best and biggest,[b] is called *iu-glans* from *Iu*-piter
and *glans* ' acorn.' The same word *nux* ' nut ' is so
called because its juice makes a person's skin black,[c]
just as *nox* ' night ' makes the air black.

103.[a] Of those which are grown in gardens, some
are called by foreign names, as, by Greek names,
ocimum ' basil,' *menta* ' mint,' *ruta* ' rue,' which they
now call πήγανον ; likewise *caulis* ' cabbage,' *lapathium*
' sorrel,' *radix* ' radish ' : for thus the ancient Greeks
called what they now call ῥάφανος ; likewise these
from Greek names : *serpyllum* [b] ' thyme,' *rosa* ' rose,'
each with one letter changed ; likewise Latin names
from these Greek names : κολίανδρον [c] ' coriander,'
μαλάχη, κύμινον ' cummin ' ; likewise *lilium* ' lily ' from
λείριον and *malva* ' mallow ' from μαλάχη and *sisym-
brium* ' mint ' from σισύμβριον.

104.[a] Native words : *lactuca* ' lettuce ' from *lact*
' milk,' because this herb contains milk ; *brassica*
' cabbage ' as though *praesica*, because from its stalk
praesicatur ' leaves are cut off ' one by one ; *asparagi*
' asparagus shoots,' because they are gathered from
aspera ' rough ' bushes and the stems themselves are
rough, not smooth : unless it is a Greek name, for in
Greece also they say ἀσπάραγος. *Cucumeres* ' cucum-
bers ' are named from their *curvor* ' curvature,' as
though *curvimeres*. *Fructus* ' fruits ' are named from
ferre [b] ' to bear,' namely those things which the farm
and those things which are on the farm bear, that

Mediterranean region.   [b] With initial *s* rather than *h*,
by assimilation to Latin *serpere*.   [c] Usually κορίανδρον,
but here with dissimilative change of the prior *r* to *l*.

§ 104.   [a] Correct on *lactuca, fructus, mola* ; wrong on
brassica, cucumeres, uva ; *asparagus* is from Greek.   [b] *Cf.*
v. 37, and note *e*.

VARRO

Hinc declinatae fruges et frumentum, sed ea e terra ;
etiam frumentum, quod ⟨ad⟩[7] exta ollicoqua[8] solet
addi ex mola, id est ex sale et farre molito.   Uvae
ab uvore.

XXII. 105.   Quae manu facta sunt dicam, de
victu, de vestitu, de instrumento, et si quid aliud
videbitur his aptum.   De victu antiquissima puls ;
haec appellata vel quod ita Graeci vel ab eo unde
scribit Apollodorus, quod ita sonet cum aqua⟨e⟩[1]
ferventi insipitur.   Panis, quod primo figura faciebant, ut mulieres in lanificio, panus ; posteaquam ei
figuras facere instituerunt alias, a pane et faciendo
panificium c⟨o⟩eptum dici.   Hinc panarium, ubi id
servabant, sicut granarium, ubi granum frumenti
condebant, unde id dictum : nisi ab eo quod Graeci
id κράνον,[2] a quo a Graecis quoque gran⟨ari⟩um[3]
dictum in quo ea quae conduntur.

106.   Hord*eum*[1] ab *h*orrido.   Triticum, quod tritum e spicis.   Far a faciendo, quod in pistrino fit.

---

[7] *Added by Turnebus.*   [8] *Turnebus, for* ollico quo.
   § 105.   [1] *Turnebus, for* aqua.   [2] *Kent, for* κροκεν.
[3] *Kent, for* granum.
   § 106.   [1] *For* horreum.

---

[c] The relation of this to *frumentum* is not clear.
   § 105.   [a] An old Latin word, which probably did not come
from Greek πόλτος.   [b] *Frag. Hist. Graec.* i. 462 Mueller.
[c] *Panis* may be of Messapian origin ; Varro's etymology is
certainly wrong.   [d] The thin, flat wafer-like Oriental bread,
made in great sheets.   [e] *Pa⟨n⟩nus,* gen. of the 4th decl.
[f] The word meant originally ' bread-making,' but came to
mean bread or cake of any kind ; note that in formation
panificium is modelled on *lanificium.*   [g] Normally ' bread-
basket ' ; but the context indicates the meaning ' bread-
closet.'   [h] Meaning ' cornel cherry ' ; it may have denoted
a cereal seed as well as the cherry stone.

100

we may enjoy them. From this are derived *fruges* 'field products' and *frumentum* 'corn,' but these come out of the earth: even *frumentum*, because [c] to the pot-boiled vitals it is customary to add some of the *mola* 'grits,' that is, salt and spelt *molitum* 'ground up' together. *Uvae* 'grapes,' from *uvor* 'moisture.'

XXII. 105. I shall now speak of things which are made by human hands: food, clothing, tools, and anything else which seems to be associated with them. Of foods the most ancient is *puls* [a] 'porridge'; this got its name either because the Greeks called it thus, or from the fact which Apollodorus [b] mentions, that it makes a sound like *puls* when it is thrown into boiling water. *Panis* [c] 'bread,' because at first they made it [d] in the shape of a *panus* [e] 'cloth' such as women make in weaving; after they began to make it in other shapes, they started saying *panificium* [f] 'pastry,' from *panis* 'bread' and *facere* 'to make.' From this, *panarium* [g] 'bread-closet,' where they kept it, like *granarium* 'granary,' where they stored the *granum* 'grain' of the corn, from which *granarium* was derived —unless it came from the fact that the Greeks called the grain κράνον [h]; and in this case it was from the Greeks also that the place in which are kept the grains that are stored, was called a *granarium*.

106.[a] *Hordeum* 'barley,' from *horridus* 'bristling.'[b] *Triticum* 'wheat,' because it was *tritum* 'threshed out' from the ears. *Far* 'emmer,' from *facere* 'to make,' because it is made into flour in the mill. *Milium*

§ 106. [a] Wrong on *far*; *libare* is derived from *libum*, instead of the reverse; the other etymologies in this section are correct. [b] That is, with the awns that form the beard of the ear.

VARRO

Milium a Graeco: nam id μελίνη. Libum, quod ut libaretur, priusquam essetur,[2] erat coctum. Testuacium, quod in testu caldo coquebatur, ut etiam nunc Matralibus id faciunt matronae. Circuli, quod mixta farina et caseo et aqua circuitum aequabiliter fundebant.

107. Hos[1] quidam qui magis incondite faciebant vocabant lixulas et similixulas vocabulo Sabino: quae[2] frequentia Sabinis. A globo farinae dilatato, item in oleo cocti, dicti a globo globi. Crustulum a crusta pultis, cuius ea, quod ut corium et uritur, crusta dicta. Cetera fere aper⟨t⟩a[3] a vocabulis Graecis sumpta, ut thrion et placenta.

108. Quod edebant cum pulte, ab eo pulmentum, ut Plautus; hinc pulmentarium dictum: hoc primum defuit[1] pastoribus. Caseus a coacto lacte ut co⟨a⟩xeus[2] dictus. Dein posteaquam desierunt esse contenti his quae suapte natura ferebat sine igne, in quo erant poma, quae minus cruda esse poterant decoque-

---

[2] *Turnebus, for* esset ut.
§ 107. [1] *L. Sp. and Mommsen, for* hoc. [2] *Kent, for* itaque. [3] *Groth, for* opera.
§ 108. [1] *A. Sp., for* debuit. [2] *Aug., with B, for* coxeus.

---

[c] A festival to the Mater Matuta, celebrated on June 11: not to be confused with the *Matronalia*, celebrated by the matrons on March 1, in honour of Mars.
§ 107. [a] Diminutive to fem. *lixa* 'boiled,' *cf. e-lixus.* [b] Probably for *semi-lixulae* 'half-rings,' while *lixulae* are 'rings,' being varieties of *circuli.* [c] The crust which forms on the inside of the pot in which porridge is regularly cooked, unless the pot is carefully scraped. [d] An absurd etymology. [e] Greek θρῖον 'fig-leaf'; also a mixture of eggs, milk, lard, flour, honey, and cheese, so called because it was wrapped in fig-leaves. [f] Greek πλακοῦς, a flat cake.

'millet,' from the Greek : for it is μελίνη. *Libum* 'cake,' because, after it was baked, *libabatur* 'there was an offering of some ' of it to the gods before it was eaten. *Testuacium* ' pot-cake,' because it was baked in a heated earthen *testu* 'pot,' as even now the matrons do this at the Matralia.[c] *Circuli* 'rings,' because they poured into the pan a regular *circuitus* ' circuit ' of a batter made of flour, cheese, and water.

107. Certain persons who used to make these rather carelessly called them *lixulae* [a] ' softies ' and *similixulae* [b] ' half-softies,' by the Sabine name, such was their general use among the Sabines. Those that consist of a leavened *globus* ' ball ' of dough and are cooked in oil, are from *globus* called *globi* ' globes.' *Crustulum* ' cookie,' from the *crusta* ' crust ' of the porridge,[c] whose *crusta* is so named because it is, as it were, a *corium* ' hide ' and it *uritur* ' is burnt.' [d] The other confections are in general of obvious origin, being taken from Greek words, like *thrion* [e] ' omelette ' and *placenta* ' sand-tart.' [f]

108. That which they ate with their *puls* ' porridge,' was from that fact called *pulmentum* [a] ' side-dish,' as Plautus says [b] ; from this was said *pulmentarium* ' relish ' : this the shepherds lacked in the early times. *Caseus* [c] ' cheese ' was named from *coactum* ' coagulated ' milk, as though *coaxeus*. Then after they ceased to be satisfied with those foods which nature supplied of her own accord without the use of fire, among which were apples and like fruits, they boiled down in a pot those which they

§ 108. [a] Rather from *pulpa* 'flesh, meat.' 316; *Miles Gl.*, 349 ; *Pseudolus*, 220 ; etc. word with no close etymological connexions.   [b] *Aulularia*,   [c] A country

VARRO

bant in olla. Ab olla *h*olera dicta, quo⟨d ea⟩rum ⟨m⟩ace*rare*[3] cruda *h*olera. E quis ad coquendum quod e terra eru⟨itu⟩r,[4] ruapa, unde rapa. Olea ab ἐλαία[5] ; olea grandis orchitis quod eam Attici[6] ὄρχιν μορ⟨ί⟩α⟨ν⟩.[7]

109. Hinc ad pecudis carnem perventum est. ⟨Ut ab sue⟩[1] suilla, sic ab ⟨a⟩*li*is[2] generibus cognominata. Hanc[3] primo assam, secundo elixam, tertio e iure uti c⟨o⟩episse natura docet. Dictum assum, quod id ab igni assud⟨escit, id est uv⟩escit[4] : uvidum enim quod humidum, et ideo ubi id non est, sucus abest ; et ideo sudandum assum destillat calore,[5] et ut crudum nimium habet humoris, sic excoctum parum habet suci. Elixum e liquore aquae dictum ; et ex iure,[6] quod iucundum magis conditione.

110. Succidia ab suibus caedendis : nam id pecus primo occidere coeperunt[1] domini et ut servarent sallere.[2] Tegus suis ab eo quod eo tegitur. Perna

---

[3] *A. Sp., for* quorum agerere.   [4] *GS. ;* e terra erueretur *Turnebus ; for* eterrae rure.   [5] *Kent, for* elea.   [6] *L. Sp., for* attico.   [7] *Canal, for* orchen mora.

§ 109.   [1] *Added by A. Sp. ;* ut *added by Mue., with* B.   [2] *Mue., for* ilis.   [3] *Aug., with* B, *for* hinc.   [4] *GS., for* assudescit.   [5] *Aug., with* B, *for* calorem.   [6] *G, Laetus, for* iuro.

§ 110.   [1] *For* caeperunt.   [2] *c, Mue., for* sallire *; cf. Diomedes,* i. 375. 21 *Keil.*

---

[d] Wrong on *holera* and *rapa*, but right about olives.

§ 109.   [a] *For arsum,* participle of *ardere* ' to be on fire.'   [b] Participle of a compound of the root seen in *liquor* ; but *ius* ' juice ' has nothing to do with *iucundum.*

§ 110.   [a] *Correct.*   [b] Properly *tergus,* and without connexion with *tegere* ; but in the form *tergoribus* it seems to have lost the first *r* by dissimilation : *tegoribus* is metrically

could less easily eat raw. From *olla* ' pot ' the *holera* [d]
' vegetables ' were named, because it is the task
of *ollae* ' pots ' to soften the raw *holera* ' vegetables.'
One of these, because it *eruitur* ' is dug out ' of the
earth for cooking, was called *ruapa*, from which
comes *rapa* ' turnip.' *Olea* ' olive berry,' from ἐλαία ;
the *orchitis* is a large kind of olive, so called because
the Athenians call it ὄρχις μορία ' the sacred olive-
berry.'

109. From here they came to domestic animals as
meat for the table. As *suilla* ' pork ' is said from *sus*
' swine,' so other meats are named from the other
kinds of animals. The nature of things shows us
that men began to use this first roasted, second boiled,
third cooked in its own juice. *Assum* [a] ' roasted ' is said
because as a result of the fire it *assudescit* ' begins to
sweat,' that is *uvescit* ' becomes moist ' : for *uvidum* is
the same as *humidum* ' moist,' and therefore where this
moisture is not present, there is a lack of juice ; and
therefore the roast that is to sweat drips on account of
the heat, and just as the raw meat has an excess of
moisture, so the thoroughly cooked meat has very
little juice. *Elixum* [b] ' boiled ' is said from the *liquor*
' fluid ' of the water ; and *ex iure* ' cooked in its own
juice ' is said because this is more *iucundum* ' tasty '
than seasoning.

110. *Succidia* [a] ' leg of pork ' is said from *sues
caedendae* ' the cutting up of the swine ' ; for this was
the first domestic animal that the owners began to
slaughter and to salt in order to keep the meat un-
spoiled. *Tegus* [b] ' piece of the back ' of swine, from
this, that by this piece the animal *tegitur* ' is covered.'

assured in Plautus, *Captivi*, 902, and is found also in *Captivi*
915, *Pseudolus* 198.

105

a pede. Sueris a nomine eius. Offula ab offa,
minima suere. Insicia ab eo quod insecta caro, ut in
Carmine Saliorum ⟨prosicium⟩[3] est, quod in extis
dicitur nunc prosectum. Murtatum a murta, quod
ea[4] ad⟨ditur⟩[5] large fartis.

111. Quod fartum intestinum ⟨e⟩[1] crassundiis,
Lucan⟨ic⟩am[2] dicunt, quod milites a Lucanis didi-
cerint, ut quod Faleriis Faliscum ventrem ; fundolum
a fundo, quod ⟨non⟩[3] ut reliquae *lactes*,[4] sed ex una
parte sola apertum ; ab hoc Graecos puto τυφλὸν
ἔντερον appellasse. Ab eadem fartura farcimina
⟨in⟩[5] extis appellata, a quo ⟨farticulum⟩[6] : in eo quod
tenuissimum intestinum fartum, hila ab hilo dicta
i⟨l⟩lo[7] quod ait Ennius :

> Neque dispendi[8] facit hilum.

Quod in hoc farcimine summo quiddam eminet, ab eo
quod ut in capite apex, apexabo dicta. Tertium
fartum est longavo, quod longius quam duo illa.

[3] *Added by GS. ; cf. Festus*, 225. 15 *M.*   [4] *Laetus. for* eo.
[5] *A. Sp., for* ad.
      § 111.   [1] *Added by Mue.*   [2] *Laetus, for* lucanam.
[3] *Added by Aldus.*   [4] *Fay, for* partes.   [5] *Added by
Aug., with B.*   [6] *Added by GS.*   [7] *Lachmann, for* hilo.
[8] *For* dispendii.

[c] *Perna* has no connexion with *pes* ; but the remaining
etymologies of this section seem to be correct.   [d] The
precise meaning of this word is unknown ; perhaps ' pork-
chop,' *cf.* W. Heraeus, *Archiv f. Lat. Lex.* 14. 124-125.
[e] Meaning assured by *offulam cum duobus costis*, Varro,
De Re Rustica, ii. 4. 11.   [f] Page 345 Maurenbrecher ;
page 3 Morel.
      § 111.   [a] The preceding etymologies in this section are
correct, but *hila* is properly *hilla*, diminutive of *hira* ' empty

Perna [c] ' ham,' from *pes* ' foot.' *Sueris*,[d] from the
animal's name. *Offula* ' rib-roast,' [e] from *offa*, a very
small *sueris*. *Insicia* ' minced meat ' from this, that
the meat is *insecta* ' cut up,' just as in the *Song of the
Salii* [f] the word *prosicium* ' slice ' is used, for which,
in the offering of the vitals, the word *prosectum* is
now used. *Murtatum* ' myrtle-pudding,' from *murta*
' myrtle-berry,' because this berry is added plentifully
to its stuffings.

111. An intestine of the thick sort that was stuffed,
they call a *Lucanica* ' Lucanian,' because the soldiers
got acquainted with it from the Lucanians, just as
what they found at Falerii they call a Faliscan haggis ;
and they say *fundolus* ' bag-sausage ' from *fundus*
' bottom,' because this is not like the other intestines,
but is open at only one end : from this, I think, the
Greeks called it the blind intestine. From the same
fartura ' stuffing ' were called the *farcimina* ' stuffies '
in the case of the vital organs for the sacrifice, whence
also *farticulum* ' stufflet ' ; in this case, because it is
the most slender intestine that is stuffed, it is called
hila [a] from that *hilum* ' whit ' which Ennius [b] uses :

And of loss not a whit does she suffer.

Because at the top of this stuffy there is a little projection, it is called an *apexabo*,[c] because the projection is
like the *apex* ' pointed cap ' on a human head. The
third kind of sausage is the *longavo*,[c] because it is
longer than those two others.

intestine ' ; *cf.* Festus, 101. 6 M.   [b] Annales, 14 Vahlen[2] ;
R.O.L. i. 6-7 Warmington ; quoted also v. 60 and ix. 54.
[c] *Apexabo* and *longavo* doubtless have the same suffix, differing only through the late Latin confusion of *b* and *v* ; unless
indeed both words are further corrupt.

VARRO

112. Augmentum, quod ex immolata hostia desectum in iecore ⟨imponitur⟩[1] in por⟨ric⟩iendo[2] a⟨u⟩gendi[3] causa. Magmentum[4] a magis, quod ad religionem magis pertinet : itaque propter hoc ⟨mag⟩mentaria[5] fana constituta locis certis quo id imponeretur. Mattea[6] ab eo quod ea Graece ματτύη. Item ⟨a⟩[7] Graecis . . . singillatim haec[8] : . . .[9] ovum, bulbum.

XXIII. 113. Lana Graecum, ut Polybius et Callimachus scribunt. Purpura a purpurae maritumae colore, ut[1] P⟨o⟩enicum, quod a Poenis primum dicitur allata. Stamen a stando, quod eo stat omne in tela velamentum. Subtemen, quod subit stamini. Trama, quod tram⟨e⟩at[2] frigus id genus vestimenti. Densum a dentibus pectinis quibus feritur. Filum, quod minimum est hilum : id enim minimum est in vestimento.

---

§ 112. [1] *Added by A. Sp.* [2] *L. Sp., for* im poriendo.
[3] *Turnebus, for* agendi. [4] *B, M, Aug., for* magnentum.
[5] *Turnebus, for* mentarea. [6] *Popma, for* mattae.
[7] *Added by L. Sp.* [8] *For* heae. [9] *The lacuna was noted by Scaliger ; the exact arrangement is by Kent, after Mue.'s indication of the probable contents.*
§ 113. [1] *Lachmann ;* colore *G, Laetus ; for* colerent.
[2] *Aug. (quoting a friend), for* tramat.

---

§ 112. [a] Correct, unless the purpose was to increase, that is, glorify the god. [b] Properly connected with *mactare* ' to sacrifice,' though popular association with *magis* affected its meaning. [c] A highly seasoned dish of hashed meat, poultry, and herbs, served cold as a dessert.
108

112. The *augmentum* [a] ' increase-cake ' is so called because a piece of it is cut out and put on the liver of the sacrificed victim at the presentation to the deity, for the sake of *augendi* ' increasing ' it. *Magmentum* [b] ' added offering,' from *magis* ' more,' because it attaches *magis* ' more ' closely to the worshipper's piety : for this reason *magmentaria fana* ' sanctuaries for the offering of *magmenta* ' have been established in certain places, that the added offering may there be laid on the original and offered with it. *Mattea* [c] ' cold meat-pie ' is so named because in Greek it is ματτύη. Likewise from the Greeks is another meat-dish called . . . , which contains item by item the following : . . . , an egg, a truffle.

XXIII. 113. *Lana* [a] ' wool ' is a Greek word, as Polybius [b] and Callimachus [c] write. *Purpura* [d] ' purple,' from the colour of the *purpura* ' purple-fish ' of the sea : a Punic word, because it is said to have been first brought to Italy by the Phoenicians. *Stamen* ' warp,' from *stare* ' to stand,' because by this the whole fabric on the loom *stat* ' stands ' up. *Subtemen* [e] ' woof,' because it *subit* ' goes under ' the *stamen* ' warp.' *Trama* [f] ' wide-meshed cloth,' because the cold *trameat* ' goes through ' this kind of garment. *Densum* [g] ' close-woven cloth,' from the *dentes* ' dents ' of the sley with which it is beaten. *Filum* [g] ' thread,' because it is the smallest *hilum* ' shred '; for this is the smallest thing in a garment.

§ 113.   [a] An old Italic word cognate to English *wool* ; *cf.* v. 130.   [b] *Frag. inc.* 99 (104) Hultsch.   [c] *Frag.* 408 Schneider.   [d] Quite possibly a Phoenician word, but transmitted to Italy by the Greeks (πορφύρα).   [e] From *subtexere* ' to weave underneath.'   [f] From *trahere* ' to pull.'   [g] Wrong.

114. Pannus *Graecum*,[1] ubi E A[2] fecit. Panuvellium dictum a pano et volvendo filo. Tunica ab tuendo corpore, tunica ut ⟨tu⟩endica.[3] Toga a tegendo. Cinctus et cingillum a cingendo, alterum viris, alterum mulieribus attributum.

XXIV. 115. Arma ab arcendo, quod his arcemus hostem. Parma, quod e medio in omnis partis par. Conum, quod cogitur in cacumen versus. Hasta, quod astans solet[1] ferri. Iaculum, quod ut iaciatur fit. Tragula a traiciendo. Scutum ⟨a⟩[2] sectura ut secutum, quod a minute consect*is*[3] fit tabellis. Umbones[4] a Graeco, quod ἄμβωνες.[5]

116. Gladiu*m*[1] C in G[2] commutato a clade, quod fit ad hostium cladem gladium ; similiter ab omine[3] pilum, qui host*is* *p*eriret,[4] ut perilum. Lorica, quod e loris de corio crudo pectoralia faciebant ; postea subcidit galli⟨ca⟩[5] e ferro sub id vocabulum, ex anulis

§ 114. [1] *Aug.*, *with* B, *for* grecus. [2] *Fay, for* ea. [3] *GS., for* indica.

§ 115. [1] *For* sollet. [2] *Added by Laetus.* [3] *Aug., for* consectum. [4] *For* umbonis. [5] *Turnebus, for* ambonis.

§ 116. [1] *L. Sp., for* gladius. [2] *For* G in C. [3] *Aug., for* homine. [4] *Aug.* (hostis B), *for* hostem feriret. [5] *Mue., for* galli.

---

§ 114. [a] Not *pannus* ' cloth,' but *pannus* ' bobbin,' in view of what follows ; there is a Greek πῆνος ' web,' and its diminutive πηνίον ' bobbin,' which in the Doric form would have A and not E. [b] Possibly right, if, as A. Spengel thinks, the word is really *panuvollium.* [c] From Semitic, either directly or through Etruscan.

§ 115. [a] *Arma, parma, conum, hasta, tragula, scutum, umbones* : all wrong etymologies. [b] Not from *traicere*, but from *trahere* ' to pull, drag ' ; perhaps because the thong wound round it for throwing (like the string used in starting a peg-top) ' pulls ' the javelin.

110

114. *Pannus* [a] ' bobbin,' is a Greek word, where
E has become A. *Panuvellium* [b] ' bobbin with thread'
was said from *panus* ' bobbin ' and *volvere* ' to wind '
the thread. *Tunica* [c] ' shirt,' from *tuendo* ' protecting ' the body : *tunica* as though it were *tuendica*.
Toga ' toga ' from *tegere* ' to cover.' *Cinctus* ' belt '
and *cingillum* ' girdle,' from *cingere* ' to gird,' the one
assigned to men and the other to women.

XXIV. 115. *Arma* [a] ' arms,' from *arcere* ' to ward
off,' because with them we *arcemus* ' ward off ' the
enemy. *Parma* ' cavalry shield,' because from the
centre it is *par* ' even ' in every direction. *Conum*
' pointed helmet,' because it *cogitur* ' is narrowed '
toward the top. *Hasta* ' spear,' because it is usually
carried *astans* ' standing up.' *Iaculum* ' javelin,' because
it is made that it may *iaci* ' be thrown.' *Tragula* [b]
' thong-javelin,' from *traicere* ' to pierce.' *Scutum*
' shield,' from *sectura* ' cutting,' as though *secutum*,
because it is made of wood cut into small pieces.
Umbones ' bosses ' from a Greek word, namely
ἄμβωνες.

116.[a] *Gladium* ' sword,' from *clades* ' slaughter,'
with change of C to G, because the *gladium* [b] is made
for a slaughter of the enemy ; likewise from its omen
was said *pilum*, by which the enemy *periret* ' might
perish,' as though *perilum*. *Lorica* ' corselet,' because
they made chest-protectors from *lora* ' thongs ' of
rawhide ; afterwards the Gallic corselet of iron was

§ 116. [a] All etymologies wrong except those of *lorica* and
(with reserves) of *galea*. [b] Varro prefers (*cf.* viii. 45, ix. 81,
De Re Rust. i. 48. 3) the unfamiliar neuter form, which may
be due to the influence of the associated words *scutum*, *pilum*,
telum. The word is of Celtic origin, but may have an ulti-
mate connexion with the root of *clades*.

111

VARRO

ferrea tunica.⁶ Balteum, quod cingulum e corio
habebant bullatum, balteum dictum. Ocrea, quod
opponebatur ob crus. Galea ab galero, quod multi
usi antiqui.

117. Tubae ab tubis, quos etiam nunc ita appellant
tubicines sacrorum. Cornua, quod ea quae nunc sunt
ex aere, tunc fiebant bubulo e cornu. Vallum vel
quod ea varicare nemo posset vel quod singula ibi
extrema bacilla furcillata habent figuram litterae V.
Cervi ab similitudine cornuum cervi ; item reliqua
fere ab similitudine ut vineae, testudo, aries.

XXV. 118. Mensam escariam cillibam appellabant ; ea erat¹ quadrata ut etiam nunc in castris est ;
a cibo cilliba dicta ; postea rutunda facta, et quod a
nobis media et a Graecis μέσα, mensa dict⟨a⟩² potest ;
nisi etiam quod ponebant pleraque in cibo mensa.
Trulla a similitudine truae, quae quod magna et haec

⁶ *Turnebus, for* ferream tunicam.

§ 118. ¹ *For* erant. ² *Mue., for* dici.

ᶜ Rather *galerum* from *galea*, which looks like a borrowing
from Greek γαλέη ' weasel'; the objection is that caps of
weasel-skin are nowhere attested.

§ 117. ᵃ Wrong etymology. ᵇ Thrust into the embank-
ment, to increase its defensive strength ; can they be the
stakes, *pali* or *valli*, forming a fence along its top ? But
these are not elsewhere spoken of as forked. ᶜ Used by
Caesar, who inserted such forked branches into the face of
his wall at Alesia, *Bell. Gall.* vii. 72. 4, 73. 2. ᵈ Otherwise
' grape-arbours '; in military use, sheds under the protection
of which soldiers could advance up to the enemy's fortifica-
tions. ᵉ A close formation of overlapping shields.

§ 118. ᵃ Borrowed from Greek κιλλίβας ' three-legged
table,' a derivative of κίλλος ' ass.' ᵇ Or perhaps *mesa*,
since *n* was weak before *s* ; Priscian, i. 58. 17 Keil, states
that Varro used both spellings. *Mensa* seems to be the

112

included under this name, an iron shirt made of links. *Balteum* ' sword-belt,' because they used to wear a leather belt *bullatum* ' with an amulet attached,' was called *balteum*. *Ocrea* ' shin-guard' was so called because it was set in the way *ob crus* ' before the shin.' *Galea* [c] ' leather helmet,' from *galerum* ' leather bonnet,' because many of the ancients used them.

117. *Tubae* ' trumpets,' from *tubi* ' tubes,' a name by which even now the trumpeters of the sacrifices call them. *Cornua* ' horns,' because these, which are now of bronze, were then made from the *cornu* ' horn ' of an ox. *Vallum* [a] ' camp wall,' either because no one could *varicare* ' straddle ' over it, or because the ends of the forked sticks [b] used there had individually the shape of the letter V. *Cervi* [c] ' chevaux-de-frise,' from the likeness to the horns of a *cervus* ' stag ' ; so the rest of the terms in general, from a likeness, as *vineae* ' mantlets,' [d] *testudo* ' tortoise,' [e] *aries* ' ram.'

XXV. 118. The eating-table they used to call a *cilliba* [a] ; it was square, as even now it is in the camp ; the name *cilliba* came from *cibus* ' victuals.' Afterwards it was made round, and the fact that it was *media* ' central ' with us and μέσα ' central ' with the Greeks, is the probable reason for its being called a *mensa* [b] ' table ' ; unless indeed they used to put on, amongst the victuals, many that were *mensa* ' measured out.' *Trulla* [c] ' ladle,' from its likeness to a *trua* ' gutter,' but because this is big and the other is small, they named it as if it were *truella* ' small *trua* ' ; this

feminine of *mensus* ' measured ' ; perhaps from *tabula mensa* ' measured board.'   [c] *Trulla* is of uncertain origin, and yielded *trua* by back-formation ; Greek τρυήλη seems to have been borrowed from Latin, as Varro states.

pusilla, ut true⟨l⟩la[3] ; hanc[4] Graeci τρυήλην.[5] Trua
qu⟨a⟩ e[6] culina in lavatrinam aquam fundunt[7] ; trua,
quod travolat ea aqua. Ab eodem est appellatum
truleum : simile enim figura, nisi quod latius est,
quod concipiat aquam, et quod manubrium cavum
non est nisi in vinario truleo.[8]

119. Accessit mateellio[1] a matula dictus et fictus,[2]
qui, posteaquam longius a figura matulae discessit, et
ab aqua aqualis dictus. Vas aquarium vocant futim,
quod in triclinio allatam aquam infundebant ; quo
postea accessit nanus[3] cum Graeco nomine et cum
Latino nomine Graeca figura barbatus. Pelvis pede-
⟨l⟩uis[4] a pedum lavatione. Candelabrum a candela :
ex his enim funiculi ardentes figebantur. Lucerna
post inventa, quae dicta a luce aut quod id vocant
λύχνον[5] Graeci.

120. Vasa in mensa escaria : ubi pultem[1] aut
iurulenti quid ponebant, a capiendo catinum nominarunt, nisi quod Siculi dicunt κάτινον ubi assa pone-

---

[3] *Klotz, for* troula.   [4] *L. Sp., for* hinc.   [5] *L. Sp., for*
trullan.   [6] *Mue., for* truae que.   [7] *Here begins the lost
quaternion in* F, *running to* vi. 61 finit ; *but before its loss
Victorius collated it, and his readings are cited as* Fv.
There is also a careful copy of F *extant in Laurent.* 51. 5,
cited as f.   [8] *Christ, for* uinaria trulla Fv.
  § 119.   [1] *Aldus, for* matiolio Fv.   [2] *A. Sp., for* dictus
et dictus.   [3] *Turnebus, for* magnus.   [4] *Scaliger ;* pede-
lauis *Aldus ; for* pedeuis.   [5] *For* licnon.
  § 120.   [1] *For* pultes Fv.

---

[d] The next statements seem to eliminate from this passage the
usual meaning of *trua* : 'ladle, stirring-spoon.'   [e] Vari-
ously spelled, but clearly a derivative of *trulla.*   [f] Apparently the wine *truleum* had a channelled handle which
could be used as a spout in pouring.

the Greeks call a τρυήλη. A *trua* ' gutter ' [d] is that by which they pour the water from the kitchen into the privy : *trua*, because by it the water *travolat* ' flies across.' From the same is named the *truleum* [e] ' basin ' ; for it is like in shape, except that it is broader because it is to hold water, and that the handle is not channelled except in the case of a wine-*truleum*.[f]

119. There was also the *matellio* ' pot,' named as well as modelled after the *matula* ' chamber-pot,' which, after it had got quite far away from the shape of a *matula*, was called also an *aqualis* ' wash-basin,' from *aqua* ' water.' A jar for water they called a *futis*,[a] because with it in the dining-room they *infundebant* ' poured on ' the guests' hands the water that had been brought ; for the performance of this same service there was afterward added a vessel [b] with the Greek name of *nanus* ' dwarf ' and the Latin name *barbatus* ' bearded man,' because of the Greek figure. *Pelvis* [c] ' basin ' was earlier *pedeluis*, from the *lavatio* ' washing ' of the *pedes* ' feet.' *Candelabrum* ' candlestick,' from *candela* ' taper ' ; for from these blazing cords were hung. The *lucerna* [d] ' lamp ' was invented later ; it was named from *lux* ' light ' or because the Greeks call it λύχνος.

120. Vessels on the eating-table : The vessel in which they set on the table porridge or anything with a great deal of juice, they called a *catinus* ' pot,' from *capere* [a] ' to contain,' unless it is because the Sicilians call that in which they put their roasts a κάτινος.

§ 119.   [a] Correct etymology.   [b] A jar in the form of a bearded dwarf.   [c] Wrong etymology.   [d] A native word, from the root of *lux*.
§ 120.   [a] Wrong ; and the Sicilian word was borrowed from Latin.

bant ; magidam aut langulam alterum a magnitudine
alterum a latitudine finxerunt. Patenas a patulo
dixerunt, ut pusillas, quod his libarent cenam, patellas.
Tryblia² et canistra quod putant esse Latina, sunt
Graeca : τρύβλιον³ enim et κανοῦν⁴ d⟨i⟩c⟨untur⟩⁵
Graece.⁶ Reliqua quod aperta sunt unde sint
relinquo.

XXVI. 121. Mensa vinaria rotunda nominabatur
ci⟨l⟩liba ⟨a⟩nte,¹ ut etiam nunc in castris. Id videtur
declinatum a Graeco κυλικείῳ,² ⟨id⟩³ a poculo cylice
qui ⟨in⟩³ illa. Capid⟨es⟩⁴ et minores capulae a
capiendo, quod ansatae ut prehendi possent, id est
capi. Harum figuras in vasis sacris ligneas ac fictiles
antiquas etiam nunc videmus.

122. Praeterea in poculis erant paterae, ab eo
quod late ⟨pate⟩nt¹ ita² dictae. Hisce etiam nunc in
publico convivio antiquitatis retinendae causa, cum
magistri fiunt, potio circumfertur, et in sacrificando
deis hoc poculo magistratus dat deo vinum. Pocula a
potione, unde potatio et etiam posca.³ Haec possunt
a πότῳ,⁴ quod πότος potio Graece.

² *Aug., with B, for* triplia.   ³ *Aug., with B, for* triplion.
⁴ *L. Sp., for* canunun *Fv.*   ⁵ *GS., for* de.   ⁶ *Canal, for*
greca.
§ 121.   ¹ *GS., for* cilibantum.   ² *Turnebus, for* culiceo.
³ *Added by Mue.*   ⁴ *L. Sp. ;* capis *Turnebus ; for* capit.
§ 122.   ¹ *GS. ;* patent *L. Sp. ;* pateant latine *Aldus ; for*
latini.   ² *After* ita, *Aldus deleted* dicunt.   ³ *Turnebus,*
for postea.   ⁴ *Mue., for* poto.

ᵇ From Greek μαγίς ' a round pan.'   ᶜ Better *lancula,*
diminutive of *lanx* ' platter.'   ᵈ Correct, except that *canis-*
trum is from Greek κάνιστρον ' bread-basket,' made of κάνναι
' reeds '; page 117 Funaioli.
§ 121.   ᵃ *Cf.* § 118, where a different etymology is given.
§ 122.   ᵃ Not from Greek, but from an Indo-European
root inherited by Latin as well as by Greek.   ᵇ The Greek
word means properly not a ' draught,' but a ' drinking-bout.'

The *magida*[b] and the *langula*,[c] both meaning 'platter,'
they named from the *magnitudo* ' size ' of the one and
the *latitudo* ' width ' of the other. *Patenae* ' plates '
they called from *patulum* ' spreading,' and the little
plates, with which they offered the gods a preliminary
sample of the dinner, they called *patellae* ' saucers.'
Tryblia ' bowls ' and *canistra* ' bread-baskets,' though
people think that they are Latin, are really Greek [d] :
for τρύβλιον and κανοῦν are said in Greek. The
remaining terms I pass by, since their sources are
obvious.

XXVI. 121. A round table for wine was formerly
called a *cilliba*,[a] as even now it is in the camp. This
seems to be derived from the Greek κυλικεῖον
' buffet,' from the cup *cylix* which stands on it. The
capides ' bowls ' and smaller *capulae* ' cups ' were
named from *capere* ' to seize,' because they have
handles to make it possible for them *prehendi* ' to be
grasped,' that is, *capi* ' to be seized.' Their shapes we
even now see among the sacred vessels, old-fashioned
shapes in wood and earthenware.

122. In addition there were among the drinking-
cups the *paterae* ' libation-saucers,' named from this,
that they *patent* ' are open ' wide. For the sake of
preserving the ancient practice, they use cups of this
kind even now for passing around the *potio* ' draught '
at the public banquet, when the magistrates enter
into their office ; and it is this kind of cup that the
magistrate uses in sacrificing to the gods, when he
gives the wine to the god. *Pocula* ' drinking-cups,'
from *potio* ' draught,' whence *potatio* ' drinking bout '
and also *posca* ' sour wine.' [a] These may however
come from πότος, because πότος is the Greek for
potio.[b]

VARRO

123. Origo potionis aqua, quod *a*equa summa. Fons unde funditur e terra aqua viva, ut fistula a qua fusus aquae. Vas vinarium grandius sinum ab sinu, quod sinum maiorem cav⟨a⟩tionem[1] quam pocula habebant. Item dicta*e* lepesta*e*,[2] quae etiam nunc in diebus sacris Sabinis vasa vinaria in mensa deorum sunt posita ; apud antiquos scriptores Graecos inveni appellari poculi genus δεπέσταν[3] : quare vel inde radices in agrum Sabinum et Romanum sunt profectae.

124. Qui vinum dabant ut minutatim funderent, a guttis guttum appellarunt ; qui sumebant minutatim, a sumendo simpu*i*um[1] nominarunt. In huiusce locum in conviviis e Graecia successit ep*i*ch*y*sis et cyathus ; in sacruficiis remansit guttus et simpu*i*um.[1]

125. Altera vasaria[1] mensa erat[2] lapidea quadrata oblonga una columella ; vocabatur cartibulum. Haec in aedibus ad compluvium apud multos me puero ponebatur et in ea et ⟨cir⟩cum ea⟨m⟩[3] aenea vasa : a gerendo cartibulum[4] potest dictum.

§ 123. [1] *Aldus, for* cautionem. [2] *Mue. ;* dicta lepeste *Sciop. ; for* dicta flepeste *f.* [3] *For* depestam *Fv.*
§ 124. [1] *Brinkmann, for* simpulum.
§ 125. [1] *For* uasaria, *with* uin *written above, both in Fv and in f.* [2] *For* erant *f.* [3] *Christ, for* cum ea. [4] cartibum *f, H, V, a, p* (cartibum unde cartibulum *Laetus ;* gertibulum unde cartibulum *B, Aug.*).

---

§ 123. [a] Wrong on *aqua, fons, fistula, sinum* (note the quantities in *sīnum* and *sĭnus*). [b] From Greek λεπαστή, a drinking-cup shaped like a λεπάς 'limpet.' [c] Not elsewhere attested with *d*.
§ 124. [a] From a Greek word, but popularly remodelled to resemble *gutta* 'drop.'

118

123.[a] The source of a drink is *aqua* ' water,' so called because its surface is *aequa* ' level.' A *fons* ' spring ' is that from which running water *funditur* ' is poured ' out of the earth, just as a *fistula* ' pipe ' is that from which there is a *fusus* ' outpour ' of water. The *sinum* is a wine-jar of a larger sort, called from *sinus* ' belly,' because the *sinum* had a greater cavity than cups. Likewise there are those called *lepestae*,[b] the kind of wine-jars that are even now, on the days of the Sabine festivals, placed on the table of the gods ; I have found in ancient Greek writers a kind of cup called δεπέστα,[c] for which reason the source of the name quite certainly set out from there into the Sabine and Roman territory.

124. Those who were giving wine in such a way as to pour it little by little, called the vessel a *guttus* [a] ' cruet,' from the *guttae* ' drops ' ; those who were taking it little by little from a larger container, called the instrument a *simpuvium* ' dipping ladle,' from *sumere* ' to take out.' Into its place, in banquets, there came from Greece the *epichysis* ' pouring ladle ' and the *cyathus* ' dipping ladle ' ; but in the sacrifices the *guttus* and the *simpuvium* remained in use.

125. A second kind of table for vessels was of stone, an oblong rectangle with one pedestal ; it was called a *cartibulum*. When I was a boy this used to be placed in many persons' houses near the opening in the roof of the court, and on and around it were set bronze vessels ; perhaps *cartibulum* [a] was said from *gerere* ' to carry.' [b]

§ 125. [a] Of unknown etymology ; commonly spelled *gartibulum* (for early C in value of *g*, *cf.* v. 64, note *f*), but not connected with *gerere*. [b] That is, from carrying the vessels.

VARRO

XXVII. 126. Praeterea erat tertium genus mensae *it*⟨em⟩[1] quadratae vasorum ; voca⟨ba⟩tur[2] urnarium, quod urnas cum aqua positas ibi potissimum habebant in culina. Ab eo etiam nunc ante balineum locus ubi poni solebat urnarium vocatur. Urnae dictae, quod urinant in aqua *h*aurienda ut *u*rinator. *U*rinare[3] est mergi in aquam.

127. *Amburvo*⟨m⟩[1] fictum ab urvo,[2] quod ita flexum ut redeat sursum versus *u*t[3] in aratro quod est *u*rvum.[4] Calix a caldo, quod in eo calda puls[5] apponebatur et caldum eo bibebant. Vas ubi coquebant cibum, ab eo caccabum appellarunt. Ver*u*[6] a versando.

XXVIII. 128. Ab sedendo appellatae sedes, sedile, so*l*ium,[1] sellae, siliquastrum ; deinde ab his subsellium : ut subsipere quod non plane sapit, sic quod non plane erat sella, subsellium. Ubi in eiusmodi duo, bisellium dictum. Arca, quod arcebantur

---

§ 126. [1] *GS.*, *for* et.   [2] uocabatur, *with* ba *expunged*, *V ;* uocatur *other* MSS.   [3] *Bentinus, for* orinator orinare.

§ 127. [1] *Kent ;* imburvom *Mue. ;* imburum *Aldus, with* B *; for* impurro.   [2] *Mue., for* urbo.   [3] *Aldus, for* est.   [4] *B, for* aruum.   [5] *Laetus, for* plus.   [6] *Aldus, for* uera.

§ 128. [1] *Aug., for* souum.

---

§ 126. [a] Wrong etymology.   [b] Derivative of *urina* at an early date when *urina* still meant merely ' water,' and not specifically ' urine.'

§ 127. [a] ' Bent about,' a vessel shaped like a gravy-boat ; if my conjecture as to the spelling of the word is right, there is basis for Varro's etymology.   [b] Of uncertain etymology, but popularly derived by the Romans from Greek κύλιξ ' cup,' the normal meaning also of Latin *calix*, but not the meaning in this passage.   [c] From Greek κάκκαβος, a pot with three legs, to stand over the fire.   [d] Wrong.

XXVII. 126. Besides there was a third kind of table for vessels, rectangular like the second kind ; it was called an *urnarium*, because it was the piece of furniture in the kitchen on which by preference they set and kept the *urnae* ' urns ' filled with water. From this even now the place in front of the bath where the urn-table is wont to be placed, is called an *urnarium*. *Urnae* ' urns ' got their name [a] from the fact that they *urinant* [b] ' dive ' in the drawing of water, like an *urinator* ' diver.' *Urinare* means to be plunged into water.

127. *Amburvum*,[a] a pot whose name is made from *urvum* ' curved,' because it is so bent that it turns up again like the part of the plough which is named the *urvum* ' beam.' *Calix* [b] ' cooking-pot,' from *caldum* ' hot,' because hot porridge was served up in it, and they drank hot liquid from it. The vessel in which they *coquebant* ' cooked ' their food, from that they called a *caccabus*.[c] *Veru* ' spit,' from *versare* ' to turn.' [d]

XXVIII. 128. From *sedere* ' to sit ' were named *sedes* ' seat,' *sedile* ' chair,' *solium* ' throne,' *sellae* [a] ' stools,' *siliquastrum* [b] ' wicker chair ' ; then from these *subsellium* ' bench ' : as *subsipere* is said a thing does not *sapit* ' taste ' clearly, so *subsellium* because it was not clearly [c] a *sella* ' stool.' Where two had room on a seat of this sort, it was called a *bisellium* ' double seat.' An *arca* ' strong-chest,' because thieves *arcebantur* ' were kept away ' from it when it

---

§ 128. [a] With *ll* from *dl*. [b] Probably *seliquastrum* (or *selli-*), as in Festus, 340 b 10, 341. 5 ; Fay suggests ' seat-basket ' (*sella* + *qualum* + suffix), citing certain types of Mexican chairs. [c] Rather ' under-seat,' that is, a seat below the tribunal.

fures ab ea clausa. Armarium et armamentarium ab eadem origine, sed declinata aliter.

XXIX. 129. Mundus ⟨ornatus⟩¹ muliebris dictus a munditia. Ornatus quasi ab ore natus : hinc enim maxime sumitur quod eam deceat, itaque id paratur speculo.² Calamistrum, quod his calfactis in cinere capillus ornatur. Qui ea ministrabat, a cinere cinerarius est appellatus. Discerniculum, quo discernitur capillus. Pecten, quod per eum explicatur capillus. Speculum a speciendo,³ quod ibi ⟨s⟩e spectant.⁴

130. Vestis a vellis vel¹ ab eo quod vellus lana tonsa universa ovis : id dictum, quod vellebant.² Lan⟨e⟩a,³ ex lana facta. Quod capillum contineret, dictum a rete reticulum ; rete ab raritudine ; item texta fasciola, qua capillum in capite alligarent, dictum capital a capite, quod sacerdotulae in capite etiam nunc solent habere. Sic rica ab ritu, quod Romano ritu sacrificium feminae cum faciunt, capita velant.

---

§ 129. ¹ *Added by GS.; cf. Festus*, 143. 1 *M.* ² *A. Sp., for* speculum. ³ *Laetus, for* spiciendo. ⁴ *a, b, Turnebus, for* espectant.
§ 130. ¹ *Laetus, for* uela. ² *B, Laetus, for* uellabant. ³ *Turnebus, for* lana.

ᵈ Both *arca* and *arcere* are derived from *arx* ' stronghold.'
ᵉ Not connected with *arca*; but belonging together.
§ 129. ᵃ *Munditia* is derived from *mundus*. ᵇ Wrong etymologies.
§ 130. ᵃ Both etymological suggestions for *vestis* are wrong ; for the meaning, see A. Spengel, *Bemerkungen*, 264.

was locked.*d* *Armarium* ' closet ' and *armamentarium*
' warehouse,' from the same source,*e* but with different
suffixes.

XXIX. 129. *Mundus* is a woman's toilet set,
named *a* from *munditia* ' neatness.' *Ornatus* ' toilet
set,' as if *natus* ' born ' from the *os* ' face ' *b* ; for
from this especially is taken that which is to
beautify a woman, and therefore this is handled
with the help of a mirror. *Calamistrum* ' curling-
iron,' because the hair is arranged with irons when
they have been *calfacta* ' heated ' in the embers.*b*
The one who attended to them was called a *cinerarius*
' ember-man,' from *cinis* ' embers.' *Discerniculum*
' bodkin,' with which the hair *discernitur* ' is parted.'
Pecten ' comb,' because by it the hair *explicatur* ' is
spread out.' *b* *Speculum* ' mirror,' from *specere* ' to
look at,' because in it they *spectant* ' look at ' themselves.

130. *Vestis* ' garment ' *a* from *velli* *b* ' shaggy hair,'
or from the fact that the shorn wool of a sheep, taken
as a whole, is a *vellus* ' fleece ' : this was said because
they formerly *vellebant* ' plucked ' it. *Lanea* ' woollen
headband,' *c* because made from *lana* ' wool.' That
which was to hold the hair, was called a *reticulum* ' net-
cap,' from *rete* ' net ' ; *rete*, from *raritudo* ' looseness
of mesh.' *d* Likewise the woven band with which
they were to fasten the hair on the head, was called
a *capital* ' headband,' from *caput* ' head ' ; and this
the sub-priestesses are accustomed to wear on their
heads even now. So *rica* ' veil,' from *ritus* ' fashion,' *d*
because according to the Roman *ritus*, when women
make a sacrifice, they veil their heads. The *mitra*

b *Vellis*, dialectal for *villis*.   *c* For meaning, see A. Spengel, *Bemerkungen*, 264.   *d* Wrong etymologies.

Mitra et reliqua fere in capite postea addita cum
vocabulis Graecis.

XXX. 131.   Prius deinde ⟨ind⟩utui,[1] tum amictui
quae sunt tangam.   Capitium ab eo quod capit pec-
tus, id est, ut antiqui dicebant, comprehendit.   Indutui alterum quod subtus, a quo subucula; alterum
quod supra, a quo supparus, nisi id quod item dicunt
Osce.   Alterius generis item duo, unum quod foris
ac palam, palla; alterum quod intus, a quo ⟨indusium,
ut⟩[2] intusium, id quod Plautus dicit :

> Indusiatam[3] patagiatam caltulam[4] ac crocotulam.

Multa post luxuria attulit, quorum vocabula apparet
esse Graeca, ut asbest⟨in⟩on.[5]

132.   Amictui dictum quod a⟨m⟩biectum[1] est, id
est circumiectum,[2] a quo etiam quo[3] vestitas se invol-
vunt, circumiectui appellant, et quod amictui habet
purpuram circum, vocant circumtextum.   Antiquis-
simi amictui ricinium ; id quod eo utebantur duplici,

---

§ 131.   [1] *B, Turnebus, for* deinde utui *Fv, f.*   [2] *Added
by GS.*   [3] *GS., for* intusiatam *; after the text of Plautus.*
[4] *Laetus, for* caltulum *; after the text of Plautus.*   [5] *GS.,
for* asbeston *; cf. Pliny, Nat. Hist. xix. 4. 20.*
§ 132.   [1] *Mue., for* abiectum.   [2] *Aug., for* circumlectum.
[3] *G, Aug., for* quod.

---

§ 131.   [a] The datives *indutui, amictui,* and *circumiectui,* are
used in § 131 and § 132 as indeclinables, like *frugi* ' thrifty,'
cordi ' pleasant,' original datives of purpose that have become
stereotyped.   [b] From *caput* ' head,' because it was put on
over the head like a sweater.   [c] From *sub* and the verb in
ind-uere, ' to put on,' *ex-uere* ' to take off.'   [d] Probably
Oscan.   [e] Of unknown etymology.   [f] From *induere*
' to put on.'   [g] *Epidicus,* 231.   [h] The Latin words are
adjectives modifying *tunicam* in the preceding line.   [i] Made
of a mineral substance called ἄσβεστος.

' turban ' and in general the other things that go on the head, were later importations, along with their Greek names.

XXX. 131. Next I shall first touch upon those things which are for putting on,[a] then those which are for wrapping about the person. *Capitium* [b] ' vest,' from the fact that it *capit* ' holds ' the chest, that is, as the ancients said, it *comprehendit* ' includes ' it. One kind of put-on goes *subtus* ' below,' from which it is called *subucula* [c] ' underskirt ' ; a second kind goes *supra* ' above,' from which it is called *supparus* [d] ' dress,' unless this is so called because they say it in the same way in Oscan. Of the second sort there are likewise two varieties, one called *palla* [e] ' outer dress,' because it is outside and *palam* ' openly ' visible ; the other is *intus* ' inside,' from which it is called *indusium* [f] ' under-dress,' as though *intusium*, of which Plautus speaks [g] :

> Under-dress, a bordered dress, of marigold and saffron
>   hue.[h]

There are many garments which extravagance brought at later times, whose names are clearly Greek, such as *asbestinon* [i] ' fire-proof.'

132. *Amictui* ' wrap ' is thus named because it is *ambiectum* ' thrown about,' that is, *circumiectum* ' thrown around,' from which moreover they gave the name of *circumiectui* ' throw-around ' to that with which women envelop themselves after they are dressed ; and any wrap that has a purple edge around it, they call *circumtextum* ' edge-weave.' Those of very long ago called a wrap a *ricinium* ' mantilla ' ; it was called *ricinium* from *reicere* ' to throw back,' [a] because they

§ 132.   [a] Properly from *rica* (§ 130) ; it was a square piece of cloth worn folded over the head in sign of mourning.

VARRO

ab eo quod dimidiam partem retrorsum *ia*ciebant,[4] ab reiciendo ricinium dictum.

133. ⟨Pallia⟩[1] hinc, quod facta duo simplicia paria, parilia primo dicta, R exclusum[2] propter levitatem. Parapechia,[3] *ch*lamydes,[4] sic multa, Graeca. L*ae*na,[5] quod de lana multa, duarum etiam togarum instar ; ut antiquissimum mulierum ricinium, sic hoc duplex virorum.

XXXI. 134. Instrumenta rustica quae serendi aut colendi fructus causa facta. Sarculum ab serendo ac sar*ie*ndo.[1] Ligo, quod eo propter latitudinem quod sub terra facilius legitur. Pala a pangendo, ⟨L⟩[2] GL quod fuit. Rutrum ruitrum a ruendo.

135. Aratrum, quod a⟨r⟩ruit[1] terram. Eius ferrum vomer, quod vomit eo plus terram. Dens, quod eo mordetur terra ; super id regula quae stat, stiva ab stando, et in ea transversa regula manicula, quod manu bubulci tenetur. Qui quasi temo est inter

---

[4] *Laetus, for* faciebant.

§ 133. [1] *Added by Canal.* [2] *Mue. ;* R esclusum *Turnebus ; for* resclusum *f,* resculum *Fv.* [3] *For* parapecchia *Fv.* [4] *Ed. Veneta, for* clamides. [5] *Aldus, for* lena.

§ 134. [1] *Aldus, for* sarcendo. [2] *Added by Ellis.*

§ 135. [1] *Turnebus, for* aruit ; *cf. Varro, De Re Rustica,* i. 35, terra adruenda.

---

§ 133. [a] Probably of Greek origin. [b] Greek παράπηχυς 'beside the elbow,' also 'woman's garment with purple border on each side.' The Latin word seems to come from the diminutive παραπήχιον 'radius, small bone below the elbow,' which however may also have denoted the woman's garment, though this is not attested. [c] Probably from Greek χλαῖνα, perhaps with an Etruscan intermediary.

wore it doubled, throwing back one half of it over the other.

133. *Pallia* [a] ' cloaks ' from this, that they consisted of two single *paria* ' equal ' pieces of cloth, called *parilia* at first, from which R was eliminated for smoothness of sound. *Parapechia* [b] ' elbow-stripes,' *chlamydes* ' mantles,' and many others, are Greek. *Laena* [c] ' overcoat,' because they contained much *lana* ' wool,' even like two togas : as the *ricinium* was the most ancient garment of the women, so this double garment is the most ancient garment of the men.

XXXI. 134. Farming tools which were made for planting or cultivating the crops. *Sarculum* [a] ' hoe,' from *serere* ' to plant ' and *sarire* ' to weed.' *Ligo* [b] ' mattock,' because with this, on account of its width, what is under the ground *legitur* ' is gathered ' more easily. *Pala* [c] ' spade ' from *pangere* ' to fix in the earth ' ; the L was originally GL. *Rutrum* ' shovel,' previously *ruitrum*, from *ruere* ' to drop in a heap.'

135.[a] *Aratrum* ' plough,' because it *arruit* [b] ' piles up ' the earth. Its iron part is called *vomer* ' ploughshare,' because with its help it the more *vomit* ' spews up ' the earth. The *dens* ' colter,' because by this the earth is bit ; the straight piece of wood which stands above this is called the *stiva* ' handle,' from *stare* ' to stand,' and the wooden cross-piece on it is the *manicula* ' hand-grip,' because it is held by the *manus* ' hand ' of the ploughman. That which is so to speak a wagon-tongue between the oxen, is called a *bura*

§ 134.   [a] From *sarire*.   [b] Of uncertain origin.   [c] Correct ; but from *pag + slā*, with loss of the extra consonants in the group.

§ 135.   [a] Wrong on *aratrum, vomer, stiva, bura, urvum*.   [b] Really from *arat* ' it ploughs.'

VARRO

boves, bura a bubus ; alii hoc a curvo urvum² appellant. Sub iugo medio cavum, quod bura extrema
addita oppilatur, vocatur cou*m*³ a *ca*vo.⁴ Iugum et
iumentum ab iunctu.

136. Irpices regula compluribus dentibus, quam
item ut plaustrum boves trahunt, ut eruant quae in
terra ser⟨p⟩unt¹ ; sirpices, postea ⟨irpices⟩² S detrito,
a quibusdam dicti. Rastelli ut irpices serrae leves ;
itaque³ homo in pratis per fenisecia⁴ eo festucas
corradit, quo ab rasu rastelli dicti. Rastri, quibus
dentatis⁵ penitus eradunt terram atque eruunt, a quo
rutu r*ua*⟨s⟩tri⁶ dicti.

137. Falces a farre littera¹ commutata ; hae in
Campania seculae a secando ; a quadam similitudine
harum aliae, ut quod apertum unde, falces fenariae
et arbor⟨ar⟩iae² et, quod non apertum unde, falces
lumaria⟨e⟩³ et sirpiculae. Lumariae sunt quibus
secant lumecta, id est cum in agris serpunt spinae ;
quas quod ab terra agricolae solvunt, id est luunt,
lumecta. Falces sirpiculae vocatae ab sirpando, id

---

² *Turnebus, for* curuum.   ³ *Aug., with B, for* cous *Fv.*
⁴ *Rhol., for* couo.

§ 136.   ¹ *Turnebus, for* serunt.   ² *Added by Mue.*
³ *Aug., with B, for* ita qua.   ⁴ *Aug., for* fenisecta.
⁵ *Turnebus, for* dentalis.   ⁶ *Kent ;* rutu rastri *Scaliger ;*
erutu rastri *Turnebus ; for* ruturbatri *Fv.*

§ 137.   ¹ *For* litera *in Fv, as often.*   ² *Georges, for*
arboriae ; *cf. Varro, De Re Rust.* i. 22. 5, *and Cato, De Agric.*
10. 3.   ³ *For* lumaria.

ᶜ The earlier form of *cavus* ' hollow ' was in fact *covos.*

§ 136.   ᵃ Properly *hirpices,* from *hirpus,* the Samnite word
for ' wolf.'   ᵇ Roots of weeds and grasses.   ᶜ Diminutive of *rastrum* ; therefore ultimately from *radere.*   ᵈ Masculine plural of neuter singular *rastrum,* from *radere* ' to
scrape.'

' beam,' from *boves* ' oxen ' ; others call this an *urvum*, from the *curvum* ' curve.' The hole under the middle of the yoke, which is stopped up by inserting the end of the beam, is called *coum*, from *cavum* ' hole.' [c] *Iugum* ' yoke ' and *iumentum* ' yoke-animal,' from *iunctus* ' joining or yoking.'

136. *Irpices* [a] ' harrows ' are a straight piece of wood with many teeth, which oxen draw just like a wagon, that they may pull up the things [b] that *serpunt* ' creep ' in the earth ; they were called *sirpices* and afterwards, by some persons, *irpices*, with the S worn off. *Rastelli* [c] ' hay-rakes,' like harrows, are saw-toothed instruments, but light in weight ; therefore a man in the meadows at haying time *corradit* ' scrapes together ' with this the stalks, from which *rasus* ' scraping ' they are called *rastelli*. *Rastri* [d] ' rakes ' are sharp-toothed instruments by which they scratch the earth deep, and *eruunt* ' dig it up,' from which *rutus* ' digging ' they are called *ruastri*.

137. *Falces* ' sickles,' from *far* ' emmer,' [a] with the change of a letter ; in Campania, these are called *seculae*, from *secare* ' to cut ' ; from a certain likeness to these are named others, the *falces fenariae* ' hay scythes ' and *arborariae* ' tree pruning-hooks,' of obvious origin, and *falces lumariae* and *sirpiculae*, whose source is obscure. *Lumariae* [b] are those with which *lumecta* are cut, that is when thorns grow up in the fields ; because the farmers *solvunt* ' loosen,' that is, *luunt* ' loose,' them from the earth, they are called *lumecta* ' thorn-thickets.' *Falces sirpiculae* [c] are named

§ 137. [a] Wrong. [b] Possibly for *dumariae* and *dumecta*, with Sabine *l* for *d* ; *cf.* Festus, 67. 10 M. [c] Apparently from *sirpus* ' rush,' collateral form of *scirpus*.

VARRO

est ab alligando ; sic sirp*ata*[4] dolia quassa, cum alligata his, dicta. Utuntur in vinea alligando fasces, incisos fustes, faculas. Has *z*anclas[5] Cher*s*o⟨ne⟩si*c*e.[6]

138. Pilum, quod eo far pisunt, a quo ubi id fit dictum pistrinum (*L*[1] et S inter se saepe locum commutant), inde post in Urbe Lucili pistrina et pistrix. Trap*et*es[2] molae oleariae ; vocant trapetes a terendo, nisi Graecum est ; ac molae a mol⟨l⟩iendo[3] : harum enim motu eo coniecta mol⟨l⟩iuntur.[4] Vallum a volatu, quod cum id iactant volant inde levia. Ventilabrum, quod ventilatur in aere frumentum.

139. Quibus conportatur fructus ac necessariae res : de his fiscina a ferendo dicta. Corbes ab eo quod eo spicas aliudve quid corruebant ; hinc minores corbulae dictae. De his quae iumenta ducunt, tragula, quod ab eo trahitur per terram ; sirpea, quae virgis sirpatur, id est colligando implicatur, in qua stercus aliudve quid vehitur.

[4] *Aug., with B, for* sirpita.   [5] *Mue. ;* zanculas *Scaliger, for* phanclas *f, G,* fanclas *H, V, p.*   [6] *Aug., with B, for* chermosie *f,* chermosioe *G, a.*
§ 138. [1] *Aug., for* R.   [2] *For* trapetas *Fv.*   [3] *Scaliger, for* moliendo.   [4] *Scaliger, for* moliuntur.

---

[d] *Cf.* the *fiaschi vestiti* or ' clothed wine-flasks ' of modern Italy.   [e] Messana in Sicily was before the Greek colonization named *Zancle* ' sickle,' from the shape of the cape on which it stood. There is no other evidence that this cape was called a Chersonesus, but as over twenty peninsulas are referred to by this name, it is possible that the name was applied here also.
§ 138. [a] Varro's basis for this statement is not apparent.   [b] *Cf.* 521 and 1250 Marx ; one must assume that one of the *Satires* of Lucilius was entitled *Urbs.*   [c] From Greek.   [d] From *molere* ' to grind.'   [e] Diminutive of *vannus* ' fan.'
§ 139. [a] Wrong on *fiscina* and *corbes.*   [b] *Cf.* § 137, note *c.*

from *sirpare* ' to plait of rushes,' that is, *alligare* ' to fasten '; thus broken jars are said to have been *sirpata* ' rush-covered,' when they are fastened together with rushes.[d] They use rushes in the vineyard for tying up bundles of fuel, cut stakes, and kindling. These sickles they call *zanclae* in the peninsular dialect.[e]

138. The *pilum* ' pestle ' is so named because with it they *pisunt* ' pound ' the spelt, from which the place where this is done is called a *pistrinum* ' mill '—L and S often change places with each other[a]—and from that afterwards *pistrina* ' bakery ' and *pistrix* ' woman baker,' words used in Lucilius's *City*.[b] *Trapetes* [c] are the mill-stones of the olive-mill : they call them *trapetes* from *terere* ' to rub to pieces,' unless the word is Greek ; and *molae* [d] from *mollire* ' to soften,' for what is thrown in there is softened by their motion. *Vallum* [e] ' small winnowing-fan,' from *volatus* ' flight,' because when they swing this to and fro the light particles *volant* ' fly ' away from there. *Ventilabrum* ' winnowing-fork,' because with this the grain *ventilatur* ' is tossed ' in the air.

139. Those means with which field produce and necessary things are transported. Of these, *fiscina* [a] ' rush-basket' was named from *ferre* ' to carry '; *corbes* ' baskets,' from the fact that into them they *corruebant* ' piled up ' corn-ears or something else ; from this the smaller ones were called *corbulae*. Of those which animals draw, the *tragula* ' sledge,' because it *trahitur* ' is dragged ' along the ground by the animal ; *sirpea* [b] ' wicker wagon,' which *sirpatur* ' is plaited ' of osiers, that is, is woven by binding them together, in which dung or something else is conveyed.

140. Vehiculum, in quo faba aliudve quid vehitur, quod e[1] viminibus vietur[2] aut eo vehitur. Brevius[3] vehiculum dictum est aliis ut[4] arcera, quae etiam in Duodecim Tabulis appellatur ; quod ex tabulis vehiculum erat factum ut arca,[5] arcera dictum. Plaustrum ab eo quod non ut in his quae supra dixi ⟨ex quadam parte⟩,[6] sed ex omni parte palam est, quae in eo vehuntur quod perluce⟨n⟩t,[7] ut lapides, asseres, tignum.

XXXII. 141. Aedificia nominata a parte ut multa : ab aedibus et faciendo maxime aedificium. Et oppidum ab opi dictum, quod munitur opis causa ubi sint et quod opus est ad vitam gerendam ubi habeant tuto. Oppida quod opere[1] muniebant, moenia ; quo moenitius esset quod exaggerabant, aggeres dicti, et qui aggerem contineret, moerus.[2] Quod muniendi causa portabatur, munus[3] ; quod sepiebant oppidum eo moenere,[4] moerus.[5]

142. Eius summa pinnae ab his quas insigniti

§ 140. [1] GS. ; ex Laetus ; for est.   [2] Turnebus, for utetur.   [3] A. Sp., for breui est.   [4] A. Sp., for uel. [5] Laetus, for arcar Fv.   [6] Added by L. Sp.   [7] Aug., for perlucet.

§ 141. [1] Aug., for operi.   [2] Sciop., for moerum Fv. [3] Laetus, for manus.   [4] Turnebus, for eae omoencre Fv. [5] Sciop., for murus.

§ 140.   [a] From vehere ' to carry.'   [b] Page 116 Schoell. [c] From plaudere ' to creak.'

§ 141.   [a] Whence ' temple ' in the singular, ' house ' in the plural.   [b] From prefix ob + pedom ' place '; cf. πέδον, Sanskrit padam.   [c] Munire, moenia, murus, munus all belong together ; oe is the older spelling, preserved in moenia in classical Latin. It is a question how far we ought to restore moe- for mu- in this passage ; possibly in all the

140. *Vehiculum* [a] 'wagon,' in which beans or something else is conveyed, because it *vietur* ' is plaited ' or because *vehitur* ' carrying is done ' by it. A shorter kind of wagon is called by others, as it were, an *arcera* ' covered wagon,' which is named even in the *Twelve Tables* [b]; because the wagon was made of boards like an *arca* ' strong box,' it was called an *arcera*. *Plaustrum* [c] ' cart,' from the fact that unlike those which I have mentioned above it is *palam* ' open ' not to a certain degree but everywhere, for the objects which are conveyed in it *perlucent* ' shine forth to view,' such as stone slabs, wooden beams, and building material.

XXXII. 141. *Aedificia* ' buildings ' are, like many things, named from a part : from *aedes* [a] ' hearths ' and *facere* ' to make ' comes certainly *aedificium*. *Oppidum* [b] ' town ' also is named from *ops* ' strength,' because it is fortified for *ops* ' strength,' as a place where the people may be, and because for spending their lives there is *opus* ' need ' of place where they may be in safety. *Moenia* [c] ' walls ' were so named because they *muniebant* ' fortified ' the towns with *opus* ' work.' What they *exaggerabant* ' heaped up ' that it might be *moenitius* ' better fortified,' was called *aggeres* [d] ' dikes,' and that which was to support the dike was called a *moerus* ' wall.' Because carrying was done for the sake of *muniendi* ' fortifying,' the work was a *munus* ' duty '; because they enclosed the town by this *moenus*, it was a *moerus* ' wall.'

142. Its top was called *pinnae* [a] ' pinnacles,' from those feathers which distinguished soldiers are accus-

words, since Varro had a fondness for archaic spellings.
[d] *Exaggerare* is from *agger*, which is from *ad* ' to ' and *gerere* ' to carry.'
  § 142. [a] Literally, ' feathers.'

VARRO

milites in galeis habere solent et in gladiatoribus Samnites. Turres a torvis, quod eae proiciunt ante alios. Qua viam relinquebant in muro, qua in oppidum portarent, portas.

143. Oppida condebant in Latio Etrusco ritu multi, id est iunctis bobus, tauro et vacca interiore, aratro circumagebant sulcum (hoc faciebant religionis causa die auspicato), ut fossa et muro essent muniti. Terram unde exculpserant, fossam vocabant et introrsum *i*actam[1] murum. Post ea[2] qui fiebat orbis, urbis principium ; qui quod erat post murum, postmoerium dictum, e*o* usque[3] auspicia urbana finiuntur. Cippi pomeri stant et circum Ar*i*ciam et[4] circum[5] Romam. Quare et oppida quae prius erant circumducta aratro ab *o*rbe[6] et urvo urb⟨e⟩s ; et[7] ideo coloniae nostrae omnes in litteris antiquis scribuntur urb*e*s,[8] quod item conditae ut Roma ; et ideo coloniae et urbes conduntur, quod intra pomerium ponuntur.

144. Oppidum quod primum conditum in Latio stirpis Romanae, Lavinium : nam ibi dii Penates

---

§ 143. [1] *Mue.*, for factam *Fv.* [2] *Mue.*, for postea. [3] *Mommsen*, for eiusque. [4] *Sciop., for* ars clamet. [5] *B, Laetus, for* circoum *Fv.* [6] *Laetus, for* urbe. [7] *Aldus, for* urbs est. [8] *For* urbis.

---

[b] Heavy-armed fighters who were matched against light-armed *pinnirapi* ' feather-snatchers.' [c] An Asiatic word brought by the Etruscans. [d] *Portare* is from *porta*.
§ 143. [a] That is, with the cow between the bull and the wall ; but GS. take *interiore* with *aratro*, interpreting, " with the plough throwing up the earth on the inside." [b] The old form of *pomerium*. [c] An ancient Latin town on the Appian Way between the Alban Lake and the Lake of Nemi. [d] An attempt to explain the phrase *urbes conduntur* ; in reality, *condere* means merely to set down in a
134

tomed to wear on their helmets, and among the gladiators the Samnites [b] wear. *Turres* [c] ' towers,' from *torvi* ' fiercely staring eyes,' because they stand out in front of the rest. Where they left a way in the wall, by which they might *portare* ' carry ' goods into the town, these they called *portae* [d] ' gates.'

143. Many founded towns in Latium by the Etruscan ritual; that is, with a team of cattle, a bull and a cow on the inside,[a] they ran a furrow around with a plough (for reasons of religion they did this on an auspicious day), that they might be fortified by a ditch and a wall. The place whence they had ploughed up the earth, they called a *fossa* ' ditch,' and the earth thrown inside it they called the *murus* ' wall.' The *orbis* ' circle ' which was made back of this, was the beginning of the *urbs* ' city '; because the circle was *post murum* ' back of the wall,' it was called a *post-moerium* [b]; it sets the limits for the taking of the auspices for the city. Stone markers of the pomerium stand both around Aricia [c] and around Rome. Therefore towns also which had earlier had the plough drawn around them, were termed *urbes* ' cities,' from *orbis* ' circle ' and *urvum* ' curved '; therefore also all our colonies are mentioned as *urbes* in the old writings, because they had been founded in just the same way as Rome; therefore also colonies and cities *conduntur* ' are founded,' because they are placed inside the pomerium.[d]

144.[a] The first town of the Roman line which was founded in Latium, was Lavinium; for there are our

secure place where there is no danger of displacement or of theft.

§ 144. [a] This section embodies the old Roman tradition; the etymologies in it are purely aetiological.

nostri. Hoc a Latini filia, quae coniuncta Aeneae,
Lavinia, appellatu⟨m⟩.[1] Hinc post triginta annos
oppidum alterum conditur, Alba ; id ab sue alba
nominatum. Haec e navi Aeneae cum fu⟨g⟩isset[2]
Lavinium, triginta parit porcos ; ex hoc prodigio post
Lavinium conditum annis triginta haec urbs facta,
propter colorem suis et loci naturam Alba Longa dicta.
Hinc mater Romuli Rhea, ex hac Romulus, hinc
Roma.

145. In oppido vici a via, quod ex ⟨u⟩traque[1] parte
viae sunt aedificia. Fundulae[2] a fundo, quod exitum
non habe⟨n⟩t[3] ac pervium non est. Angiportum,
si⟨ve quod⟩ id[4] angustum, ⟨sive⟩[5] ab agendo et portu.
Quo conferrent suas controversias et quae vende-
rentur vellent quo ferrent, forum appellarunt.

146. Ubi quid generatim, additum ab eo cognomen, ut Forum Bovarium, Forum *H*olitorium : hoc
erat antiquum Macellum, ubi *h*olerum copia ; ea loca
etiam nunc Lacedaemonii vocant μάκελλον, sed Iones
ostia[1] *h*ortorum μακελλώτας *h*ortorum, et castelli

§ 144. [1] *Stanley, for* appellata. [2] *Aug., with B, for*
fuisset.
§ 145. [1] *Aug., with B, for* dextra qui. [2] *L. Sp., for*
fundullae. [3] *B, for* habet. [4] *Mue., for* si id.
[5] *Added by Mue.*
§ 146. [1] *For* hostia.

---

[b] It lay on the edge of the old volcanic crater containing the
Alban Lake.

§ 145. [a] A *vicus* is apparently a street on the ridge of a
hill, with houses on each side ; this forms virtually the entire
village. The word is not connected with *via*. [b] From the
first part of *angustum,* + *portus* in its old meaning of ' pas-

small fortified villages. Along the Tiber, at the sanctuary of Portunus, they call it the *Forum Piscarium* ' Fish Market '; therefore Plautus says [b] :

Down at the Market that sells the fish.

Where things of various kinds are sold, at the Cornel-Cherry Groves, is the *Forum Cuppedinis* ' Luxury Market,' from *cuppedium* ' delicacy,' that is, from *fastidium* ' fastidiousness '; many [c] call it the *Forum Cupidinis* ' Greed Market,' from *cupiditas* ' greed.'

147. After all these things which pertain to human sustenance had been brought into one place, and the place had been built upon, it was called a Macellum, as certain writers say,[a] because there was a garden there ; others say that it was because there had been there a house of a thief with the cognomen Macellus,[b] which had been demolished by the state, and from which this building has been constructed which is called from him a Macellum.

148. In the Forum is the *Lacus Curtius* ' Pool of Curtius '; it is quite certain that it is named from Curtius, but the story about it has three versions : for Procilius [a] does not tell the same story as Piso,[b] nor did Cornelius [c] follow the story given by Procilius. Procilius states [d] that in this place the earth yawned open, and the matter was by decree of the senate referred to the haruspices ; they gave the answer that the God of the Dead demanded the fulfilment of a forgotten vow, namely that the bravest citizen be sent down to him. Then a certain Curtius, a brave man, put on his war-gear, mounted his horse, and turning away from the Temple of Concord, plunged into the

author of a work on Roman history. [c] Identity quite uncertain. [d] *Hist. Rom. Frag.*, page 198 Peter.

locum coisse atque eius corpus divinitus humasse ac reliquisse genti suae monumentum.

149. Piso in Annalibus scribit Sabino bello, quod fuit Romulo et Tatio, virum fortissimum Met⟨t⟩ium Cur*t*ium[1] Sabinum, cum Romulus cum suis ex superiore parte impressionem fecisset,[2] in locum[3] palustrem, qui tum fuit in Foro antequam cloacae sunt factae, secessisse atque ad suos in Capitolium recepisse ; ab eo lacum ⟨Curtium⟩[4] invenisse nomen.

150. Cornelius et Lutatius[1] scribunt eum locum esse fulguritum et ex S. C. septum esse : id quod factum es⟨se⟩t[2] a Curtio consule, cui M. Genucius[3] fuit collega, Curtium appellatum.

151. Arx ab arcendo, quod is locus munitissimus Urbis, a quo facillime possit hostis prohiberi. Carcer a coercendo, quod exire prohibentur. In hoc pars quae sub terra Tullianum, ideo quod additum a Tullio rege. Quod Syracusis, ubi de⟨licti⟩[1] causa custodiuntur, vocantur latomiae, ⟨in⟩de[2] lautumia

---

§ 149. [1] *For* curcium *Fv*.   [2] *After* fecisset, *Popma deleted* curtium.   [3] *Laetus, for* lacum.   [4] *Added by GS*.

§ 150. [1] *Aug., with B, for* luctatius.   [2] *Mue., for* est.   [3] *For* genutius.

§ 151. [1] *Bergmann, for* de.   [2] *Mue. ;* exinde *Turnebus ; for* et de.

---

§ 149. [a] *Hist. Rom. Frag.*, page 79 Peter.   [b] Traditionally built by the first Tarquin ; *cf.* Livy, i. 38. 6.   [c] *Cf.* Livy, i. 10-13, especially i. 12. 9-10 and i. 13. 5.

§ 150. [a] Q. Lutatius Catulus, 152-87 B.C., consul 102 as colleague of Marius in the victory over the Cimbri at Vercellae ; a writer on etymology and antiquities.   [b] *Hist. Rom. Frag.*, page 126 Peter ; *Gram. Rom. Frag.*, page 105 Funaioli.   [c] C. Curtius Chilo and M. Genucius Augurinus were colleagues in the consulship in 445 B.C.

gap, horse and all ; upon which the place closed up and gave his body a burial divinely approved, and left to his clan a lasting memorial.

149. Piso in his *Annals* [a] writes that in the Sabine War between Romulus and Tatius, a Sabine hero named Mettius Curtius, when Romulus with his men had charged down from higher ground and driven in the Sabines, got away into a swampy spot which at that time was in the Forum, before the sewers [b] had been made, and escaped from there to his own men on the Capitoline [c] ; and from this the pool found its name.

150. Cornelius and Lutatius [a] write [b] that this place was struck by lightning, and by decree of the senate was fenced in : because this was done by the consul Curtius,[c] who had M. Genucius as his colleague, it was called the *Lacus Curtius*.

151. The *arx* [a] ' citadel,' from *arcere* ' to keep off,' because this is the most strongly fortified place in the City, from which the enemy can most easily be kept away. The *carcer* [b] ' prison,' from *coercere* ' to confine,' because those who are in it are prevented from going out. In this prison, the part which is under the ground is called the *Tullianum*, because it was added by King Tullius. Because at Syracuse the place where men are kept under guard on account of transgressions is called the *Latomiae* [c] ' quarries,' from

§ 151. [a] The northern summit of the Capitoline, on which stood the temple of Juno Moneta. [b] Beneath the Arx, at the corner of the Forum ; etymology wrong. [c] Greek λατομίαι, contracted from λαοτομίαι, which gave the Latin word ; there were old tufa-quarries on the slopes of the Capitoline, and the excavation which formed the dungeon was probably a part of the quarry.

translatum, quod hic quoque in eo loco lapidicinae
fuerunt.

152. In ⟨Aventi⟩no[1] Lauretum ab eo quod ibi
sepultus est Tatius rex, qui ab Laurentibus inter-
fectus est, ⟨aut⟩[2] ab silva laurea, quod ea ibi excisa et
aedificatus vicus : ut inter Sacram Viam et Macellum
editum Corneta ⟨a cornis⟩,[3] quae abscisae loco reliquerunt nomen, ut *A*esculetum ab *a*esculo[4] dictum
et Fagutal a fago, unde etiam Iovis Fagutalis, quod
ibi sacellum.

153. Armilustr⟨i⟩um[1] ab ambitu lustri : locus
idem Circus M*aximu*s[2] dictus, quod circum spectaculis
aedificatus *u*bi[3] ludi fiunt, et quod ibi circum metas
fertur pompa et equi currunt. Itaque dictum in
Cornicula⟨ria⟩[4] milit*i*s[5] adventu, quem circumeunt
ludentes :

> Quid cessamus ludos facere ?   Circus noster ecce
> adest.

§ 152. [1] *Groth, for* in eo.   [2] *Added by Sciop.*
[3] *Added by Aug., with B.*   [4] *Laetus, for* escula.
§ 153. [1] *For* armilustrum.   [2] *Laetus, for* mecinus.
[3] *Aug., with B, for* ibi.   [4] *Vertranius, for* cornicula.
[5] *Turnebus, for* milites.

§ 152. [a] There is here a lacuna, or else the *in eo* of the
manuscripts stands for *in Aventino* ; for the Lauretum was
on the Aventine.
§ 153. [a] The word denotes both the ceremony, held on
October 19, and the place where it was performed, which
seems originally to have been on the Aventine ; according to
Varro, it was later held in the Circus, in the valley between
the Aventine and the Palatine.   According to Servius, *in
Aen.* i. 283, the name was *ambilustrum*, so called because the
ceremony was not legal unless performed by both (*ambo*)
censors jointly ; it is possible that the word should be so
emended here and at vi. 22.   [b] *Circum* is merely the ac-

that the word was taken over as *lautumia*, because here also in this place there were formerly stone-quarries.

152. On the Aventine [a] is the *Lauretum* 'Laurel-Grove,' called from the fact that King Tatius was buried there, who was killed by the *Laurentes* 'Laurentines,' or else from the *laurea* 'laurel' wood, because there was one there which was cut down and a street run through with houses on both sides : just as between the Sacred Way and the higher part of the Macellum are the *Corneta* 'Cornel-Cherry Groves,' from *corni* 'cornel-cherry trees,' which though cut away left their name to the place ; just as the *Aesculetum* 'Oak-Grove' is named from *aesculus* 'oak-tree,' and the *Fagutal* 'Beech-tree Shrine' from *fagus* 'beech-tree,' whence also Jupiter *Fagutalis* ' of the Beech-tree,' because his shrine is there.

153. *Armilustrium* [a] ' purification of the arms,' from the going around of the *lustrum* ' purificatory offering'; and the same place is called the *Circus Maximus*, because, being the place where the games are performed, it is built up *circum* [b] ' round about ' for the shows, and because there the procession goes and the horses race *circum* 'around' the turning-posts. Thus in *The Story of the Helmet-Horn* [c] the following is said at the coming of the soldier, whom they encircle and make fun of :

Why do we refrain from making sport ? See, here's
   our circus-ring.

cusative of *circus*. [c] Frag. I of Plautus's *Cornicularia*, which may be taken as the *Story of the Corniculum*, a horn-shaped ornament on the helmet, bestowed for bravery ; here apparently assumed by a braggart soldier, the *miles* of the text.

VARRO

In circo primum unde mittuntur equi, nunc dicuntur carceres, Naevius oppidum appellat. Carceres dicti, quod coercentur[6] equi, ne inde exeant antequam magistratus signum misit. Quod a⟨d⟩ muri sp*ecie*m[7] pinnis[8] turribusque[9] carceres olim fuerunt, scripsit poeta :

> Dictator ubi currum insidit, pervehitur usque ad
> oppidum.

154. Intumus circus ad Murci*ae*[1] vocatu*r*,[2] ut Procilius aiebat, ab urceis, quod is locus esset inter figulos ; alii dicunt a murteto declinatum, quod ibi id fuerit ; cuius vestigium manet, quod ibi est sacellum etiam nunc Murteae Veneris. Item simili de causa Circus Flaminius dicitur, qui circum aedificatus est Flaminium Campum, et quod ibi quoque Ludis Tauriis equi circum metas currunt.

155. Comitium ab eo quod coibant eo comitiis curiatis et litium causa.[1] Curiae duorum generum : nam et ubi curarent sacerdotes res divinas, *ut*[2] curiae

---

[6] *p, Ed. Veneta* (cohercentur *Laetus*), *for* coercuntur.
[7] *Mue., for* a muris partem. [8] *Laetus, for* pennis.
[9] *Aug., for* turribus qui.

§ 154. [1] *L. Sp., for* murcim *Fv.* [2] *Sciop., for* uocatum.
§ 155. [1] *Mue. ; *caussa *Aug., with B ;* causae *Fv.* [2] *For* et.

---

[d] Merely the plural of *carcer* ' prison ' ; not related to *coercere.* [e] Naevius, *Comic. Rom. Frag., inc. fab.* II Ribbeck[3] ; *R.O.L.* ii. 148-149 Warmington.

§ 154. [a] *Hist. Rom. Frag.,* page 3 Peter. [b] Page 116 Funaioli. [c] In the level ground of the Campus Martius, through which C. Flaminius Nepos as censor in 220 B.C. built the *Via Flaminia,* the great highway from Rome to the north, and near it the *Circus Flaminius ;* he was consul in 217 and was killed in the battle with Hannibal at Lake

In the Circus, the place from which the horses are let go at the start, is now called the *Carceres* 'Prison-stalls,' but Naevius called it the Town. *Carceres* [d] was said, because the horses *coercentur* 'are held in check,' that they may not go out from there before the official has given the sign. Because the Stalls were formerly adorned with pinnacles and towers like a wall, the poet wrote [e] :

When the Dictator mounts his car, he rides the whole way to the Town.

154. The very centre of the Circus is called *ad Murciae* 'at Murcia's,' as Procilius [a] said, from the *urcei* 'pitchers,' because this spot was in the potters' quarter ; others [b] say that it is derived from *murtetum* 'myrtle-grove,' because that was there : of which a trace remains in that the chapel of Venus *Murtea* 'of the Myrtle' is there even to this day. Likewise for a similar reason the *Circus Flaminius* 'Flaminian Circus' got its name, for it is built [c] *circum* 'around' the Flaminian Plain, and there also the horses race *circum* 'around' the turning-posts at the Taurian Games.[d]

155. The *Comitium* 'Assembly-Place' was named from this, that to it they *coibant* 'came together' for the *comitia curiata* [a] 'curiate meetings' and for law-suits. The *curiae* [b] 'meeting-houses' are of two kinds : for there are those where the priests were to attend to affairs of the gods, like the old meeting-

Trasumennus.   [d] Games in honour of the deities of the netherworld.

§ 155.   [a] Long before Varro's time, practically replaced by the *comitia centuriata*.   [b] *Curia* denoted first a group of *gentes* ; then a meeting-place for such groups ; then any meeting-place.

VARRO

veteres, et ubi senatus humanas, ut Curia Hostilia,
quod primus aedificavit Hostilius rex. Ante hanc
Rostra ; cuius id vocabulum, ex hostibus capta fixa
sunt rostra ; sub dextra huius a Comitio locus sub-
structus, ubi nationum subsisterent legati qui ad
senatum essent missi ; is Graecostasis appellatus a
parte, ut multa.

156. Senaculum supra Graecostasim, ubi Aedis
Concordiae et Basilica Opimia ; Senaculum vocatum,
ubi senatus aut ubi seniores consisterent, dictum ut
γεροντία[1] apud Graecos. Lautolae ab lavando, quod
ibi ad Ianum Geminum aquae caldae fuerunt. Ab
his palus fuit in Minore Velabro, a quo, quod ibi
vehebantur lintribus,[2] velabrum, ut illud de quo supra
dictum est.

157. Aequimaelium, quod a⟨e⟩quata[1] Maeli domus
publice,[2] quod regnum occupare voluit is. Locus ad
Busta Gallica, quod Roma recuperata Gallorum ossa

§ 156.   [1] *Rhol.*, *for* ierusia (gerusia *G*).   [2] *Laetus*, *for*
luntribus *Fv*.
§ 157.   [1] *Rhol.*, *for* aquata.   [2] *Aldus*, *for* publico.

[c] The third king of Rome ; for his building of the *curia*,
see Livy, i. 30. 2.   [d] This was the old stand, erected at
least one hundred years before it was decorated in 338 by
C. Maenius with six beaks of war-vessels taken in a battle
with Antium ; *cf.* Livy, viii. 14. 8.   [e] Presumably because
the Greeks were the first to send such embassies ; when
other nations began to send them, the name of the place
had been established.

§ 156.   [a] As the two stands were at the foot of the Capitoline and the end of the Forum, the *senaculum* must have lain
just in front of them.   [b] Those over forty-six years of age,
in distinction from the *iuniores*.   [c] This temple lay apparently a little to the east of the Comitium, at the side of the
Forum or slightly away from it.   [d] The tense of *fuerunt*
and *fuit* indicates that the hot springs and the pool were no
longer there in Varro's time.   [e] *Cf.* v. 43-44.

146

houses, and those where the senate should attend to affairs of men, like the Hostilian Meeting-House, so called because King Hostilius *c* was the first to build it.   In front of this is the *Rostra* ' Speaker's Stand '*d* : of which this is the name—the *rostra* ' beaks ' taken from the enemy's ships have been fastened to it. A little to the right of it, in the direction of the Comitium, is a lower platform, where the envoys of the nations who had been sent to the senate were to wait ; this, like many things, was called from a part of its use, being named the *Graecostasis* 'Stand of the Greeks.' *e*

156.   Above the Graecostasis was the *Senaculum a* ' Senate-Stand,' where the Temple of Concord and the Basilica Opimia are ; it was called *Senaculum* as a place where the senate or the *seniores b* ' elders ' were to take their places, named like γερουσία ' assembly of elders ' among the Greeks.   *Lautolae* ' baths,' from *lavare* ' to wash,' because there near the Double Janus *c* there once were *d* hot springs. From these there was *d* a pool in the Lesser Velabrum, from which fact it was called *velabrum* because there they *vehebantur* ' were conveyed ' by skiffs, like that greater Velabrum of which mention has been made above. *e*

157.   The *Aequimaelium* ' Maelius-Flat,' because the house of Maelius was *aequata* ' laid flat ' by the state since he wished to seize the power and be king. *a*   The place *Ad Busta Gallica* ' At the Gauls' Tombs,' because on the recovery of Rome the bones of the Gauls who

§ 157.   *a* Spurius Maelius, suspected of aiming at royal power, was slain by C. Servilius Ahala, *magister equitum*, in 439 B.C., by direction of the dictator L. Quinctius Cincinnatus ; *cf.* Livy, iv. 13-14.

VARRO

qui possederunt urbem ibi coacervata ac consepta.
Locus qui vocatur Doliola ad Cluacam Maxumam, ubi
non licet despuere, a doliolis sub terra. Eorum duae
traditae historiae, quod alii inesse aiunt ossa cada-
verum, alii Numae Pompilii religiosa quaedam post
mortem eius infossa. Argiletum³ sunt qui scripserunt ab Argo La⟨ri⟩saeo,⁴ quod is huc venerit
ibique sit sepultus, alii ab argilla, quod ibi id genus
terrae sit.

158. Clivos Public⟨i⟩us¹ ab aedilibus plebei Pu-
blici⟨i⟩s qui eum publice aedificarunt. Simili de causa
Pullius et Cosconius, quod ab his viocuris dicuntur
aedificati. Clivus proximus a Flora susus² versus
Capitolium Vetus, quod ibi sacellum Iovis Iunonis
Minervae, et id antiquius quam aedis quae in Capitolio facta.

159. Esquiliis¹ Vicus Africus, quod ibi obsides ex
Africa bello Punico dicuntur custoditi. Vicus Cyprius
a cypro, quod ibi Sabini cives additi consederunt, qui

---

³ *Laetus, for* argeletum.   ⁴ *Kent, for* argola seu.

§ 158.   ¹ *Aug., for* publicus.   ² *Victorius and Turnebus,*
for a floras usus.

§ 159.   ¹ *For* exquiliis.

ᵇ In 390 (or 388 ?) B.C.; *cf.* Livy, v. 37 ff.   ᶜ Livy, v. 40. 8,
and Festus, 69. 8 M., say that the burial of the sacred objects
was at the time of the Gallic invasion.   ᵈ A street alongside the Comitium ; clearly ' Clay-pit,' from *argilla*, but
commonly understood as *Argi letum* 'death of Argus.'
According to Servius *in Aen.* viii. 345, Argus was murdered
while he was a guest of Evander ; Evander gave him honourable burial.   ᵉ Page 115 Funaioli.   ᶠ My suggestion for
the impossible *argola seu* of the text is based on the fact
that both Argus the guardian of Io and Argus the son of
Niobe were connected with the city Argos, whose citadel

had held Rome [b] were heaped up there and fenced in. The place near the Cloaca Maxima which is called *Doliola* ' The Jars,' where spitting is prohibited, from some *doliola* ' jars ' that were buried under the earth. Two stories about these are handed down : some say that bones of dead men were in them, others that certain sacred objects belonging to Numa Pompilius were buried in them after his death.[c] The Argiletum,[d] according to some writers,[e] was named from Argus of Larisa,[f] because he came to this place and was buried there ; according to others, from the *argilla* ' clay,' because this kind of earth is found at this place.

158. The *Clivus* [a] *Publicius* ' Publician Incline,' from the members of the Publician gens [b] who as plebeian aediles constructed it by state authority. For like reasons the *Clivus Pullius* and the *Clivus Cosconius*, because they are said to have been constructed by men of these names as Street-Overseers. The Incline that goes up close by the Temple of Flora is Old Capitol, because there is in that place a chapel of Jupiter, Juno, and Minerva, and this is older than the temple which has been built on the Capitol.

159. On the Esquiline there is a *Vicus Africus* ' African Row,' because there, it is said, the hostages from Africa in the Punic War were kept under guard. The *Vicus Cyprius* ' Good Row,' from *cyprum*, because there the Sabines who were taken in as citizens settled, and they named it from the good omen :

was named *Larisa* or *Larissa* ; and Evander's guest may well have been represented as coming thence.

§ 158. [a] A street running steeply up a hill. [b] Two brothers Lucius and Marcus Publicius Malleolus, according to Festus, 238 b 28 M.

VARRO

a bono omine id appellarunt: nam cyprum Sabine
bonum. Prope hunc Vicus Sceleratus, dictus a Tullia
Tarquini Superbi uxore, quod ibi cum iaceret pater
occisus, supra eum carpentum mulio ut inigeret[2]
iussit.

XXXIII. 160. Quoniam vicus constat ex domibus,
nunc earum[1] vocabula vide⟨a⟩mus.[2] Domus Graecum
et ideo in aedibus sacris ante cellam, ubi sedes dei
sunt, Graeci dicunt πρόδομον,[3] quod po⟨s⟩t est,[4]
ὀπισθόδομ⟨ον⟩.[5] Aedes[6] ab aditu, quod plano pede
adibant. Itaque ex aedibus efferri indictivo[7] funere
praeco etiam eos dicit qui ex tabernis efferuntur, et
omnes in censu villas inde ⟨de⟩dicamus[8] aedes.

161. Cavum aedium dictum qui locus tectus intra
parietes relinquebatur patulus, qui esset ad com-
⟨m⟩unem omnium usum. In hoc locus si nullus
relictus erat, sub divo qui esset, dicebatur testudo ab
testudinis similitudine, ut est in praetorio et castris.
Si relictum erat in medio ut lucem caperet,[1] deorsum
quo impluebat, dictum impluium, susum qua com-
pluebat, compluium: utrumque a pluvia. Tuscanicum dictum a Tuscis, posteaquam illorum cavum

[2] *Ursinus, for* iniceret.

§ 160. [1] *p, Aug., for* eorum. [2] *For* uidemus *Fv.*
[3] *For* prodomum *Fv.* [4] *GS.; post* Victorius; *for* potest.
[5] *Victorius, for* opisthodum *Fv.* [6] *For* aedis. [7] *Aug.,*
with B, for inductiuo. [8] *Mue., for* inde dicamus.

§ 161. [1] *Aug., with B, for* carperet *Fv.*

§ 159. [a] The Sabine word for 'good' was *cupro-*; and
Vicus Cyprius, if correctly written, must mean 'Cyprian
Row' or 'Copper Row.' [b] *Cf.* Livy, i. 48. 7.

§ 160. [a] Latin *domus* is akin to, not derived from, Greek
δόμος. [b] Wrong; an *aedes* is a building with a fireplace,
150

for *cyprum* means ' good ' in Sabine.*ᵃ* Near this is the *Vicus Sceleratus* ' Accursed Row,' named from Tullia wife of Tarquin the Proud, because when her father was lying dead in it she ordered her muleteer to drive her carriage on over his body.*ᵇ*

XXXIII. 160. Since a Row consists of houses, let us now look at the names of these. *Domus* ' house ' is a Greek word,*ᵃ* and therefore in the temples the room in front of the hall where the abode of the god is the Greeks call πρόδομος ' front room,' and that which is behind they call ὀπισθόδομος ' back room.' *Aedes* ' house,' from *aditus* ' approach,' because they *adibant* ' approached ' it on level footing.*ᵇ* Therefore the herald at an announced funeral even says that those who are carried out of any building made of boards, are carried *ex aedibus* ' from the house ' ; and all the country-houses in the census-list we from that fact *ᶜ* call *aedes.*

161. The *cavum aedium* ' inner court ' is said of the roofed part which is left open within the house-walls, for common use by all. If in this no place was left which is open to the sky, it was called a *testudo* ' tortoise ' from the likeness to the *testudo,* as it is at the general's headquarters and in the camps. If some space was left in the centre to get the light, the place into which the rain fell down was called the *impluvium,* and the place where it ran together up above was called the *compluvium* ; both from *pluvia* ' rain.' The *Tuscanicum* ' Tuscan-style ' was named from the *Tusci* ' Etruscans,' after the Romans

cf. Greek αἴθειν ' to blaze.'   *ᶜ* Because such *villae* were wooden buildings, and normally owned by Romans whose prominence would authorize them to have publicly announced funerals.

VARRO

aedium simulare coeperunt. Atrium appellatum ab
Atriatibus Tuscis : illinc enim exemplum sumptum.

162. Circum cavum aedium erat unius cuiusque
rei utilitatis causa parietibus dissepta : ubi quid conditum esse volebant, a celando cellam appellarunt;
penariam ubi penus ; ubi cubabant cubiculum ; ubi
cenabant cenaculum vocitabant, ut etiam nunc
Lanuvi apud aedem Iunonis et in cetero Latio ac
Faleri⟨i⟩s et Cordubae dicuntur. Posteaquam in
superiore parte cenitare coeperunt, superioris domus
universa cenacula dicta ; posteaquam ubi cenabant
plura facere coeperunt, ut in castris ab hieme hiberna,
hibernum domus vocarunt ; contraria . . .

HIC DEFECIT EXEMPLAR FOLIIS DUOBUS[1]

XXXIV. 163. . . . ⟨quam re⟩ligionem[1] Porcius
designat cum de Ennio scribens dicit eum coluisse
Tutilinae loca. Sequitur Porta Naevia, quod in
nemoribus Naevii*s*[2] : etenim loca, ubi ea, sic dicta.

§ 162.   [1] *Thus Fv.*
§ 163.   [1] *Aug., for* ligionem.   [2] *Laetus, for* naevius.

---

§ 161.   [a] *Atrium* either from *Atria*, as Varro states, or
from *ater* ' black,' because the roof was blackened by the
smoke from the hearth-fire, which originally had to escape
by the opening in the roof.

§ 162.   [a] In Spain, the modern Cordova.   [b] Varro
doubtless stated that a dining-room for summer use was
called an *aestivum*.

§ 163.   [a] The lost passage concluded with an account of
the gates of the wall of Servius Tullius ; the extant text
resumes just at the end of this description, giving the gates
on the Aventine.   [b] Page 44 Huschke. Porcius Licinus
was a poet who flourished about 100 B.C. or slightly earlier.
[c] Ennius lived on the Aventine ; according to Varro, near

152

began to imitate their style of inner court. The *atrium* ' reception hall ' was named [a] from the Etruscans of Atria ; for from them the model was taken.

162. Around the inner court the house was divided by walls, making rooms useful for different purposes : where they wished something to be stored away, they called it a *cella* ' store-room,' from *celare* ' to conceal ' ; a *penaria* ' food-pantry,' where *penus* ' food ' was kept ; a *cubiculum* ' sleeping-chamber,' where they *cubabant* ' lay down ' for rest ; where they *cenabant* ' dined,' they called it a *cenaculum* ' dining-room,' as even now such rooms are named at Lanuvium in the Temple of Juno, in the rest of Latium, at Falerii, and at Corduba.[a] After they began to take dinner upstairs, all the rooms of the upper story were called *cenacula* ; still later, when they began to have several rooms for dining, they called one the *hibernum* ' winter-room ' of the house, as in camps they speak of the *hiberna* ' winter camp,' from *hiems* ' winter ' ; and on the other hand . . .[b]

HERE THE MODEL COPY LACKED TWO LEAVES

XXXIV. 163.[a] . . . which worship Porcius [b] means when, speaking of Ennius, he says that he dwelt in the locality of Tutilina.[c] Next comes the Naevian Gate,[d] so called because it is in the Naevian Woods : for the locality where it is, is called by this name. Then the *Porta Rauduscula* [e] ' Copper Gate,'

the sanctuary of Tutilina, a goddess of protection. This must be near the Porta Capena or somewhat to the west of it, in the circuit of the Servian walls, before reaching the *Porta Naevia*. [d] On the south-east slope of the Aventine. [e] Or *Raudusculana*, whereby the road led over the central depression of the Aventine to the Ostian road.

Deinde Rauduscula, quod aerata fuit. Aes raudus
dictum ; ex eo[3] veteribus in mancipiis scriptum :

Raudusculo libram ferito.

Hinc Lavernalis ab ara Lavernae, quod ibi ara eius.

164. Praeterea intra muros video portas dici in
Palatio Mucionis a mugitu, quod ea pecus in buceta
tum ⟨ante⟩ antiquum[1] oppidum exigebant ; alteram
Romanulam, ab Roma dictam, quae habet gradus in
Nova *V*ia[2] ad Volupiae sacellum.

165. Tertia est Ianualis, dicta ab Iano, et ideo ibi
positum Iani signum et ius institutum a Pompilio, ut
scribit in Annalibus Piso, ut sit aperta semper, nisi
cum bellum sit nusquam. Traditum est memoriae
Pompilio rege fuisse opertam[1] et post Tito Manlio[2]
consule bello Cart*h*aginiensi primo confecto, et eodem
anno apertam.

XXXV. 166. Super lectulis origines quas adverti,
hae : lectica, quod legebant unde *eam*[1] facerent

---

[3] *After* eo, *L. Sp. deleted* in.
    § 164.   [1] *L. Sp., for* bucitatum antiquum (bucita tum
Scaliger).   [2] *Scaliger, for* noualia.
    § 165.   [1] *Scaliger, for* apertam.   [2] *Aug.* (manlio *B*),
for titio manilio.
    § 166.   [1] *Victorius, for* iam.

---

[f] The oldest " money " consisted of slabs or bars of *aes rude*
' rough copper,' to which reference is here made.   [g] A
goddess of the netherworld, patroness of thieves ; the
location of the gate with her altar is not known.
    § 164.   [a] The three gates in the old walls of the Palatine.
[b] Or *Porta Mugonia* ; in the divine name *Mucio* the C has
the early value of *g*. This gate was at the top of the Nova
Via.   [c] Leading up from the foot of the Nova Via.   [d] A
goddess of pleasure.

because it was at one time covered with copper. Copper is called *raudus* ; from this the ancients had it written in their formula for symbolic sales :

> Let him strike the balance-pan with a piece of
> *raudus.*[f]

From here, the Lavernal Gate, from the altar of Laverna,[g] because her altar is there.

164. Besides, inside the walls, I see, there are gates[a] on the Palatine : the Gate of Mucio,[b] from *mugitus* ' lowing,' because by it they drove the herds out into the cow-pastures which were then in front of the ancient town ; a second called the *Romanula* ' Little Roman,' named from Rome, which has steps[c] in New Street at the Chapel of Volupia.[d]

165. The third gate is the Janual Gate, named from Janus, and therefore a statue of Janus[a] was set up there, and the binding practice was instituted by Pompilius, as Piso[b] writes in his *Annals*, that the gate should always be open except when there was no war anywhere. The story that has come down to us is that it was closed when Pompilius was king, and afterwards when Titus Manlius was consul, at the end of the first war with Carthage, and then opened again in the same year.[c]

XXXV. 166. On the subject of beds,[a] the origins of the names, so far as I have observed them, are the following : *Lectica* ' couch,' because they *legebant*

§ 165. ^a The archway of Janus, placed at the end of the Argiletum where it debouched into the Forum ; *cf.* Livy, i. 19. 2. ^b *Hist. Rom. Frag.*, page 79 Peter. ^c In 235 B.C. ; but it was closed three times in the reign of Augustus.

§ 166. ^a *Lectus, lectulus, lectica*, all from a root meaning ' to lie,' not otherwise found in Latin, but seen in English *lie* and *lay*, and in Greek.

stramenta atque herbam, ut etiam nunc fit in castris ;
lecticas, ne essent in terra,[2] sublimis in his ponebant ;
nisi ab eo quod Graeci antiqui dicebant λέκτρον
lectum potius.   Qui[3] lecticam involvebant, quod fere
stramenta erant e segete, segestria appellarunt, ut
etiam nunc in castris, nisi si a Graecis : nam στέγαστρον ibi.[4]   Lectus mortui ⟨quod⟩[5] fertur, dicebant
feretrum nostri, Graeci φέρετρον.

167.   Posteaquam transierunt ad culcitas, quod in
eas acus[1] aut tomentum aliudve quid calcabant, ab
inculcando culcita dicta.   Hoc quicquid insternebant
ab sternendo stragulum appellabant.   Pulvinar vel a
plumis vel a pellulis[2] declinarunt.   Quibus operibantur, operimenta, et pallia opercula dixerunt.   In his
multa peregrina, ut sagum, reno Gallica, ut[3] gaunaca[4]
et amphimallum Graeca ;   contra Latinum toral,[5]
ante torum, et torus a torto,[6] quod is in promptu.

[2] *Aug.*, *for* terras.   [3] *Ed. Veneta*, *for* quam.   [4] *L. Sp.*,
for ubi.   [5] *Added by L. Sp.*
  § 167.   [1] *Turnebus*, *for* ea sagus.   [2] *Aldus*, *for* a
pluribus uel a pollulis.   [3] *GS.* ; gallica *Turnebus* ; *for*
galli quid.   [4] *GS.* ; gaunacum *Scaliger*, *for* gaunacuma.
[5] *A. Sp.* ; toral quod *Aug.* ; torale quod *Aldus* ; *for* tore
uel.   [6] *Meursius*, *for* toruo.

[b] That is, on additional straw and grass (if the text be
correct).   [c] From the Greek, with dissimilative loss of the
prior *t*.   [d] The standing grain ; then, the stems of the
grain-plants, not merely of wheat.   [e] From the Greek
word, which is from φέρω ' I bear.'
  § 167.   [a] Wrong.   [b] *Hoc* = *huc* ' into this.'   [c] From
156

' gathered ' the straw-coverings and the grass with which to make them, as even now is done in camp ; these couches, that they might not be on the earth, they raised up on these materials [b] ;—unless rather from the fact that the ancient Greeks called a bed a λέκτρον. Those who covered up a couch, called the coverings *segestria*,[c] because the coverings in general were made from the *seges* [d] ' wheat-stalks,' as even now is done in the camp ; unless the word is from the Greeks, for there it is στέγαστρον. Because the bed of a dead man *fertur* ' is carried,' our ancestors called it a *feretrum* [e] ' bier,' and the Greeks called it a φέρετρον.

167. After they had passed to the use of *culcitae* ' mattresses and pillows,' because into them they *calcabant* ' pressed ' chaff or stuffing or something else, the article was called a *culcita* from *inculcare* ' to press in.' [a] Whatever they spread upon this,[b] they called a *stragulum* ' cover ' from *sternere* ' to spread.' The *pulvinar* [c] ' cushioned seat of honour ' they derived either from *plumae* ' feathers ' or from *pellulae* ' furs.' That with which they *operibantur* ' were covered,' they called *operimenta* ' covers,' and *pallia* ' covers of a Greek sort ' they called *opercula*. Among these there are many foreign words, such as *sagum* ' soldier's blanket ' and *reno* ' cloak of reindeer skin,' which are Gallic, and *gaunaca* [d] ' heavy Oriental cloak ' and *amphimallum* ' cloak shaggy on both sides,' which are Greek ; and on the other hand *toral* ' valance,' in front of the *torus* ' bolster,' is Latin, and so in *torus* ' bolster,' from *tortum* ' twisted,' because it is ready for

pulvinus ' pillow,' a word of undetermined origin.
[d] Correct sources ; but *gaunaca* came into Greek from Persian.

157

VARRO

Ab hac similitudine toru*l*us[7] in mulieris capite
ornatus.

168. Qua simplici scansione scandebant in lectum
non al*t*um,[1] scabellum ; in altiorem, scamnum. Duplicata scansio gradus dicitur, quod gerit in inferiore[2]
superiorem. Graeca sunt peristromata et peripetasmata, sic ali⟨a⟩ qu*ae*[3] item convivii causa ibi multa.

XXXVI. 169.[1] Pecuniae signatae vocabula sunt
aeris et argenti haec : as ab aere ; dupondius ab[2]
duobus ponderibus, quod unum pondus assipondium
dicebatur ; id ideo quod as erat libra pond*o*.[3] Deinde
ab numero reliquum dictum usque ad centussis,[4] ut
as[5] singulari numero, ab tribus assibus tressis, et sic
proportione usque ad nonussis.

170. In denario numero hoc mutat, quod primum
est ab decem assibus decussis, secundum ab duobus
decussibus *v*icessis,[1] quod dici sol⟨it⟩um[2] a duobus

---

[7] *Aug., for* toruius.
   § 168.   [1] *M, Laetus, for* alium.   [2] *Laetus, for* inferiora.
[3] *L. Sp., for* aliquid.
   § 169.   [1] *Priscian*, iii. 410. 10 *Keil, quotes from this point,
beginning with* multa *at the end of* § 168, *placed with* § 169
by wrong division ; he continues through decuma libella *in
the first line of* § 174.   *As the best manuscript of Priscian is
at least three centuries older than F of Varro. his text is
useful here, though it omits some words and phrases, and has
one considerable insertion.*   [2] *Priscian, for* a.   [3] *Gronov.,
for* pondus.   [4] *Priscian has* centussem.   [5] *After* as,
Laetus deleted a.
   § 170.   [1] *Turnebus, for* bicessis.   [2] *Turnebus, for* solum.

---

[*] Wrong ; he apparently means that the *torus*, a bolster
originally of twisted rushes, was ready when it was properly
158

use.[e] From likeness [f] to this is named the *torulus* 'knob,' [g] an ornament on a woman's head.

168. That by which they *scandebant* 'mounted' by a single *scansio* 'step' into a bed that was not high, they called a *scabellum* 'bed step'; that by which they mounted into a higher bed, a *scamnum* 'bed steps.' [a] A double step is called a *gradus* 'pace,' because it *gerit* 'carries' a higher step on the lower.[b] *Peristromata* 'bedspreads' and *peripetasmata* 'bed-curtains' are Greek words, so are other things which are used for banquets as well—and of them there are quite a number.

XXXVI. 169. The names of stamped money of bronze and silver are the following : *as* [a] from *aes* 'copper'; *dupondius* 'two-*as* piece' from *duo pondera* 'two weights,' because one weight was called an *assipondium* '*as* piece'; this for the reason that an *as* was a *libra* 'unit' *pondo* 'by weight.' From this the rest were named from the number up to *centussis* 'one hundred *asses*,' as *as* when the number is one, *tressis* from three *asses*, and so by regular analogy up to *nonussis* 'nine *asses*.'

170. At the number ten this changes, because first there is the *decussis* from *decem asses* 'ten *asses*,' second the *vicessis* [a] 'twenty *asses*' from two *decusses*, which

twisted, like a *tormentum* or piece of artillery which was ready to fire when the ropes, its source of propulsion, had been twisted. [f] That is, similarity in shape. [g] The shape in which the hair was arranged.

§ 168. [a] Wrong etymology; but *scabellum* is a diminutive of *scamnum*. [b] Wrong.

§ 169. [a] Not from *aes*, but a word borrowed from some unknown source. The etymologies from here on through § 174 are correct except as noted.

§ 170. [a] Properly from *viginti* 'twenty,' *vicies* 'twenty times.'

bicessis ; reliqua conveniunt, quod est ut tricessis[3]
proportione usque ad centussis, quo maius aeris
proprium vocabulum non est : nam ducenti⟨s⟩ et sic[4]
proportione quae dicuntur non magis asses quam
denarii aliaeve quae[5] res significantur.

171.   Aeris minima pars sextula, quod sexta pars
unciae.   Semuncia, quod dimidia pars unciae : se[1]
valet dimidium, ut in selibra et semodio.   Uncia ab
uno.   Sextans ab eo quod sexta pars assis, ut quadrans quod quarta, et triens quod tertia pars.   Semis,
quod semi⟨a⟩s,[2] id est[3] dimidium assis, ut supra
dictum est.   Septunx a septem et uncia conclusum.

172.   Reliqua obscuriora, quod ab deminutione, et
ea quae deminuuntur ita sunt, ut extremas syllabas
habeant : ut ⟨un⟩de una[1] dempta uncia deunx,

---

[3] *Priscian, for* tricensis.   [4] *L. Sp. ;* ducenti et sic *Priscian ,
for* ducenti in.   [5] alieuae quae *Fv ;* aliaeque *Priscian.*
  § 171.   [1] *Bentinus, for* sic.   [2] *Turnebus, for* semis.
[3] *After* est, *Laetus deleted* ut, *which Priscian also omits.*
  § 172.   [1] ut unde una *Kent ;* unde una *Mue. ; for* ut de
una (*Priscian omits* ut de).

---

[b] It is hardly likely that *vicessis* became *bicessis* (influenced
by ' two ' in the form *bi-* as prefix) until the confusion of B
and V in pronunciation ; this began about a century after
Varro wrote this work.   The clause therefore seems to be
an interpolation.   [c] After *centussis*, Priscian inserts : *quod
et Persius ostendit " et centum Graecos uno centusse licetur,"*
' and on one hundred Greeks he sets the value of just one
hundred *asses.*'   The quotation is Persius, 5. 191, where
the text has *curto* ' clipped ' instead of *uno.*
  § 171.   [a] Apparently named as the smallest coin, one
seventy-second of the *as* ; but no such coin is actually attested.   [b] Really *semi-*, with the vowel elided : *sem-uncia.*

is customarily pronounced *bicessis*, from *duo* ' two ' *b* ; the rest harmonize, in that the formation is like *tricessis* regularly up to *centussis*,*c* after which there is no special word for larger sums of copper money : for *ducenti* ' two hundred ' and higher numbers which are made analogically do not indicate *asses* any more than they do *denarii* or any other things.

171. The smallest piece of copper is a *sextula*,*a* so named because it is the *sexta* ' sixth ' part of an ounce. The *semuncia* ' half-ounce,' because it is the half of an ounce : *se* equals *dimidium* ' half,' *b* as in *selibra* *c* ' half-pound ' and *semodius* ' half-peck.' *Uncia* ' ounce,' from *unum* ' one.' *d* *Sextans* ' sixth,' from the fact that it is the sixth part of an *as*, as the *quadrans* ' fourth ' is that which is a fourth, and the *triens* ' third ' that which is a third.*e* *Semis* ' half-*as*,' because it is a *semi-as*, that is, the half of an *as*, as has been said above. The *septunx* ' seven ounces,' contracted from *septem* and *uncia*.

172. The remaining words are less clear, because they are expressed by subtraction, and those elements from which the subtraction is made are such that they keep their last syllables *a* : as that from which one *dempta uncia* ' ounce is taken,' is a *deunx* ' eleven twelfths ' ; if a *sextans* is taken away, it is a *dextans*

---

c *Se-libra* after the model of *se-modius*, which is for *semi-modius*, with loss of one of the two similar syllables.   *d* For *oinikia*, as *unus* is from *oinos* ; the ounce was one twelfth of the *as* ' pound.'   *e* *Quincunx*, from *quinque* and *uncia*, is expected here, and may have fallen out of the text.

§ 172.   *a* The " keeping of the last syllables " is seen in *de-*(*se*)*xtans*, in *de-*(*qua*)*drans* becoming *dodrans*, in *de-*(*tri*)*es* becoming *des*. In reality, *des* or *bes* is for *duo assis*, short for *duo partes assis* ' two parts (that is, two thirds) of an *as*,' with various phonetic changes.

dextans dempto sextante, dodrans dempto quadrante,
bes, ut olim des, dempto triente.

173. In argento nummi, id ab Siculis : denarii,
quod[1] denos aeris valebant ; quinarii, quod quinos ;
sestertius,[2] quod semis tertius. Dupondius enim et
semis antiquus sestertius[2] : est et veteris consuetu-
dinis, ut retro aere dicerent, ita ut semis tertius,
⟨semis⟩[3] quartus, semis ⟨quintus⟩[3] pronuntiarent.
Ab semis tertius ⟨sestertius⟩[4] dictus.

174. Nummi denarii decuma libella, quod libram
pondo as valebat et erat ex argento parva. Simbella,
quod libellae dimidium, quod semis assis. Terruncius
a tribus unciis, quod libellae ut haec quarta pars, sic
quadrans assis.

175. Eadem pecunia vocabulum mutat : nam
potest item dici dos, arrabo, merces, corollarium.
Dos, si nuptiarum causa data ; haec Graece δωτίνη :
ita enim hoc Siculi. Ab eodem donum : nam Graece

---

§ 173. [1] *After* quod, *Ed. Veneta deleted a repeated* denarii quod (*omitted by Priscian*). [2] *For* sextertius *Fv.*
[3] *Added by GS., following Priscian.* [4] *Added by L. Sp.,*
following Priscian.

---

§ 173. [a] Not connected with *as* or *aes*. [b] The customary unit of Roman business ; in Varro's time, worth about
3¼d. sterling, or $0.07 (standard of 1936). [c] After a
number of reductions, the copper *as* was in 217 B.C. reduced
to one ounce of metal ; at the same time the silver *denarius*
was fixed at ten *asses*, and the *sestertius* at four *asses*.
[d] " The third half-*as* " implies that the first two *asses* were
complete while the third was not, as though " two *asses* and
the third half-*as* " ; *cf.* German *drittehalb* ' 2½,' and similar
formations.

§ 174. [a] Diminutive of *libra*, because of small bulk as

'five sixths'; if a *quadrans* is taken away, it is a *dodrans*; it is a *bes* 'two thirds,' or as it once was, a *des*, if a *triens* is *demptus* 'taken off.'

173. In silver, there are coins called *nummi*, this word from the Sicilians : *denarii*,[a] because they were worth *deni aeris* 'ten *asses* of copper'; *quinarii*, because they were worth *quini* 'five *asses* each'; and the *sestertius* [b] 'sesterce,' so called because it is *semis tertius* 'the third half-*as*.' For the old-time sesterce [c] was a *dupondius* and a *semis*; it is also a part of ancient practice, that they should speak of coin in reverse order, so that they named them the *semis tertius* 'two and a half *asses*,' [d] *semis quartus* 'the fourth half, three and a half *asses*' *semis quintus* 'the fifth half, four and a half *asses*.' From *semis tertius* they said *sestertius*.

174. The tenth part of a *nummus denarius* 'silver coin of ten *asses*' is a *libella*,[a] because the *as* was worth a pound by weight, and the *as* of silver was a small one. The *simbella* [b] is so called because it is the half of a *libella*, as the *semis* is half of an *as*. The *terruncius* [c] 'three-ounce piece,' from *tres unciae* 'three ounces,' because as this is the fourth part of a *libella*, so the *quadrans* is the fourth of an *as*.

175. This same money changes its name : for it can likewise be called *dos* 'dower,' *arrabo* 'earnest-money,' *merces* 'wages,' *corollarium* 'bonus.' *Dos* [a] 'dower,' if it is given for the purpose of a marriage ; this in Greek is δωτίνη, for thus the Sicilians call it. From the same comes *donum* 'gift'; for in Greek it

---

compared with the *libra* of aes.   [b] Or perhaps *sembella*; for *sem(i-li)bella*.   [c] The first element is *ter* 'three times' (earlier *terr* if before a vowel).

§ 175.   [a] A native Latin word, akin to *donum* and the Greek words.

VARRO

ut ⟨Aeol⟩is δόνειον[1] et ut alii δόμα et ut Attici δόσιν.
Arrabo sic data, ut reliquum reddatur : hoc verbum
item a Graeco ἀῤῥαβών. Reliquum, quod ex eo quod
debitum reliquum.

176. Damnum a demptione, cum minus re factum
quam quanti constat. Lucrum ab luendo, si amplius
quam ut exsolveret, quanti esset, ⟨re⟩ceptum.[1]
Detrimentum a detritu, quod ea quae trita minoris
pretii. Ab eodem ⟨tri⟩mento,[2] intertrimentum ab
eo, quod duo quae inter se trita, et deminuta ; a
quo etiam in⟨ter⟩trigo[3] dicta.

177. Multa ⟨e⟩a[1] pecunia quae a magistratu dicta,
ut exigi posset ob peccatum ; quod singulae dicuntur,
appellatae eae multae,[2] ⟨et⟩[3] quod olim v⟨i⟩num[4]
dicebant multam[5] : itaque cum ⟨in⟩[6] dolium aut
culleum vinum addunt rustici, prima urna addita
dicunt etiam nunc. Poena a poeniendo aut quod post
peccatum sequitur. Pretium, quod emptionis aesti-
mationisve causa constituitur, dictum a peritis, quod
hi soli facere possunt recte id.

§ 175. [1] *Bergk, for* issedonion.
§ 176. [1] *L. Sp., for* ceptum. [2] *A. Sp., for* ab eadem
mente. [3] *Bentinus, for* intrigo (intrigo dicta et intertrigo
B and Aug.).
§ 177. [1] *Groth, for* a. [2] *Aug., for* multas. [3] *Added
by Mue.* [4] *B, Laetus, for* unum. [5] *Goeschen, for*
multae. [6] *Added by Aug., with B.*

§ 176. [a] Wrong.
§ 177. [a] *Multa* ' fine,' possibly taken from Sabine, but
probably from the root in *mulcare* ' to beat.' Varro seems
to identify it with *multae* ' many,' supply perhaps *pecuniae* :
the magistrate imposed one *multa* after another, just as the
countrymen poured one *multa* of wine after another into

164

is δόνειον with the Aeolians, and δόμα as others say it, and δόσις of the Athenians. *Arrabo* ' earnest-money,' when money is given on this stipulation, that a balance is to be paid : this word likewise is from the Greek, where it is ἀρραβών. *Reliquum* ' balance,' because it is the *reliquum* ' remainder ' of what is owed.

176. *Damnum* ' loss,' from *demptio* ' taking away,' *a* when less is brought in by the sale of the object than it cost. *Lucrum* ' profit ' from *luere* ' to set free,' if more is taken in than will *exsolvere* ' release ' the price at which it was acquired. *Detrimentum* ' damage,' from *detritus* ' rubbing off,' because those things which are *trita* ' rubbed ' are of less value. From the same *trimentum* comes *intertrimentum* ' loss by attrition,' because two things which have been *trita* ' rubbed ' *inter se* ' against each other ' are also diminished ; from which moreover *intertrigo* ' chafing of the skin ' is said.

177. A *multa* ' fine ' is that money named by a magistrate, that it might be exacted on account of a transgression ; because the fines are named one at a time, they are called *multae* as though ' many,' and because of old they called wine *multa* : thus when the countrymen put wine into a large jar or wine-skin, they even now call it a *multa* after the first pitcherful has been put in.*a* *Poena* ' penalty,' from *poenire* *b* ' to punish ' or because it follows *post* ' after ' a transgression.*c* *Pretium* ' price ' is that which is fixed for the purpose of purchase or of evaluation ; it is named from the *periti* *d* ' experts,' because these alone can set a price correctly.

the storage jars or skins.   *b Poena* from Greek : *poenire* (classical *punire*) from *poena*.   *c* As though from *pone* ' behind,' =*post*.   *d* Wrong etymology.

178. Si quid datum pro opera aut opere, merces, a merendo. Quod manu factum erat et datum pro eo, manupretium, a manibus et pretio. Corollarium, si additum praeter quam quod debitum ; eius vocabulum fictum a corollis, quod eae, cum placuerant actores, in scaena dari solitae. Praeda est ab hostibus capta, quod manu parta, ut parida praeda. Praemium a praeda, quod ob recte quid factum concessum.

179. Si datum quod reddatur, mutuum, quod Siculi μοῖτον : itaque scribit Sophron

Μοῖτον ἄντιμο⟨ν⟩.[1]

Et munus quod mutuo animo qui sunt dant officii causa ; alterum munus, quod muniendi causa imperatum, a quo etiam municipes, qui una munus fungi debent, dicti.

180. Si es⟨t⟩[1] ea pecunia quae in iudicium[2] venit in litibus, sacramentum a sacro ; qui[3] petebat et qui infitiabatur,[4] de aliis rebus ut⟨e⟩rque[5] quingenos aeris ad pont⟨ific⟩em[6] deponebant, de aliis rebus item certo

§ 179.   [1] Fay, with haplology, for Scaliger's ἀντίτιμον ; for moeton antimo ; cf. Hesychius, s.v. μοῖτοι.
§ 180.   [1] A. Sp., for is.   [2] For indicium.   [3] For quis.   [4] GS., for inficiabatur.   [5] Aug., with B, for utrique.   [6] Aug., for pontem.

§ 178.   [a] Dubious etymology.   [b] From the elements in pre-hendere ' to grasp.'   [c] From prae + emere ' to take before (some one else).'
§ 179.   [a] The two words are connected, but the Latin is not from the Sicilian.   [b] Fragment 168 Kaibel ; the text is uncertain.   [c] Munus, mutuus, munire, municeps all have the same root.   [d] Including (kind) services and favours.   [e] Apparently obligatory citizen service on streets and walls.   [f] Citizens of a municipium.
§ 180.   [a] Probably because each party took a sacramentum ' oath ' to the justice of his case when he made the deposit.   [b] This depositing with the pontifex is not known from other

178. If any payment is made for services or for labour, it is *merces* ' wages,' from *merere* ' to earn.' *ᵃ* What was done by hand and what was paid for the work, were both called *manupretium* ' workmanship ' and ' workman's pay,' from *manūs* ' hands ' and *pretium* ' price.' *Corollarium* ' bonus,' if anything is added beyond what is due ; this word was made from *corollae* ' garlands,' because the spectators were in the habit of throwing flowers on the stage when they liked the actors' performance. *Praeda ᵇ* ' booty ' is that which has been taken from the enemy, because it is *parta* ' won ' by the work of the hands : *praeda* as though *parida*. *Praemium ᶜ* ' reward,' from *praeda* ' booty,' because it is granted for something well done.

179. If money is given which is to be paid back, it is a *mutuum* ' loan,' so called because the Sicilians call it a μοῖτος *ᵃ* ; thus Sophron writes *ᵇ*

Loan to be repaid.

Also *munus ᶜ* ' present,' because those who are on terms of *mutuus* ' mutual ' affection give presents *ᵈ* out of kindness ; a second *munus* ' duty,' *ᵉ* because it is ordered for the *muniendum* ' fortification ' of the town, from which moreover the *municipes* ' townspeople ' *ᶠ* are named, who must jointly perform the *munus*.

180. If it is that money which comes into court in lawsuits, it is called *sacramentum* ' sacred deposit,' *ᵃ* from *sacrum* ' sacred ' : the plaintiff and the defendant each deposited with the pontifex *ᵇ* five hundred copper *asses* for some kinds of cases, and for other kinds the trial was conducted likewise under a deposit

sources, and here rests upon an emendation, but may have been regular in early times ; in Varro's time, the deposit was made with the praetor who acted as judge.

alio legitimo numero ac*tum*[7] ; qui iudicio vicerat,
suum sacramentum e sacro auferebat, victi ad aerarium redibat.

181. Tributum dictum a tribubus, quod ea pecunia,
quae populo imperata erat, tributim a singulis pro
portione census exigebatur.[1] Ab hoc ea quae assig-
nata erat attributum dictum ; ab eo quoque quibus
attributa erat pecunia, ut militi reddant, tribuni
aerarii dicti ; id quod attributum erat, aes militare ;
hoc est quod ait Plautus :

> Cedit miles, aes petit.

Et hinc dicuntur milites aerarii ab aere, quod stipendia
facerent.

182. Hoc ipsum stipendium a stipe dictum, quod
aes quoque stipem dicebant : nam quod asses librae[1]
pondo erant, qui acceperant maiorem numerum non
in arca ponebant, sed in aliqua cella stipabant, id est
componebant, quo minus loci occuparet ; ab stipando
stipem dicere coeperunt. Stip*s*[2] ab στοιβή fortasse,
Graeco verbo. Id apparet, quod ut tum institutum
etiam nunc diis cum thesauris asses dant stipem

---

[7] *C. F. W. Mueller, for* assum.

§ 181. [1] *Aldus, for* exigebantur.

§ 182. [1] *Laetus, for* libras. [2] *L. Sp., with* b, *for* stipa.

---

[c] 500 if the case involved an amount of 1000 *asses* or more ;
50 if the case involved a smaller amount or the personal
freedom of an individual. [d] The phrase *e sacro* confirms
the statement that deposit was made with the pontifex.

§ 181. [a] Derivation probable, but not certain. [b] *Aulularia*, 526 ; but Plautus means a bailiff collecting a bad debt !
[c] The phrase means also ' to serve years in the army,' since
each *stipendium* is one year's pay.

§ 182. [a] *Stips* (not from Greek) is the basis of the other

of some other fixed amount specified by law *c* ; he who won the decision got back his deposit from the temple,*d* but the loser's deposit passed into the state treasury.

181. *Tributum* ' tribute ' was said from the *tribus* ' tribes,' *a* because that money which was levied on the people, was exacted *tributim* ' tribe by tribe ' individually, in proportion to their financial rating in the census. From this, that money which was allotted was *attributum* ' assigned ' ; from this also, those to whom the money was assigned, that they may pay it to the soldiery, were called *tribuni aerarii* ' treasury tribunes ' ; that which was assigned, was the *aes militare* ' soldier's pay-fund ' ; this is what Plautus means *b* :

> Comes the soldier, asks for cash.

And from this comes the term *milites aerarii* ' paid soldiers,' from the *aes* ' cash-pay,' because they earned stipends.*c*

182. This very word *stipendium* ' stipend ' is said from *stips* ' coin,' because they also called an *aes* ' copper coin ' a *stips* *a* ; for because the *asses* were a pound each in weight, those who had received an unusual number of them did not put them in a strong-box, but *stipabant* ' packed,' that is, *componebant* ' stored,' them away in some chamber, that they might take up less space *b* ; they started the use of the word *stips* from *stipare* ' to pack.' *Stips* is perhaps from the Greek word στοιβή ' heap.' This is clear, because, as was then started, so even now they speak of a *stips* when they give money to the temple treasuries for the gods, and those who make a contract about

words in this section.   *b* *Stips* ' stamped coin ' and *stipare* ' to press, stamp ' may belong together etymologically.

dicunt, et qui pecuniam alligat, stipulari et restipulari. Milit*i*s stipendia[3] ideo, quod eam stipem
pendebant ; ab eo etiam Ennius scribit :

Poeni stipendia pendunt.

183. Ab eodem aere pendendo dispensator, et in
tabulis scribimus expensum et in⟨de⟩[1] prima pensio
et sic secunda aut quae alia, et dispendium, ideo quod
in dispendendo solet minus fieri ; compendium quod
cum compend*i*tur[2] una fit ; a quo usura, quod in sorte
accedebat, impendium appellatum ; quae cum ⟨non⟩[3]
accederet ad sortem usu,[4] usura dicta, ut sors quod
suum fit sorte. Per trutinam solvi solitum : vestigium etiam nunc manet in aede Saturni, quod ea
etiam nunc[5] propter pensuram trutinam habet posi-
tam. Ab aere Aerarium appellatum.

XXXVII. 184. Ad vocabula quae pertinere sumus
rati ea quae loca et ea quae in locis sunt satis ut
arbitror dicta, quod neque parum multa sunt aperta
neque, si amplius velimus, volumen patietur. Quare
in proximo, ut in primo libro dixi, quod sequitur de
temporibus dicam.

[3] *Sciop., for* milites stipendii.
    § 183. [1] *Aug., with B, for* in.   [2] *Laetus, for* compende-
tur.   [3] *Added by Mue.*   [4] *Aldus, for* usum.   [5] *Aug.,
for* ea iam nunc et.

[c] *Stipendium* from *stipi-pendium*, with haplology ; the earliest payments must have been made by weighing, the word
then coming to mean ' pay.'   [d] *Ann.* 265 Vahlen[2] ; *R.O.L.*
i. 116-117 Warmington.
    § 183.   [a] That is, " and kept in one's possession."
[b] The fundamental meaning of *sors*, according to Varro ;
cf. vi. 65 and notes.   [c] In the Temple of Saturn.
    § 184.   [a] Its length limits the *liber* ' book.'   [b] v. 11-12.

money are said to *stipulari* ' stipulate ' and *restipulari* ' make counter-stipulations.' Therefore the soldier's *stipendia*[c] ' stipends,' because they *pendebant* ' weighed' the *stips* ; from this moreover Ennius writes [d] :

> The Phoenicians pay out the stipends.

183. From the same *pendere* ' to weigh or pay,' comes *dispensator* ' distributing cashier,' and in our accounts we write *expensum* ' expense ' and therefrom the first *pensio* ' payment ' and likewise the second and any others, and *dispendium* ' loss by distribution,' for this reason, that money is wont to become less in the *dispendendo* ' distributing of the payments ' ; *compendium* ' saving,' which is made when it *compenditur* ' is weighed all together ' [a] ; from which the *usura* ' interest,' because it was added *in* ' on ' the principal, was called *impendium* ' outlay ' ; when it was not added to the principal, it was called *usura* ' interest ' because of the *usus* ' use ' of the money, just as *sors* ' principal ' is said because it becomes one's own by *sors* ' union.' [b] It was once the custom to pay by the use of a pair of scales ; a trace of this remains even now in the Temple of Saturn, because it even now has a pair of scales set up ready for weighing purposes. From *aes* ' copper money ' the *Aerarium* [c] ' Treasury ' was named.

XXXVII. 184. What we have thought to pertain to names which are places and those which express things in places, has been, as I think, adequately set forth, because a great many are perspicuous and if we should wish to write further the roll [a] will not permit it. Therefore in the next book, as I said at the beginning of this book,[b] I shall speak of the next topic, namely about times.

171

M. TERENTI VARRONIS
DE LINGUA LATINA

LIBER V EXPLICIT ; INCIPIT

LIBER VI

I. 1. Origines verborum qua⟨e⟩[1] sunt[2] locorum et ea
quae in his in priore libro scripsi. In hoc dicam de
vocabulis temporum et earum rerum quae in agendo
fiunt aut dicuntur cum tempore aliquo ut sedetur,
ambulatur, loquontur ; atque si qua erunt ex diverso
genere adiuncta, potius cognationi verborum quam
auditori calumnianti geremus[3] morem.

2. Huius rei auctor satis mihi Chrysippus et
Antipater et illi in quibus, si non tantum acuminis, at
plus litterarum, in quo est Aristophanes et Apollodorus, qui omnes verba ex verbis ita declinari scribunt,
ut verba litteras alia assumant, alia mittant, alia

§ 1. [1] *For* qua.   [2] *p, Rhol., for* sint.   [3] *G, V, Aldus,
for* oremus.

---

§ 2. [a] Of Soli in Cilicia (280–207 B.C.), who followed
Cleanthes as leader of the Stoic school of philosophy in
Athens ; page 154 von Arnim.   [b] Of Tarsus, who succeeded
Diogenes of Seleucia as head of the Stoic school in the first
part of the second century B.C. ; page 17 von Arnim.   [c] Of
Byzantium (262–185 B.C.), eminent grammarian at Alex-

MARCUS TERENTIUS VARRO'S
ON THE LATIN LANGUAGE

BOOK V ENDS, AND HERE BEGINS

BOOK VI

I. 1. The sources of the words which are names of places and are names of those things which are in these places, I have written in the preceding book. In the present book I shall speak about the names of times and of those things which in the performance take place or are said with some time-factor, such as sitting, walking, talking : and if there are any words of a different sort attached to these, I shall give heed rather to the kinship of the words than to the rebukes of my listener.

2. In this subject I rely on Chrysippus [a] as an adequate authority, and on Antipater,[b] and on those in whom there was more learning even if not so much insight, among them Aristophanes [c] and Apollodorus [d] : all these write that words are so derived from words, that the words in some instances take on letters, in others lose them, in still others change them, as in the case of *turdus* ' thrush ' takes place

andria ; page 269 Nauck. [d] Of Athens, pupil of Aristarchus the grammarian and of Diogenes of Seleucia ; *Frag. Hist. Graec.* i. 462 Mueller.

commutent, ut fit in turdo, in turdario et turdelice. Sic declinantes Graeci nostra nomina dicunt Lucienum[1] Λευκιηνόν[2] et Quinctium Κοΐντιον, et ⟨nostri illorum⟩[3] Ἀρίσταρχον Aristarchum et Δίωνα Dionem ; sic, inquam, consuetudo nostra multa declinavit[4] a vetere, ut ab solu solum, ab *Loebeso*[5] Liberum, ab Lasibus Lares : quae obruta vetustate ut potero eruere conabor.

II. 3. Dicemus primo de temporibus, *tum*[1] quae per ea fiunt, sed ita ut ante de natura eorum : ea enim dux fuit ad vocabula imponenda homini. Tempus esse dicunt in⟨ter⟩vallum[2] mundi[3] motus. Id divisum in partes aliquot maxime ab solis et lunae cursu. Itaque ab eorum tenore temperato tempus dictum, unde tempestiva ; et a motu[4] eorum qui toto caelo coniunctus mundus.

4. Duo motus ⟨solis : alter cum caelo, quod movetur ab Iove rectore, qui Graece Δία appellatur, cum ab oriente ad oc⟩casu⟨m⟩ venit,[1] quo tempus id

§ 2.   [1] *B, Laetus, for* leucienum.   [2] *Mue. ; Λευκιενόν Sciop. ; for* leucienon.   [3] *Added by GS. ; nos illorum L. Sp. ; after Laetus, who set* nos illi *after* Ἀρίσταρχον.   [4] *After* declinavit, *Popma deleted* ut.   [5] *Mue., for* libero.
§ 3.   [1] *A. Sp., for* quam.   [2] *Laetus, for* inuallum.   [3] *After* mundi, *Turnebus deleted* et.   [4] *H, Aldus, for* motor *Fv.*
§ 4.   [1] solis ; alter cum caelo, quo ab oriente ad occasum venit *Mue. ; the balance with Kriegshammer, based on Festus,* 74. 7 *M.*

---

* Meaning found in certain S. Italian derivatives ; formation, *turdela* + -*ix* as in *cornix*, etc. (Whatmough, *C.P.* xxxiv. 381, xxxv. 84) ; hardly right is Fay, *A.J.P.* xxxv. 245, as ' spiral entrance for thrushes,' despite *cocliam* in Varro, *De Re Rustica*, iii. 5. 3.   *f* Varro had a friend Q. Lucienus, a Roman senator, well versed in Greek ; he appears as a speaker in Varro's *De Re Rustica*, ii. (5. 1, etc.).   *g* With

in *turdarium* ' thrush-cote ' and *turdelix* [e] ' magpie.'
Thus the Greeks, in adapting our names, make
Λευκιηνός of *Lucienus* [f] and Κοίντιος of *Quinctius*, and
we make *Aristarchus* of their Ἀρίσταρχος and *Dio* of
their Δίων. In just this way, I say, our practice has
altered many from the old form, as *solum* [g] ' soil ' from
solu, *Liberum* [h] ' God of Wine ' from *Loebesom*, *Lares* [i]
' Hearth-Gods ' from *Lases* : these words, covered up
as they are by lapse of time, I shall try to dig out as
best I can.

II. 3. First we shall speak of the time-names, then
of those things which take place through them, but in
such a way that first we shall speak of their essential
nature : for nature was man's guide to the imposition
of names. Time, they say, is an interval in the
motion of the world. This is divided into a number
of parts, especially from the course of the sun and the
moon. Therefore from their *temperatus* ' moderated '
career, *tempus* ' time ' is named,[a] and from this comes
tempestiva ' timely things '; and from their *motus*
' motion,' the *mundus* [b] ' world,' which is joined with
the sky as a whole.

4. There are two motions of the sun : one with the
sky, in that the moving is impelled by Jupiter as ruler,
who in Greek is called Δία, when it comes from east to
west [a] ; wherefore this time is from this god called a

change from the fourth declension to the second (if the text is
correct).   [h] With change of the vowel as well as rhotacism ;
the accusative form must be kept in the translation, to show
this clearly.   [i] With rhotacism (change of intervocalic
s to *r*).

§ 3.   [a] The converse is true: *temperare* is from *tempus*.
[b] Wrong.

§ 4.   [a] This insertion in the text gives the needed sense ;
the second *motus* is in § 8.

VARRO

ab hoc deo dies appellatur. Meridies ab eo quod
medius dies. D antiqui, non R in hoc dicebant, ut
Praeneste incisum in solario vidi. Solarium dictum
id, in quo horae in sole inspiciebantur, ⟨vel horologium
ex aqua⟩,² quod Cornelius in Basilica Aemilia et
Fulvia inumbravit. Diei principium mane, quod
*tum*³ manat dies ab oriente, nisi potius quod bonum
antiqui dicebant manum, ad cuiusmodi religionem
Graeci quoque cum lumen affertur, solent dicere φῶς
ἀγαθόν.

5. Suprema summum diei, id ab superrimo. Hoc
tempus XII Tabulae dicunt occasum esse solis ; sed
postea lex Plaetoria¹ id quoque tempus esse iubet
supremum quo praetor in Comitio supremam pronun-
tiavit populo. Secundum hoc dicitur crepusculum a
crepero : id vocabulum sumpserunt a Sabinis, unde
veniunt Crepusci nominati Amiterno, qui eo tempore
erant nati, ut Luci⟨i⟩² prima luce in Reatino ³ ; crepusculum significat dubium ; ab eo res dictae dubiae
creperae, quod crepusculum dies etiam nunc sit an
iam nox multis dubium.

² *Added by GS.*   ³ *For* cum.
§ 5.   ¹ *Aug., for* praetoria.   ² *Laetus, for* luci.   ³ *Mue.,*
for reatione *or* creatione.

ᵇ *Dies* is cognate with Greek Δία, but not derived from it.
ᶜ P. Cornelius Scipio Nasica Corculum, when censor in
159 B.C. with M. Popilius Laenas, set up the first water-clock
in Rome in this Basilica, which was erected in 179 on the
north side of the Forum by the censors M. Aemilius Lepidus
and M. Fulvius Nobilior, from whom it was named.
ᵈ Both etymologies wrong.
§ 5.   ᵃ Approximately correct.   ᵇ Page 119 Schoell.
176

dies ' day.' [b]   *Meridies* ' noon,' from the fact that it is the *medius* ' middle ' of the *dies* ' day.'   The ancients said D in this word, and not R, as I have seen at Praeneste, cut on a sun-dial.   *Solarium* ' sun-dial ' was the name used for that on which the hours were seen in the *sol* ' sunlight '; or also there is the water-clock, which Cornelius[c] set up in the shade in the Basilica of Aemilius and Fulvius.   The beginning of the day is *mane* ' early morning,' because then the day *manat* ' trickles ' from the east, unless rather because the ancients called the good *manum* [d] : from a superstitious belief of the same kind as influences the Greeks, who, when a light is brought, make a practice of saying, " Goodly light ! "

5.   *Suprema* means the last part of the day ; it is from *superrimum*.[a]   This time, the *Twelve Tables* say,[b] is sunset ; but afterwards the Plaetorian Law [c] declares that this time also should be ' last ' at which the praetor in the Comitium has announced to the people the *suprema* ' end of the session.'   In line with this, *crepusculum* ' dusk ' is said from *creperum* ' obscure ' ; this word they took from the Sabines, from whom come those who were named *Crepusci*, from Amiternum, who had been born at that time of day, just like the *Lucii*, who were those born at dawn (*prima luce*) in the Reatine country.   *Crepusculum* means doubtful : from this doubtful matters are called *creperae* ' obscure,' [d] because dusk is a time when to many it is doubtful whether it is even yet day or is already night.

[c] A law for the protection of minors, named from Plaetorius, a tribune of the people.   [d] All etymologically sound, but a meaning ' doubtful ' must have proceeded from a word *crepus* ' dusk.'

6. Nox, quod, ut *Pacuius*[1] ait,

> Omnia nisi interveniat sol pruina obriguerint,

quod nocet, nox, nisi quod Graece νύξ nox. Cum stella prima exorta (eum Graeci vocant ἕσπερον, nostri Vesperuginem ut Plautus :

> Neque Vesperugo neque Vergiliae occidunt),

id tempus dictum a Graecis ἑσπέρα, Latine vesper ; ut ante solem ortum quod eadem stella vocatur iubar, quod iubata, Pacui dicit pastor :

> Exorto iubare, noctis decurso itinere ;

Enni[2] Aiax :

> Lumen—iubarne ?—in caelo cerno.

7. Inter vesperuginem et iubar dicta nox intempesta, ut in Bruto Cassii quod dicit Lucretia :

> Nocte intempesta nostram devenit domum.

Intempestam Aelius dicebat cum tempus agendi est nullum, quod alii concubium[1] appellarunt, quod omnes fere tunc cubarent ; alii ab eo quod sileretur

§ 6.   [1] *Ribbeck ;* Pacuvius *Scaliger ; for* catulus.   [2] *GS. ;* Ennii *Laetus ; for* ennius.
§ 7.   [1] *Laetus, for* inconcubium.

§ 6.   [a] *Antiopa, Trag. Rom. Frag.* 14 Ribbeck[3] ; *R.O.L.* ii. 170-171 Warmington ; *cf.* Funaioli, page 123.   Ribbeck's *nocti ni* for *nisi* is probably Pacuvius's wording ; Varro, as often, paraphrases the quotation.   [b] *Nox* and νύξ come from the same source ; connexion with *nocere* is dubious.   [c] *Amphitruo*, 275.   [d] Correct etymologies.   [e] *Iubar* and *iuba* 'mane' are not related, despite vii. 76.   [f] *Trag. Rom. Frag.* 347 Ribbeck[3] ; *R.O.L.* ii. 320-321 Warmington.   [g] *Trag. Rom. Frag.* 336 Ribbeck[3] ; *R.O.L.* i. 226-227 Warmington ; *cf.* vi. 81 and vii. 76.
§ 7.   [a] A writer of *praetextae*, otherwise unknown : the name recurs at vii. 72 ; possibly Victorius's emendation to

6. *Nox* ' night ' is called *nox*, because, as Pacuvius says,[a]

> All will be stiff with frost unless the sun break in,

because it *nocet* ' harms ' ; unless it is because in Greek night is νύξ.[b] When the first star has come out (the Greeks call it Hesperus, and our people call it *Vesperugo*, as Plautus does [c] :

> The evening star sets not, nor yet the Pleiades),

this time is by the Greeks called ἑσπέρα, and *vesper* ' evening ' in Latin [d] ; just as, because the same star before sunrise is called *iubar* ' dawn-star,' because it is *iubata* ' maned,' [e] Pacuvius's herdsman says [f] :

> When morning-star appears and night has run her course.

And Ennius's Ajax says [g] :

> I see light in the sky—can it be dawn ?

7. The time between dusk and dawn is called the *nox intempesta* ' dead of night,' as in the *Brutus* of Cassius,[a] in the speech of Lucretia :

> By dead of night he came unto our home.

Aelius [b] used to say that *intempesta* means the period when it is not a time for activity, which others have called the *concubium* [c] ' general rest,' because practically all persons then *cubabant* ' were lying down ' ; others, from the fact that *silebatur* ' silence was observed,' have called it the *silentium* ' still ' of the night,

---

Accii is correct. The passage is listed among the fragments of the *Brutus* of Accius by Ribbeck[3], *Trag. Rom. Frag.*, page 331, and by Warmington, *R.O.L.* ii. 562-563.   [b] Page 60 Funaioli.   [c] The early part of the night ; *cf.* vii. 78, which quotes Plautus, *Trinummus*, 886. *Cf.* also Funaioli, page 115.

silentium noctis, quod idem Plautus tempus conticinium[2] : scribit enim :

Videbimus[3] : factum volo. Redito[4] conticinio.[5]

8.   Alter motus solis est, al⟨i⟩ter ⟨ac⟩ caeli,[1] quod
movetur a bruma ad solstitium.   Dicta bruma, quod
brevissimus tunc dies est ; solstitium, quod sol eo die
sistere videbatur, quo[2] ad nos versum proximus est.
Sol[3] cum venit in medium spatium inter brumam et
solstitium, quod dies aequus fit ac nox, aequinoctium
dictum.   Tempus a bruma ad brumam dum sol redit,
vocatur annus, quod ut parvi circuli anuli, sic magni
dicebantur circites ani, unde annus.

9.   Huius temporis pars prima hiems, quod tum
multi imbres ; hinc hibernacula, hibernum ; vel, quod
tum anima quae flatur omnium apparet, ab hiatu
hiems.   Tempus secundum ver, quod tum virere[1]
incipiunt virgulta ac vertere se tempus anni ; nisi
quod Iones dicunt ἦρ[2] ver.   Tertium ab aestu aestas ;
hinc aestivum ; nisi forte a Graeco αἴθεσθαι. Quartum autumnus, ⟨ab augendis hominum opibus dictus
frugibusque coactis, quasi auctumnus⟩.[3]

[2] *For* conticinnium *f.*   [3] uidebitur *Plautus.*   [4] redito
huc *Plautus.*   [5] *For* conticinnio *f.*

§ 8.   [1] *Mue., for* alter caeli.   [2] quo *A. Sp. ;* quod *Mue. ;*
for aut quod.   [3] *A. Sp. ;* proximus est sol, solstitium
L. Sp. ; for proximum est solstitium.

§ 9.   [1] *Aldus, for* uiuere.   [2] *L. Sp. ;* ἔαρ *Victorius ; for*
et.   [3] *Added by GS., after Kriegshammer, and Fest.*
23. 11 *M.*

---

[d] *Asinaria,* 685.

§ 8.   [a] For the first motion, see § 4.   [b] The winter and
the summer solstices.   [c] *Annus* is not connected with *anus*
or *anulus* ' ring.'

§ 9.   [a] Wrong.   [b] Cognate with the Greek, not derived
from it.

the time which Plautus likewise calls the *conticinium* ' general silence ' : for he writes [d] :

> We'll see, I want it done. At general-silence time
> come back.

8. There is a second motion of the sun,[a] differing from that of the sky, in that the motion is from *bruma* ' winter's day ' to *solstitium* ' solstice.' [b] *Bruma* is so named, because then the day is *brevissimus* 'shortest': the *solstitium*, because on that day the *sol* ' sun ' seems *sistere* ' to halt,' on which it is nearest to us. When the sun has arrived midway between the *bruma* and the *solstitium*, it is called the *aequinoctium* ' equinox,' because the day becomes *aequus* ' equal ' to the *nox* ' night.' The time from the *bruma* until the sun returns to the *bruma*, is called an *annus* ' year,' because just as little circles are *anuli* ' rings,' so big circuits were called *ani*, whence comes *annus* ' year.' [c]

9. The first part of this time is the *hiems* ' winter,' so called because then there are many *imbres* ' showers ' [a] ; hence *hibernacula* ' winter encampment,' *hibernum* ' winter time ' ; or because then everybody's breath which is breathed out is visible, *hiems* is from *hiatus* ' open mouth.' [a] The second season is the *ver* [b] ' spring,' so called because then the *virgulta* ' bushes ' begin *virere* ' to become green ' and the time of year begins *vertere* ' to turn or change ' itself [a] ; unless it is because the Ionians say ἦρ for spring. The third season is the *aestas* ' summer,' from *aestus* ' heat ' ; from this, *aestivum* ' summer pasture ' ; unless perhaps it is from the Greek αἴθεσθαι ' to blaze.' [b] The fourth is the *autumnus* ' autumn,' named from *augere* ' to increase ' the possessions of men and the gathered fruits, as if *auctumnus*.[a]

181

VARRO

10. ⟨Ut annus⟩[1] ab sole, sic[2] mensis a lunae motu
dictus, dum ab sole profecta rursus redit ad eum.
Luna quod Graece olim dicta μήνη, unde illorum μῆνες,
ab eo nostri.   A mensibus intermestris dictum, quod
putabant inter prioris mensis senescentis extremum
diem et novam lunam esse diem, quem diligentius
Attici ἕνην καὶ νέαν[3] appellarunt, ab eo quod eo die
potest videri extrema et prima luna.

11.   Lustrum nominatum tempus quinquennale a
luendo, id est solvendo, quod quinto quoque anno
vectigalia et ultro tributa per censores persolve-
bantur.   Seclum spatium annorum centum vocarunt,
dictum a sene, quod longissimum spatium senescen-
dorum hominum id putarunt.   Aevum ab aetate
omnium annorum (hinc aeviternum, quod factum est
aeternum) : quod Graeci αἰῶνα, id ait Chrysippus
esse ⟨ἀ⟩ε⟨ὶ⟩ ὄν.[1]   Ab eo Plautus :

> Non omnis aetas ad perdiscendum est satis,[2]

hinc poetae :

> Aeterna templa caeli.[3]

§ 10.   [1] *See* § 9, *critical note* 3.   [2] *B, Laetus, for* sicut.
[3] *Aldus, for* menencenean.
  § 11.   [1] *Turnebus, for* eon.   [2] sat est *Plautus.*
[3] *Laetus, for* caeli celi.

---

§ 10.   [a] Cognate with the Greek.   [b] The end of the
astronomical day would normally not coincide with the end
of the 24-hour day, and the last day of the month was therefore regarded by the Greeks as including parts of two days,
the old day closing the old month, and the new day beginning
the new month.
  § 11.   [a] Most   probably   from   *lavare* ' to   wash.'
[b] Properly *saeculum* ; ultimately from the root ' to sow,' seen

10. As the year is named from the motion of the sun, so the month is named from the motion of the moon, until after departing from the sun she returns again to him. Because the moon was in Greek formerly called μήνη, whence their μῆνες ' months ' —from this word we named the *menses* ' months.' *ᵃ* From *menses* is named the *intermestris* ' day between the months,' because they thought that between the last day of the preceding expiring month and the new moon there was a day, which with more care the Athenians called the ' old and new,' *ᵇ* because on that day the very last of the old moon and the first beginnings of the new moon can both be seen.

11. A five-year period was called a *lustrum*,*ᵃ* from *luere* ' to set free,' that is, *solvere* ' to release,' because in every fifth year the taxes and the voluntary tribute payments were completely discharged, through the activity of the censors. A *seclum* *ᵇ* ' century ' was what they called the space of one hundred years, named from *senex* ' old man,' because they thought this the longest stretch of life for *senescendi* ' aging ' men. *Aevum* *ᶜ* ' eternity,' from an *aetas* ' period ' of all the years (from this comes *aeviternum*, which has become *aeternum* ' eternal ') : which the Greeks call an αἰών—Chrysippus says that this is ⟨ἀ⟩ε⟨ὶ⟩ ὄν ' always existing.' *ᵈ* From this Plautus says *ᵉ* :

All time is not enough for thorough learning,

and from this the poets say :

The everlasting temples of the sky.

in *semen* ' seed.'   *ᶜ Aevum* is the basis for the other Latin words, and is cognate with the Greek word, not derived from it.   *ᵈ* Chrysippus (163 von Arnim) was wrong.   *ᵉ Truculentus*, 22.

VARRO

III. 12. A⟨d⟩ naturale discrimen[1] civilia vocabula die⟨ru⟩m[2] accesserunt. Dicam prius qui deorum causa, tum qui hominum sunt instituti. Dies Agonales per quos rex in Regia arietem immolat, dicti ab " agon," eo quod interrogat ⟨minister sacrificii " agone ? " : nisi si a Graeca lingua, ubi ἄγων princeps, ab eo quod immolat⟩ur[3] a principe civitatis et princeps gregis immolatur. Carmentalia nominantur quod sacra tum et feriae Carmentis.

13. Lupercalia dicta, quod in Lupercali Luperci sacra faciunt. Rex cum ferias menstruas Nonis Februariis edicit, hunc diem februatum appellat ; februm Sabini purgamentum, et id in sacris nostris verbum non ⟨ignotum : nam pellem capri, cuius de loro caeduntur puellae Lupercalibus, veteres februm vocabant⟩,[1] et Lupercalia Februatio, ut in Antiquitatum libris demonstravi. Quirinalia a Quirino, quod

§ 12.   [1] *GS.*, *for* a naturali discrimine (ad *with Sciop.*).
[2] *Sciop., for* diem.   [3] *Added by Krumbiegel, who recognized that alternative etymologies stood here.*
§ 13.   [1] *Added by GS., after Serv. Dan. in Aen.* viii. 343 *ff.*

§ 12.   [a] There were four *Agonia* in the year, celebrated on January 9, March 17, May 21, December 11, respectively to Janus, Mars, Vediovis, and an unknown god. The name *Agonium* came from *agere* ' to do one's work,' through a noun *ago* ' performer,' formed like *praeco* ' herald.'   [b] The traditional palace of Numa, at the end of the Forum ; used as the residence of the pontifex maximus, and for certain important religious ceremonies.   [c] That is, slay the sacrificial victim ; the formulaic answer was, " *Hoc age !* " [d] Celebrated on January 11 and 15 in honour of *Carmentis* or *Carmenta*, an old Italic goddess of childbirth, with prophetic powers ; one later legend made her the mother of Evander, whom she accompanied from Arcadia to Rome.
§ 13.   [a] Celebrated on March 15 by the priests of Mars

184

III. 12. To the division made by nature there have been added the civic names for the days. First I shall give those which have been instituted for the sake of the gods, then those instituted for the sake of men. The *dies Agonales* ' days of the Agonia,' [a] on which the high-priest sacrifices a ram in the Regia,[b] were named from *agon* for this reason, because the helper at the sacrifice asks " *agone?* " ' Shall I do my work ? ' [c] : unless it is from the Greek, where ἄγων means *princeps* ' leader,' from the fact that the sacrificing is done by a leader of the state and the leader of the flock is sacrificed. The *Carmentalia* [d] are so named because at that time there are sacrifices and a festival of Carmentis.

13. The *Lupercalia* [a] was so named because the Luperci make sacrifice in the Lupercal. When the High-priest announces the monthly festivals on the Nones of February, he calls the day of the Lupercalia *februatus* : for *februm* is the name which the Sabines give to a purification, and this word is not unknown in our sacrifices ; for a goat hide, with a thong of which the young women are flogged at the Lupercalia, the ancients called a *februs*, and the Lupercalia was called also *Februatio* ' Festival of Purification,' as I have shown in the *Books of the Antiquities*. *Quirinalia* [b] ' Festival of Quirinus,' from Quirinus,[c] because it is a

called *Luperci*, beginning with the sacrifice of a buck in the *Lupercal*, the cave on the Palatine where traditionally the she-wolf suckled Romulus and Remus ; after which the *Luperci*, naked except for breech-clouts made of the buck's hide, ran around the Palatine, where the people had massed themselves, striking the women with thongs which also were cut from the hide of the slaughtered animal, a process supposed to ensure the fertility of those struck. [b] On February 17. [c] The deified Romulus.

⟨e⟩i deo[2] feriae et eorum hominum, qui Furnacalibus suis non fuerunt feriati.   Feralia[3] ab inferis et ferendo, quod ferunt tum epulas ad sepulcrum quibus ius ibi[4] parentare.   Terminalia, quod is dies anni extremus constitutus : duodecimus enim mensis fuit Februarius et cum intercalatur inferiores quinque dies duodecimo demuntur mense.   Ecurria ab equorum cursu : eo die enim ludi currunt in Martio Campo.

14.   Liberalia dicta, quod per totum oppidum eo die sedent ⟨ut⟩[1] sacerdotes Liberi anus hedera coronatae cum libis et foculo pro emptore sacrificantes.   In libris Saliorum quorum cognomen Agonensium, forsitan hic dies ideo appelletur potius Agonia.   Quinquatrus : hic dies unus ab nominis errore observatur proinde ut sint quinque[2] ; dictus, ut ab Tusculanis post diem sextum Idus similiter vocatur Sexatrus et post diem septimum Septimatrus, sic[3] hic, quod

[2] *Aug., with B, for* ideo.   [3] *Aldus, for* ferialia.   [4] *Aug., with B, for* sibi.

§ 14.   [1] *Added by GS.*   [2] *Punctuation of Mue.*   [3] *Laetus, for* septematruus sit.

---

[d] Or *Fornacalia*, in honour of an alleged goddess *Fornax* ' Spirit of the Bake-oven '; celebrated early in February, on various dates in different curiae.   [e] On February 21, the official part of the *Parentalia* (February 18-21, otherwise for private ceremonies) ; etymology obscure.   [f] God of Endings.   [g] On February 23 : Varro is speaking of the old Roman year of 355 days (before the reform of Julius Caesar in 45 B.C.), in which an extra month of 22 or 23 days was inserted in alternate years after February 23 ; which thereby became the last date in the year which was common to all years, the remaining five days of February being placed at the end of the extra month.   [h] Or *Equirria* ; on February 27 and March 14, in honour of Mars.

§ 14.   [a] On March 17, the day when the boys assumed the toga of manhood.   [b] Frag. inc. 2, page 351 Maurenbrecher ; page 5 Morel.   [c] This sentence seems to belong

festival to that god and also of those men who did not get a holiday on their own *Furnacalia*^d ' Bakers' Festival.' The *Feralia*^e ' Festival of the Dead,' from *inferi* ' the dead below ' and *ferre* ' to bear,' because at that time they *ferunt* ' bear ' viands to the tomb of those to whom it is a duty to offer ancestor-worship there. The *Terminalia* ' Festival of Terminus,'^f because this day^g is set as the last day of the year; for the twelfth month was February, and when the extra month is inserted the last five days are taken off the twelfth month. The *Ecurria* ' Horse-Race,'^h from the *equorum cursus* ' running of horses '; for on that day they *currunt* ' run ' races in the sports on the Campus Martius.

14. The *Liberalia* ' Festival of Liber,'^a because on that day old women wearing ivy-wreaths on their heads sit in all parts of the town, as priestesses of Liber, with cakes and a brazier, on which they offer up the cakes on behalf of any purchaser. In the books of the Salii^b who have the added name *Agonenses*, this day is for this reason, perhaps, called rather the *Agonia.*^c The *Quinquatrus*: this day, though one only, is from a misunderstanding of the name observed as if there were five days in it.^d Just as the sixth day after the Ides is in similar fashion called the *Sexatrus* by the people of Tusculum, and the seventh day after is the *Septimatrus*, so this day was named here, in that

in § 12. The proper name of the festival was *Agonium*, plural *Agonia*; popularly corrupted to *Agonalia*, in imitation of other festival names. ^d On March 19-23, five days instead of merely the fifth day after the Ides (March 15; fifth by Roman counting of both ends); etymology, the ' fifth black (*ater*) day,' perhaps *Quinquatrus* for *Quintatrus*, with dissimilative change of one *t*, and concurrent influence of the cardinal *quinque*.

erat post diem quintum Idus, Quinquatrus. Dies Tubulustrium appellatur, quod eo die in Atrio Sutorio sacrorum tubae lustrantur.

15. Megalesia dicta a Graecis, quod ex Libris Sibyllinis arcessita ab Attalo rege Pergama; ibi prope murum Megalesion, *id est*[1] templum eius deae, unde advecta Romam. Fordicidia a fordis bubus; bos forda quae fert in ventre; quod eo die publice immolantur boves praegnantes in curiis complures,[2] a fordis caedendis Fordicidia dicta. Palilia dicta a Pale, quod ei[3] feriae, ut Cerialia a Cerere.

16. Vinalia a vino; hic dies Iovis, non Veneris. Huius rei cura non levis in Latio: nam aliquot locis vindemiae primum ab sacerdotibus publice fiebant, ut Romae etiam nunc: nam flamen Dialis auspicatur vindemiam et ut iussit vinum legere, agna Iovi facit, inter cuius exta caesa et porrecta[1] flamen pr⟨im⟩us[2] vinum legit. In Tusculanis *portis*[3] est scriptum:

Vinum novum ne vehatur in urbem ante quam
Vinalia kalentur.[4]

§ 15. [1] *GS., for* in. [2] *For* compluris. [3] *Victorius, or* et.

§ 16. [1] *Aug., with B, for* proiecta. [2] *Mue., for* porus. [3] *Bergk, for* sortis. [4] *Aug., for* calentur.

---

[e] March 23; also May 23.

§ 15. [a] Celebrated on April 4 in honour of Cybele, the *Magna Mater* (μεγάλη 'magna,' whence the name of the festival), whose worship was brought to Rome from Pergamum (here *Pergama*, fem.) in Mysia, in 204 B.C. [b] On April 15. [c] Often written *Parilia*; on April 21. [d] Often written *Cerealia*; on April 19.

§ 16. [a] On April 23, and again on August 19. [b] That is, not before the priests fix the date and the ceremony has been performed.

the fifth day after the Ides was the *Quinquatrus*. The *Tubulustrium* ' Purification of the Trumpets ' is named from the fact that on this day *e* the *tubae* ' trumpets ' used in the ceremonies *lustrantur* ' are purified ' in Shoemakers' Hall.

15. The *Megalesia* *a* ' Festival of the Great Mother ' is so called from the Greeks, because by direction of the Sibylline Books the Great Mother was brought from King Attalus, from Pergama ; there near the city-wall was the *Megalesion*, that is, the temple of this goddess, whence she was brought to Rome. The *Fordicidia* *b* was named from *fordae* cows : a *forda* cow is one that is carrying an unborn calf ; because on this day several pregnant cows are officially and publicly sacrificed in the curiae, the festival was called the Fordicidia from *fordae caedendae* ' the pregnant (cows) which were to be slaughtered.' The *Palilia* *c* ' Festival of Pales ' was named from Pales, because it is a holiday in her honour, like the *Cerialia*,*d* named from *Ceres*.

16. The *Vinalia* *a* ' Festival of the Wine,' from *vinum* ' wine ' ; this is a day sacred to Jupiter, not to Venus. This feast receives no slight attention in Latium : for in some places the vintages were started by the priests, on behalf of the state, as at Rome they are even now : for the special priest of Jupiter makes an official commencement of the vintage, and when he has given orders to gather the grapes, he sacrifices a lamb to Jupiter, and between the cutting out of the victim's vitals and the offering of them to the god he himself first plucks a bunch of grapes. On the gates of Tusculum there is the inscription :

The new wine shall not be carried into the city until
the *Vinalia* has been proclaimed.*b*

189

Robigalia[5] dicta ab Robigo ; secundum segetes huic
deo sacrificatur, ne robigo occupet segetes.

17.   Dies Vestalia ut virgines Vestales a[1] Vesta.
Quinquatrus minusculae dictae Iuniae Idus ab similitudine maiorum, quod tibicines *tum*[2] feriati vagantur
per urbem et conveniunt ad Aedem Minervae.   Dies
Fortis Fortunae appellatus ab Servio Tullio rege, quod
is fanum Fortis Fortunae secundum Tiberim extra
urbem Romam dedicavit Iunio mense.

18.   Dies Poplifugia videtur nominatus, quod eo
die tumultu repente fugerit populus : non multo enim
post hic dies quam decessus Gallorum ex Urbe, et qui
tum sub Urbe populi, ut Ficuleates ac Fidenates et
finitimi alii, contra nos coniurarunt.   Aliquot huius
d⟨i⟩ei vestigia fugae in sacris apparent, de quibus
rebus Antiquitatum Libri plura referunt.   Nonae
Caprotinae, quod eo die in Latio Iunoni Caprotinae
mulieres sacrificant et sub caprifico faciunt ; e capri-

[5] Rubigalia *B*, *Laetus*, *for* robicalia.
   § 17.   [1] *A. Sp. ;* ab *L. Sp. ; for* aut.   [2] *Laetus, for*
cum.

---

[c] On April 25.   [d] The passage containing the festivals
of May has here been lost.
   § 17.   [a] On June 9.   [b] On June 13.   [c] See § 14.
[d] On June 24.
   § 18.   [a] On July 5, according to the *Fasti* of Amiternum.
[b] Ficulea, a town near Fidenae ; Fidenae, on the Tiber about
five miles above Rome.   [c] July 7 ; it is not necessary to
conclude that the *Poplifugia* and the ceremony of the *Nonae
Caprotinae* were on the same day : the Flight may well have
preceded the Fig-Tree Signal (see note *d*) by two days.
190

The *Robigalia* [c] ' Festival of Robigus ' was named from Robigus ' God of Rust ' ; to this god sacrifice is made along the cornfields, that rust may not seize upon the standing corn.[d]

17. The *Vestalia* [a] ' Festival of Vesta,' like the Vestal Virgins, from Vesta. The Ides of June are called the Lesser *Quinquatrus*,[b] from the likeness to the Greater *Quinquatrus*,[c] because the pipes-players take a holiday, and after roaming through the City, assemble at the Temple of Minerva. The day of *Fors Fortuna* [d] ' Chance Luck ' was named by King Servius Tullius, because he dedicated a sanctuary to Fors Fortuna beside the Tiber, outside the city Rome, in the month of June.

18. The *Poplifugia* [a] ' People's Flight ' seems to have been named from the fact that on this day the people suddenly fled in noisy confusion : for this day is not much after the departure of the Gauls from the City, and the peoples who were then near the City, such as the Ficuleans and Fidenians [b] and other neighbours, united against us. Several traces of this day's flight appear in the sacrifices, of which the *Books of the Antiquities* give more information. The Nones of July [c] are called the Caprotine Nones, because on this day, in Latium, the women offer sacrifice to Juno Caprotina, which they do under a *caprificus* ' wild fig-tree ' ; they use a branch from the fig-tree.[d]

---

[d] The invaders demanded from the Romans, who were helpless after the ravages of the Gauls, that they surrender their wives and daughters. The maid-servants volunteered to go disguised as their mistresses, and plied their captors with wine. When they were asleep, the women signalled to the Romans from the branches of a *caprificus*, and a sudden attack routed the invaders. See Macrobius, *Sat.* i. 11. 36-40 and iii. 2. 14.

VARRO

fico adhibent virgam. Cur hoc, toga[1] praetexta data
eis Apollinaribus Ludis docuit populum.

19. Neptunalia a Neptuno : eius enim dei[1] feriae.
Furrinalia ⟨a⟩ Furrina,[2] quod ei deae feriae publicae[3]
dies is ; cuius deae honos apud antiquos : nam ei
sacra instituta annua et flamen attributus ; nunc vix
nomen notum paucis. Portunalia dicta a Portuno,
cui eo die aedes in portu Tiberino facta et feriae
institutae.

20. Vinalia rustica dicuntur ante diem XII⟨II⟩[1]
Kalendas Septembres, quod tum Veneri dedicata
aedes et horti ei deae dicantur[2] ac tum sunt feriati
holitores. Consualia dicta a Conso, quod tum feriae
publicae ei deo et in Circo ad aram eius ab sacerdotibus ludi illi, quibus virgines Sabinae raptae. Volcanalia a Volcano, quod ei tum feriae et quod eo die
populus pro se in ignem animalia mittit.

21. Opeconsiva dies ab dea Ope Consiva, cuius in
Regia sacrarium quod adeo[1] artum,[2] ut eo praeter

§ 18.   [1] M, Laetus, for togata.
§ 19.   [1] Laetus, for die.   [2] a Furrina Aug., for furrinae.
[3] Aldus, for publice.
§ 20.   [1] quartum decimum Aug., after inscc., for XII.
[2] Mue., for dicuntur.
§ 21.   [1] GS., for ideo.   [2] Canal, for actum.

---

[e] The ancillae had been richly dressed when they were sent
off representing the wives and daughters of the aristocratic
Romans ; and after they had thus saved the state, the Senate
rewarded them with freedom and other gifts, including the
rich garments which they had worn.   The presentation of a
toga praetexta at the Games of Apollo seems to have sym-
bolized this gift.   [f] Celebrated on July 12 (at the time
when Varro wrote).

Why this was done, the bordered toga *e* presented to them at the Games of Apollo *f* enlightened the people.

19. The *Neptunalia* *a* ' Festival of Neptune,' from Neptune ; for it is the holiday of this god. The *Furrinalia* *b* ' Festival of Furrina,' from Furrina, for this day is a state holiday for this goddess ; honour was paid to her among the ancients, who instituted an annual sacrifice for her, and assigned to her a special priest, but now her name is barely known, and even that to only a few. The *Portunalia* *c* ' Festival of Portunus ' was named from Portunus, to whom, on this day, a temple was built at the *portus* ' port ' on the Tiber, and a holiday instituted.

20. The nineteenth of August was called the Country *Vinalia* *a* ' Wine-Festival,' because at that time a temple was dedicated to Venus and gardens were set apart for her, and then the kitchen-gardeners went on holiday. The *Consualia* *b* ' Festival of Consus ' was called from Consus, because then there was the state festival to that god, and in the Circus at his altar those games were enacted by the priests in which the Sabine maidens were carried off. The *Volcanalia* *c* ' Festival of Vulcan,' from Vulcan, because then was his festival and because on that day the people, acting for themselves, drive their animals over a fire.

21. The day named *Opeconsiva* *a* is called from *Ops Consiva* *b* ' Lady Bountiful the Planter,' whose shrine is in the Regia ; it is so restricted in size that no one

§ 19. *a* On July 23. *b* On July 25 ; *Furrina*, an ancient Italic goddess. *c* On August 17.
§ 20. *a* *Vinalia* from *vinum*, not from *Venus* ; on August 19. *b* On August 21 ; *cf.* Livy, i. 9. 6. *c* On August 23.
§ 21. *a* August 25. *b* Goddess of Abundance, the wife of Saturn, as planter or sower ; another aspect of *Terra*.

VARRO

virgines Vestales et sacerdotem publicum introeat
nemo. "Is cum eat, suffibulum ut[3] habeat," scriptum : id dicitur ut[4] ab suffi⟨g⟩endo[5] subfigabulum.[6]
Volturnalia[7] a deo Volturno,[8] cuius feriae tum. Octo-
bri mense Meditrinalia dies dictus a medendo, quod
Flaccus flamen Martialis dicebat hoc die solitum
vinum ⟨novum⟩[9] et vetus libari et degustari medica-
menti causa ; quod facere solent etiam nunc multi
cum dicunt [10] :

Novum vetus vinum bibo : novo veteri [11] morbo medeor.

22. Fontanalia a Fonte, quod is dies feriae eius ;
ab eo tum et in fontes coronas iaciunt et puteos
coronant. Armilustrium ab eo quod in Armilustrio
armati sacra faciunt, nisi locus potius dictus ab his ;
sed quod de his prius, id ab lu⟨d⟩endo[1] aut lustro,
id est quod circumibant ludentes ancilibus armati.

---

[3] L. Sp., for aut.   [4] Aldus, for diciturne.   [5] Skutsch,
for suffiendo.   [6] Kent, for subligaculum.   [7] For uor-
turnalia ; cf. volturn. in the Fasti.   [8] For uorturno ; cf.
preceding note.   [9] Added by Laetus.   [10] L. Sp., for
dicant.   [11] After veteri, G, V, f, Aldus deleted uino ; cf.
Festus, 123. 16 M.

§ 22.   [1] Vertranius, for luendo.

---

[6] An oblong piece of white cloth with a coloured border,
which the Vestal Virgins fastened over their heads with a
fibula ' clasp ' when they offered sacrifice ; cf. Festus, 348 a 25
and 349. 8 M.   [d] On August 27 ; the god Volturnus
cannot be identified unless he is identical with Vortumnus
(Vertumnus), since he can hardly be the deity of the river
Volturnus in Campania or of the mountain Voltur, in Apulia,
near Horace's birthplace.   [e] On October 3 ; Meditrina,

194

may enter it except the Vestal Virgins and the state priest. " When he goes there, let him wear a white veil," is the direction ; this *suffibulum* *c* ' white veil ' is named as if *sub-figabulum* from *suffigere* ' to fasten down.' The *Volturnalia* ' Festival of Volturnus,' from the god Volturnus,*d* whose feast takes place then. In the month of October, the *Meditrinalia* *e* ' Festival of Meditrina ' was named from *mederi* ' to be healed,' because Flaccus the special priest of Mars used to say that on this day it was the practice to pour an offering of new and old wine to the god, and to taste of the same,*f* for the purpose of being healed ; which many are accustomed to do even now, when they say :

> Wine new and old I drink, of illness new and old
> I'm cured.*g*

22. The *Fontanalia* ' Festival of the Springs,' from *Fons* ' God of Springs,' because that day *a* is his holiday ; on his account they then throw garlands into the springs and place them on the well-tops. The *Armilustrium* *b* ' Purification of the Arms,' from the fact that armed men perform the ceremony in the *Armilustrium*, unless the place *c* is rather named from the men ; but as I said of them previously, this word comes from *ludere* ' to play ' or from *lustrum* ' purification,' that is, because armed men went around *ludentes* ' making sport ' with the sacred shields.*d*

Goddess of Healing.   *f* The ceremonial first drinking of the new wine.   *g* *Frag. Poet. Lat.*, page 31 Morel.
    § 22.   *a* October 13.   *b* October 13.   *c* The place was named from the ceremony ; cf. v. 153.   *d* The first *ancile* is said to have fallen from heaven in the reign of Numa, who had eleven others made exactly like it, to prevent its loss or to prevent knowledge of its loss ; for the safety of the City depended on the preservation of that shield which fell from heaven.

Saturnalia dicta ab Saturno, quod eo die feriae eius,
ut post diem tertium Opalia Opis.

23. Angeronalia ab Angerona, cui sacrificium fit
in Curia Acculeia et cuius feriae publicae is dies.
Larentinae, quem diem quidam in scribendo Larentalia appellant, ab Acca Larentia nominatus, cui
sacerdotes nostri publice parentant e sexto die,[1] qui
ab ea[2] dicitur die*s*[3] Parent⟨ali⟩um[4] Accas Larentinas.[5]

24. Hoc sacrificium fit in Velabro, qua[1] in Novam
Viam exitur, ut aiunt quidam ad sepulcrum Accae, ut
quod ibi prope faciunt diis Manibus servilibus sacerdotes ; qui uterque locus extra urbem antiquam fuit
non longe a Porta Romanula, de qua in priore libro
dixi. Dies Septimontium nominatus ab his septem
montibus, in quis sita Urbs est ; feriae non populi, sed
montanorum modo, ut Paganalibus, qui sunt alicuius
pagi.

25. De statutis diebus dixi ; de annalibus nec

§ 23. [1] parentant *Aug.*, e sexto die *Fay*, *for* parent ante
sexto die. [2] *Mue.*, *for* atra. [3] L. *Sp.*, *for* diem.
[4] *Mommsen, for* tarentum. [5] *L. Sp., for* tarentinas.
§ 24. [1] *Laetus, for* quia.

---

[e] December 17, and the following days. [f] December 19.
§ 23. [a] On December 21. [b] Goddess of Suffering and
Silence. [c] On December 23 ; supply *feriae* with *Larentinae.* [d] Wife of Faustulus ; she nursed and brought up
the twins Romulus and Remus. [e] " Sixth " is wrong if
the Saturnalia began on December 17, unless in this instance
both ends are counted, or the allusion is to an earlier practice
by which the Saturnalia began one day later. On the phrase
e sexto die, cf. Fay, *Amer. Journ. Phil.* xxxv. 246
[f] Archaic genitive singular ending in *-as.*

The *Saturnalia* ' Festival of Saturn ' was named from Saturn, because on this day *e* was his festival, as on the second day thereafter the *Opalia*,*f* the festival of Ops.

23. The *Angeronalia*,*a* from Angerona,*b* to whom a sacrifice is made in the Acculeian Curia and of whom this day is a state festival. The Larentine Festival,*c* which certain writers call the *Larentalia*, was named from Acca Larentia,*d* to whom our priests officially perform ancestor-worship on the sixth day after the Saturnalia,*e* which day is from her called the Day of the *Parentalia* of Larentine Acca.*f*

24. This sacrifice is made in the Velabrum, where it ends in New Street, as certain authorities say, at the tomb of Acca, because near there the priests make offering to the departed spirits of the slaves *a* : both these places *b* were outside the ancient city, not far from the Little Roman Gate, of which I spoke in the preceding book.*c* Septimontium Day *d* was named from these *septem montes* ' seven hills,' *e* on which the City is set ; it is a holiday not of the people generally, but only of those who live on the hills, as only those who are of some *pagus* ' country district ' have a holiday *f* at the *Paganalia* *g* ' Festival of the Country Districts.'

25. The fixed days are those of which I have spoken ; now I shall speak of the annual festivals

§ 24. *a* Faustulus and Acca were, of course, slaves of the king. *b* The tomb of Acca and the place of sacrifice to the *Manes serviles*. *c* v. 164. *d* On December 11. *e* Not the usual later seven ; Festus, 348 M., lists Capitoline with Velia and Cermalus, three spurs of the Esquiline—Oppius, Fagutal, Cispius—and the Subura valley between. *f* Supply *feriantur*. *g* Early in January, but not on a fixed date.

d⟨i⟩e¹ statutis dicam. Compitalia dies attributus
Laribus *vialibus*² : ideo ubi viae competunt tum in
competis sacrificatur. Quotannis is dies concipitur.
Similiter Latinae Feriae dies conceptivus³ dictus a
Latinis populis, quibus ex Albano Monte ex sacris
carnem⁴ petere fuit ius cum Romanis, a quibus Latinis
Latinae dictae.

26. Sementivae¹ Feriae dies is, qui a pontificibus
dictus, appellatus a semente, quod sationis causa sus-
cepta⟨e⟩.² Paganicae eiusdem agriculturae causa
susceptae, ut haberent in agris omn*is*³ pagus, unde
Paganicae dictae. Sunt praeterea feriae conceptivae
quae non sunt annales, ut hae quae dicuntur sine
proprio vocabulo aut cum perspic*uo*,⁴ ut Novendiales⁵
sunt.

IV. 27. De his diebus ⟨satis⟩¹ ; nunc iam, qui
hominum causa constituti, videamus. Primi dies
mensium nominati *K*alendae,² quod his diebus calan-

§ 25. ¹ *Mommsen, for* de.   ² *Bongars, for* ut alibi.
³ *Laetus, for* conseptivus.   ⁴ *Victorius, for* carmen.
§ 26. ¹ *f, Vertranius, for* sementinae.   ² *Aldus, for*
suscepta.   ³ *Aldus, for* omnes.   ⁴ *Aug., for* perspicio.
⁵ *For* novendialis.
§ 27. ¹ *Added by Sciop.*   ² *Aug., with B, for* cal-.

§ 25. *a* That is, set by special proclamation, and not
always falling on the same date.   *b* By the praetor, not far
from January 1.   *c* Written *competa* in the text, to make
the association with *competunt*.   *d* The festival of the
league of the Latin cities; its date was set by the Roman
consuls (or by a consul) as soon as convenient after entry
into office.

§ 26. *a* In January, on two days separated by a space
of seven days ; as they were days of sowing, the choice
depended upon the weather.   *b* Collective singular with

which are not fixed on a special day.[a] The *Compitalia* is a day assigned [b] to the Lares of the highways ; therefore where the highways *competunt* ' meet,' sacrifice is then made at the *compita* [c] ' crossroads.' This day is appointed every year. Likewise the *Latinae Feriae* ' Latin Holiday ' [d] is an appointed day, named from the peoples of Latium, who had equal right with the Romans to get a share of the meat at the sacrifices on the Alban Mount : from these Latin peoples it was called the Latin Holiday.

26. The *Sementivae Feriae* ' Seed-time Holiday ' [a] is that day which is set by the pontiffs ; it was named from the *sementis* ' seeding,' because it is entered upon for the sake of the sowing. The *Paganicae* ' Country-District Holiday ' was entered upon for the sake of this same agriculture, that the whole *pagus* [b] ' country-district ' might hold it in the fields, whence it was called *Paganicae*. There are also appointive holidays which are not annual, such as those which are set without a special name of their own,[c] or with an obvious one, such as is the *Novendialis* ' Ceremony of the Ninth Day.' [d]

IV. 27. About these days this is enough [a] ; now let us see to the days which are instituted for the interests of men. The first days of the months are named the *Kalendae*,[b] because on these days the

plural verb. [c] Such as the *supplicationes* voted for Caesar's victories in Gaul ; *cf. Bell. Gall.* ii. 35. 4, iv. 38. 5, vii. 90. 8. [d] The offerings and feasts for the dead on the ninth day after the funeral ; also, a festival of nine days proclaimed for the purpose of averting misfortunes whose approach was indicated by omens and prodigies.

§ 27. [a] The insertion of *satis* makes the chapter beginning conform to those at v. 57, 75, 95, 184, vi. 35, etc. [b] The K in *Kalendae* and *kalo*, before A, is well attested.

tur eius mens*i*s³ Nonae a pontificibus, quintanae an
septimanae sint futurae, in Capitolio in Curia Calabra
sic : " Die te quin*ti*⁴ *k*alo⁵ Iuno Covella " ⟨aut⟩⁶ " Sep-
t*im*⟨i⟩ d*i*e te⁷ *k*alo⁵ Iuno Covella."

28.   Nonae appellatae aut quod ante diem nonum
Idus semper, aut quod, ut novus annus Kalendae¹
Ianuariae ab novo sole appellatae, novus mensis ⟨ab⟩²
nova luna Non*ae*³ ; eodem di*e*⁴ in Urbe⟨m⟩⁵ ⟨qui⟩⁶ in
agris ad regem conveniebat populus.   Harum rerum
vestigia apparent in sacris Nonalibus in Arce, quod
tunc ferias primas menstruas, quae futurae sint eo
mense, rex edicit populo.   Idus ab eo quod Tusci
Itus, vel potius quod Sabini Idus dicunt.

29.   Dies postridie Kalendas, Nonas, Idus appellati
atri, quod per eos dies ⟨nihil⟩¹ novi inciperent.   Dies
fasti, per quos praetoribus omnia verba sine piaculo
licet fari ; comitiales dicti, quod tum ut ⟨in Comitio⟩²

---

³ *Aug., with B, for* menses.   ⁴ *Mommsen ;* die te V
Christ ; for dictae quinque.   ⁵ *See note* 2, § 27.   ⁶ *Added
by Zander.*   ⁷ *Mommsen ;* VII die te *Christ ; for* septem
dictae.

§ 28.   ¹ *Aug., with B, for* calendae.   ² a *added by Sciop.*
³ *Sciop., for* nonis.   ⁴ *After* die, *Mue. deleted* enim.
⁵ *Laetus, for* urbe.   ⁶ *Added by L. Sp.*

§ 29.   ¹ *Added by Turnebus.*   ² *Added by Bergk.*

ᶜ See v. 13.   ᵈ The statement of Macrobius, *Sat.* i. 15. 10,
that *kalo Iuno Covella* was repeated five or seven times respectively, may rest merely on a corrupted form of this passage
which was in the copy used by Macrobius.   ᵉ ' Juno of the
New Moon ' ; *Covella*, diminutive from *covus* ' hollow,'
earlier form of *cavus* (*cf.* v. 19)—unless it be corrupt for
Novella, as Scaliger thought.   For the New Moon has a
concave shape.

§ 28.   ᵃ The north-eastern summit of the Capitoline.
ᵇ Origin uncertain ; perhaps from Etruscan, as Varro says.

Nones of this month *calantur* ' are announced ' by the pontiffs on the Capitoline in Announcement Hall,[c] whether they will be on the fifth or on the seventh, in this way [d] : " Juno Covella,[e] I announce thee on the fifth day " or " Juno Covella, I announce thee on the seventh day."

28. The Nones are so called either because they are always the *nonus* ' ninth ' day before the Ides, or because the Nones are called the *novus* ' new ' month from the new moon, just as the Kalends of January are called the new year from the new sun ; on the same day the people who were in the fields used to flock into the City to the King. Traces of this status are seen in the ceremonies held on the Nones, on the Citadel,[a] because at that time the high-priest announces to the people the first monthly holidays which are to take place in that month. The *Idus* [b] ' Ides,' from the fact that the Etruscans called them the *Itus*, or rather because the Sabines call them the *Idus*.

29. The days next after the Kalends, the Nones, and the Ides, were called *atri* ' black,' [a] because on these days they might not start anything new. *Dies fasti* [b] ' righteous days, court days,' on which the praetors [c] are permitted *fari* ' to say ' any and all words without sin. *Comitiales* ' assembly days ' are so called because then it is the established law that the

§ 29. [a] *Cf.* Macrobius, *Sat.* i. 15. 22 ; the use of *ater* was appropriate after the Ides, when the moon was not visible in the day nor in the early evening, nor was it visible immediately after the Kalends. [b] That is, when it was *fas* to hold court and make legal decisions; Varro connects with *fari* ' to say,' with which the Romans associated *fas* etymologically, but the connexion has recently been questioned. [c] Who functioned as judges.

esset populus constitutum est ad suffragium ferundum, nisi si quae feriae conceptae essent, propter quas non liceret, ⟨ut⟩[3] Compitalia et Latinae.

30. Contrarii horum vocantur dies nefasti, per quos dies nefas fari praetorem " do," " dico," " addico " ; itaque non potest agi : necesse est aliquo ⟨eorum⟩[1] uti verbo, cum lege qui⟨d⟩[2] peragitur. Quod si tum imprudens id verbum emisit ac quem manumisit, ille nihilo minus est liber, sed vitio, ut magistratus vitio creatus nihilo setius[3] magistratus. Praetor qui tum fatus[4] est, si imprudens fecit, piaculari hostia facta piatur ; si prudens dixit, Quintus Mucius aiebat[5] eum expiari ut impium non posse.

31. Intercisi[1] dies sunt per quos mane et vesperi est nefas, medio tempore inter hostiam caesam et exta porrecta[2] fas ; a quo quod fas tum intercedit aut eo[3] intercisum nefas, intercisi.[4] Dies qui vocatur sic " Quando[5] rex comitiavit fas," is[6] dictus ab eo quod

[3] *Added by Laetus.*

§ 30. [1] *Added by Laetus, with B.* [2] *Laetus, for* qui. [3] *A. Sp. ;* secius *Victorius ; for* sed ius. [4] *Turnebus, for* factus. [5] *L. Sp., for* abigebat.

§ 31. [1] *Laetus, for* intercensi. [2] *Aug., with B, for* proiecta. [3] *L. Sp. ;* eo est *Mue. ; for* eos. [4] *A. Sp., for* intercisum. [5] *Before* quando, *B inserts* Q R C F, *the abbreviation found in the Fasti.* [6] fas is *Victorius, for* fassis.

§ 30. [a] For the meaning of *vitio*, see Dorothy M. Paschall, " The Origin and Semantic Development of Latin *Vitium*," *Trans. Amer. Philol. Assn.* lxvii. 219-231. [b] i. 19 Huschke.

§ 31. [a] March 24 and May 24. [b] The *caedere* ' to cut ' in *intercidere* and the *cedere* ' to go on ' in *intercedere* are not etymologically connected.

people should be in the Comitium to cast their votes—unless some holidays should have been proclaimed on account of which this is not permissible, such as the *Compitalia* and the Latin Holiday.

30. The opposite of these are called *dies nefasti* 'unrighteous days,' on which it is *nefas* 'unrighteousness' for the praetor to say *do* 'I give,' *dico* 'I pronounce,' *addico* 'I assign'; therefore no action can be taken, for it is necessary to use some one of these words, when anything is settled in due legal form. But if at that time he has inadvertently uttered such a word and set somebody free, the person is none the less free, but with a bad omen[a] in the proceeding, just as a magistrate elected in spite of an unfavourable omen is a magistrate just the same. The praetor who has made a legal decision at such a time, is freed of his sin by the sacrifice of an atonement victim, if he did it unintentionally; but if he made the pronouncement with a realization of what he was doing, Quintus Mucius[b] said that he could not in any way atone for his sin, as one who had failed in his duty to God and country.

31. The *intercisi dies* 'divided days' are those[a] on which legal business is wrong in the morning and in the evening, but right in the time between the slaying of the sacrificial victim and the offering of the vital organs; whence they are *intercisi* because the *fas* 'right' *intercedit*[b] 'comes in between' at that time, or because the *nefas* 'wrong' is *intercisum* 'cut into' by the *fas*. The day which is called thus: "When the high-priest has officiated in the Comitium, Right," is named from the fact that on this day the high-priest pronounces the proper formulas for the sacrifice in the

eo die rex sacrificio *ius*[7] dicat ad Comitium, ad quod tempus est nefas, ab eo fas : itaque post id tempus lege actum saepe.

32. Dies qui vocatur " Quando stercum delatum fas,"[1] ab eo appellatus, quod eo die ex Aede Vestae stercus everritur et per Capitolinum Clivum in locum defertur certum. Dies Alliensis ab Allia[2] fluvio dictus : nam ibi exercitu nostro fugato Galli obsederunt Romam.

33. Quod ad singulorum dierum vocabula pertinet dixi. Mensium nomina fere sunt aperta, si a Martio, ut antiqui constituerunt, numeres : nam primus a Marte. Secundus, ut Fulvius scribit et Iunius, a Venere, quod ea sit *Aph*rodite[1] ; cuius nomen ego antiquis litteris quod nusquam inveni, magis puto dictum, quod ver omnia aperit, Aprilem. Tertius a maioribus Maius, quartus a iunioribus dictus Iunius.

34. Dehinc quintus Quintilis et sic deinceps usque ad Decembrem a numero. Ad hos qui additi, prior a principe deo Ianuarius appellatus ; posterior, ut idem dicunt scriptores, ab diis inferis Februarius appellatus,

---

[7] *Other codices, for* sacrificiolus *Fv.*

§ 32. [1] *Before* quando, *B inserts* Q S D F, *the abbreviation found in the Fasti.* [2] *B,* Laetus, *for* allio (auio *f*).

§ 33. [1] *For* afrodite.

---

§ 32. [a] June 15. [b] July 18 ; anniversary of the battle of 390 B.C., at the place where the Allia flows into the Tiber, eleven miles above Rome.

§ 33. [a] Probably from an adjective *apero*- ' second,' not otherwise found in Latin. [b] Servius Fulvius Flaccus, consul 135 B.C., skilled in law, literature, and ancient history. [c] Page 121 Funaioli ; page 11 Huschke. [d] From *Maia*, mother of Mercury. [e] From the goddess Juno ; page 121 Funaioli.

§ 34. [a] Varro wrote before *Quintilis* was renamed *Iulius*

presence of the assembly, up to which time legal business is wrong, and from that time on it is right : therefore after this time of day actions are often taken under the law.

32. The day *a* which is called " When the dung has been carried out, Right," is named from this, that on this day the dung is swept out of the Temple of Vesta and is carried away along the Capitoline Incline to a certain spot. The *Dies Alliensis* *b* ' Day of the Allia ' is called from the Allia River ; for there our army was put to flight by the Gauls just before they besieged Rome.

33. With this I have finished my account of what pertains to the names of individual days. The names of the months are in general obvious, if you count from March, as the ancients arranged them ; for the first month, *Martius*, is from Mars. The second, *Aprilis,a* as Fulvius *b* writes and Junius also,*c* is from Venus, because she is Aphrodite ; but I have nowhere found her name in the old writings about the month, and so think that it was called April rather because spring *aperit* ' opens ' everything. The third was called *Maius* *d* ' May ' from the *maiores* ' elders,' the fourth *Iunius* *e* ' June ' from the *iuniores* ' younger men.'

34. Thence the fifth is *Quintilis* *a* ' July ' and so in succession to December, named from the numeral. Of those which were added to these, the prior was called *Ianuarius* ' January ' from the god *b* who is first in order ; the latter, as the same writers say,*c* was called *Februarius* *d* ' February ' from the *di inferi* ' gods

and *Sextilis* was renamed *Augustus.* *b* Janus. *c* Page 16 Funaioli ; page 11 Huschke. *d* From a lost word *feber* ' sorrow.'

quod tum his paren⟨te⟩tur[1] ; ego magis arbitror
Februarium a die februato, quod tum februatur
populus, id est Lupercis nudis lustratur antiquum
oppidum Palatinum gregibus humanis cinctum.

V. 35. Quod ad temporum vocabula Latina
attinet, hactenus sit satis dictum ; nunc quod ad eas
res attinet quae in tempore aliquo fieri animadver-
terentur, dicam, ut haec sunt : legisti, cursus,[1] ludens ;
de quis duo praedicere volo, quanta sit multitudo
eorum et quae sint obscuriora quam alia.

36. Cum verborum declinatuum[1] genera sint quattuor, unum quod tempora adsignificat neque habet
casus, ut ab lego leges, lege[2] ; alterum quod casus
habet neque tempora adsignificat, ut ab lego lectio
et lector ; tertium quod habet utrunque et tempora
et casus, ut ab lego legens, lecturus ; quartum quod
neutrum habet, ut ab lego lecte ac lectissime : horum
verborum si primigenia sunt ad mille,[3] ut Cosconius
scribit, ex eorum declinationibus verborum discrimina
quingenta milia esse possunt ideo, quod a[4] singulis
verbis primigenii⟨s⟩[5] circiter quingentae species declinationibus fiunt.

§ 34. ¹ *Aug. ;* parentent *Laetus ; for* parent.
§ 35. ¹ *Mue., with* G, H, *for* currus.
§ 36. ¹ B, *Laetus, for* declinatiuum.   ² V, *b, for* lego
Fv.   ³ *Victorius, for* admitte.   ⁴ *L. Sp., for* quia.
⁵ *Aug., for* primigenii.

ᵉ Three different ceremonies are confounded here : one of
purification, one of expiation to the gods of the Lower World,
one of fertility ; *cf.* vi. 13, note *a.*
§ 35.   ᵃ That is, all verbal forms, and the derivatives from
the verbal roots.
§ 36.   ᵃ The verb has both meanings ; some of the derivatives have only one or the other.   ᵇ Q. Cosconius, orator

of the Lower World,' because at that time expiatory sacrifices are made to them ; but I think that it was called February rather from the *dies februatus* ' Purification Day,' because then the people *februatur* ' is purified,' that is, the old Palatine town girt with flocks of people is passed around by the naked Luperci.[e]

V. 35. As to what pertains to Latin names of time ideas, let that which has been said up to this point be enough. Now I shall speak of what concerns those things which might be observed as taking place at some special time [a]—such as the following : *legisti* ' thou didst read,' *cursus* ' act of running,' *ludens* ' playing.' With regard to these there are two things which I wish to say in advance : how great their number is, and what features are less perspicuous than others.

36. The inflections of words are of four kinds : one which indicates the time and does not have case, as *leges* ' thou wilt gather or read,' [a] *lege* ' read thou,' from *lego* ' I gather or read ' ; a second, which has case and does not indicate time, as from *lego lectio* ' collection, act of reading,' *lector* ' reader '; the third, which has both, time and case, as from *lego legens* ' reading,' *lecturus* ' being about to read ' ; the third, which has neither, as from *lego lecte* ' choicely,' *lectissime* ' most choicely.' Therefore if the primitives of these words amount to one thousand, as Cosconius [b] writes, then from the inflections of these words the different forms can be five hundred thousand in number for the reason that from each and every primitive word about five hundred forms are made by derivation and inflection.

and authority on grammar and literature, who flourished about 100 B.C. ; page 109 Funaioli.

VARRO

37. Primigenia dicuntur verba ut lego, scribo, sto, sedeo et cetera, quae non sunt ab ali⟨o⟩ quo[1] verbo, sed suas habent radices. Contra verba declinata sunt, quae ab ali⟨o⟩ quo[2] oriuntur, ut ab lego legis, legit, legam et sic[3] indidem hinc permulta. Quare si quis primigeniorum verborum origines ostenderit, si ea mille sunt, quingentum milium simplicium verborum causas aperuerit una ; sin[4] nullius, tamen qui ab his reliqua orta ostenderit, satis dixerit de originibus verborum, cum unde nata sint, principia erunt pauca, quae inde nata sint, innumerabilia.

38. A quibus iisdem principiis antepositis praeverbiis paucis immanis verborum accedit numerus, quod praeverbiis ⟨in⟩mutatis[1] additis atque commutatis aliud atque aliud fit : ut enim ⟨pro⟩cessit[2] et recessit, sic accessit et abscessit ; item incessit et excessit, sic successit et decessit, ⟨discessit⟩[3] et concessit. Quod si haec decem sola praeverbia essent, quoniam ab uno verbo declinationum quingenta discrimina fierent, his decemplicatis coniuncto praeverbio ex uno quinque milia numero efficerent⟨ur⟩,[4] ex mille ad quinquagies centum milia discrimina fieri possunt.

§ 37. [1] *Mue.;* alio *Aug., G ; for* aliquo. [2] *Mue., for* aliquo. [3] *After* sic, *Laetus deleted* in. [4] *Turnebus, for* unas in.

§ 38. [1] *GS., for* mutatis. [2] *Fritzsche, for* cessit.
[3] *Added by GS* (et discessit *added by Vertranius*). [4] *Aldus, for* efficerent.

---

§ 37. [a] That is, cannot be referred to a simpler radical element.

208

37. Primitive is the name applied to words like *lego* ' I gather,' *scribo* ' I write,' *sto* ' I stand,' *sedeo* ' I sit,' and the rest which are not from some other word,[a] but have their own roots. On the other hand derivative words are those which do develop from some other word, as from *lego* come *legis* ' thou gatherest,' *legit* ' he gathers,' *legam* ' I shall gather,' and in this fashion from this same word come a great number of words. Therefore, if one has shown the origins of the primitive words, and if these are one thousand in number, he will have revealed at the same time the sources of five hundred thousand separate words ; but if without showing the origin of a single primitive word he has shown how the rest have developed from the primitives, he will have said quite enough about the origins of words, since the original elements from which the words are sprung are few and the words which have sprung from them are countless.

38. There are besides an enormous number of words derived from these same original elements by the addition of a few prefixes, because by the addition of prefixes with or without change a word is repeatedly transformed ; for as there is *processit* ' he marched forward ' and *recessit* ' drew back,' so there is *accessit* ' approached ' and *abscessit* ' went off,' likewise *incessit* ' advanced ' and *excessit* ' withdrew,' so also *successit* ' went up ' and *decessit* ' went away,' *discessit* ' departed ' and *concessit* ' gave way.' But if there were only these ten prefixes, from the thousand primitives five million different forms can be made inasmuch as from one word there are five hundred derivational forms and when these are multiplied by ten through union with a prefix five thousand different forms are produced out of one primitive.

VARRO

39. Democritus, E⟨pi⟩curus,[1] item alii qui infinita principia dixerunt, quae unde sint non dicunt, sed cuiusmodi sint, tamen faciunt magnum : quae ex his constant in mundo, ostendunt. Quare si etymolog*us*[2] principia verborum postulet mille, de quibus ratio ab se non poscatur, et reliqua ostendat, quod non postulat, tamen immanem verborum expediat numerum.

40. De multitudine quoniam quod satis esset admonui,[1] de obscuritate pauca dicam. Verborum quae tempora adsignificant ideo locus[2] difficillimus ἔτυμα,[3] quod neque his fere societas cum Graeca lingua, neque vernacula ea quorum in partum memoria adfuerit nostra ; e[4] quibus, ut dixi,[5] quae poterimus.

VI. 41. Incipiam hinc primu*m*[1] quod dicitur ago. Actio ab agitatu facta. Hinc dicimus " agit gestum tragoedus,"[2] et " agitantur quadrigae " ; hinc " agitur pecus pastum." Qua[3] vix agi potest, hinc angiportum ; qua nil potest agi, hinc angulus, ⟨vel⟩[4] quod in eo locus angustissimus, cuius loci is angulus.

42. Actionum trium primus agitatus mentis, quod

§ 39. [1] *Turnebus, for* secutus *Fv*, securus *G, H*. [2] etymologos *B, Rhol., for* ethimologos *Fv*, ethimologus *G*.

§ 40. [1] *Laetus, for* admonuit. [2] *f, Aldus, for* locutus. [3] est ἔτυμα *Sciop.* (*L. Sp. deleted* est), *for* est TYMa *Fv*. [4] *A. Sp., for* nostrae. [5] *M, Laetus, for* dixit.

§ 41. [1] *Laetus, for* primus. [2] *For* tragaedus. [3] *Aldus, for* quia. [4] *Added by Mue., whose punctuation is here followed.*

§ 39. [a] Of Abdera (about 460–373 B.C.), originator of the atomic theory. [b] Of Athens (341–270 B.C.), founder of the Epicurean school of philosophy ; Epic. 201. 33 Usener. [c] That is, does not postulate that they are original elements (*quod* for *quot*).

§ 40. [a] For *adfuerit* with the goal construction, *cf.* Vergil, *Ecl.* 2. 45 *huc ades*, etc. [b] v. 10.

39. Democritus,[a] Epicurus,[b] and likewise others who have pronounced the original elements to be unlimited in number, though they do not tell us whence the elements are, but only of what sort they are, still perform a great service : they show us the things which in the world consist of these elements. Therefore if the etymologist should postulate one thousand original elements of words, about which an interpretation is not to be asked of him, and show the nature of the rest, about which he does not make the postulation,[c] the number of words which he would explain would still be enormous.

40. Since I have given a sufficient reminder of the number of existing words, I shall speak briefly about their obscurity. Of the words which also indicate time the most difficult feature is their radicals, for the reason that these have in general no communion with the Greek language, and those to whose birth [a] our memory reaches are not native Latin ; yet of these, as I have said,[b] we shall say what we can.

VI. 41. I shall start first from the word *ago* ' I drive, effect, do.' *Actio* ' action ' is made from *agitatus* ' motion.' [a] From this we say " The tragic actor *agit* ' makes ' a gesture," and " The chariot-team *agitantur* ' is driven ' " ; from this, " The flock *agitur* ' is driven ' to pasture." Where it is hardly possible for anything *agi* ' to be driven,' from this it is called an *angiportum* [b] ' alley ' ; where nothing can *agi* ' be driven,' from this it is an *angulus* ' corner,' or else because in it is a very narrow (*angustus*) place to which this corner belongs.

42. There are three *actiones* ' actions,' and of these

§ 41. [a] All these words are derivatives of *agere*, except *angiportum* and *angulus* ; but *actio* does not develop by loss of the *i* in *agitatus*. [b] *Cf.* v. 145.

primum ea quae sumus acturi cogitare debemus,
deinde tum dicere et facere. De his tribus minime
putat volgus esse actionem cogitationem ; tertium, in
quo quid facimus, id maximum. Sed et cum cogitamus[1] quid et eam rem agitamus[2] in mente, agimus,
et cum pronuntiamus, agimus. Itaque ab eo orator
agere dicitur causam et augures augurium agere
dicuntur, quom in eo plura dicant quam faciant.

43. Cogitare a cogendo dictum : mens plura in
unum cogit, unde eligere[1] possit. Sic e lacte coacto
caseus nominatus ; sic ex hominibus contio dicta, sic
coemptio, sic compitum nominatum. A cogitatione
concilium, inde consilium ; quod ut vestimentum
apud fullonem cum cogitur, conciliari[2] dictum.

44. Sic reminisci, cum ea quae tenuit mens ac
memoria, cogitando repetuntur. Hinc etiam comminisci dictum, a con et mente, cum finguntur in
mente quae non sunt ; et ab hoc illud quod dicitur
eminisci,[1] cum commentum pronuntiatur. Ab eadem

§ 42.   [1] *Sciop.*, *for* hos agitamus *Fv.*   [2] *L. Sp., for*
cogitamus.
§ 43.   [1] *a, p, Rhol., for* elicere.   [2] *Aug.. for* consiliari.
§ 44.   [1] *Heusinger, for* reminisci.

---

§ 42.   [a] Page 16 Regell.
§ 43.   [a] Here Varro gives a parenthetic list of words with
the prefix *co-* or *com-* ; though he is wrong in including
caseus.   [b] *Cogitatio, concilium, consilium* have nothing in
common except the prefix.

the first is the *agitatus* ' motion ' of the mind, because
we must first *cogitare* ' consider ' those things which
we are *acturi* ' going to do,' and then thereafter say
them and do them.   Of these three, the common folk
practically never thinks that *cogitatio* ' consideration '
is an action ; but it thinks that the third, in which we
do something, is the most important.   But also when
we *cogitamus* ' consider ' something and *agitamus*
' turn it over ' in mind, we *agimus* ' are acting,' and
when we make an utterance, we *agimus* ' are acting.'
Therefore from this the orator is said *agere* ' to plead '
the case, and the augurs are said *[a]* *agere* ' to practice '
augury, although in it there is more saying than
doing.

43.   *Cogitare* ' to consider ' is said from *cogere* ' to
bring together ' :   the mind *cogit* ' brings together '
several things into one place, from which it can
choose.   Thus *[a]* from milk that is *coactum* ' pressed,'
caseus ' cheese ' was named ; thus from men brought
together was the *contio* ' mass meeting ' called, thus
coemptio ' marriage by mutual sale,' thus *compitum*
' cross-roads.'   From *cogitatio* ' consideration ' came
concilium ' council,' and from that came *consilium*
' counsel ' ; *[b]* and the *concilium* is said *conciliari* ' to be
brought into unity ' like a garment when it *cogitur* ' is
pressed ' at the cleaner's.

44.   Thus *reminisci* ' to recall,' when those things
which have been held by mind and memory are fetched
back again by considering (*cogitando*).   From this also
comminisci ' to fabricate a story ' is said, from *con* ' together ' and *mens* ' mind,' when things which are not,
are devised in the mind ; and from that comes the
word *eminisci* ' to use the imagination,' when the
commentum ' fabrication ' is uttered.   From the same

mente meminisse dictum et amens, qui a mente sua discedit.[2]

45. Hinc etiam metu*s*[1] ⟨a⟩ mente quodam modo mota,[2] *ut*[3] metuisti ⟨te⟩[4] amovisti ; sic, quod frigidus timor, tremuisti timuisti. Tremo dictum a similitudine vocis, quae tunc cum valde tremunt apparet, cum etiam in corpore pili, ut arista in spica *h*ordei, horrent.

46. Curare a cura dictum. Cura, quod cor urat ; curiosus, quod hac praeter modum utitur. Recordar*i*,[1] rursus in cor revocare. Curiae, ubi senatus rempublicam curat, et illa ubi cura sacrorum publica ; ab his curiones.

47. Volo a voluntate dictum et a volatu, quod animus ita est, ut puncto temporis pervolet quo volt. L*u*bere[1] ab labendo dictum, quod lubrica mens ac prolabitur, ut dicebant olim. Ab lubendo libido, libidinosus ac Venus Libentina et Libitina, sic alia.

[2] *Aug., for* descendit.

§ 45. [1] *GS., for* metuo. [2] *Canal, for* mentem quodam modo motam. [3] *L. Sp., for* uel. [4] *Added by Kent, after Fay.*

§ 46. [1] *Aug., with B, for* recordare.

§ 47. [1] *L. Sp.,* for libere.

---

§ 45. [a] According to Mueller, the sequence of the topics indicates that this section and § 49 have been interchanged in the manuscripts. All etymologies in this section are wrong.

§ 46. [a] Three etymologically distinct sets of words are here united : *cura, curare, curiosus* ; *cor, recordari* ; *curia, curio.*

§ 47. [a] *Volo* ' I wish ' is distinct from *volo* ' I fly.' [b] *Lubet,* later *libet,* is distinct from *labi* and from *lubricus.* [c] Either as a euphemism, or from the fact that the funeral apparatus was kept in the storerooms of the Temple of Venus, which caused the epithet to acquire a new meaning.

word *mens* ' mind ' come *meminisse* ' to remember ' and *amens* ' mad,' said of one who has departed *a mente* ' from his mind.'

45.[a] From this moreover *metus* ' fear,' from the *mens* ' mind ' somehow *mota* ' moved,' as *metuisti* ' you feared,' equal to *te amovisti* ' you removed yourself.' So, because *timor* ' fear ' is cold, *tremuisti* ' you shivered ' is equal to *timuisti* ' you feared.' *Tremo* ' I shiver ' is said from the similarity to the behaviour of the voice, which is evident then when people shiver very much, when even the hairs on the body bristle up like the beard on an ear of barley.

46.[a] *Curare* ' to care for, look after ' is said from *cura* ' care, attention.' *Cura*, because it *cor urat* ' burns the heart ' ; *curiosus* ' inquisitive,' because such a person indulges in *cura* beyond the proper measure. *Recordari* ' to recall to mind,' is *revocare* ' to call back ' again into the *cor* ' heart.' The *curiae* ' halls,' where the senate *curat* ' looks after ' the interests of the state, and also there where there is the *cura* ' care ' of the state sacrifices ; from these, the *curiones* ' priests of the curiae.'

47. *Volo* ' I wish ' is said from *voluntas* ' free-will ' and from *volatus* ' flight,' because the spirit is such that in an instant it *pervolat* ' flies through ' to any place whither it *volt* ' wishes.' [a] *Lubere* [b] ' to be pleasing ' is said from *labi* ' to slip,' because the mind is *lubrica* ' slippery ' and *prolabitur* ' slips forward,' as of old they used to say. From *lubere* ' to be pleasing ' come *libido* ' lust,' *libidinosus* ' lustful,' and Venus *Libentina* ' goddess of sensual pleasure ' and *Libitina* [c] ' goddess of the funeral equipment,' so also other words.

VARRO

48. Metuere a quodam motu animi, cum id quod malum casurum putat refugit mens. Cum vehementius in movendo ut ab se abeat foras fertur, formido ; cum ⟨parum movetur⟩[1] pavet, et ab eo pavor.

49. Meminisse a memoria, cum ⟨in⟩ id quod remansit in mente[1] rursus movetur ; quae a manendo[2] ut manimoria[3] potest esse dicta. Itaque Salii quod cantant :

Mamuri Veturi,[4]

significant memoriam veterem.[5] Ab eodem monere,[6] quod is qui monet, proinde sit ac memoria ; sic monimenta quae in sepulcris, et ideo secundum viam, quo praetereuntis admoneant[7] et se fuisse et illos esse mortalis. Ab eo cetera quae scripta ac facta memoriae causa monimenta dicta.

50. Maerere a marcere, quod etiam corpus marcescere⟨t⟩[1] ; hinc etiam macri dicti. Laetari ab eo

§ 48.   [1] *Added by L. Sp.*
§ 49.   [1] *A. Sp., for* id quod remansit in mente in id quod *; the omission, with Sciop.*   [2] *Rhol., for* manando.
[3] *Other codices, for* maniomoria *Fv.*   [4] *Turnebus, for* memurii ueterum *or* ueteri.   [5] *Maurenbrecher ;* veterem memoriam *Aug., with B ; where, according to Victorius, F had* memoriam *followed by an illegible word.*   [6] *For* monerem.   [7] *For* admoueant *Fv,* admoneat *B.*
§ 50.   [1] *L. Sp., for* marcescere.

---

§ 48.   [a] All etymologies in the section are wrong.
§ 49.   [a] See note on § 45. *Meminisse, mens, monere, monimentum* (or *monumentum*) are from the same root ; *memoria* is perhaps remotely connected with them ; but *manere* is to be kept apart.   [b] Frag. 8, page 339 Maurenbrecher; page 4 Morel.   [c] The traditional smith who made the best of the duplicate *ancilia* (see vi. 22, note *d*), and at his request was rewarded by the insertion of his name in the *Hymns* of the Salii (Festus, 131. 11 M.).   But Varro seems
216

48.[a] *Metuere* ' to fear,' from a certain *motus* 'emotion' of the spirit, when the mind shrinks back from that misfortune which it thinks will fall upon it. When from excessive violence of the emotion it is borne *foras* ' forth ' so as to go out of itself, there is *formido* ' terror ' ; when *parum movetur* ' the emotion is not very strong,' it *pavet* ' dreads,' and from this comes *pavor* ' dread.'

49.[a] *Meminisse* ' to remember,' from *memoria* ' memory,' when there is again a motion toward that which *remansit* ' has remained ' in the *mens* ' mind ' : and this may have been said from *manere* ' to remain,' as though *manimoria*. Therefore the Salii,[b] when they sing

O Mamurius Veturius,[c]

indicate a *memoria vetus* ' memory of olden times.' From the same is *monere* ' to remind,' because he who *monet* ' reminds,' is just like a memory. So also the *monimenta* ' memorials ' which are on tombs, and in fact alongside the highway, that they may *admonere* ' admonish ' the passers-by that they themselves were mortal and that the readers are too. From this, the other things that are written and done to preserve their *memoria* ' memory ' are called *monimenta* ' monuments.'

50.[a] *Maerere* ' to grieve,' was named from *marcere* ' to wither away,' because the body too would *marcescere* ' waste away ' ; from this moreover the *macri* ' lean ' were named. *Laetari* ' to be happy,' from this,

to feel an etymological connexion between *Mamuri Veturi* and *memoriam veterem*.

§ 50. [a] All etymologies wrong, except the association of *laetari, laetitia, laeta*.

quod latius gaudium propter magni boni opinionem diffusum. Itaque Iuventius ait :

Gaudia
Sua si omnes homines conferant unum in locum.
Tamen mea exsuperet laetitia.

Sic cum se habent, laeta.

VII. 51. Narro, cum alterum facio narum,[1] a quo narratio, per quam cognoscimus rem gesta⟨m⟩.[2] Quae pars agendi est ab dicendo[3] ac sunt aut coniuncta cum temporibus aut ab his : eorum[4] hoc genus videntur ἔτυμα.

52. Fatur is qui primum homo significabilem ore mittit vocem. Ab eo, ante quam ita faciant, pueri dicuntur infantes ; cum id faciunt, iam fari ; cum hoc vocabulum,[1] ⟨tum⟩ a similitudine vocis pueri ⟨fariolus⟩ ac fatuus dictum.[2] Ab hoc tempora[3] quod tum pueris constituant Parcae fando, dictum fatum et res fatales. Ab hac eadem voce[4] qui facile fantur facundi dicti, et qui futura praedivinando soleant fari fatidici ; dicti idem vaticinari, quod vesana mente faciunt :

§ 51. [1] *Victorius, for* narrum.   [2] *For* gesta *Fv*.   [3] *L. Sp. ;* a dicendo *Ursinus ; for* ab adiacendo *Fv*.   [4] *Aug., for* earum.
§ 52. [1] *Aug., for* uocabulorum.   [2] *GS., for* a similitudine uocis pueri ac fatuus fari id dictum.   [3] *Popma, for* tempore.   [4] *Canal, for* ad haec eandem uocem.

---

[b] *Com. Rom. Frag.*, verses 2-4 Ribbeck[3]. Juventius was a writer of comedies from the Greek, in the second century B.C.
§ 51. [a] Varro wrote *naro*, with one R, according to Cassiodorus, vii. 159. 8 Keil ; the etymology is correct.   [b] *Cf.* vi. 42.
§ 52. [a] The etymologies in this section are correct, except those of *fariolus* and *vaticinari*.   [b] Dialectal form, prob-

that joy is spread *latius* 'more widely' because of the idea that it is a great blessing. Therefore Juventius says [b] :

> Should all men bring their joys into a single spot,
> My happiness would yet surpass the total lot.

When things are of this nature, they are said to be *laeta* ' happy.'

VII. 51. *Narro* [a] ' I narrate,' when I make a second person *narus* ' acquainted with ' something ; from which comes *narratio* ' narration,' by which we make acquaintance with an occurrence. This part of acting is in the section of saying,[b] and the words are united with time-ideas or are from them : those of this sort seem to be radicals.

52.[a] That man *fatur* ' speaks ' who first emits from his mouth an utterance which may convey a meaning. From this, before they can do so, children are called *infantes* ' non-speakers, infants ' ; when they do this, they are said now *fari* ' to speak ' ; not only this word, but also, from likeness to the utterance of a child, *fariolus* [b] ' soothsayer ' and *fatuus* ' prophetic speaker ' are said. From the fact that the Birth-Goddesses by *fando* ' speaking ' then set the life-periods for the children, *fatum* ' fate ' is named, and the things that are *fatales* ' fateful.' From this same word, those who *fantur* ' speak ' easily are called *facundi* ' eloquent,' and those who are accustomed *fari* ' to speak ' the future through presentiment, are called *fatidici* ' sayers of the fates '; they likewise are said *vaticinari* [c] ' to prophesy,' because they do this with frenzied

ably Faliscan, for *hariolus*, which is connected with *haruspex*.
[c] As though *fati-* ; but properly from the stems of *vates* ' bard ' and *canere* ' to sing.'

sed de hoc post erit usurpandum, cum de poetis
dicemus.

53. Hinc fasti dies, quibus verba certa legitima
sine piaculo praetoribus licet fari ; ab hoc nefasti,
quibus diebus ea fari ius non est et, si fati sunt, pia-
culum faciunt. Hinc effata dicuntur, qui augures
finem auspiciorum caelestum extra urbem agri⟨s⟩[1]
sunt effati ut esset ; hinc effari templa dicuntur : ab
auguribus effantur qui in his fines sunt.

54. Hinc fana nominata, quod[1] pontifices in sac-
rando fati sint finem ; hinc profanum, quod est ante
fanum coniunctum fano ; hinc profanatum quid in
sacrificio atque[2] Herculi decuma appellata ab eo est
quod sacrificio quodam fanatur, id est ut fani lege *f*it.[3]
Id dicitur pollu⟨c⟩tum,[4] quod a porriciendo est fictum:
cum enim ex mercibus libamenta porrecta[5] sunt
Herculi in aram, tum pollu⟨c⟩tum[4] est, ut cum pro-
fan⟨at⟩um[6] dicitur, id est proinde ut sit fani factum :
itaque *i*bi[7] olim ⟨in⟩[8] fano consumebatur omne quod

§ 53. [1] *Laetus, for* agri.
§ 54. [1] *Laetus, for* quae.   [2] *M, V, Laetus, for* ad quae
Fv. [3] *Canal, for* sit.   [4] *Aug. (quoting a friend), for*
pollutum.   [5] *Aug., with B, for* proiecta.   [6] *Turnebus,
for* profanum.   [7] *Vertranius, for* ubi.   [8] *Added by
Vertranius.*

---

[d] *Cf.* vii. 36.
§ 53. [a] *Fastus* and *nefastus*, from *fas* and *nefas* ; but
whether *fas* and *nefas* are from the root of *fari*, is question-
able.   [b] *Cf.* vi. 29-30.   [c] Page 19 Regell.   [d] *Effari* is
used both with active and with passive meaning.
§ 54. [a] *Fanum* (whence adj. *profanus*), from *fas*, not from
fari.   [b] *Profanus* was used also of persons who remained
' before the sanctuary ' because they were not entitled to go
inside, or because admission was refused ; therefore ' uninitiated ' or ' unholy,' respectively.   [c] Wrong etymology.
[d] Any edibles or drinkables were appropriate offerings to

mind : but this will have to be taken up later, when we speak about the poets.[d]

53. From this the *dies fasti* [a] ' righteous days, court days,' on which the praetors are permitted *fari* ' to speak ' without sin certain words of legal force ; from this the *nefasti* ' unrighteous days,' on which it is not right for them to speak them, and if they have spoken these words, they must make atonement.[b] From this those words are called *effata* ' pronounced,' by which the augurs [c] have *effati* ' pronounced ' the limit that the fields outside the city are to have, for the observance of signs in the sky ; from this, the areas of observation are said *effari* [d] ' to be pronounced ' ; by the augurs,[c] the boundaries *effantur* ' are pronounced ' which are attached to them.

54. From this the *fana* [a] ' sanctuaries ' are named, because the pontiffs in consecrating them have *fati* ' spoken ' their boundary ; from this, *profanum* ' being before the sanctuary,' [b] which applies to something that is in front of the sanctuary and joined to it ; from this, anything in the sacrifice, and especially Hercules's tithe, is called *profanatum* ' brought before the sanctuary, dedicated,' from this fact that it *fanatur* ' is consecrated ' by some sacrifice, that is, that it becomes by law the property of the sanctuary. This is called *polluctum* ' offered up,' a term which is shaped [c] from *porricere* ' to lay before ' : for when from articles of commerce first fruits [d] are laid before Hercules, on his altar, then there is a *polluctum* ' offering-up,' just as, when *profanatum* is said, it is as if the thing had become the sanctuary's property. So formerly all that was *profanatum* [e] ' dedicated ' used to be consumed in

Hercules ; *cf.* Festus, 253 a 17-21 M.   [e] That is, so far as it was not burned on the altar, in the god's honour.

221

VARRO

profan⟨at⟩um[9] erat, ut etiam ⟨nunc⟩[10] fit quod praetor urb⟨an⟩us[11] quotannis facit, cum Herculi immolat publice iuvencam.

55. Ab eodem verbo fari fabulae, ut tragoediae et comoediae,[1] dictae. Hinc fassi ac confessi, qui fati id quod ab is[2] quaesitum. Hinc professi ; hinc fama et famosi. Ab eodem falli, sed et falsum et fallacia, quae propterea, quod fando quem decipit ac contra quam dixit facit. Itaque si quis re fallit, in hoc non proprio nomine fallacia, sed tralati⟨ci⟩o,[3] ut a pede nostro pes lecti ac betae. Hinc etiam famigerabile[4] et sic compositicia[5] alia item ut declinata multa, in quo et Fatuus et Fatuae.[6]

56. Loqui ab loco dictum.[1] Quod qui primo dicitur iam fari[2] vocabula et reliqua verba dicit ante quam suo quique[3] loco ea dicere potest,[1] hunc Chrysippus negat loqui, sed ut loqui : quare ut imago hominis non sit hon o, sic in corvis, cornicibus, pueris primitus incipientibus fari verba non esse verba, quod

[9] L. Sp., for profanum.   [10] Added by L. Sp.   [11] Aug., with B, for P. R. urbis Fv.

§ 55.   [1] For tragaediae et comaediae.   [2] For his.
[3] A. Sp.; tralatitio Sciop.; for tranlatio.   [4] M, V, p, Aldus, for famiger fabile Fv.   [5] A. Sp., for composititia Fv.   [6] B, G, f, for fatue Fv.

§ 56.   [1] Punctuation by Stroux.   [2] For farit Fv.   [3] L. Sp.; quidque Aug.; for quisque.

§ 55.   [a] The preceding words all belong with fari : but falli, falsum, fallacia form a distinct group.   [b] Instead of by speaking.   [c] That is, beet-root.   [d] Faunus and the Nymphs.
§ 56.   [a] Wrong.   [b] Page 143 von Arnim.   [c] Ravens

the sanctuary, as even now is done with that which the City Praetor offers every year, when on behalf of the state he sacrifices a heifer to Hercules.

55. From the same word *fari* ' to speak,' the *fabulae* ' plays,' such as tragedies and comedies, were named. From this word, those persons have *fassi* ' admitted ' and *confessi* ' confessed,' who have *fati* ' spoken ' that which was asked of them. From this, *professi* ' openly declared ' ; from this, *fama* ' talk, rumour,' and *famosi* ' much talked of, notorious.' [a] From the same, *falli* ' to be deceived,' but also *falsum* ' false ' and *fallacia* ' deceit,' which are so named on this account, that by *fando* ' speaking ' one misleads someone and then does the opposite of what he has said. Therefore if one *fallit* ' deceives ' by an act,[b] in this there is not *fallacia* ' deceit ' in its own proper meaning, but in a transferred sense, as from our *pes* ' foot ' the *pes* ' foot ' of a bed and of a beet [c] are spoken of. From this, moreover, *famigerabile* ' worth being talked about,' and in this fashion other compounded words, just as there are many derived words, among which are *Fatuus* ' god of prophetic speaking ' and the *Fatuae* ' women of prophecy.' [d]

56. *Loqui* ' to talk,' is said from *locus* ' place.'[a] Because he who is said to speak now for the first time, utters the names and other words before he can say them each in its own *locus* ' place,' such a person Chrysippus says [b] does not *loqui* ' talk,' but quasi-talks ; and that therefore, as a man's sculptured bust is not the real man, so in the case of ravens, crows,[c] and children making their first attempts to speak, their words are not real words, because they are not

and crows were the chief speaking birds of the Romans ; *cf.* Macrobius, *Sat.* ii. 4. 29-30.

non loquantur.[4]   Igitur is loquitur, qui suo loco quod-
que verbum sciens ponit, et is tum[5] prolocutus,[6] quom
in animo quod habuit extulit loquendo.

57.   Hinc dicuntur eloqui ac reloqui[1] in fanis
Sabinis, e cella dei qui loquuntur.[2]   Hinc dictus
loquax, qui nimium loqueretur ; hinc eloquens, qui
copiose loquitur ; hinc colloquium, cum veniunt in
unum locum loquendi causa ; hinc adlocutum mulieres
ire aiunt, cum eunt ad aliquam locutum consolandi[3]
causa ; hinc quidam loquelam dixerunt verbum quod
in loquendo efferimus.   Concinne loqui dictum a
concinere,[4] ubi inter se conveniunt partes ita ⟨ut⟩[5]
inter se concinant[6] aliud alii.

58.   Pronuntiare dictum ⟨a pro⟩[1] et nuntiare ; pro
idem valet quod ante, ut in hoc : proludit.   Ideo
actores pronuntiare dicuntur, quod in proscaenio
enuntiant poeta⟨e⟩ cogitata,[2] quod maxime tum[3]
dicitur proprie, novam fabulam cum agunt.   Nuntius
enim est a ⟨n⟩ovis[4] rebus nominatus, quod a verbo

[4] *Aug., for* loquebantur.   [5] *Canal, for* istum.   [6] *Fay,*
for prolocutum.

§ 57.   [1] *Aug., with B, for* eloquium ac reliqui.   [2] *Lach-*
mann, for eloquuntur.   [3] *G, Aug., for* consulendi.
[4] *Scaliger, for* concinne.   [5] *Added by Mue. ; added after*
inter se *by L. Sp.*   [6] *Mue., for* condeant.

§ 58.   [1] *Added by Groth.*   [2] *Sciop., for* poeta cogitante.
[3] *After* tum, *Laetus deleted* id.   [4] *Turnebus, for* quis.

---

[d] That is, do not convey ideas to others.

§ 57.   [a] *Concinne,* adverb to *concinnus* ' neatly fitted,' has
nothing in common with *concinere* ' to sing in harmony,'
except the prefix.

§ 58.   [a] *Nuntiare* and its compounds are derived from

talking.*d* Therefore he *loquitur* 'talks,' who with understanding puts each word in its own place, and he has then *prolocutus* ' spoken forth,' when he has by *loquendo* ' talking ' expressed what he had in his spirit.

57. From this, they are said *eloqui* ' to speak forth ' and *reloqui* ' to speak in reply ' in the Sabine sanctuaries, who *loquuntur* ' speak ' from the chamber of the God. From this he was called *loquax* ' talkative,' who talked too much ; from this, *eloquens* ' eloquent,' who talks profusely ; from this, *colloquium* ' conference,' when persons come into one place for the purpose of talking ; from this, they say that women go *adlocutum* ' to talk to her,' when they go to someone, to talk for purposes of consolation ; from this, a word which we utter in talking has been by some called a *loquela* ' talk-unit.' To talk *concinne* *a* ' neatly ' is said from *concinere* ' to harmonize,' where the parts agree with each other in such a way that they mutually *concinunt* ' harmonize ' one with another.

58. *Pronuntiare* *a* ' to make known publicly ' is said from *pro* and *nuntiare* ' to announce ' ; *pro* means the same as *ante* ' before,' as in *proludit* ' he plays beforehand.' Therefore actors are said *pronuntiare* ' to declaim,' because they *enuntiant* ' make known ' on the *proscaenium* ' stage ' the poet's thoughts *b* ; and the word is used with the most literal meaning, when they act a new play.*c* For a *nuntius* ' messenger ' was named from *novae res* *d* ' new things,' which is perhaps

---

nuntius.   *b* As though *pronuntiare* united the *pro* of *proscenium* and the *nuntiare* of *enuntiare.*   *c* A play not previously acted.   *d* A *nuntius* is a *novo-vent-ios*, but is not from Greek ; Latin *novus* and Greek *νέος* are from a common original.

VARRO

Graeco potest declinatum ; ab eo itaque Neapolis illorum Novapolis ab antiquis vocitata nostris.

59. A quo etiam extremum novissimum quoque dic*i*[1] coeptum volgo, quod mea memoria ut Aelius sic senes aliquot, nimium novum verbum quod esset, vitabant ; cuius origo, ut a vet⟩re vetust⟨i⟩us ac veterrimu*m*,[2] sic ab novo declinatum ⟨novius et⟩[3] novissimum, quod extremum. Sic ab eadem origine novitas et novicius et novalis in agro et " sub Novis " dicta pars in Foro aedificiorum, quod vocabulum ei pervetust*um*,[4] ut Novae Viae, quae via iam diu vetus.

60. Ab eo quoque potest dictum nominare, quod res novae in usum quom[1] additae erant, quibus ea⟨s⟩[2] novissent, nomina ponebant. Ab eo nuncupare, quod tunc ⟨pro⟩[3] civitate vota nova suscipiuntur. Nuncupare nominare valere apparet in legibus, ubi " nuncupatae pecuniae " sunt scriptae ; item in Choro in quo est :

Aenea !—Quis ⟨is⟩[4] est qui meum nomen nuncupat ?

§ 59. [1] *Aug., from Gellius,* x. 21. 2, *for* dico. [2] *Bentinus, from Gellius, l.c., for* uetustus ac ueterrimus. [3] *Added by Aug., from Gellius, l.c.* [4] *B, Laetus, for* peruetustas.
§ 60. [1] *Aug. (quoting a friend), for* quomodo. [2] *Vertranius, for* ea. [3] *Added by L. Sp.* [4] *Added by Grotius.*

---

[e] Naples ; *Nova-polis* is a half-way translation into Latin.
§ 59. [a] Page 57 Funaioli. [b] The *Tabernae Novae* were the shops on the north side of the Forum which replaced those burned in the fire of 210 B.C.; those on the south side, which escaped the fire, were called the *Tabernae Veteres.*
§ 60. [a] *Nomen* and *nominare* are distinct from *novus,* and

derived from a Greek word ; from this, accordingly, their *Neapolis* *^e* ' New City ' was called *Nova-polis* ' New-polis ' by the old-time Romans.

59. From this, moreover, *novissimum* ' newest ' also began to be used popularly for *extremum* ' last,' a use which within my memory both Aelius *^a* and some elderly men avoided, on the ground that this superlative of the word was too new a formation ; its origin is just like *vetustius* ' older ' and *veterrimum* ' oldest ' from *vetus* ' old,' thus from *novum* were derived *novius* ' newer ' and *novissimum*, which means ' last.' So, from the same origin, *novitas* ' newness ' and *novicius* ' novice ' and *novalis* ' ploughed anew ' in the case of a field, and a part of the buildings in the Forum was called *sub Novis* *^b* ' by the New Shops ' ; though it has had the name for a very long time, as has the *Nova Via* ' New Street,' which has been an old street this long while.

60. From this can be said also *nominare* *^a* ' to call by name,' because when *novae* ' new ' things were brought into use, they set *nomina* ' names ' on them, by which they *novissent* ' might know ' them. From this, *nuncupare* *^b* ' to pronounce vows publicly,' because then *nova* ' new ' vows are undertaken for the state. That *nuncupare* is the same as *nominare*, is evident in the laws, where sums of money are written down as *nuncupatae* ' bequeathed by name ' ; likewise in the *Chorus*, in which there is *^c* :

Aeneas !—Who is this who calls me by my name ?

also from *novisse* ' to know.'   *^b* Containing the elements of *nomen* and *capere* ' to take.'   *^c* *Trag. Rom. Frag.*, page 272 Ribbeck³ ; *R O.L.* ii. 608–609 Warmington ; possibly belonging to a play entitled *Proserpina*, *cf.* vi. 94. But the title is perhaps hopelessly corrupt.

VARRO

Item in Medo [5]:

Quis tu es, mulier, quae me insueto nuncupasti nomine ?

61. Dico originem habet Graecam, quod Graeci
δεικνύω.[1] Hinc ⟨etiam dicare, ut ait⟩[2] Ennius :

Dico VI hunc dicare ⟨circum metulas⟩.[3]

Hinc iudicare, quod tunc ius dicatur ; hinc iudex,
quod iu⟨s⟩ dicat[4] accepta potestate ; ⟨hinc dedicat⟩,[5]
id est quibusdam verbis dicendo finit : sic[6] enim aedis
sacra a magistratu pontifice prae⟨e⟩un*te*[7] dicendo
dedicatur. Hinc, ab dicendo,[8] indicium ; hinc illa :
indicit ⟨b⟩ellum,[9] indixit funus, prodixit diem, addixit
iudicium ; hinc appellatum dictum in mimo,[10] ac
dictiosus ; hinc in manipulis castrensibus ⟨dicta[11]
ab⟩[12] ducibus ; hinc dictata in ludo ; hinc dictator
magister populi, quod is a consule debet dici ; hinc
antiqua illa ⟨ad⟩dici[13] numo et dicis causa et addictus.

[5] *Aldus,* for medio.
§ 61. [1] *L. Sp. ;* δεικνύναι *Mue. ;* δείκω *Scaliger ; for*
NIδIhcε *Fv.* [2] *Added by Kent.* [3] *Fay, for* qui hunc
dicare *; cf. Festus,* 153 a 15-21 *M., and Livy,* xli. 27. 6.
[4] *Aug., with* B, *for* iudicat. [5] *Added by Stroux.* [6] *With*
sic enim, F *resumes ; cf.* v. 118, *crit. note* 7. [7] *Bentinus*
(*or earlier*) *;* praeunte *f, Laetus ; for* prae unce F. [8] *L.*
Sp., for dicando. [9] *Turnebus, for* illum. [10] B, *Aldus,*
for minimo. [11] *Added by Aug., with* B. [12] *Added by*
Kent ; a *added by Fay.* [13] *Budaeus, for* dici.

---

[d] Pacuvius, *Trag. Rom. Frag.* 239 Ribbeck[3] ; *R.O.L.* ii. 260-
261 Warmington ; the play was named from one of Medea's
sons.
§ 61. [a] All the words explained in this section belong
together ; but *dicere* is cognate with the Greek word, not
derived from it. [b] Inc. frag. 39 Vahlen[2] ; see critical note.
[c] Rather, because he *dictat* ' gives orders ' to the people.
[d] *Numo* in the text is the older spelling, in which consonants
were never doubled. [e] Applied to the fictitious sale of an

And likewise in the *Medus* [d] :

> Who are you, woman, who have called me by an
> unaccustomed name?

61. *Dico* [a] ' I say ' has a Greek origin, that which the Greeks call δεικνύω ' I show.' From this moreover comes *dicare* ' to show, dedicate,' as Ennius says [b] :

> I say this circus shows six little turning-posts.

From this, *iudicare* ' to judge,' because then *ius* ' right ' *dicitur* ' is spoken ' ; from this, *iudex* ' judge,' because he *ius dicat* ' speaks the decision ' after receiving the power to do so ; from this, *dedicat* ' he dedicates,' that is, he finishes the matter by *dicendo* ' saying ' certain fixed words : for thus a temple of a god *dedicatur* ' is dedicated ' by the magistrate, by *dicendo* ' saying ' the formulas after the pontiff. From this, that is from *dicere*, comes *indicium* ' information ' ; from this, the following : *indicit* ' he declares ' war, *indixit* ' he has invited to ' a funeral, *prodixit* ' he has postponed ' the day, *addixit* ' he has awarded ' the decision ; from this was named a *dictum* ' bon mot ' in a farce, and *dictiosus* ' witty person ' ; from this, in the companies of soldiers in camp, the *dicta* ' orders ' of the leaders ; from this, the *dictata* ' dictation exercises ' in the school ; from this, the *dictator* [c] ' dictator,' as master of the people, because he must *dici* ' be appointed ' by the consul; from this, those old phrases *addici nummo* [d] ' to be made over to somebody for a shilling,' [e] and *dicis causa* ' for the sake of judicial form,' and *addictus* ' bound over [f] ' to somebody.

inheritance to the heir. [f] Said of a defendant who was unable to pay the amount of debt or damages, and was delivered to the custody of the plaintiff as a virtual slave until he could arrange payment.

VARRO

62. Si dico quid ⟨sciens[1] ne⟩scienti,[2] quod *ei*[3] quod ignoravit trado, hinc doceo declinatum vel quod cum docemus[4] dicimus vel quod qui docentur inducuntur[5] in id quod docentur. Ab eo quod scit ducere[6] qui est dux aut ductor ; ⟨hinc[7] doctor⟩[8] qui ita inducit, ut doceat. Ab ducendo[9] docere disciplina discere litteris commutatis paucis. Ab eodem principio documenta, quae exempla docendi causa dicuntur.

63. Disputatio et computatio e[1] propositione putandi, quod valet purum facere ; ideo antiqui purum putum appellarunt ; ideo putator, quod arbores puras facit ; ideo ratio putari dicitur, in qua summa fit pura : sic is sermo in quo pure disponuntur verba, ne sit confusus atque ut diluceat, dicitur disputare.

64. Quod dicimus disserit item translati⟨ci⟩o[1] aeque[2] ex agris verbo : nam ut *h*olitor disserit in areas sui cuiusque generis res, sic in oratione qui facit, disertus. Sermo, opinor, est a serie, unde serta ; etiam in vestimento sartum, quod comprehensum :

§ 62. [1] *Added by L. Sp.* [2] *Scaliger, for* scienti. [3] *Sciop., for* det. [4] *After* docemus, *Laetus deleted* ut. [5] *Reiter, for* inducantur. [6] *M, Laetus, for* ducare. [7] *Added by GS.* [8] *Added by L. Sp.* [9] *Fay, for* docendo.
§ 63. [1] *L. Sp., for* et.
§ 64. [1] *A. Sp.;* translatitio *Aug.; for* translatio. [2] *Aug., for* atque.

§ 62. [a] *Docere* is quite independent of *dicere*, and also of *ducere*. [b] *Disciplina* was popularly associated with *discere*, but was really a derivative of *discipulus*, which came from *dis* + *capere* ' to take apart (for examination).'
§ 64. [a] There are in Latin two verbs *sero serere*, distinct in etymology : *serere sevi satus* ' to sow, plant,' and *serere serui sertus* ' to join together, intertwine.' The derivatives in this section are all from the second verb, except *sartum*, the participle of *sarcio*, which is distinct from both.

62. If I *dico* ' say ' something that I know to one who does not know it, because I *trado* ' hand over ' to him what he was ignorant of, from this is derived *doceo* [a] ' I teach,' or else because when we *docemus* ' teach ' we *dicimus* ' say,' or else because those who *docentur* ' are taught ' *inducuntur* ' are led on ' to that which they *docentur* ' are taught.' From this fact, that he knows how *ducere* ' to lead,' is named the one who is *dux* ' guide ' or *ductor* ' leader ' ; from this, *doctor* ' teacher,' who so *inducit* ' leads on ' that he *docet* ' teaches.' From *ducere* ' to lead,' come *docere* ' to teach,' *disciplina* [b] ' instruction,' *discere* ' to learn,' by the change of a few letters. From the same original element comes *documenta* ' instructive examples,' which are said as models for the purpose of teaching.

63. *Disputatio* ' discussion ' and *computatio* ' reckoning,' from the general idea of *putare*, which means to make *purum* ' clean ' ; for the ancients used *putum* to mean *purum*. Therefore *putator* ' trimmer', because he makes trees clean ; therefore a business account is said *putari* ' to be adjusted,' in which the sum is *pura* ' net.' So also that discourse in which the words are arranged *pure* ' neatly,' that it may not be confused and that it may be transparent of meaning, is said *disputare* ' to discuss ' a problem or question.

64. Our word *disserit* [a] is used in a figurative meaning as well as in relation to the fields : for as the kitchen-gardener *disserit* ' distributes ' the things of each kind upon his garden plots, so he who does the like in speaking is *disertus* ' skilful.' *Sermo* ' conversation,' I think, is from *series* ' succession,' whence *serta* ' garlands ' ; and moreover in the case of a garment *sartum* ' patched,' because it is held together : for

231

VARRO

sermo enim non potest in uno homine esse solo, sed ubi ⟨o⟩ratio[3] cum altero coniuncta. Sic conserere manu⟨m⟩[4] dicimur cum hoste ; sic ex iure manu⟨m⟩[5] consertum vocare ; hinc adserere manu[6] in libertatem cum prendimus. Sic augures dicunt :

Si mihi auctor es[7] verbenam[8] manu[9] asserere,
dicit⟨o⟩[10] consortes.

65. Hinc etiam, a quo[1] ipsi consortes, sors ; hinc etiam sortes, quod in his iuncta tempora cum hominibus ac rebus ; ab his sortilegi ; ab hoc pecunia quae in faenore sors est, impendium quod inter se iung*it*.[2]

66. Legere dictum, quod leguntur ab oculis litterae ; ideo etiam legati, quod ⟨ut⟩[1] publice mittantur leguntur. Item ab legendo leguli, qui oleam aut qui uvas legunt ; hinc legumina in frugibus variis ; etiam leges, quae lectae et ad populum latae quas observet. Hinc legitima et collegae, qui una lecti, et qui in eorum locum suppositi, sublecti ; additi allecti et collecta, quae ex pluribus locis in unum lecta. Ab

[3] *Aug., for* ratio. [4] *Other codd., for* manu *F.* [5] *Sciop., for* manu *; cf.* Gellius, xx. 10. [6] *p, Aug., for* manum. [7] *Aug., for* est. [8] *Bergk, for* verbi nam. [9] *Aug., for* manum. [10] *A. Sp., for* dicit.
§ 65. [1] *L. Sp., for* ad qui. [2] *Groth, for* iungat.
§ 66. [1] *Added by B, Aldus.*

---

[b] Genitive plural. [c] Page 18 Regell.
§ 65. [a] These words belong to *serere*, but Varro's reason for the meaning of *sors* may not be correct. [b] To Varro, the fundamental meaning in *sors* is one of ' joining ' ; *cf.* v. 183.
§ 66. [a] All words discussed in this section are from various forms of the root seen in *legere*, which means ' to gather, pick, select, choose, read ' ; except *legumen*. [b] Properly participle of *legare* ' to appoint,' a derivative of *legere*. [c] More exactly, *legumina* are, according to Varro, fruits of various kinds that have to be picked (rather than cut, like cabbage,

sermo ' conversation ' cannot be where one man is alone, but where his speech is joined with another's. So we are said *conserere manum* ' to join hand-to-hand fight ' with an enemy ; so to call for *manum* [b] *consertum* ' a laying on of hands ' according to law ; from this, *adserere manu in libertatem* ' to claim that so-and-so is free,' when we lay hold of him. So the augurs say [c] :

> If you authorize me to take in my hand the sacred bough, then name my colleagues (*consortes*).

65. From this, moreover, *sors* [a] ' lot,' from which the *consortes* ' colleagues ' themselves are named ; from this, further, *sortes* ' lots,' because in them time-ideas are joined with men and things ; from these, the *sortilegi* ' lot-pickers, fortune-tellers ' ; from this, the money which is at interest is the *sors* ' principal,' because it joins [b] one expense to another.

66.[a] *Legere* ' to pick or read,' because the letters *leguntur* ' are picked ' with the eyes ; therefore also *legati* [b] ' envoys,' because they *leguntur* ' are chosen ' to be sent on behalf of the state. Likewise, from *legere* ' to pick,' the *leguli* ' pickers,' who *legunt* ' gather ' the olives or the grapes ; from this, the *legumina* [c] ' beans ' of various kinds ; moreover, the *leges* ' laws,' which are *lectae* ' chosen ' and brought before the people for them to observe. From this, *legitima* ' lawful things ' ; and *collegae* ' colleagues,' who have been *lecti* ' chosen ' together, and those who have been put into their places, are *sublecti* ' substitutes ' ; those added are *allecti* ' chosen in addition,' and things which have been *lecta* ' gathered ' from several places into one, are *collecta* ' collected.' From *legere* ' to gather '

or mowed, like wheat) ; but the resemblance to *legere* seems to be only accidental.

legendo ligna quoque, quod ea caduca legebantur in agro quibus in focum uterentur. Indidem ab legendo legio et diligens et dilectus.^d

67. Murmur*ari*[1] a similitudine sonitus dictus, qui ita leviter loquitur, ut magis e sono id facere quam ut intellegatur videatur. Hinc etiam poetae

> Murmurantia litora.

Similiter fremere, gemere, clamare, crepare ab similitudine vocis sonitus dicta. Hinc illa

> Arma sonant, fremor oritur ;

hinc

> Nihil[2] me increpitando commoves.

68. Vicina horum quiritare, iubilare. Quiritare dicitur is qui Quiritum fidem clamans inplorat. Quirites a Curensibus ; ab his cum Tatio rege in societatem venerunt civita*t*is.[1] Ut quiritare urbanorum, sic iubilare rusticorum : itaque hos imitans Aprissius ait :

> Io bucco !—Quis me iubilat ?—
> Vicinus tuus antiquus.

Sic triumphare appellatum, quod cum imperatore

---

§ 67. [1] *L. Sp., for* murmuratur dictum. [2] *For* nichil.
§ 68. [1] *Sciop., for* civitates.

---

^d Better spelling, *delectus.*
§ 67. ^a Some, but not all, of the words discussed in this section are onomatopoeic. ^b *Lěviter* ' lightly.' ^c *Trag. Rom. Frag.*, page 314 Ribbeck[3] ; but the words look like part of a dactylic hexameter, in which case it should read *Arma sonant, oritur fremor.* ^d *Trag. Rom. Frag.*, page 314 Ribbeck[3].
§ 68. ^a Frequentative of *queri* ' to complain,' and not connected with *Quirites.* ^b *Cures,* ancient capital city of the Sabines. ^c The name is corrupt, but no probable

comes also *ligna* ' firewood,' because the wood that had fallen was gathered in the field, to be used on the fireplace. From the same source, *legere* ' to gather,' came *legio* ' legion,' and *diligens* ' careful,' and *dilectus*[d] ' military levy.'

67.[a] From likeness to the sound, he is said *murmurari* ' to murmur,' who speaks so softly[b] that he seems more as the result of the sound to be doing it, than to be doing it for the purpose of being understood. From this, moreover, the poets say

> Murmuring sea-shore.

Likewise, *fremere* ' to roar,' *gemere* ' to groan,' *clamare* ' to shout,' *crepare* ' to rattle ' are said from the likeness of the sound of the word to that which it denotes. From this, that passage[c] :

> Arms are resounding, a roar doth arise.

From this, also,[d]

> By your rebuking you alarm me not.

68. Close to these are *quiritare*[a] ' to shriek,' *iubilare* ' to call joyfully.' He is said *quiritare*, who shouts and implores the protection of the *Quirites*. The Quirites were named from the *Curenses* ' men of Cures '[b] ; from that place they came with King Tatius to receive a share in the Roman state. As *quiritare* is a word of city people, so *iubilare* is a word of the countrymen ; thus in imitation of them Aprissius[c] says :

> Oho, Fat-Face !—Who is calling me ?—
> Your neighbour of long standing.

So *triumphare* ' to triumph ' was said, because the

emendation has been suggested ; *Com. Rom. Frag.*, page 332 Ribbeck³.

milites redeuntes clamitant per Urbem in Capitolium
cunti " ⟨I⟩o² triumphe "; id a θριάμβῳ³ ac Graeco
Liberi cognomento potest dictum.

69. Spondere est dicere spondeo, a sponte: nam id
⟨idem⟩¹ valet et a voluntate. Itaque Lucilius scribit
de Cretaea,² cum ad se cubitum venerit sua voluntate,
sponte ipsam suapte adductam, ut tunicam et cetera³
reiceret. Eandem voluntatem Terentius significat,
cum ait satius esse

> Sua sponte recte facere quam alieno metu.

Ab eadem sponte, a qua dictum spondere, declinatum
⟨de⟩spondet⁴ et respondet et desponsor et sponsa,
item sic alia. Spondet enim qui dicit a sua sponte
" spondeo "; ⟨qui⟩ spo⟨po⟩ndit,⁵ est sponsor; qui
⟨i⟩dem⁶ ⟨ut⟩⁷ faciat obligatur sponsu,⁸ consponsus.

70. Hoc Naevius significat cum ait " consponsi."
⟨Si⟩¹ spondebatur pecunia aut filia nuptiarum causa,

---

² *Laetus, for* o.   ³ *Aldus, for* triambo.
   § 69.   ¹ *Added by Fay.*   ² *For* Gretea.   ³ *For* ceterae.
⁴ *GS, after Lachmann, for* spondit.   ⁵ *L. Sp., for* spondit.
⁶ *B, Ed. Veneta, for* quidem.   ⁷ *Added by Aug., with B.*
⁸ *L. Sp., for* sponsus.
   § 70.   ¹ *Added by Fay.*

ᵈ From the Greek, through the Etruscan.   ᵉ *Ac*, intro-
ducing an appositive.
   § 69.   ᵃ Verses 925-927 Marx. *Cretaea* was a *meretrix*,
named from the country of her origin. Varro has para-
phrased the quotation, which was thus restored to metrical
form by Lachmann, the first two words being added by Marx:

> *Cretaea nuper, cum ad me cubitum venerat,*
> *Sponte ipsa suapte adducta ut tunicam et cetera*
> *Reiceret.*

soldiers shout " Oho, triumph ! " as they come back with the general through the City and he is going up to the Capitol; this is perhaps derived [d] from θρίαμβος, as [e] a Greek surname of Liber.

69. *Spondere* is to say *spondeo* ' I solemnly promise,' from *sponte* ' of one's own inclination ' : for this has the same meaning as from *voluntas* ' personal desire.' Therefore Lucilius writes of the Cretan woman,[a] that when she had come of her own desire to his house to lie with him, she was of her own *sponte* ' inclination ' led to throw back her tunic and other garments. The same *voluntas* ' personal desire ' is what Terence means [b] when he says that it is better

> Of one's own inclination right to do,
> Than merely by the fear of other folk.

From the same *sponte* from which *spondere* is said, are derived *despondet* ' he pledges ' and *respondet* ' he promises in return, answers,' and *desponsor* ' promiser' and *sponsa* ' promised bride,' and likewise others in the same fashion. For he *spondet* ' solemnly promises' who says of his own *sponte* ' inclination ' *spondeo* ' I promise '; he who *spopondit* ' has promised' is a *sponsor* ' surety '; he who is by *sponsus* ' formal promise ' bound to do the same thing as the other party, is a *consponsus* ' co-surety.'

70. This is what Naevius means [a] when he says *consponsi*. If money [b] or a daughter *spondebatur* ' was promised ' in connexion with a marriage, both the

----

While this might accord with the Lucilian prototype of Horace, *Sat.* i. 5. 82-85, the meter forbids, and because of the subject matter A. Spengel proposed *Licinius*, writer of comedies, for *Lucilius*.   [b] *Adelphoe*, 75.

§ 70.   [a] *Com. Rom. Frag.*, page 34 Ribbeck[3]; *R.O.L.* ii. 598 Warmington.   [b] As dower.

appellabatur et pecunia et quae desponsa erat sponsa;
quae pecunia inter se contra sponsu[2] rogata erat, dicta
sponsio ; cui desponsa qu*ae*[3] erat, sponsus ; quo die
sponsum erat, sponsalis.

71. Qu*i*[1] spoponderat filiam, despondisse[2] dicebant, quod de sponte eius, id est de voluntate,
exierat : non enim si volebat, dabat, quod sponsu erat
alligatus : nam ut in com⟨o⟩ediis vides dici :

> Sponde⟨n⟩[3] tuam gnatam[4] filio uxorem meo ?

Quod tum et praetorium ius ad legem et censorium
iudicium ad aequum existimabatur. Sic despondisse
animum quoque dicitur, ut despondisse filiam, quod
suae spontis statuerat finem.

72. A *s*ua sponte dicere cum spondere, ⟨respon-
dere⟩[1] quoque dixerunt, cum a⟨d⟩ sponte⟨m⟩[2] re-
sponderent, id est ad voluntatem rogatoris.[3] Itaque
qui ad id quod rogatur non dicit, non respondet, ut
non spondet ille statim qui dixit spondeo, si iocandi

[2] *L. Sp., for* sponsum.   [3] *Mue., for* quo.
  § 71.   [1] *G, B, Laetus, for* quo.   [2] *B, Aldus, for* dispon-
disse.   [3] *Aug.;* spondem *Rhol.; for* sponde.   [4] *Rhol.,
for* agnatam.
  § 72.   [1] *Lachmann, for* a qua sponte dicere cumspondere.
[2] *Turnebus, for* a sponte.   [3] *L. Sp., for* rogationis.

---

[c] To be forfeited to the other party as damages by that party
which might break the agreement.
  § 71.   [a] *Com. Rom. Frag.,* page 134 Ribbeck[3].

money and the girl who had been *desponsa* ' pledged ' were called *sponsa* ' promised, pledged ' ; the money which had been asked under the *sponsus* ' engagement ' for their mutual protection against the breaking of the agreement,[c] was called a *sponsio* ' guarantee deposit ' ; the man to whom the money or the girl was *desponsa* ' pledged,' was called *sponsus* ' betrothed ' ; the day on which the engagement was made, was called *sponsalis* ' betrothal day.'

71. He who *spoponderat* ' had promised ' his daughter, they said. *despondisse* ' had promised her away,' because she had gone out of the power of his *sponte* ' inclination,' that is, from the control of his *voluntas* ' desire ' : for even if he wished not to give her, still he gave her, because he was bound by his *sponsus* ' formal promise ' : for you see it said, as in comedies [a] :

Do you now promise your daughter to my son as wife?

This was at that time considered a principle established by the praetors to supplement the statutes, and a decision of the censors for the sake of fairness. So a person is said *despondisse animum* ' to have promised his spirit away, to have become despondent,' just as he is said *despondisse filiam* ' to have promised his daughter away,' because he had fixed an end of the power of his *sponte* ' inclination.'

72. Since *spondere* was said from *sua sponte dicere* ' to say of one's own inclination,' they said also *respondere* ' to answer,' when they *responderunt* ' promised in return ' to the other party's *spontem* ' inclination,' that is, to the desire of the asker. Therefore he who says " no " to that which is asked, does not *respondere*, just as he does not *spondere* who has immediately said

239

causa dixit, neque agi potest cum eo ex sponsu. Itaqu⟨e⟩ is⁴ qu⟨o⟩i dicit⟨ur⟩⁵ in *comoedia* ⁶ :

> Meministin⁷ te spondere⁸ mihi gnatam⁹ tuam ?

quod sine sponte sua dixit, cum eo non potest agi ex sponsu.

73. Etiam spes a sponte potest esse declinata, quod tum sperat cum quod¹ volt fieri putat : nam quod non volt si putat, metuit, non sperat. Itaque hi² quoque qui dicunt in Astraba Plauti :

> N*unc*³ sequere adseque, Polybadisce, meam spem
> cupio consequi.—
> Sequor hercle ⟨e⟩quidem,⁴ nam libenter mea⟨m⟩
> sperata⟨m⟩⁵ consequor :

quod sine sponte dicunt, vere neque ille sperat qui dicit adolescens neque illa ⟨quae⟩⁶ sperata est.

74. Sponsor et pr*ae*s et vas neque ide*m*,¹ neque res a quibus hi, sed e re simili.² Itaque pr*ae*s qui a magistratu interrogatus, in publicum ut praestet ; a quo et cum respondet, dicit "praes." Vas appel-

---

⁴ *L. Sp., for* itaquis.   ⁵ *Kent, for* qui dicit *F* (d'r *a* =dicitur).   ⁶ *L. Sp., for* tragoedia.   ⁷ *Aug., for* meministine.
⁸ *Lachmann, metri gratia, for* despondere.   ⁹ *Rhol., for* agnatam.
§ 73.   ¹ *Aug., for* quod cum.   ² *L. Sp., for* hic.   ³ *L. Sp., for* ne.   ⁴ *L. Sp., for* quidem.   ⁵ *Ritschl, for* mea sperata.   ⁶ *Added by Kent.*
§ 74.   ¹ *Laetus, for* ideo.   ² *Sciop., for* simile.

---

§ 72.   ᵃ Hanging nominative, resumed by *cum eo* after the quotation.   ᵇ *Trag. Rom. Frag.*, page 305 Ribbeck³ ; but as the content indicates that it came from a comedy rather than from a tragedy, I have accepted L. Spengel's emendation *comoedia* for the manuscript *tragoedia.*
§ 73.   ᵃ Wrong.   ᵇ Frag. I Ritschl.   ᶜ *Adseque,* active imperative form ; *cf.* Neue-Wagener, *Formenlehre der lat.*

spondeo, if he said it for a joke, nor can legal action be taken against him as a result of such a *sponsus* 'promise.' Thus he [a] to whom someone says in a comedy,[b]

> Do you recall you pledged your daughter unto me?

which he had said without his *sponte* 'inclination,' cannot be proceeded against under his *sponsus*.

73. *Spes* 'hope' is perhaps also derived [a] from *sponte* 'inclination,' because a person then *sperat* 'hopes,' when he thinks that what he wishes is coming true ; for if he thinks that what he does not wish is coming true, he fears, not hopes. Therefore these also who speak in the *Astraba* of Plautus [b] :

> Follow now closely,[c] Polybadiscus, I wish to overtake
>   my hope.—
> Heavens I surely do : I'm glad to overtake her whom
>   I hope :

because they speak without *sponte* ' feeling of success,' the youth who speaks does not truly ' hope,' nor does the girl who is ' hoped for.' [d]

74. *Sponsor* and *praes* and *vas* are not the same thing, nor are the matters identical from which these terms come; but they develop out of similar situations.[a] Thus a *praes* is one who is asked by the magistrate that he *praestat* ' make a guarantee ' to the state ; from which, also when he answers, he says, " I am your *praes*." He was called a *vas*

Spr.[3] iii. 89.   [d] *Sperata*, a regular term for the object of a young man's love.

§ 74.   [a] Varro apparently says that a *sponsor* is one who undertakes an engagement toward an individual or individuals ; a *praes* is one who undertakes an engagement on his own behalf, toward the state ; a *vas* is one who guarantees another person's engagement toward the state.

latus, qui pro altero vadimonium promittebat. Consuetudo erat, cum re*us*[3] parum esset idoneus inceptis rebus, ut pro se alium daret ; a quo caveri[4] postea lege coeptum[5] est ab his, qui praedia venderent, vadem ne darent ; ab eo ascribi coeptum[5] in lege mancipiorum :

> Vadem ne poscerent nec dabitur.

75. Canere,[1] accanit et succanit ut canto et cantatio ex Camena permutato pro M N.[2] Ab eo quod semel, canit, si s*a*epius, cantat. Hinc cantitat, item alia ; nec sine canendo ⟨tubicines, liticines, cornicines⟩,[3] tibicines dicti : omnium enim horum quoda⟨m⟩[4] canere ; etiam bucinator a vocis similitudine et cantu dictus.

76. Oro ab ore et perorat et exorat et oratio et orator et osculum dictum. Indidem omen, ornamentum ; alterum quod ex ore primum elatum est, osmen dictum; alterum nunc cum propositione dicitur vulgo ornamentum, quod sicut olim ornamenta[1]

---

[3] *For* reos.   [4] *For* cavari.   [5] *For* caeptum.
§ 75. [1] *For* canerae.   [2] *Mue., for* N.M.   [3] *Added by L. Sp., after Mue. recognized the lacuna and its contents, but set it after* tibicines *; cf.* v. 91.   [4] *Kent ;* quoddam Canal *; for* quod a.
§ 76. [1] *GS., for* ornamentum.

---

§ 75.   [a] The words explained in this section belong together, except *Camena*, which stands apart.   [b] Either ' sing ' or ' play on an instrument.'   [c] Usually in the plural ; Italian goddesses of springs and waters, regularly identified with the Greek Muses.   [d] The insertion in the text is rendered necessary by *omnium horum* ; *cf.* also critical note.   [e] *Quodam,* ablative with *canere.*
§ 76.   [a] These words are from *os,* except *omen, ornamentum, oscines.*
242

' bondsman ' who promised bond for another. It was the custom, that when a party in a suit was not considered capable of fulfilling his engagements, he should give another as bondsman for him ; from which they later began to provide by law against those who should sell their real estate, that they should not offer themselves as bondsmen. From this, they began to add the provision in the law about the transfer of properties, that

> " they should not demand a bondsman, nor will a
> bondsman be given."

75.*a* *Canere* *b* ' to sing,' *accanit* ' he sings to ' something, and *succanit* ' he sings a second part,' like *canto* ' I sing ' and *cantatio* ' song,' from *Camena* *c* ' Muse,' with N substituted for M. From the fact that a person sings once, he *canit* ; if he sings more often, he *cantat*. From this, *cantitat* ' he sings repeatedly,' and likewise other words ; nor without *canere* ' singing, playing ' are the *tubicines* ' trumpeters,' named, and the *liticines* ' cornetists,' *cornicines* ' horn-blowers,' *d* *tibicines* ' pipes-players ' : for *canere* ' playing ' on some special instrument *e* belongs to all these. The *bucinator* ' trumpeter ' also was named from the likeness of the sound and the *cantus* ' playing.'

76.*a* *Oro* ' I beseech ' was so called from *os* ' mouth,' and so were *perorat* ' he ends his speech ' and *exorat* ' he gains by pleading,' and *oratio* ' speech ' and *orator* ' speaker ' and *osculum* ' kiss.' From the same, *omen* ' presage ' and *ornamentum* ' ornament ' : because the former was first uttered from the *os* ' mouth,' it was called *osmen* ; the latter is now commonly used in the singular with the general idea of ornament, but as formerly most of the scenic poets use it in

VARRO

scaenici plerique dicunt. Hinc oscines dicuntur apud
augures, quae ore faciunt auspicium.

VIII. 77.   Tertium gradum agendi esse dicunt, ubi
quid faciant ; in eo propter similitudinem agendi et
faciendi et gerendi quidam error his qui putant esse
unum.   Potest enim aliquid facere et non agere, ut
poeta facit fabulam et non agit, contra actor agit et
⟨non⟩[1] facit, et sic a poeta fabula fit, non agitur, ab
actore agitur, non fit.   Contra imperator quod dicitur
res gerere, in eo neque facit neque agit, sed gerit, id
est sustinet, tralatum ab his qui onera[2] gerunt, quod
hi sustinent.

78.   Proprio nomine dicitur facere a facie, qui rei
quam facit imponit faciem.   Ut fictor cum dicit fingo,
figuram imponit, quom dicit formo,[1] formam, sic cum
dicit facio, faciem imponit ; a qua facie discernitur, ut
dici possit aliud esse vestimentum, aliud vas, sic item
quae fiunt apud fabros, fictores, item alios alia.   Qui
quid[2] amministrat, cuius opus non extat quod sub

§ 77.   [1] *Omitted in F.*   [2] *G, H, for* honera *F.*
§ 78.   [1] *L. Sp., for* informo.   [2] *Aug., for* quicquid.

---

[b] Found only in the plural in the scenic poets, who used
it of ornaments for the head and face (*os*) ; it is a derivative
of *ornare* ' to adorn,' which comes from *ordo ordinis.*
[c] From prefix *ops*+*can*- ' sing ' ; *cf. o(p)s-tendere* ' to show.'
§ 77.   [a] *Cf.* vi. 41-42.   [b] The distinction is almost
impossible to imitate in translation, but the argument is good
so far as the examples in the text are concerned.
§ 78.   [a] *Facies* is from *facere.*

244

the plural.[b] From this, *oscines* [c] ' singing birds ' are spoken of among the augurs, which indicate their premonitions by the *os* ' mouth.'

VIII. 77. The third stage of action [a] is, they say, that in which they *faciunt* ' make ' something : in this, on account of the likeness among *agere* ' to act ' and *facere* ' to make ' and *gerere* ' to carry or carry on,' a certain error is committed by those who think that it is only one thing.[b] For a person can *facere* something and not *agere* it, as a poet *facit* ' makes ' a play and does not act it, and on the other hand the actor *agit* ' acts ' it and does not make it, and so a play *fit* ' is made ' by the poet, not acted, and *agitur* ' is acted ' by the actor, not made. On the other hand, the general, in that he is said to *gerere* ' carry on ' affairs, in this neither *facit* ' makes ' nor *agit* ' acts,' but *gerit* ' carries on,' that is, supports, a meaning transferred from those who *gerunt* ' carry ' burdens, because they support them.

78. In its literal sense *facere* ' to make ' is from *facies* [a] ' external appearance ' : he is said *facere* ' to make ' a thing, who puts a *facies* ' external appearance ' on the thing which he *facit* ' makes.' As the *fictor* ' image-maker,' when he says " *Fingo* ' I shape,' " puts a *figura* ' shape ' on the object, and when he says " *Formo* ' I form,' " puts a *forma* ' form ' on it, so when he says " *Facio* ' I make,' " he puts a *facies* ' external appearance ' on it ; by this external appearance there comes a distinction, so that one thing can be said to be a garment, another a dish, and likewise the various things that are made by the carpenters, the image-makers, and other workers. He who furnishes a service, whose work does not stand out in concrete form so as to come under the observation of our

245

sensu⟨m⟩[3] veniat, ab agitatu, ut dixi, magis agere
quam facere putatur ; sed quod his magis promiscue
quam diligenter consuetudo est usa, translaticiis
utimur verbis : nam et qui dicit, facere verba dicimus,
et qui aliquid agit, non esse inficientem.

79. ⟨Et facere lumen,[1] faculam⟩[2] qui adlucet,
dicitur. Lucere ab luere, ⟨quod⟩ et[3] luce dissolvuntur tenebrae ; ab luce Noctiluca,[4] quod propter lucem
amissam is cultus institutus. Acquirere est ad et
qu*a*erere ; ipsum qu*a*erere ab eo quod quae res ut
reciperetur datur opera ; a qu*a*erendo qu*a*estio, ab
his *tum* qu*a*estor.[5]

80. Video a visu, ⟨id a vi⟩[1] : qui⟨n⟩que[2] enim
sensuum maximus in oculis : nam cum sensus nullus
quod abest mille passus sentire possit, oculorum
sensus vis usque pervenit ad stellas. Hinc :

> Visenda vigilant, vigilium invident.

Et Acci[3] :

[3] H, *Aldus, for* sensu.
  § 79. [1] *Added by GS.* [2] *Added by Fay, from Plautus,
Persa,* 515. [3] quod et *Kent;* quod *A. Sp.; for* et.
[4] *After* Noctiluca, *L. Sp. deleted* lucere item ab luce, *a marginal gloss that had crept into the text.* [5] *Kent, for* con-
questor.
  § 80. [1] *Added by L. Sp.* [2] *For* qui que. [3] *Kent, for*
atti.

[b] vi. 41-42.
  § 79. [a] *Wrong etymology.* [b] This sentence, if properly
reconstructed, goes with the preceding section. [c] Wrong.
[d] As *dis-so-luuntur,* which is in fact its origin. [e] This
sentence is out of place, but its proper place cannot be determined ; *cf.* v. 81. [f] Correct etymologies, except that of
quaerere itself.
  § 80. [a] *Video* is to be kept distinct from *vis* and from
vigilium. [b] Part of a verse from an unknown play, in

physical senses, is, from his *agitatus* ' action, motion,' as I have said,[b] thought rather *agere* ' to act ' than *facere* ' to make ' something ; but because general practice has used these words indiscriminately rather than with care, we use them in transferred meanings ; for he who *dicit* ' says ' something, we say *facere* ' makes ' words, and he who *agit* ' acts ' something, we say is not *inficiens* ' failing to do ' something.

79. And he who lights a *faculam* [a] ' torch,' is said to *facere* ' make ' a light.[b] *Lucere* ' to shine,' from *luere* [c] ' to loose,' because it is also by the light that the shades of night *dissolvuntur* [d] ' are loosed apart ' ; from *lux* ' light ' comes *Noctiluca* ' Shiner of the Night,' because this worship was instituted on account of the loss of the daylight. *Acquirere* [e] ' to acquire ' is *ad* ' in addition ' and *quaerere* ' to seek ' ; *quaerere* itself is from this, that attention is given to *quae res* ' what thing ' is to be got back ; from *quaerere* comes *quaestio* ' question ' ; then from these, *quaestor* ' investigator, treasurer.' [f]

80. *Video* [a] ' I see,' from *visus* ' sight,' this from *vis* ' strength ' ; for the greatest of the five senses is in the eyes. For while no one of the senses can feel that which is a mile away, the strength of the sense of the eyes reaches even to the stars. From this [b] :

> They watch for what is to be seen, but hate to
> stay awake.[c]

Also the verse of Accius [d] :

which the persons are watching the night sky for omens. [e] *Invidere* ' to look at with dislike ' originally took a direct object, as here ; *cf.* Cicero, *Tusc.* iii. 9. 20. [d] If properly reconstituted, an iambic tetrameter catalectic, referring to Actaeon, who inadvertently beheld Artemis bathing with the nymphs.

VARRO

Cum illud o⟨c⟩*uli*⟨s⟩ violav*it*[4] ⟨is⟩,[5] qui in*vidit*[6]
invidendum.

A quo etiam violavit virginem pro vit⟨i⟩avit dicebant ;
aeque eadem modestia potius cum muliere fuisse
quam concubuisse dicebant.

81. Cerno idem valet : itaque pro video ait Ennius :

Lumen—iubarne ?—in caelo cerno.

Ca*ss*ius[1] :

Sensumque inesse et motum in membris cerno.

Dictum cerno a cereo, id est a creando ; dictum ab eo
quod cum quid creatum est, tunc denique videtur.
Hinc fines capilli d*i*scripti,[2] quod finis videtur, discrimen ; et qu*o*d[3] in testamento ⟨cernito⟩,[4] id est
facito videant te esse heredem : itaque in cretione
adhibere iubent testes. Ab eodem est quod ait
Medea :

Ter sub armis malim v*i*tam[5] cernere,
Quam semel modo parere ;

quod, ut decernunt de vita eo tempore, multorum
videtur vitae finis.

[4] *Mue.*, *for* obliuio lavet (obviolavit *Aug.*, *with B*).
[5] *Added by Kent, metri gratia.* [6] *Kent ;* vidit *Mue. ;*
for incidit.
§ 81. [1] *Schoell, marginal note in his copy of A. Sp.'s
edition, for* canius. [2] *A. Sp., for* descripti. [3] *Turnebus,
for* qui id. [4] *Added by Turnebus.* [5] *Bentinus, from
Nonius Marc. 261. 22 M., for* multa.

---

[6] See note *c.* [1] *Invidendum* with negative prefix *in-*,
unlike the preceding word ; *cf. infectum* meaning both
' stained ' and ' not done.'
§ 81. [a] Literally ' separate ' ; hence ' distinguish, see,'
and also ' discriminate, decide.' *Cerno* has no connexion

> When that he violated with his eyes,
> Who looked upon *e* what ought not to be seen.*f*

From which moreover they used to say *violavit* ' he did violence to ' a girl instead of *vitiavit* ' ruined ' her ; and similarly, with the same modesty, they used to say rather that a man *fuit* ' was ' with a woman, than that he *concubuit* ' lay ' with her.

81. *Cerno* *a* has the same meaning ; therefore Ennius *b* uses it for *video* :

> I see light in the sky—can it be dawn ?

Cassius *c* says :

> I see that in her limbs there's feeling still and motion.

Cerno ' I see ' is said from *cereo*, that is, *creo* ' I create '; it is said from this fact, that when something has been created, then finally it is seen. From this, the boundary-lines of the parted hair,*d* because a boundary-line is seen, got the name *discrimen* ' separation '; and the *cernito* ' let him decide,' *e* which is in a will, that is, make them see that you are heir : therefore in the *cretio* ' decision ' they direct that the heir bring witnesses. From the same is that which Medea says *f* :

> I'd rather thrice decide, in battle wild,
> My life or death, than bear but once a child.

Because, when they *decernunt* ' decide ' about life at that time, the end of many persons' lives is seen.

with *creo*. *b* *Trag. Rom. Frag.*, verse 338 Ribbeck³ ; *R.O.L.* i. 226-227 Warmington ; from the *Ajax* ; *cf.* vi. 6 and vii. 76. *c* Fitting Cassius's play *Lucretia* ; *cf.* vi. 7 and vii. 72. *d* *Capillus* in the singular was used as a collective by Varro, according to Charisius, i. 104. 20 Keil. *e* *Cf.* Gaius, *Institut.* ii. 174. *f* Ennius, *Medea*, 222-223 Ribbeck³ ; *R.O.L.* i. 316-317 Warmington ; translated from Euripides, *Medea*, 250-251.

82. Spectare dictum ab ⟨specio⟩[1] antiquo, quo etiam Ennius usus :

⟨Q⟩uos[2] Epulo postquam spexit,

et quod in auspiciis distributum est qui habent spectionem, qui non habeant, et quod in auguriis etiam nunc augures dicunt avem specere. Consuetudo com⟨m⟩unis quae cum praeverbi⟨i⟩s coniun⟨c⟩ta fuerunt etiam nunc servat, ut aspicio, conspicio, respicio, suspicio, despicio,[3] sic alia ; in quo etiam expecto quod spectare volo. Hinc speculo⟨r⟩,[4] hinc speculum, quod in eo specimus imaginem. Specula, de quo prospicimus. Speculator, quem mittimus ante, ut respiciat quae volumus. Hinc qui oculos inunguimus quibus specimus, specillum.

83. Ab auribus verba videntur dicta audio et ausculto ; au*res*[1] ab a*veo*,[2] quod his avemus di⟨s⟩cere[3] semper, quod Ennius videtur ἔτυμον ostendere velle in Alexandro cum ait :

Iam dudum ab ludis animus atque aures avent,
Avide expectantes nuntium.

Propter hanc aurium aviditatem theatra replentur. Ab audiendo etiam auscultare declinatum, quod hi

§ 82. [1] *Added by Aug.* [2] *A. Sp., from Festus,* 330 b 32 M., *for* uos. [3] *M, Laetus, for* didestspicio. [4] *Canal. for* specula.
§ 83. [1] *Mue., for* audio. [2] *Laetus, for* abaucto. [3] *Aug., for* dicere.

§ 82. [a] *Annales,* 421 Vahlen[2]: *R.O.L.* i. 148-149 Warmington; given in better form by Festus, 330 b 32 M. : *Quos ubi rex* ⟨Ep⟩*ulo spexit de cotibus* (=*cautibus*) *celsis.* Epulo was a king of the Istrians, who fought against the Romans in 178–177 B.C. ; *cf.* Livy, xli. 1, 4, 11. [b] Page 20 Regell. [c] Page 17 Regell.
§ 83. [a] *Auris, audio, ausculto* belong ultimately together,

82. *Spectare* ' to see ' is said from the old word *specere*, which in fact Ennius used [a] :

> After Epulo saw them,

and because in the taking of the auspices [b] there is a division into those who have the *spectio* ' watch-duty ' and those who have not ; and because in the taking of the auguries even now the augurs say [c] *specere* ' to watch ' a bird. Common practice even now keeps the compounds made with prefixes, as *aspicio* ' I look at,' *conspicio* ' I observe,' *respicio* ' I look back at,' *suspicio* ' I look up at,' *despicio* ' I look down upon,' and similarly others ; in which group is also *expecto* ' I look for, expect ' that which I wish *spectare* ' to see.' From this, *speculor* ' I watch ' ; from this, *speculum* ' mirror,' because in it we *specimus* ' see ' our image. *Specula* ' look-out,' that from which we *prospicimus* ' look forth.' *Speculator* ' scout,' whom we send ahead, that he *respiciat* ' may look attentively ' at what we wish. From this, the instrument with which we anoint our eyes by which we *specimus* ' see,' is called a *specillum* ' eye-spatula.'

83. From the *aures* ' ears ' seem to have been said the words *audio* ' I hear ' and *ausculto* ' I listen, heed ' ; *aures* ' ears ' from *aveo* [a] ' I am eager,' because with these we are ever eager to learn, which Ennius seems to wish to show as the radical in his *Alexander*,[b] when he says :

> A long time eager have been my spirit and my ears,
> Awaiting eagerly some message from the games.

It is on account of this eagerness of the ears that the theatres are filled. From *audire* ' to hear ' is derived also *auscultare* ' to listen, heed,' because they are said

but are not to be connected with *aveo*.   [b] *Trag. Rom. Frag.* 34-35 Ribbeck[3]; *R.O.L.* i. 236-237 Warmington.

auscultare dicuntur qui auditis parent, a quo dictum
poetae :

Audio, ⟨h⟩aut[4] ausculto.[5]

Littera commutata dicitur odor olor, hinc olet et
odorari et odoratus[6] et odora res, sic al⟨ia⟩.[7]

84. Ore edo, sorbeo, bibo, poto. Edo a Graeco
ἔδω,[1] hinc esculentum et esca ⟨et⟩ edulia[2] ; et quod
Graece γεύεται,[3] Latine gustat. Sorbere, item bibere a vocis sono, ut fervere aquam ab eius rei simili
sonitu. Ab eadem lingua, quod πότον, potio, unde
poculum, potatio, repotia.[4] Indidem puteus, quod
sic Graecum antiquum, non ut nunc φρέαρ dictum.

85. A manu manupretium[1] ; mancipium, quod
manu capitur ; ⟨quod⟩[2] coniungit plures manus,
manipulus ; manipularis, manica. Manubrium, quod
manu tenetur. Mantelium, ubi manus terguntur. . . .[3]

---

[4] *Aug. (quoting a friend), for* aut.   [5] *B, Laetus, for* ob-
sculto.   [6] *L. Sp., for* odoratur.   [7] sic alia ab ore *A. Sp.,
for* sic ab ore (*Mue. deleted* sic, *and set* ab ore *at the beginning of the next section*).

§ 84.   [1] *Aldus, for* edon.   [2] *Canal ;* escae edulia *Aldus ;
for* escaedulia.   [3] *Victorius, for* geuete.   [4] *Aug. (quoting a friend), for* repotatio.

§ 85.   [1] *Victorius, for* mantur praetium.   [2] *Added by
G, H.*   [3] *Lacuna recognized by Aug.*

---

[6] After *susculto,* seemingly a lacuna, as the transition from
hearing to smell is abrupt. *Odor* is not connected with
audio ; olor, with the well-known change of *d* to *l,* is not
attested elsewhere in Latin literature, but is found in the
glosses and survives in the Romance languages.

§ 84.   [a] The etymological connexions are correct (except
for *puteus ; cf.* v. 25 note *a*), but the Latin words are cognate

252

auscultare who obey what they have heard ; from which comes the poet's saying :

I hear, but do not heed.

With the change of a letter are formed *odor* ^c or *olor* ' smell ' ; from this, *olet* ' it emits an odour,' and *odorari* ' to detect by the odour,' and *odoratus* ' perfumed,' and an *odora* ' fragrant ' thing, and similarly other words.

84.^a With the mouth *edo* ' I eat,' *sorbeo* ' I suck in,' *bibo* ' I drink,' *poto* ' I drink.' *Edo* from Greek ἔδω ' I eat ' ; from this, *esculentum* ' edible ' and *esca* ' food ' and *edulia* ' eatables ' ; and because in Greek it is γεύεται ' he tastes,' in Latin it is *gustat*. *Sorbere* ' to suck in,' and likewise *bibere* ' to drink,' from the sound ^b of the word, as for water *fervere* ' to boil ' is from the sound like the action. From the same language, because there it is πότον ' drink,' is *potio* ' drink,' whence *poculum* ' cup,' *potatio* ' drinking-bout,' *repotia* ' next day's drinking.' From the same comes *puteus* ' well,' because the old Greek word was like this, and not φρέαρ as it is now.

85. From *manus* ' hand ' comes *manupretium* ' workman's wages ' ; *mancipium* ' possession of property,' because it *capitur* ' is taken ' *manu* ' in hand ' ; *manipulus* ' maniple,' because it unites several *manus* ' hands ' ; *manipularis* ' soldier of a maniple,' *manica* ' sleeve.' *Manubrium* ' handle,' because it is grasped by the *manus* ' hand.' *Mantelium* ' towel,' on which the *manus* ' hands ' *terguntur* ' are wiped.' . . .^a

with the Greek, not derived from it.   ^b These words are not onomatopoeic.

§ 85.   ^a The gap is serious : the subject matter shifts abruptly, and many appropriate topics are missed, such as the actions of the feet, and some further discussion of the distinctions among *agere*, *facere*, *gerere*, *cf.* § 77.

VARRO

IX. 86. Nunc primum ponam ⟨de⟩[1] Censoriis
Tabulis :

Ubi noctu in templum censor[2] auspicaverit atque de
caelo nuntium erit, praeconi[3] sic imperato[4] ut viros vocet :
" Quod bonum fortunatum felix salutareque siet[5] populo Romano Quiriti*bus*[6] reique publicae populi Romani Quiritium
mihique collegaeque meo, fidei magistratuique nostro :
omnes Quirites pedites armatos, privatosque, curatores
omnium tribuum, si quis pro se sive *pro*[7] altero rationem dari
volet, voca[8] inlicium huc ad me."
87. Praeco in templo primum vocat, postea de moeris[1]
item vocat. Ubi lu*cet*,[2] censor⟨es⟩[3] scribae magistratus
murra unguentisque unguentur. Ubi praetores tribunique
plebei quique in*licium*[4] vocati sunt venerunt, censores inter
se sortiuntur, uter lustrum faciat. Ubi templum factum est,
post tum conventionem habet qui lustrum conditurus est.

88. In Commentariis Consularibus scriptum sic
inveni :

Qui exercitum imperaturus erit, accenso dicito : " C.[1]
Calpurni, voca inlicium omnes Quirites huc ad me." Accensus
dicit sic : " Omnes Quirites, inlicium vos ite[2] huc ad iudices."
" C. Calpurni," cos.[3] dicit, " voca ad conventionem omnes
Quirites huc ad me." Accensus dicit sic : " Omnes Quirites,

§ 86. [1] *Added by Laetus.* [2] *Aldus, for* censora *F*[1]
(censura *F*[2]). [3] *Aldus, for* praeconis. [4] *Possibly the
verbs coordinate to* imperato *in this section and in* § 87
*should all be imperatives ; but the manuscript reading sup-
ports this only for* imperato *and partially for* dicito, § 88.
[5] *Laetus, for* salutare quesierit. [6] *Brissonius, with b, for*
quiritium. [7] *Sciop., for* si uerbo. [8] *Aug., with B, for*
uocat.
§ 87. [1] *Aug., with B, for* post eadem aeris. [2] *Aug., for*
licet. [3] *L. Sp., for* censor. [4] *Sciop., for* in consilium.
§ 88. [1] *Bruns-Mommsen, for* dicit hoc. [2] *A. Sp. ;* ite
Sciop. ; for visite. [3] *Sciop., for* calpurnicos (*punctuation
by Mue., after Gronov.*).

§ 86. [a] The preparation for the *lustratio*, at the com-
pletion of the census. [b] Page 21 Regell. [c] Technical

IX. 86. Now first I shall put down some extracts from the *Censors' Records* [a] :

When by night the censor has gone into the sacred precinct to take the auspices,[b] and a message has come from the sky, he shall thus command the herald to call the men: "May this be good, fortunate, happy, and salutary to the Roman people—the Quirites—and to the government of the Roman people—the Quirites—and to me and my colleague, to our honesty and our office : All the citizen soldiers under arms and private citizens as spokesmen of all the tribes, call hither to me with an *inlicium* [c] 'invitation,' in case any one for himself or for another wishes a reckoning [d] to be given."

87. The herald calls them first in the sacred precinct, afterwards he calls them likewise from the walls. When it is dawn, the censors, the clerks, and the magistrates are anointed with myrrh and ointments. When the praetors and the tribunes of the people and those who have been called to the invitation meeting have come, the censors cast lots with each other, as to which one of them shall conduct the ceremony of purification. When the sacred precinct [a] has been determined, then after that he who is to perform the purification conducts the assembly.

88. In the *Consular Commentaries* I have found the following account :

He who is about to summon the citizen-army, shall say to his assistant, "Gaius Calpurnius,[a] call all the citizens hither to me, with an *inlicium* 'invitation.'" The assistant speaks thus : "All citizens, come ye hither to the judges,[b] to an invitation meeting." "Gaius Calpurnius," says the consul, "call all the citizens hither to me, to a gathering." The assistant speaks thus : "All citizens, come hither to the judges, to a

---

name for an invitation to a specially called assembly ; *cf.* § 93–§ 94. With *vocare*, *inlicium* is an inner object. [d] That is, makes a protest against the censor's rating.

§ 87. [a] This is another *templum*, in the Campus Martius.

§ 88. [a] Used as a type name, or taken from the records of some specific instance. [b] An old name for the consuls ; *cf.* Livy, iii. 55. 11.

ite ad conventionem huc ad iudices." Dein consul eloquitur ad exercitum: "Impero qua convenit ad comitia centuriata."

89. Quare hic[1] accenso, illic praeconi dicit, haec est causa : in aliquot rebus item[2] ut praeco accensus acciebat,[3] a quo accensus quoque dictus. Accensum[4] solitum ciere Boeotia ostendit, quam comoediam[5] alii ⟨Plauti, alii Aquili⟩[6] esse dicunt, hoc versu :

Ubi primum accensus clamarat meridiem.

Hoc idem Cosconius in Actionibus scribit praetorem accensum solitum tum esse iubere, ubi ei videbatur horam esse tertiam, inclamare horam tertiam esse, itemque meridiem et horam nonam.

90. Circum muros[1] mitti solitum[2] quo modo inliceret populum in eum ⟨locum⟩,[3] unde vocare posset ad contionem, non solum ad consules et censores, sed etiam quaestores, Commentarium indicat vetus Anquisitionis[4] M'.[5] Sergii, Mani filii, quaestoris,[6] qui capitis accusavit ⟨T⟩rogum[7] ; in qua[8] sic est :

§ 89. [1] *Aldus, for* hinc. [2] *Bentinus, for* idem. [3] *Lactus, for* accipiebat. [4] *Laetus, for* ad censum. [5] *For* commaediam. [6] *Added by Riese.*

§ 90. [1] moeros *Ursinus, for* auras. [2] *Aug., for* solitus. [3] *Added by Aug., cf.* § 94. [4] *Aug., for* inquisitionis *; cf.* § 92. [5] *L. Sp., for* M. [6] *For* questores. [7] *B, Vertranius, for* rogum *; cf.* § 92. [8] *Aug., for* in aqua.

[c] From early times, the chief deliberative and legislative assembly of the Roman people.

§ 89. [a] Properly, passive participle of *ac-censere* ' to reckon thereto,' hence one assigned to help another ; it has no connexion with *acciere*. [b] Gellius, iii. 3. 4, says that Varro, on the basis of style, attributed the *Boeotia* to Plautus, though it was reputed to be a work of Aquilius. [c] *Com. Rom. Frag.* II, page 39 Ribbeck[3] ; Plautus, *Frag.* verse 30

gathering." Then the consul makes declaration to the army: " I order you to go by the proper way to the centuriate assembly.[c] "

89. Why the latter speaks to the *accensus* ' assistant ' and the former to the herald—this is the reason: in some affairs the *accensus* [a] ' assistant ' *acciebat* ' gave the call ' just like a herald, from which the *accensus* also got his name. That the *accensus* was accustomed *ciere* ' to give the call,' is shown by the *Boeotia*,[b] a comedy which some say is a work of Plautus, and others say is a work of Aquilius, in this verse [c] :

Soon as the aide had called that 'twas the hour of noon.

Cosconius [d] records the same in his work on *Civil Cases*, that the praetor had the habit of ordering his *accensus*, at the time when he thought that it is the third hour, to call out that it is the third hour, and likewise midday and the ninth hour.[e]

90. That someone was regularly sent around the walls, *inlicere* ' to entice ' [a] the people to that place from which he might call them to the gathering, not only before the consuls and the censors, but also before the quaestors, is shown by an old *Commentary on the Indictment* which the quaestor Manius Sergius [b] son of Manius brought against Trogus, accusing him of a capital offence ; in which there is the following :

Ritschl.   [d] Page 109 Funaioli ; page 10 Huschke.   [e] If he wished to divide the day evenly, this means the end (not the beginning) of the third and the ninth hours.

§ 90.   [a] The origin of *inlicium* seems to be, as Varro says, from the fact that the announcer *inliciebat* ' enticed ' the people to the meeting.   [b] Sergius and his commentary, and the case against Trogus, are entirely unknown except from this passage and § 92 ; but the mention of praetors sets the incident after 242 B.C., when the number of praetors was increased from one to two.

257

VARRO

91. Auspicio o⟨pe⟩ram des *et*[1] in templo auspic*es*,[2]
*t*um[3] aut ad praetorem aut ad consulem mittas auspicium
petitum ; com*i*⟨ti⟩atum[4] praetor ⟨r⟩e*um*[5] vocet ad te, et eum
de muris vocet praeco ; id imperare ⟨o⟩portet.[6] Corni-
c⟨in⟩em[7] ad privati ianuam et in Arcem mittas, ubi canat.[8]
Collegam[9] rog*es*[10] ut comitia edicat[11] de rostris et argentarii
tabe⟨r⟩nas occludant. Patres censeant exqu*ae*ras et adesse
iubeas ; magistratus censea⟨n⟩t[12] ex⟨qua⟩*e*ra⟨s⟩,[13] consules
praetores tribunosque plebis collegasque ⟨t⟩uos,[14] et in
templo adesse iubeas omnes[15] ; ac cum mittas, contionem
a⟨d⟩voces.[16]

92. In eodem Commentario A*n*quisitionis[1] ad extremum scriptum caput edicti hoc est :

Item quod attingat qui de ce*n*soribus[2] classicum ad
comitia centuriata redemptum habent, uti curent eo die quo
die comitia erunt, in Arce classicus canat[3] circumque muros
et ante privati huiusce T. Quinti Trogi scelerosi ostium[4] canat,
et ut in Campo cum primo luci adsiet.[5]

93. Inter id cum circum muros mittitur et cum
contio advocatur, interesse tempus apparet ex his
quae interea fieri in*l*icium[1] scriptum est ; sed ad
comitiatum[2] vocatur populus ideo, quod alia de causa
hic magistratus non potest exercitum urbanum con-

§ 91. [1] *Bergk, for* orande sed. [2] *Mommsen, for* auspiciis. [3] *L. Sp., for* dum. [4] *Sciop., for* commeatum.
[5] *Kent ;* praeco reum *Aug. ; for* praetores. [6] *Laetus, for*
portet. [7] *Aug., with B, for* cornicem. [8] *Aldus, for*
cannat. [9] *Rhol., for* colligam. [10] *Mue., for* rogis.
[11] *Victorius, for* comitiae dicat. [12] *Mue., for* censeat.
[13] *Bergk ;* exquiras *Mue. ; for* extra. [14] *Sciop., for* uos.
[15] *Sciop., for* homines. [16] *B, G, Aug., for* auoces.
§ 92. [1] *Aug., with B, for* acquisitionis. [2] *Aug., with
B, for* decessoribus. [3] *Victorius, for* cannatum.
[4] *Sciop., for* hostium. [5] *Sciop., for* adsit et.
§ 93. [1] *Aldus, for* illicitum *F*[1] (illicium *F*[2]). [2] *Sciop.,
for* comitia tum.

§ 91. [a] The document is addressed to Sergius as quaestor.
[b] Page 21 Regell. [c] The northern summit of the Capito-
258

91. You[a] shall give your attention to the auspices,[b] and take the auspices in the sacred precinct ; then you shall send to the praetor or to the consul the favourable presage which has been sought. The praetor shall call the accused to appear in the assembly before you, and the herald shall call him from the walls : it is proper to give this command. A horn-blower you shall send to the doorway of the private individual and to the Citadel,[c] where the signal is to sound. Your colleague you shall request that from the speaker's stand he proclaim an assembly, and that the bankers shut up their shops.[d] You shall seek that the senators express their opinion, and bid them be present ; you shall seek that the magistrates express their opinion, the consuls, the praetors, the tribunes of the people, and your colleagues, and you shall bid them all be present in the temple ; and when you send the request, you shall summon the gathering.

92. In the same *Commentary on the Indictment*, this is the summing up of the edict written at the end :

Likewise in what pertains to those who have received from the censors the contract for the trumpeter who gives the summons to the centuriate assembly, they shall see to it that on that day, on which the assembly shall take place, the trumpeter shall sound the trumpet on the Citadel and around the walls, and shall sound it before the house-entrance of this accursed Titus Quintius Trogus, and that he be present in the Campus Martius at daybreak.[a]

93. That between the sending around the walls and the calling of the gathering some time elapses, is clear from those things the doing of which in the meantime is written down as the *inlicium* 'invitation' ; but the people is called to appear in the assembly because for any other reason this magistrate[a] cannot call together the citizen-army of the City. The

line. [d] These shops (*cf.* § 59 and note), on both sides of the Forum, were to be closed during the trial of Trogus.

§ 92. [a] In early Latin, *lux* was normally masculine, as in Plautus, *Aul.* 748, *Cist.* 525, *Capt.* 1008 ; Terence, *Adel.* 841.

§ 93. [a] The praetor.

VARRO

vocare ; censor, consul, dictator, interrex potest, quod censor[3] exercitum centuriato constituit quinquennalem, cum lustrare[4] et in urbem ad vexillum ducere debet ; dictator et consul in singulos annos, quod hic exercitui imperare potest quo eat, id quod propter centuriata comitia imperare solent.

94. Quare non est dubium, *quin*[1] hoc inlicium sit, cum circum muros itur, ut populus inliciatur ad magistratus conspectum, qui ⟨vi⟩ros[2] vocare[3] potest, in eum locum unde vox ad contionem vocantis exaudiri possit. Quare una origine illici et inlicis quod in Choro Proserpinae est, et pellexit, quod in *H*ermiona est, cum ait Pacuius :

> Regni alieni cupiditas
> Pellexit.

Sic Elicii Iovis ara[4] in Aventino, ab eliciendo.

95. Hoc nunc aliter fit atque olim, quod augur consuli adest tum cum exercitus imperatur ac pr*a*eit quid eum dicere oporteat. Consul augur⟨i⟩[1] imperare solet, ut i*n*licium[2] vocet, non accenso aut praeconi. Id inceptum credo, cum non adesset accensus ; et nihil intererat cui imperaret, et dicis causa fieba⟨n⟩t[3]

---

[3] *Laetus, for* censorem.   [4] *Scaliger, for* lustraret.
§ 94.   [1] *Vertranius, for* cum.   [2] *L. Sp., for* qui ros.
[3] *Aldus, for* uocari.   [4] *Victorius, for* iobis uisa ara.
§ 95.   [1] *Victorius, for* augur.   [2] *B, Laetus, for* is licium.
[3] *Aug., with B, for* fiebat.

---

[b] This statement refers to the consul only ; the part defining the dictator's powers seems to have fallen out of the text.
§ 94.   [a] *Trag. Rom. Frag.*, page 272 Ribbeck[3], of an unknown poet ; unless *Chorus Proserpinae* is a substitute name for *Eumenides,* a tragedy of Ennius.   [b] *Trag. Rom. Frag.*, verses 170-171 Ribbeck[3] ; *R.O.L.* ii. 226-227 Warmington.
[c] A popular etymology only, since Jupiter could hardly be

censor, the consul, the dictator, the interrex can, because the censor arranges in centuries the citizen-army for a period of five years, when he must ceremonially purify it and lead it to the city under its standards; the dictator and the consul do so every year,[b] because the latter can order the citizen-army where it is to go, a thing which they are accustomed to order on account of the centuriate assembly.

94. Therefore there is no doubt that this is the *inlicium*, when they go around the walls that the people may *inlici* ' be enticed ' before the eyes of the magistrate who has the authority to call the men into that place from which the voice of the one who is calling them to the gathering can be heard. Therefore there come from the same source also *illici* ' to be enticed ' and *inlicis* ' thou enticest,' which are in the *Chorus of Proserpina*,[a] and *pellexit* ' lured,' which is in the *Hermiona*, when Pacuvius says [b] :

> Desire for another's kingdom lured him on.

So also the altar of Jupiter *Elicius* ' the Elicited ' on the Aventine, from *elicere* ' to lure forth.' [c]

95. This is now done otherwise than it was of old, because the augur is present with the consul when the citizen-army is summoned, and says in advance the formulas which he is to say. The consul regularly gives order to the augur, not to the assistant nor to the herald, that he shall call the *inlicium* ' invitation.' I believe that this was begun on an occasion when the assistant was not present; it really made no difference to whom he gave the order, and it was for form's sake

' tricked '; according to G. S. Hopkins, *Indo-European deiwos and Related Words*, 27-32, *Elicius* is a derivative of *liquere* ' to be liquid,' and Jupiter *Elicius* is a rain-god.

quaedam neque item facta neque item dicta semper. Hoc ipsum inlicium scriptum inveni in M. Iunii Commentariis ; quod tamen ⟨inlex apud Plautum in Persa est qui legi non paret⟩,[4] ibidem est quod illicit illex, ⟨f⟩it quo*d*[5] ⟨I⟩[6] cum E et C cum G magnam habet co⟨m⟩munitatem.

X. 96. Sed quoniam in hoc de paucis rebus verba feci plura, de pluribus rebus verba faciam pauca, et potissimum quae in Graeca lingua putant Latina, ut scalpere a σκαλεύειν,[1] sternere a στρωννύειν,[2] lingere a λιχμᾶσθαι,[3] i ab ἴθ⟨ι⟩,[4] ite ab ἴτε,[5] gignitur ⟨a⟩[6] γίγνεται,[7] ferte a φέρετε,[8] provider*e*[9] ⟨a⟩[10] προιδεῖν,[11] errare ab ἔρρειν,[12] ab eo quod dicunt στραγγαλᾶν[13] strangulare, tingue⟨re⟩[14] a τέγγειν.[15] Praeterea ⟨depsere⟩ a δεψῆσ⟨αι⟩[16] ; ab eo quod illi μαλάσσειν[17] nos malaxare, ut gargarissare ab ἀναγαργαρίζεσθαι,[18] putere a πύθεσθαι,[19] domare a δαμάζειν,[20] mulgere ab ἀμέλγειν,[21] pectere a πέκειν,[22] stringere a στλεγγίζειν[23] :

[4] *Added by GS.*   [5] *GS., for* illicite illexit quae *F* (quod *Mue., for* quae).   [6] *Added by Ciacconius apud Aug.*

§ 96.   [1] *Rhol., for* SCOLPSa.&.   [2] *L. Sp., for* STPONYIN.   [3] *L. Sp., for* Λημμωστε.   [4] *A. Sp., for* hϵ.   [5] *L. Sp., for* hτϵ.   [6] *Added by L. Sp.*   [7] *L. Sp., for* YhYNOITϵ.   [8] *L. Sp., for* ferete.   [9] *p, Laetus, for* prouidete.   [10] *Added by GS.*   [11] *Rhol., for* ΠΡωhδϵhN.   [12] *Scaliger, for* ϵRRϵhN.   [13] *L. Sp. (after Buttmann), for* strangalā.   [14] *B, Rhol., for* tingue.   [15] *Buttmann, for* THNKϵΔϵ.   [16] *Ellis (after L. Sp.), for* ades.ψϵC.   [17] *L. Sp., for* ΜΑΛΑΣϵΝ.   [18] *L. Sp., for* aNaPΓaPHCTϵ.   [19] *Canal, for* potare a ΠοΙΘϵCTaϵ.   [20] *L. Sp., for* ΔμαισhΝ.   [21] *Rhol., for* ΑΜϵΛΓΗΝ.   [22] *L. Sp., for* ΠϵΣϵΡϵ.   [23] *GS., for* CRHNΓHΔϵ.

§ 95.   [a] *Iurisprud. Antehadr. Rel.*, i. 39 Bremer.

only that certain things were done, but they were not always said or done in just the same way. This very word *inlicium* I have found written in the *Commentaries* of Marcus Junius [a]; that however *inlex* in Plautus's *Persa* [b] is a person who does not obey the *lex* ' law,' and in the same work *illex* is also that which *illicit* ' entices,' [c] is the result of the fact that I has much in common with E and C with G.

X. 96. But since in this connexion I have spoken at length on a few matters, I shall speak briefly on a number of topics, and especially on the Latin words whose origin they think [a] to be in the Greek tongue [b]: as *scalpere* ' to engrave ' from σκαλεύειν ' to scratch,' *sternere* ' to spread out ' from στρωννύειν, *lingere* ' to lick up ' from λιχμᾶσθαι, *i* ' go thou ' from ἴθι, *ite* ' go ye ' from ἴτε, *gignitur* ' he is born ' from γίγνεται, *ferte* ' bear ye ' from φέρετε, *providere* ' to act with foresight ' from προιδεῖν ' to see ahead, foresee,' *errare* ' to stray ' from ἔρρειν ' to go away '; *strangulare* ' to strangle ' from the word στραγγαλᾶν, *tinguere* ' to dip, dye ' from τέγγειν. Besides, there is *depsere* ' to knead ' from δεψῆσαι; from the word which they call μαλάσσειν, we say *malaxare* ' to soften,' as *gargarissare* ' to gargle ' from ἀναγαργαρίζεσθαι, *putere* ' to stink ' from πύθεσθαι ' to decay,' *domare* ' to subdue ' from δαμάζειν, *mulgere* ' to milk ' from ἀμέλγειν, *pectere* ' to comb ' from πέκειν, *stringere* ' to scrape '

[b] *Persa*, 408 and 597. [c] The insertion by GS. must be approximately correct, in view of Festus, 113. 6, Nonius, 446. 34, *Corp. Gloss. Lat.* vi-vii. s.v. *illex*.

§ 96. [a] Page 116 Funaioli. [b] These Latin words are mostly cognate with the Greek words, not derived from them; but *strangulare, depsere, malaxare, gargarissare,* and *runcina* are derived from the Greek words, and *errare* and *stringere* are not related at all to the alleged Greek sources.

id enim a στλεγγίς,[24] ut runcinare a runcina, cuius
ῥυκάνη[25] origo Graeca.

XI. 97. Quod ad origines verborum huius libri
pertinet, satis multas arbitror positas huius generis[1] ;
desistam, et quoniam de hisce rebus tri⟨s⟩[2] libros ad
te mittere institui, de oratione soluta duo, poetica
unum, et ex soluta oratione ad te misi duo, priorem
de locis et quae in locis sunt, hunc de temporibus et
quae cum his sunt coniuncta, deinceps in proximo de
poeticis verborum originibus scribere in⟨cipiam⟩.[3]

---

[24] *GS., for* CHNΓHMHC.   [25] *Scaliger, for* PHXaNε.
§ 97. [1] *For* gaeneris.   [2] *Laetus, for* tri.   [3] *Groth, with*
a, b, for in *F, after which the space of twenty lines is left*
vacant ; for incipiam, *cf.* viii. 1 *and* viii. 25.

from στλεγγίζειν : for this is from στλεγγίς ' scraper,' as *runcinare* ' to plane ' from *runcina* ' plane,' of which ῥυκάνη is the Greek source.

XI. 97. As to what concerns the sources of the words which belong to this book, sufficiently numerous examples of this kind have, I think, been set down ; I shall stop, and since I have undertaken to send you three books on these topics, two about prose composition and one about poetical, and I have sent you the two about prose, the former about places and the things that are in them, the latter about time-ideas and those things which are associated with them, I shall at last, in the next book, begin to write of the sources of words used in poetry.

⟨M. TERENTI VARRONIS
DE LINGUA LATINA

LIBER VI EXPLICIT ; INCIPIT

LIBER VII⟩[1]

HIC DEEST IN EXEMPLARI FOLIUM I IN QUO EST
PRINCIPIUM LIBRI VII[2]

I. 1. ⟨DIFFICILIA sunt explicatu poetarum vocabula.
Saepe enim significationem aliquam prioribus temporibus impositam⟩[1] repens ruina operuit,[2] ⟨a⟩ut[3]
verbum quod conditum est e quibus litteris oportet
inde post aliqua dempta, sic[4] obscurior[5] fit voluntas
impos⟨i⟩toris.[6] Non reprehendendum igitur in illis
qui in scrutando verbo litteram adiciunt aut demunt,
quo[7] facilius quid sub ea voce subsit videri[8] possit :
ut[9] enim facilius obscuram operam ⟨M⟩yrmecidis[10] ex

---

[1] *The lost heading is restored after that of Book VI.*   [2] *F
contains this statement of loss ; B and the Leipzig codex
contain an interpolated beginning :* Temporum vocabula et
eorum quae coniuncta sunt, aut in agendo fiunt, aut cum
tempore aliquo enuntiantur, priore libro dixi. In hoc dicam
de poeticis vocabulis et eorum originibus, in quis multa
difficilia : nam, *after which comes* repens ruina aperuit.

266

MARCUS TERENTIUS VARRO'S
ON THE LATIN LANGUAGE

BOOK VI ENDS, AND HERE BEGINS

BOOK VII

AT THIS POINT, IN THE MODEL COPY, ONE LEAF IS
LACKING, ON WHICH IS THE BEGINNING OF BOOK VII

I. 1. THE words of the poets are hard to expound.
For often some meaning that was fixed in olden times
has been buried by a sudden catastrophe, or in a word
whose proper make-up of letters is hidden after some
elements have been taken away from it, the intent of
him who applied the word becomes in this fashion
quite obscure. There should be no rebuking then of
those who in examining a word add a letter or take
one away, that what underlies this expression may be
more easily perceived : just as, for instance, that the
eyes may more easily see Myrmecides' indistinct

---

§ 1. ¹ *Proposed by A. Sp., as the most probable indication
of what immediately preceded.* ² *Turnebus, for* aperuit.
³ *A. Sp., for* ut. ⁴ *Turnebus, for* sit. ⁵ *Aldus, H, for*
obscurius. ⁶ *Victorius, for* in posterioris. ⁷ *Turnebus,
for* quid. ⁸ *L. Sp., for* uidere. ⁹ *Victorius, for* et.
¹⁰ *L. Sp.* ; Myrmetidis *Aldus ; for* yrmeci dum.

VARRO

ebore oculi videant, extrinsecus admovent nigras
setas.

2. Cum haec amminicula addas ad eruendum
voluntatem impositoris, tamen latent multa. Quod
si poetice ⟨quae⟩[1] in carminibus servavit[2] multa prisca
quae essent, sic etiam cur essent posuisset,[3] *f*ecundius[4]
poemata ferrent fructum ; sed ut in soluta oratione
sic in poematis verba ⟨non⟩[5] omnia quae habent[6]
ἔτυμα possunt dici, neque multa ab eo, quem non
erunt in lucubratione litterae prosecutae, multum
licet legeret. *A*elii[7] hominis in primo in litteris
Latinis exercitati interpretationem Carminum Saliorum videbis et exili littera expedita⟨m⟩[8] et praeterita
obscura[9] multa.

3. Nec mirum, cum non modo Ep*i*menides[1]
⟨s⟩opor⟨e⟩[2] post annos L experrectus a multis non
cognoscatur, sed etiam Teucer Livii post XV annos
ab suis qui sit ignoretur. A*t*[3] hoc quid ad verborum
poeticorum aetatem ? Quorum si Pompili regnum
fons in Carminibus Saliorum neque ea ab superioribus

§ 2. [1] *Added by L. Sp.* [2] *Victorius, for* servabit.
[3] *Victorius, for* posuissent. [4] *Laetus, for* secundius.
[5] *Added by Mue.* [6] *For* haberent. [7] *II, B, Ed. Veneta,
for* helii. [8] *Laetus, for* expedita. [9] *For* praeteritam
obscuram.
§ 3. [1] *Aug., with B, for* Epamenidis. [2] *GS., for* opôs.
[3] *Victorius, for* ad.

---

§ 1. [a] *Cf.* ix. 108 ; his carvings were so tiny that the
detail in the white ivory could be seen only against a black
background.
§ 3. [a] A Cretan poet and prophet, reputed to have cleansed
Athens of a plague in 596 B.C. According to one story, in his
boyhood he went into a cave to escape the noonday sun, and
fell into a sleep that lasted fifty-seven years. When he awoke,

handiwork [a] in ivory, men put black hairs behind the objects.

2. Even though you employ these tools to unearth the intent of him who applied the word, much remains hidden. But if the art of poesy, which has in the verses preserved many words that are early, had in the same fashion also set down why and how they came to be, the poems would bear fruit in more prolific measure ; unfortunately, in poems as in prose, not all the words can be assigned to their primitive radicals, and there are many which cannot be so assigned by him whom learning does not attend with favour in his nocturnal studies, though he read prodigiously. In the interpretation of the *Hymns of the Salians*, which was made by Aelius, an outstanding scholar in Latin literature, you will see that the interpretation is greatly furthered by attention to a single poor letter, and that much is obscured if such a letter is passed by.

3. Nor is this astonishing : for not only were there many who failed to recognize Epimenides [a] when he awoke from sleep after fifty years, but even Teucer's own family, in the play of Livius Andronicus,[b] do not know who he is after his absence of fifteen years. But what has this to do with the age of poetic words ? If the reign of Numa Pompilius [c] is the source of those in the *Hymns of the Salians* and those words were not received from earlier hymn-makers, they are none the

everything was changed ; his younger brother had become an old man. [b] Livius Andronicus, *Trag. Rom. Fraq.*, page 7 Ribbeck[3] ; *R.O.L.* ii. 14-15 Warmington. Teucer, son of Telamon king of Salamis, was absent from home during the Trojan War, and again during his exile after his return from that war. [c] Second king of Rome, founder of the Salian priesthood.

accepta, tamen habent DCC annos. Quare cur
scriptoris industriam reprehendas qui herois tritavum,
atavum non potuerit reperire, cum ipse tui tritavi
matrem dicere non possis ? Quod intervallum multo
tanto propius nos, quam hinc ad initium Saliorum,
quo Romanorum prima verba poetica dicunt Latina.

4. Igitur de originibus verborum qui multa dixerit commode, potius boni consulendum, quam qui
aliquid nequierit reprehendendum, praesertim quom
dicat etymologice[1] non omnium verborum posse dici
causa⟨m⟩,[2] ut qui a⟨c⟩ qua re res u⟨tilis[3] sit⟩[4] ad
medendum medicina ; neque si non norim radices
arboris, non posse me dicere pirum esse ex ramo,
ramum ex arbore, eam ex radicibus quas non video.
Quare qui ostendit equitatum esse ab equitibus,
equites ab equite, equitem ab equo neque equus unde
sit dicit, tamen hic docet plura et satisfacit grato,
quem imitari possimusne ipse liber erit indicio.

II. 5. Dicam in hoc libro de verbis quae a poetis
sunt posita, primum de locis, dein quae in locis sunt,
tertio de temporibus, tum quae cum temporibus sunt
coniuncta, ⟨se⟩d is[1] ut qu⟨ae cum his sint coniuncta,

§ 4. [1] *For* ethymologice. [2] *L. Sp., for* causa.
[3] *Ellis, for* quia quare res u *and a blank space capable of
holding about seven letters.* [4] *Added by Kent.*
§ 5. [1] *A. Sp. ;* sed ita *Mue. ; for* dis.

less seven hundred years old. Therefore why should you find fault with the diligence of a writer who has not been able to find the name of the great-grandfather or the grandfather of a demigod's great-grandfather, when you yourself cannot name the mother of your own great-grandfather's great-grandfather? This interval is much closer to us, than the stretch from the present time to the beginning of the Salians, when, they say, the first poetic words of the Romans were composed, in Latin.

4. Therefore the man who has made many apt pronouncements on the origins of words, one should regard with favour, rather than find fault with him who has been unable to make any contribution; especially since the etymologic art says that it is not of all words that the basis can be stated—just as it cannot be stated how and why a medicine is effective for curing; and that if I have no knowledge of the roots of a tree, still I am not prevented from saying that a pear is from a branch, the branch is from a tree, and the tree from roots which I do not see. For this reason, he who shows that *equitatus* ' cavalry ' is from *equites* ' cavalrymen,' *equites* from *eques* ' cavalryman,' *eques* from *equus* ' horse,' even though he does not give the source of the word *equus*, still gives several lessons and satisfies an appreciative person; whether or not we can do as much, the present book itself shall serve as testifying witness.

II. 5. In this book I shall speak of the words which have been put down by the poets, first those about places, then those which are in places, third those about times, then those which are associated with time-ideas; but in such a way that to them I shall add those which are associated with these, and

271

VARRO

adiungam, et si quid excedit[2] ex hac quadripertitione, tamen in ea ut comprehendam.

6. Incipiam hinc :

> Unus erit quem tu tolles in caerula caeli
> Templa.

Templum tribus modis dicitur : ab natura, ab auspicando,[1] a similitudine ; ⟨ab⟩[2] natura in caelo, ab auspiciis in terra, a similitudine sub terra. In caelo te⟨m⟩plum dicitur, ut in *H*ecuba :

> O magna templa caelitum, commixta stellis splendidis.

In terra, ut in Periboea :

> Scrupea saxea Ba⟨c⟩chi
> Templa prope aggreditur.

Sub terra, ut in Andromacha :

> Acherusia templa alta Orci, salvete, infera.

7. Quaqua[1] in⟨tu⟩iti era⟨n⟩t[2] oculi, a tuendo primo templum dictum : quocirca caelum qua attuimur dictum templum ; sic :

> Contremuit templum magnum Iovis altitonantis,

[2] *Sciop., for* excidit.
  § 6. [1] *Groth, with* V, p, *for* auspicando.   [2] *Added by* L. Sp.
  § 7. [1] *Aug., for* quaquia.   [2] *Sciop., for* initium erat.

  § 6. [a] Said of Romulus, by Ennius, *Ann.* 65-66 Vahlen[2]; *R.O.L.* i. 22-23 Warmington; quoted without *templa* by Ovid, *Met.* xiv. 814 and *Fast.* ii. 487.   [b] Properly a 'limited space,' for divination or otherwise ; from the root *tem-* 'cut.'   [c] Page 18 Regell.   [d] That is, likeness to a *templum* in the sky or on the earth.   [e] Ennius, *Trag. Rom. Frag.* 163 Ribbeck[3]; *R.O.L.* i. 292-293 Warmington.

that if any word lies outside this fourfold division, I shall still include it in the account.

6. I shall begin from this :

> One there shall be, whom thou shalt raise up to sky's
> azure temples.[a]

Templum [b] ' temple ' is used in three ways, of nature, of taking the auspices,[c] from likeness [d] : of nature, in the sky ; of taking the auspices, on the earth ; from likeness, under the earth. In the sky, *templum* is used as in the *Hecuba* [e] :

> O great temples of the gods, united with the shining
> stars.

On the earth, as in the *Periboea* [f] :

> To Bacchus' temples aloft
> On sharp jagged rocks it draws near.

Under the earth, as in the *Andromacha* [g] :

> Be greeted, great temples of Orcus,
> By Acheron's waters, in Hades.

7. Whatever place the eyes had *intuiti* ' gazed on,' was originally called a *templum* ' temple,' from *tueri* ' to gaze ' ; therefore the sky, where we *attuimur* ' gaze at ' it, got the name *templum*, as in this [a] :

> Trembled the mighty temple of Jove who thunders
> in heaven,

---

[f] Pacuvius, *Trag. Rom. Frag.* 310 Ribbeck[3] ; *R.O.L.* ii. 278-279 Warmington ; anapaestic ; said of a Bacchic rout.
[g] Ennius, *Trag. Rom. Frag.* 70-71 Ribbeck[3] ; *R.O.L.* i. 254-255 Warmington ; anapaestic ; quoted more fully by Cicero, *Tusc. Disp.* i. 21. 48.
§ 7. [a] Ennius, *Ann.* 541 Vahlen[2] ; *R.O.L.* i. 450-451 Warmington.

VARRO

id est, ut ait Naevius,

> Hemis*pha*erium[3] ubi conca⟨vo⟩[4]
> Caerulo[5] septum stat.

Eius templi partes quattuor dicuntur, sinistra ab oriente, dextra ab occasu, antica ad meridiem, postica ad septemtrionem.

8. In terris dictum templum locus augurii aut auspicii causa quibusdam conceptis verbis finitus. Concipitur verbis non isdem[1] usque quaque ; in Arce sic :

> Tem⟨pla⟩ tescaque[2] me ita sunto, quoad ego ea *rite*[3] lin*gu*a[4] nuncupavero.
> Olla *ver*⟨a⟩[5] arbos quirquir est, quam me sentio dixisse, templum te*s*cumque m*e* esto[6] in sinistrum.
> Olla *ver*⟨a⟩[7] arbos quirquir est, qu*am*[8] me sentio dixisse, te⟨m⟩plum te*s*cumque m*e* esto[6] ⟨in⟩[9] dextrum.
> Inter ea conregione conspicione cortumione, utique ea ⟨rit⟩e *dix*isse me[10] sensi.

9. In hoc templo faciundo arbores constitui fines apparet et intra eas regiones qua oculi conspiciant, id

---

[3] *Turnebus, B, for* hiemisferium. [4] *Mue., for* conca.
[5] *For* cherulo.
§ 8. [1] *Mue., for* hisdem. [2] *Turnebus, for* item testaque.
[3] ea rite *L. Sp., for* eas te. [4] *Victorius, p, for* linquam.
[5] *Kent, for* ullaber. [6] tescum *Turnebus,* -que me *Fay,* esto *Scaliger and Turnebus, for* tectum quem festo. [7] *Kent, for* ollaner. [8] *Mue., for* quod. [9] *Added by B, Laetus.*
[10] *L. Sp., ;* ea dixisse me *Sciop. ; for* ea erectissime.

---

[b] An uncertain fragment, not li*s*ted in the collections of the fragments of Naevius. [c] *Cf.* p. 18 Regell.
§ 8. [a] Page 18 Regell. [b] Text and translation both very problematic. I take *me* as dative (*cf.* Fest. 160. 2) ; regard *quirquir* as equal to *quisquis*, either by manuscript corruption or with rhotacism in the phrase *quisquis est*,

that is, as Naevius says,[b]

> Where land's semicircle lies,
> Fenced by the azure vault.

Of this temple [c] the four quarters are named thus : the left quarter, to the east ; the right quarter, to the west ; the front quarter, to the south ; the back quarter, to the north.

8. On the earth, *templum* is the name given to a place set aside and limited by certain formulaic words for the purpose of augury [a] or the taking of the auspices. The words of the ceremony are not the same everywhere ; on the Citadel, they are as follows [b] :

> Temples and wild lands be mine in this manner, up to where I have named them with my tongue in proper fashion.
> Of whatever kind that truthful[c] tree is, which I consider that I have mentioned, temple and wild land be mine to that point on the left.
> Of whatever kind that truthful tree is, which I consider that I have mentioned, temple and wild land be mine to that point on the right.
> Between these points, temples and wild lands be mine for direction, for viewing, and for interpreting, and just as I have felt assured that I have mentioned them in proper fashion.

9. In making this temple, it is evident that the trees are set as boundaries, and that within them the regions are set where the eyes are to view, that is we

becoming *quisquir est* (so Fay, *Amer. Journ. Phil.* xxxv. 253) ; take as datives the three words in *-one* in the last sentence (meanings, vii. 9), supplying after them *templa tescaque me sunto.* For meaning of *tescum, cf.* vii. 10-11. [c] That is, lending itself to true predictions through the auspices.

est tucamur, a quo templum dictum, et contemplare,
ut apud Ennium in Medea :

> Contempla et templum Cereris ad laevam aspice.

Contempla et conspicare id⟨em⟩[1] esse apparet, ideo
dicere *t*um, *cum* te⟨m⟩plum[2] facit, augurem conspicione, qua oculorum conspectum finiat. Quod
cum dicunt conspicionem, addunt cortumionem,
dicitur a cordis visu : cor enim cortumionis origo.

10. Quod addit templa ut si⟨n⟩t[1] *tes*ca,[2] aiunt
sancta esse qui glossas scripserunt. Id est falsum :
nam Curia Hostilia templum est et sanctum non est ;
sed hoc ut putarent aedem sacram esse templum,
⟨eo videtur⟩[3] esse factum quod in urbe Roma pleraeque aedes sacrae sunt templa, eadem sancta, et quod
loca quaedam agrestia, qu*ae*[4] alicuius dei sunt, di-
*c*untur[5] tesca.

§ 9.   [1] *Bentinus, for* id.   [2] *Turnebus, for* cum conteplum.
§ 10.   [1] *Laetus,   for* sit.   [2] *Turnebus, for* dextra.
[3] *Added by GS.*   [4] *L. Sp., for* quod.   [5] *Bentinus, for*
dicentur.

---

§ 9.   [a] As Varro derives *templum* from *tueri*, he must
insist on the meaning ' to gaze,' because in his time its usual
meaning was ' to protect.'   [b] *Trag. Rom. Frag.* 244 Ribbeck[3]; *R.O.L.* i. 324-325 Warmington. The preceding
verse ended with *Athenas anticum opulentum oppidum*,
which is the object of *contempla*, but Varro obviously understood his shortened citation as it is here translated.   [c] He
means, from *cor* and *tueri* ; but the second part is rather
from the root *tem-* ' to cut,' as in *aestimare* ' to cut bronze,
276

tueamur ' are to gaze,'[a] from which was said *templum* and *contemplare* ' to contemplate,' as in Ennius, in the *Medea* [b] :

> Contemplate and view Ceres' temple on the left.

Contempla ' do thou contemplate ' and *conspicare* ' do thou view ' are the same, it is obvious, and therefore the augur, when he makes a temple, says *conspicione* ' for viewing,' with regard to where he is to delimit the *conspectus* ' view ' of the eyes. As to their adding *cortumio* when they say *conspicio*, this term is derived from the vision of the *cor* ' heart ' ; for *cor* is the basis of *cortumio*.[c]

10. As to his adding that the temples shall be *tesca* ' wild lands,' those who have written glossaries [a] say that this means that the temples are inviolable.[b] This is quite wrong : for the Hostilian Meeting-House [c] is a temple and is not inviolable.[d] But that people should have the idea that a temple is a consecrated building, seems to have come about from the fact that in the city Rome most consecrated buildings are temples, and they are likewise inviolable, and that certain places in the country, which are the property of some god, are called *tesca*.

---

evaluate, think,' and the whole word means perhaps ' interpreting.'

§ 10. [a] Page 113 Funaioli. [b] That is, where any violence, at whatever directed, is sacrilege toward the gods. ' Temple ' is in this statement used in the wide meaning of a ' limited space,' not in the derived sense of a building for the worship of the gods or of a god, which is an *aedes sacra*. [c] In the Comitium ; traditionally built by Tullus Hostilius, third king of Rome, as a meeting place for the Senate. [d] A *locus sacer* (' consecrated to a deity ') was always *sanctus*, but a *locus sanctus* was not always *sacer*.

VARRO

11. Nam apud Accium *in*[1] Philocteta[2] Lemnio :

> Quis tu es mortalis, qui in deserta et tesca te
> appor*tes*[3] loca ?

⟨Ea⟩[4] enim loca quae sint designat, cum dicit :

> Lemnia praesto
> Litora rara,[5] et celsa Cabirum
> Delubra te*nes*,[6] mysteria quae
> Pristina castis[7] concepta sacris.

Dein :

> Volcania[8] ⟨iam⟩[9] templa sub ipsis
> Collibus, in quos delatus locos
> Dicitur alto ab limine[10] caeli.

Et :

> Nemus expirante vapore vides,
> Unde ignis[11] cluet[12] mortalibus ⟨clam⟩[13]
> Divis⟨us⟩.[14]

Quare h*a*ec quo⟨d⟩ tesca dixit, non errauit, neque ideo quod sancta, sed quod ubi mysteria fiunt attuentur,[15] tuesca dicta.

12. Tueri duo significat, unum ab aspectu ut dixi, unde est En*nii*[1] illud :

> Tueor te, senex ? Pro Iupiter !

§ 11. [1] *Laetus, for* ut. [2] *Aldus, for* philocto etatem. [3] *Aldus, for* appones (*cf.* adportas *Festus,* 356 a 26 *M.*). [4] *Added by Mue.* [5] *Aug., with B, for* prest olitor a rarat. [6] *For* teues. [7] *Aldus, for* castris. [8] *For* uolgania. [9] *Added by Ribbeck.* [10] *Aug., with B, for* lumine. [11] *Vertranius* (*from Cicero, Tusc.* ii. 10. 23), *for* ignes. [12] *Aldus, for* clauet. [13] *Added by Victorius* (*from Cicero, l.c.*). [14] *Turnebus* (*from Cicero, l.c.*), *for* diuis. [15] *Mue., for* aut tuentur.

§ 12. [1] *Sciop., for* enim.

---

§ 11. [a] *Trag. Rom. Frag.* 554 Ribbeck[3]; *R.O.L.* ii. 514-515 Warmington. [b] *Trag. Rom. Frag.* 525-534 Ribbeck[3];

11. For there is the following in Accius, in the *Philoctetes of Lemnos* [a] :

> What man are thou, who dost advance
> To places desert, places waste ?

What sort of places these are, he indicates when he says [b] :

> Around you you have the Lemnian shores,
> Apart from the world, and the high-seated shrines
> Of Cabirian Gods, and the mysteries which
> Of old were expressed with sacrifice pure.

Then :

> You see now the temples of Vulcan, close by
> Those very same hills, upon which he is said
> To have fallen when thrown from the sky's lofty sill.[c]

And :

> The wood here you see with the smoke gushing forth,
> Whence the fire—so they say—was secretly brought
> To mankind.[d]

Therefore he made no mistake in calling these lands *tesca*, and yet he did not do so because they were consecrated ; but because men *attuentur* ' gaze at ' places where mysteries take place, they were called *tuesca*.[e]

12. *Tueri* has two meanings, one of ' seeing ' as I have said, whence that verse of Ennius [a] :

> I really see thee, sire ?   Oh Jupiter !

R.O.L. ii. 506-507 Warmington; anapaestic.   [c] He fell on Lemnos, as related in *Iliad*, i. 590-594.   [d] This last portion is quoted by Cicero, *Tusc. Disp.* ii. 10. 23, who continues with a summary of the story of Prometheus.   [e] Varro means that *tesca* is for *tuesca*, waste or wild land where men may look at (*attueri*) celebrations of religious mysteries : an incorrect etymology.

§ 12.   [a] *Trag. Rom. Frag.* 335 Ribbeck³; *R.O.L.* i. 290-291 Warmington.

VARRO

Et :

> Quis pater aut cognatus volet *ros*[2] contra tueri ?

Alterum a curando ac tutela, ut cum dicimus " *vellet*[3] tueri villam," a quo etiam quidam dicunt illum qui curat aedes sacras *a*edituum, non aedit*u*mum[4] ; sed tamen hoc ipsum ab eadem est profectum origine, quod quem volumus domum curare dicimus " tu domi videbis," ut Plautus cum ait :

> Intus para, cura, vide. Qu*o*d opus⟨t⟩[5] fiat.

Sic dicta vestis⟨pi⟩ca,[6] quae vestem spiceret, id est videret vestem ac tueretur. Quare a tuendo et templa et tesca dicta cum discrimine eo quod dixi.

13.   Etiam indidem illud En*nii*[1] :

> Extemplo acceptam[2] me necato[3] et filiam.[4]

Extemplo enim est continuo, quod omne te⟨m⟩plum esse debet conti⟨nu⟩o septum nec plus unum introitum habere.

---

[2] *Aug., with B, for* nos.   [3] *Ellis, for* bell . . et (*vacant space for two letters*).   [4] *For* aeditomum.   [5] *From Plautus, Men.* 352, *for* quid opus.   [6] *Aldus, for* vestisca.
    § 13. [1] *Scaliger, for* enim.   [2] *Voss, for* acceptum. [3] *Scaliger, for* negato.   [4] *Bothe, for* filium ; *cf. Euripides, Hecuba,* 391.

---

[b] *Ann.* 463 Vahlen[2];   *R.O.L.* i. 172-173 Warmington. [c] *Aeditumus* is original, with the second part of uncertain origin.   [d] Varro compares the two meanings of *tueri* with the two meanings of *videre,* ' to see ' and ' to see after, care for.'   [e] *Men.* 352.

And [b] :

> Who will now wish, though father or kinsman, to look
>   on your faces ?

The other meaning is of ' caring for ' and *tutela* ' guardianship,' as when we say " I wish he were willing *tueri* ' to care for ' the farmhouse," from which some indeed say that the man who attends to consecrated buildings is an *aedituus* and not an *aeditumus* [c] ; but still this other form itself proceeded from the same source, because when we want some one to take care of the house we say " You will see to [d] matters at home," as Plautus does when he says [e] :

> Inside prepare, take pains, see to 't ;
> Let that be done, that's needed.

In this way the *vestispica* ' wardrobe maid ' was named, who was *spicere* ' to see ' the *vestis* ' clothing,' that is, was to see to the clothing and *tueri* ' guard ' it. Therefore, both temples and *tesca* ' wastes ' were named from *tueri*, with that difference of meaning which I have mentioned.

13. Moreover, from the same source comes the word in Ennius [a] :

> *Extemplo* take me, kill me, kill my daughter too.

For *extemplo* [b] ' on the spot ' is *continuo* ' without interval,' because every *templum* ought to be fenced in uninterruptedly and have not more than one entrance.

§ 13.   [a] *Trag. Rom. Frag.* 355 Ribbeck³ ; *R.O.L.* i. 380–381 Warmington ; perhaps spoken by the captive Hecuba, who gave her name to a tragedy by Ennius.   [b] *Templum* denotes a limited portion of time as well as of space ; in *extemplo* the application is to time.

VARRO

14.   Quod est apud Accium :

> Pervade polum, splendida mundi
> Sidera, bigis, ⟨bis⟩[1] continui⟨s⟩
> Se⟨x ex⟩pict*i* *sign*is,[2]

polus Graecum, id significat circum caeli : quare quod
est pervade polum val*et*[3] vade περὶ πόλον.   Signa
dicuntur eadem et sidera.   Signa quod aliquid
significent, ut libra aequinoctium ;   sidera, quae
⟨qua⟩si[4] insidunt atque ita significant aliquid in terris
perurendo ali*ave*[5] qua re : ut signum candens in
pecore.

15.   Quod est :

> Terrarum anfracta revis*am*,[1]

anfractum est flexum, ab origine duplici dictum, ab
ambitu et frangendo : ab eo leges iubent in directo
pedum VIII esse ⟨viam⟩,[2] in anfracto XVI, id est in
flexu.

16.   Ennius :

> Ut tibi
> Titanis Trivia dederit stirpem liberum.

Titanis Trivia Diana est, ab eo dicta Trivia, quod in

§ 14.   [1] *Added by Kent ; cf. GS.,* note.   [2] Continui se
cepit spoliis *F ;* continuis sex apti signis *Scaliger ;* picti
Ribbeck, exceptis *Fay,* expicti *Kent.*   [3] *Victorius, for*
valde.   [4] quae quasi *GS. ;* quod quasi *L. Sp. ; for* quae
si.   [5] *A. Sp., for* aliudue.
§ 15.   [1] *Aug., with* B, *for* anfractare visum.   [2] *Added
by GS ; following Sciop., who added* viam *after* iubent.

§ 14.   [a] *Trag. Rom. Frag.* 678-680 Ribbeck[3] ; *R.O.L.*
ii. 572-573 Warmington ; anapaestic. The passage is apparently addressed to Phaethon, but possibly to the Sun-God or
to the Moon-God.   The twelve signs of the zodiac are con-
ceived as taken by the Universe and worn by it as a girdle.
[b] Wrong etymology.   [c] Properly ' white-hot ' ; the Roman

14. As for what is in Accius,[a]

> With thy team do thou go through the sky, through
>   the bright
> Constellations aloft, which the universe holds,
> Adorned with its twice six continuous signs,

the word *polus* ' sky ' is Greek, it means the circle of the sky : therefore the expression *pervade polum* ' traverse the sky ' means ' go around the πόλος.' *Signa* ' signs of the zodiac ' means the same as *sidera* ' constellations.' *Signa* are so called because they *significant* ' indicate ' something, as the Balance marks the equinox ; those are *sidera* which so to speak *insidunt* ' settle down ' [b] and thus indicate something on earth by burning or otherwise : as for example a *signum candens* ' scorching sign,' [c] in the matter of the flocks.

15. In the phrase

> Again of the land I shall see the *anfracta*,[a]

anfractum means ' bent or curved,' being formed from a double source, from *ambitus* ' circuit ' and *frangere* ' to break.' Concerning this the laws [b] bid that a road shall be eight feet wide where it is straight, and sixteen at an *anfractum*, that is, at a curve.

16. Ennius says [a] :

> As surely as to thee
> Titan's daughter Trivia shall grant a line of sons.

The Trivian Titaness is Diana, called *Trivia* from the

poets often speak of the flocks as being burned by the heat of *Canicula* ' the Dog-star,' while the sun is in the sign of Leo.

§ 15. [a] Accius, *Trag. Rom. Frag.* 336 Ribbeck[3]; *R.O.L.* ii. 440-441 Warmington.   [b] *Cf. XII Tabulae*, page 138 Schoell.

§ 16. [a] *Trag. Rom. Frag.* 362 Ribbeck[3]; *R.O.L.* i. 260-261 Warmington.

VARRO

trivio ponitur fere in oppidis Graecis, vel quod luna
dicitur esse, quae in caelo tribus viis movetur, in
altitudinem et latitudinem et longitudinem. Titanis
dicta, quod eam genuit, ut ai⟨t⟩[1] Plautus, Lato ; ea,
ut scribit Manilius,

> Est Coe⟨o⟩ creata[2] Titano.

Ut idem scribit :

> Latona pari⟨e⟩t[3] casta complexu Iovis
> Deliadas[4] geminos,

id est Apollinem et Dianam. Dii, quod Titanis
⟨Deli eos peperit⟩,[5] Deliadae.

17. Eidem[1] :

> O sancte Apollo, qui umbilicum certum terrarum
> optines.

Umbilicum dictum aiunt ab umbilico nostro, quod is
medius locus sit terrarum, ut umbilicus in nobis ;
quod utrumque est falsum : neque hic locus est
terrarum medius neque noster umbilicus est hominis
medius. Itaque pingitur quae[2] vocatur ⟨ἀντ⟩ίχθων[3]
Πυθαγόρα, ut media caeli ac terrae linea ducatur infra

§ 16. [1] *Kent, after L. Sp., for* ni. [2] *Mue., for* coc-
creata. [3] *Neue, for* parit. [4] *Lachmann, for* delia dōs.
[5] *Added by L. Sp.*
§ 17. [1] *A. Sp. (nom. sing. masc.), for* eadem. [2] *Mue.,
for* qui. [3] *G. Hermann, for* IXToN.

---

[b] This first etymology is better ; it should be referred to
images set up in Italian towns, not in Greek towns.
[c] *Lato,* from which the Romans made *Latona* (*cf.* Plautus,
Bac. 893), is the Greek form in Doric and in all other
dialects except Attic-Ionic. [d] *Frag. Poet. Lat.*, page 52
Morel. [e] *Deliadae* is a word not found elsewhere ; but
it seems difficult not to admit it in this passage.
§ 17. [a] *Trag. Rom. Frag. inc. inc.* 19-20 Ribbeck[3];

fact that her image is set up quite generally in Greek towns where three roads meet,[b] or else because she is said to be the Moon, which moves in the sky by *tres viae* ' three ways,' upwards, sidewise, and onwards. She is called *Titanis* ' daughter of Titan,' because her mother was, as Plautus says, Lato [c]; and she, as Manilius writes,[d]

> Was begot by the Titan Coeus.

As the same author writes,[d]

> The chaste Latona shall give birth, by Jove's embrace,
> To Deliad twins,

that is, to Apollo and Diana. These gods were called Deliads [e] because the Titaness gave birth to them on the island of Delos.

17. The same has this [a]:

> O holy Apollo, who dost hold
> The true established *umbilicus* of the lands.

The *umbilicus*, they say,[b] was so called from our *umbilicus* ' navel,' because this is the middle place of the lands, as the navel in us. But both these are false statements : this place is not the middle of the lands, nor is the navel the middle point of a man. But in this fashion is indicated the so-called ' counter-earth of Pythagoras,' [c] so that the line which is midway in sky and earth should be drawn below the navel

---

R.O.L. ii. 602-603 Warmington, who doubtfully attributes it to Ennius, since Cicero, *de Divin.* ii. 56. 115. citing this passage more fully, had last quoted from Ennius ; preceded by *eidem* (nom. sing. masc.), it belongs to Manilius. [b] Page 117 Funaioli.   [c] Pythagoras taught that around the fire in the centre of the universe there swung the earth and a counter-earth, each forming part of a sphere, and balancing each other.

umbilicum per id quo discernitur homo mas an femina
sit, ubi ortus humanus similis ut in mundo[4] : ibi[5]
enim omnia nascuntur in medio, quod terra mundi
media.   Praeterea si quod medium id est umbilicus
pila⟨e⟩[6] terrae, non Delphi medium ;   et terrae
medium—non[7] hoc, sed quod vocant—Delphis[7] in
aede ad latus est quiddam ut thesauri specie, quod
Graeci vocant ὀμφαλόν,[8] quem Pythonos aiunt esse
tumulum[9] ;   ab eo nostri interpretes ὀμφαλόν umbilicum dixerunt.

18.   Pacuius :

Calydonia altrix terra ex⟨s⟩uperantum virum.

Ut ager Tusculanus, sic Calydonius ager est, non
terra ; sed lege poetica, quod terra Aetolia in qua
Calydon, a parte[1] totam accipi Aetoliam voluit.

19.   Acci :

Mystica ad dextram vada
Praetervecti.

Mystica a mysteriis, quae ibi in propinquis locis
nobilia fiunt.

---

[4] A dittography in F, written ubi ortus humanus situlis ut in
mundo, is here excised.   [5] Aug., for ubi.   [6] ut pilae
Mue., for ut pila F (but ut was deleted by F[1]).   [7] The
dashes were inserted by Stroux.   [8] Aldus, for ΟΜΦαΛVΝ.
[9] Lobeck, for tumulos.

§ 18.   [1] For aperte.

---

[d] Nonius, 333. 35 M., quotes Varro as using the expression
terra pila (or terrae).   [e] The "treasure-houses" at Delphi
were small buildings in which the valuable dedicatory gifts
were kept ; a number of cities had special treasure-houses
of their own.   [f] Slain here by Apollo after the flood of
Deucalion and Pyrrha.

through that by which the distinction is made whether a human being is male or female, where human life starts—and the like is true in the case of the universe: for there all things originate in the centre, because the earth is the centre of the universe. Besides, if the ball of the earth [d] has any centre, or *umbilicus*, it is not Delphi that is the centre ; and the centre of the earth at Delphi—not really the centre, but so called—is something in a temple building at one side, something that looks like a treasure-house,[e] which the Greeks call the ὀμφαλός, which they say is the tomb of the Python.[f] From this our interpreters turned the word into *umbilicus* ' navel.'

18. Pacuvius has this verse [a] :

Calydonian *terra*, nurse of mighty men.

But just as Tusculum has an *ager* ' field-land,' so Calydon has an *ager* and not a *terra* ' land ' [b] ; but by the privilege of the poets, because Aetolia in which Calydon is located is a *terra*, he wished all Aetolia to be understood from the name of the part.

19. In this of Accius,[a]

Sailing past the mystic waters [b] on the right,

mystica ' mystic ' is from the famous *mysteria* ' mysteries,' which are performed there in places close at hand.

§ 18.   [a] *Trag. Rom. Frag.* 404 Ribbeck[3]; *R.O.L.* ii. 274-275 Warmington.   [b] Varro objects to the use of *terra* with a city-name attached, since *terra* means the whole state, and cannot belong to a city : a city owns only an *ager*.

§ 19.   [a] *Trag. Rom. Frag.* 687-688 Ribbeck[3]; *R.O.L.* ii. 568-569 Warmington.   [b] Probably those at Eleusis, where mysteries of Demeter were celebrated; or possibly those near Samothrace, where the Cabiri were worshipped, *cf.* vii. 34.

VARRO

Ennii :

> Areopagitae quia[1] dedere ⟨ae⟩quam pilam.[2]

Areopagitae ab Areopago ; is locus[3] Athenis.

20.   Musae quae pedibus magnum pulsatis Olympum.

Caelum dicunt Graeci Olympum, montem in Macedonia omnes ; a quo potius puto Musas dictas
Olympiadas : ita enim ab terrestribus locis aliis
cognominatae Libethrides, Pipleides, Thespiades,[1]
Heliconides.

21.   Ca⟨s⟩si[1] :

> Hellespontum et claustra.

⟨Claustra⟩,[2] quod Xerxes[3] quondam eum locum
clausit : nam, ut Ennius ait,

> Isque Hellesponto pontem contendit in alto.

Nisi potius ab eo quod Asia et Europa ibi con⟨c⟩ludi-
t⟨ur⟩[4] mare ; inter angustias facit Propontidis fauces.

§ 19.   [1] *Ribbeck, for* quid.   [2] *Ribbeck ;* aequam pugnam
Mue. ; aequom palam *Bothe ; for* quam pudam.   [3] *Laetus,
for* his locis.
§ 20.   [1] *For* piplę idĕ (= id est) espiades, *with* h *above the*
e *of* esp-.
§ 21.   [1] *Mue. ;* Cassius *Sciop. ; for* quasi.   [2] *Added by
Scaliger.*   [3] *Bentinus, for* exerses.   [4] *A. Sp. ;* con-
cludit *Laetus ; for* colludit.

---

[c] *Trag. Rom. Frag.* 349 Ribbeck[3] ; *R.O.L.* i. 272-273
Warmington.   [d] At the trial of Orestes for the murder
of his mother.
§ 20.   [a] Ennius, *Ann.* 1 Vahlen[2] ; *R.O.L.* i. 2-3 Warmington ; opening the poem.   [b] As home of the gods.
[c] That is, not merely the Greeks.   [d] *Pipleides* or *Pim-*

In the verse of Ennius,[c]

> Since the Areopagites have cast an equal vote,[d]

Areopagitae ' Areopagites ' is from Areopagus ; this is a place at Athens.

20. Muses, ye who with dancing feet beat mighty Olympus.[a]

Olympus is the name which the Greeks give to the sky,[b] and all peoples [c] give to a mountain in Macedonia ; it is from the latter, I am inclined to think, that the Muses are spoken of as the Olympiads : for they are called in the same way from other places on earth the Libethrids, the Pipleids,[d] the Thespiads, the Heliconids.[e]

21. In this phrase of Cassius,[a]

> The Hellespont and its barriers,

claustra ' barriers ' is used because once on a time Xerxes *clausit* ' closed ' the place by barriers [b] : for, as Ennius says,[c]

> He, and none other, on Hellespont deep did fasten
>   a bridgeway.

Unless it is said rather from the fact that at this place the sea *concluditur* ' is hemmed in ' by Asia and Europe ; in the narrows it forms the entrance to the Propontis.

---

pleides.   [e] Respectively from Libethra, a fountain sacred to the Muses, near Libethrum and Magnesia, in Macedonia ; Pimpla, a place and fountain in Pieria, in Macedonia ; Thespiae, a town of Boeotia at the foot of Helicon ; and Helicon, a mountain-range in Boeotia.

§ 21.   [a] *Trag. Rom. Frag. inc. inc.* 106 Ribbeck[3] ; with the text as here emended, it belongs to Cassius.   [b] *Cf.* Herodotus, vii. 33-36.   [c] *Ann.* 378 Vahlen[2] ; *R.O.L.* i. 136-137 Warmington.

VARRO

22. Pacui :

Li⟨n⟩qui[1] in *A*egeo fretu.[2]

Dictum fretum ab similitudine ferventis aquae, quod
in fretum s*a*epe concurrat *a*estus atque effervescat.
*A*egeum dictum ab insulis, quod in eo mari scopuli in
pelago vocantur ab similitudine caprarum *a*eges.

23. Ferme aderant aequore in alto ratibus repentibus.

Mare appellatum ⟨aequor⟩,[1] quod a⟨e⟩quatum[2] cum
commotum vento non est. Ratis navis longa⟨s⟩[3]
dixit, ut N*a*evius cum ait :

⟨Ut⟩[4] conferre quea*nt*[5] ratem aeratam qui
Per *li*quidum[6] mare sudantes eunt atque sed*e*ntes.[7]

Ratis dicta navis longa propter remos, quod hi, cum
per aquam sublati sunt dextra et sinistra, duas *rates*[8]
efficere videntur : ratis enim, unde hoc tralatum, illi
ubi plures mali aut asseres ⟨iuncti aqua ducuntur.
Hinc naviculae cum remis ratariae dicuntur⟩.[9]

§ 22. [1] *Kent, for* liqui. [2] *A. Sp., for* fretum.
§ 23. [1] *Added here by A. Sp.; added before* mare *by
Laetus.* [2] *Laetus, for* aquatum. [3] *Mue., for* longa.
[4] *Added by Kent.* [5] *Turnebus, for* conferreque aut.
[6] *Scaliger, for* perit quidum. [7] *Scaliger, for* sedantes.
[8] *Mue., for* partes. [9] *Added by Mue., after Serv. Dan. in
Aen.* i. 43 *and Gellius,* x. 25. 5.

§ 22. [a] *Trag. Rom. Frag.* 420 Ribbeck[3] ; *R.O.L.* ii. 306-
307 Warmington; perhaps spoken by Ariadne, deserted
by Theseus on the island of Naxos. [b] Incorrect etymology ; *fretu*, fourth declension ablative. [c] Like goats
on a plain ; very dubious etymology. [d] Greek αἴγες.
§ 23. [a] Given as *Trag. Rom. Frag. inc. inc.* 225 Ribbeck[3] ;

22.   In the verse of Pacuvius,[a]

> To be forsaken in the Aegean strait,

fretum ' strait ' is named from the likeness to *fervens* ' boiling ' water,[b] because the tide often dashes into a strait and boils up.   The Aegean is named from the islands, because in this sea the craggy islands in the open water are called *aeges* ' goats,' [c] from their likeness to she-goats.[d]

23.   They had almost arrived ; on the *aequor* deep
      the *rates* were gliding.[a]

Aequor ' level water ' is a name given to the sea, because it is *aequatum* ' levelled ' when it is not stirred up by the wind.[b]   By *ratis* ' raft ' he meant a war-ship, as does Naevius when he says [c] :

> That they may clash 'gainst the foe
>   Their bronze-shod raft, in which
> They go o'er the liquid sea,
>   Sweating as they sit.[d]

A war-ship is called a *ratis* from the oars, because these, when they are raised through the water on the right and on the left, seem to form two rafts [e] ; for it is a *ratis*—from which this word is transferred—there where several poles or beams are joined together and floated on the water.   From this, the adjective *ratarius* is applied to small boats with oars.

---

but more probably a dactylic hexameter of Ennius, *R.O.L.* i. 458-459 Warmington :

> *Ferme aderant ratibus repentibus aequore in alto,*

quoted by Varro with wrong order of the words, as is shown by his explanation of *aequor* before he takes up *ratis* (*cf.* Vahlen, *Ennius²*, p. xxxvii.).   [b] Correct etymology. [c] *Frag. Poet. Rom.*, p. 48 Baehrens ; *R.O.L.* ii. 68-69 Warmington ; Saturnian, but text very dubious.   [d] The seated rowers.   [e] The same word *ratis* means ' ship ' and ' raft,' whether or not this explanation is correct.

VARRO

III. 24. . . . ⟨hostias⟩[1] agrestis ab agro dictas
apparet ; inful⟨at⟩as hosti*as*,[2] quod velamenta his e
lana quae adduntur, infulae : itaque tum, quod ad
sepulcrum[3] ferunt frondem ac flores, addidit :

> Non lana[4] sed velatas frondenti coma.[5]

25.   Cornu⟨t⟩a taurum umbra ⟨in pugna⟩m *laci*⟨t⟩.[1]

Dicere apparet cornutam a cornibus ; cornua a curvore dicta, quod pleraque curva.

26.   Musa*s*[1] quas memorant nosce⟨s⟩[2] nos esse
                      ⟨Camenas⟩.[2]

Ca⟨s⟩menarum[3] priscum vocabulum ita natum ac
scriptum est alibi ; Carmenae ab eadem origine sunt
declinatae.   In multis verbis in quo[4] antiqui dicebant
S, postea dicunt R, ut in Carmine Saliorum sunt haec :

---

[10] *This statement is in the margin of F, opposite a blank space
which amounts to one and one half pages.*

§ 24.   [1] *Added by L. Sp. and by Bergk.*   [2] *Mue., for*
infulas hostiis.   [3] *For* sepulchrum.   [4] *L. Sp. and Ribbeck, for* lanas.   [5] *L. Sp. and Ribbeck, for* frondentis
comas.

§ 25.   [1] *GS.* (cornutam umbram *L. Sp. ;* cornutarum
umbram *Victorius ;* iacit *Scaliger*), *for* cornua taurum
umbram iaci.

§ 26.   [1] *Scaliger, for* curuamus ac (*which includes the last
word of* § 25).   [2] *Additions by Jordan.*   [3] *Laetus, for*
camenarum.   [4] *Later codd., for* quod F.

---

§ 24.   [a] *Trag. Rom. Frag. inc. inc.* 220-221 Ribbeck³.
§ 25.   [c] *Trag. Rom. Frag. inc. inc.* 222 Ribbeck³.
[b] *Cornu* and *curvus* are not connected etymologically.
§ 26.   [a] Ennius, *Ann.* 2 Vahlen².   [b] Perhaps of Étruscan
origin ; at any rate, not connected with *canere* ' to sing.'
[c] A spelling caused by association with *carmen* and *Car-*

III. 24. . . . it is clear that *agrestes* ' rural '
sacrificial victims were so called from *ager* ' field-
land ' ; that *infulatae* ' filleted ' victims were so called,
because the head-adornments of wool which are put
on them, are *infulae* ' fillets ' : therefore then, with
reference to the carrying of leafy branches and flowers
to the burial-place, he added [a] :

> Decked not with wool, but with a hair-like shock
> of leaves.

25.   The hornèd shadow lures the bull to fight.[a]

It is clear that *cornuta* ' horned ' is said from *cornua*
' horns ' ; *cornua* is said from *curvor* ' curvature,'
because most horns are *curva* ' curved.' [b]

26.   Learn that we, the *Camenae*, are those whom
they tell of as Muses.[a]

Casmenae [b] is the early form of the name, when it
originated, and it is so written in other places : the
name *Carmenae* [c] is derived from the same origin.   In
many words, at the point where the ancients said S,
the later pronunciation is R,[d] as the following in the
Hymn of the Salians [e] :

menta ; though no etymological connexion with them exists.
[d] The well-known phenomenon of rhotacism, the change of
intervocalic S to R.   [e] *Fragg.* 2-3, pp. 332-335 Maurenbrecher ; page 1 Morel.   It is hazardous in the extreme to
attempt to restore and interpret the text of the *Hymn*.   These
sentences seem to invoke Mars not as God of War, but in his
old Italic capacity of God of Agriculture, spoken of in several
functions.   It was the view of L. Spengel, approved by A.
Spengel, that this verbatim text of the *Hymn* was an interpolation, and that *foedesum foederum* of § 27 immediately
followed *in Carmine Saliorum sunt haec.*

VARRO

Cozevi oborieso. Omnia vero ad Patulc⟨ium⟩
commisse⟨i⟩.
Ianeus iam es, duonus Cerus es, du⟨o⟩nus Ianus.
Ven⟨i⟩es po⟨tissimu⟩m melios eum recum . . .[5]

HIC SPATIUM X LINEARUM RELICTUM ERAT IN
EXEMPLARI[6]

27. . . . f⟨o⟩edesum foederum,[1] plusima plurima, meliosem meliorem, asenam arenam, ianitos
ianitor.   Quare e[2] Casmena Carmena, ⟨e⟩[3] Carmena[4]
R extrito Camena factum. Ab eadem voce canite,
pro quo in Saliari versu scriptum est cante, hoc
versu :

> Divum em pa[5] cante, divum deo supplicate.[6]

28. In Carmine Priami[1] quod est :

> Veteres Casmenas cascam rem volo profarier,[2]

[5] *F has* : Cozeulodori eso. Omnia uero adpatula coemisse.
ian cusianes duonus ceruses. dunus ianusue uet pom melios
eum recum.   *This is here emended as follows* : Cozevi *Havet ;*
oborieso *Kent ;* Patulcium *Kent, after Bergk ;* commissei
Kent ; Ianeus *GS., cf. Festus,* 103. 11 *M. ;* iam es *Kent ;*
duonus Cerus es, duonus Ianus *Bergk ;* ueniet *V,* venies
Kent ; potissimum, *cf. Festus,* 205 a 11 *M.*   [6] *At this point,
the remainder of the line and the next four lines are vacant in
F, with traces of writing in the last empty line, which must
have given the data for this statement, found in II and a.*
  § 27. [1] *For* faederum.   [2] *A. Sp. ;* ex *Ursinus ; for* ē
(=est).   [3] *Added by A. Sp.*   [4] *A. Sp., for* carmina
carmen.   [5] *Bergk, for* empta.   [6] *Grotefend, for* sup-
plicante.
  § 28. [1] *At this point, the rest of the page (three and one-
third lines) remains vacant in F, but there is no gap in the
text.*   [2] *Scaliger, for* profari et.

***

[1] Cozevi, voc. of *Consivius* (epithet of Janus, in Macrobius,
Sat. i. 9. 15), with NS developing to NTS as in Umbrian,
the N not written before the consonants (*cf.* Latin cosol for
consul), and z having the value of *ts*, as in the Umbrian
294

O Planter God,[f] arise. Everything indeed have I committed unto (thee as) the Opener.[g] Now art thou the Doorkeeper, thou art the Good Creator, the Good God of Beginnings. Thou'lt come especially, thou the superior of these kings [h] . . .

HERE A SPACE OF TEN LINES WAS LEFT VACANT IN THE MODEL COPY [i]

27. . . . ⟨In the *Hymn of the Salians* are found such old forms as⟩ *foedesum* for *foederum* ' of treaties,' *plusima* for *plurima* ' most,' *meliosem* for *meliorem* ' better,' *asenam* for *arenam* ' sand,' *ianitos* for *ianitor* [a] ' doorkeeper.' Therefore from *Casmena* came *Carmena*, and from *Carmena*, with loss of the R, came *Camena*.[b] From the same radical came *canite* ' sing ye,' for which in a Salian verse [c] is written *cante*, and this is the verse :

Sing ye to the Father [d] of the Gods, entreat the God of Gods.[e]

28. In *The Song of Priam* there is the following [a] :

I wish the ancient Muses to tell a story old.

alphabet.   [g] Epithet of Janus, in Macrobius, *Sat.* i. 9. 15. [h] The god is addressed as more powerful than all earthly lords, whether kings or (perhaps) priests. The gen. plural *eum*, equal to *eorum*, is elsewhere attested.   [i] The vacant lines in the model copy may have represented more of the text of the Hymn, too illegible to copy.

§ 27.   [a] *Fragg.* 4, 7, 20, 26, 27, pages 335, 339, 347, 349 Maurenbrecher. *Ianitos* is an incorrect form, since the word had an original R ; but all the other words have R from earlier S.   [b] *Cf.* § 26, note b.   [c] *Frag.* 1, page 331 Maurenbrecher ; page 1 Morel.   [d] Here *em pa* stands for *in patrem* ; so Th. Bergk, *Zts. f. Altertumswiss.* xiv. 138 = *Kleine Philol. Schriften*, i. 505, relying on Festus, 205 a 11 M., *pa pro parte* (read *pa're*) *et po pro potissimum positum est in Saliari Carmine.*   [e] Equal to ' father of the gods.'

§ 28.   [a] *Frag. Poet. Lat.*, page 29 Morel.

VARRO

primum cascum significat vetus ; secundo eius origo
Sabina, quae usque radices in Oscam linguam egit.
Cascum vetus esse significat Ennius quod ait :

> Quam Prisci casci populi *t*enuere[3] Latini.

Eo magis Manilius quod ait :

> Cascum duxisse cascam non mirabile est,
> Quoniam cariosas[4] conficiebat nuptias.

Item ostendit Papini epigrammation, quod in adole-
scentem fecerat Cascam :

> Ridiculum est, cum te Cascam tua dicit amic*a*,[5]
> Fili⟨a⟩[6] Potoni, sesquisenex[7] puerum.
> Dic tu *i*llam[8] pusam : sic fiet " mutua[9] muli " :
> Nam vere pusus tu, tua amica senex.

29. Idem ostendit quod oppidum vocatur Casinum
(hoc enim ab Sabinis orti Samnites tenuerunt) et[1]
nostri etiam nunc Forum Vetus appellant. Item
significat[2] in Atellanis aliquot Pappum, senem quod
Osci[3] casnar appellant.

---

[3] *Columna, for* genuere. [4] *L. Sp. and Lachmann, for*
carioras. [5] *Laetus, B, for* amici. [6] *Popma, for* fili.
[7] *Turnebus, for* potonis es qui senex. [8] *Turnebus, for* dicit
pusum puellam. [9] *Pantagathus, for* mutuam.

§ 29. [1] *L. Sp. deleted* nunc *after* et. [2] *For* significant.
[3] *For* ostii.

---

[b] The native Latin word was *cānus* ' grey-haired,' from
casnos, with the same root as in *cascus*, but a different suffix.
[c] Sabine was not a dialect of Oscan, but stood on an equal
footing with it. [d] *Ann.* 24 Vahlen[2]; *R.O.L.* i. 12-13
Warmington. [e] *Frag. Poet. Lat.*, page 52 Morel.
[f] *Frag. Poet. Lat.*, page 42 Morel ; the poet's name is
doubtful : Priscian, ii. 90. 2 K., calls him Pomponius, and
Bergk, *Opusc.* i. 88, proposes Pompilius. [g] *Casca* was
a male cognomen in the Servilian *gens* only ; for this reason
Potonius is rather to be taken as a jesting family name of
the *amica*. [h] *Pusum puellam* (see crit. note) was origin-

First, *cascum* means ' old ' ; secondly, it has its origin from the Sabine language,[b] which ran its roots back into Oscan.[c] That *cascum* is ' old,' is indicated by the phrase of Ennius [d] :

> Land that the Early Latins then held, the long-ago
> peoples.

It is even better shown in Manilius's utterance [e] :

> That Whitehead married Oldie is surely no surprise :
> The marriage, when he made it, was aged and decayed.

It is shown likewise in the epigram of Papinius,[f] which he made with reference to the youth Casca :

> Funny it is, when your mistress tenderly calls you her
> " Casca " [g] ;
> Daughter of Rummy she, old and a half—you a boy.
> Call her your " laddie " [h] ; for thus there will be the
> mule's trade of favours [i] :
> You're but a lad, to be sure ; Oldie's the name for
> your girl.

29. The same is shown by the fact that there is a town named Casinum,[a] which was inhabited by the Samnites, who originated from the Sabines,[b] and we Romans even now call it Old Market. Likewise in several Atellan farces [c] the word denotes Pappus, an old man's character, because the Oscans call an old man *casnar*.

---

ally a marginal gloss to *pusam*, since *pusus* had no normal feminine form ; *cf.* French *la garçonne*. But the gloss crept into the text.   [i] Proverbial phrase, equal to ' tit for tat,' or ' an eye for an eye.'

§ 29.   [a] A town of southeastern Latium, on the borders of Samnium.   [b] The Samnites and the Sabines were separate peoples, but their names are etymologically related, and so presumably were the two peoples.   [c] *Com. Rom. Frag. inc. nom.* vii. p. 334 Ribbeck[3] ; these farces were named from Atella, an Oscan town in Campania a few miles north of Naples.

VARRO

30. Apud Lucilium :

Quid tibi ego ambages Ambiv⟨i⟩[1] scribere coner ?

Profectum a verbo ambe, quod inest in ambitu et ambitioso.

31. Apud Valerium Soranum :

Vetus adagio est, O Publi[1] Scipio,

quod verbum usque eo evanuit, ut Graecum pro eo positum magis sit apertum : nam id⟨em⟩ est[2] quod παροιμίαν vocant Graeci, ut est :

Auribus lupum teneo ;

Canis caninam non est.

Adagio est littera commutata a⟨m⟩bagio,[3] dicta ab eo quod ambit orationem, neque in aliqua una re consistit sola. ⟨Amb⟩agio[4] dicta ut a⟨m⟩bustum,[5] quo⟨d⟩[6] circum ustum est, ut ambegna[7] bos apud augures, quam circum aliae hostiae constituuntur.

32. Cum tria sint coniuncta in origine verborum quae sint animadvertenda, a quo sit impositum et in quo et quid, saepe non minus de tertio quam de primo dubitatur, ut in hoc, utrum primum una canis

§ 30. [1] *Laetus, for* ambiu.
§ 31. [1] *Abbreviated to* P *in* F. [2] idem est *Mue. ;* idem *early edd., with later codd. ; for* id est *F.* [3] *Turnebus, for* abagio. [4] *L. Sp. ;* adagio *Laetus ; for* agio. [5] *Aug., for* adustum. [6] *Laetus, M, for* quo. [7] *Turnebus, with Festus,* 4. 16 *M., for* ambiegna.

---

§ 30. [a] 1281 Marx. [b] If the text is correctly restored, this is L. Ambivius Turpio, famous stage director and actor of Caecilius Statius and of Terence ; Lucilius puns on his name. [c] Equal to Greek ἀμφί, and found in Latin only as a prefix.

§ 31. [a] A little-known writer of the second century B.C. ; *Frag. Poet. Lat.*, page 40 Morel. [b] *Adagio*, gen. *-onis* ; not

298

30. In Lucilius [a] :

> Why should I try to tell to you Roundway's [b] round-
> about speeches ?

The word *ambages* ' circumlocutions ' comes from the word *ambe* [c] ' round about,' which is present in *ambitus* ' circuit ' and in *ambitiosus* ' going around (for votes), ambitious.'

31. In Valerius of Sora [a] is the following :

> It is an old *adagio*,[b] Publius Scipio.

This word has gone out of use to such a point that the Greek word put for it is more easily understood : for it is the same as that which the Greeks call παροιμία ' proverb,' as for example :

> I'm holding a wolf by the ears,[c]
>
> Dog doesn't eat dog-flesh.

Now *adagio* [d] is only *ambagio* with a letter changed, which is said because it *ambit* ' goes around ' the discourse and does not stop at some one thing only.[e] *Ambagio* resembles *ambustum*, which is ' burnt around,' and an *ambegna* cow [f] in the augural speech,[g] which is a cow around which other victims are arranged.

32. Whereas there are three things combined which must be observed in the origin of words, namely from what the word is applied, and to what, and what it is, often there is doubt about the third no less than about the first, as in this case, whether the word for dog in the feminine was at first *canis* or *canes* :

the more usual *adagium*.   [c] Terence, *Phor.* 506, etc.
[d] Really from *ad* ' thereto ' and the root of *aio* ' I say.'
[e] That is, it applies also to other things than that which it specifically mentions.   [f] ' Having a lamb (*agna*) on each side.'   [g] Page 17 Regell.

VARRO

aut canes si*t*[1] appellata : dicta enim apud veteres una canes.   Itaque Ennius scribit :

> Tantidem quasi feta[2] canes sine dentibus latrat.

Lucilius :

> Nequam et magnus homo, laniorum imman*is*[3] canes ut.

Impositio unius debuit esse canis, plurium canes ; sed neque Ennius consuetudinem illam sequens reprehendendus, nec is qui nunc dicit :

> Canis canina⟨m⟩[4] non est.

Sed canes quod latratu[5] signum dant, ut signa canunt, canes appellatae, et quod ea voce indicant noctu quae latent, latratus appellatus.

33.   Sic dictum a quibusdam ut una canes, una trabes :

> ⟨Trabes⟩[1] remis rostrata per altum.

Ennius :

> Utinam ne in nemore P*e*lio[2] securibus
> C*ae*sa accidisset abiegna ad terram trabes,

cuius verbi singularis casus rect*us*[3] correptus[4] ac facta trabs.

§ 32.   [1] *For* sic.   [2] *For* faeta.   [3] *Aug., with B, for* immanes.   [4] *Laetus, for* canina.   [5] *M, V, p, Laetus, for* latratus.

§ 33.   [1] *Added by Columna.*   [2] *For* polio.   [3] *Sciop., for* recte.   [4] *Laetus, for* correctus.

§ 32.   [a] *Ann.* 528 Vahlen[2]; *R.O.L.* i. 432-433 Warmington.   [b] Her bark is worse than her bite, as a pregnant bitch was proverbially harmless ; *cf.* Plautus, *Most.* 852, *Tam placidast (illa canis) quam feta quaevis.*   [c] 1221
300

for in the older writers the expression is one *canes*. Therefore Ennius writes the following, using *canes* [a]:

> Barks just as loud as a pregnant bitch : but she's toothless.[b]

Lucilius also uses *canes* [c]:

> Worthless man and huge, like the monstrous dog of the butchers.

When applied to one, the word should have been *canis*, and when applied to several it should have been *canes* ; but Ennius ought not to be blamed for following the earlier custom, nor should he who now says :

> *Canis* ' dog ' doesn't eat dog-flesh.

But because dogs by their barking give the signal, as it were, *canunt* ' sound ' the signals, they are called *canes* ; and because by this noise they make known the things which *latent* ' are hidden ' in the night, their barking is called *latratus*.[d]

33. As some have said *canes* in the singular, so others have said *trabes* ' beam, ship ' in the singular :

> The beakèd *trabes* is driven by oars through the waters.[a]

Ennius used *trabes* in the following [b]:

> I would the *trabes* of the fir-tree ne'er had fall'n
> To earth, in Pelion's forest, by the axes cut !

But now the nominative singular of this word has lost a vowel and become *trabs*.

Marx.   [d] *Canis* is not etymologically connected with *canere*, nor *latratus* with *latere*.
§ 33.   [a] Ennius, *Ann.* 616 Vahlen[2]; *R.O.L.* i. 458-459 Warmington.   [b] *Medea Exul, Trag. Rom. Frag.* 205-206 Ribbeck[3]; *R.O.L.* i. 312-313 Warmington; that is, " would that the ship Argo had never been built."

34. In Medo :

Caelitum camilla, expectata advenis : salve, hospita.

Camilla⟨m⟩¹ qui glos⟨s⟩emata interpretati dixerunt administram ; addi oportet, in his quae occultiora : itaque dicitur nuptiis camillus² qui cumerum³ fert, in quo quid sit, in ministerio plerique extrinsecus ne⟨s⟩ciun*t*.⁴   Hinc Casmilus⁵ nominatur Samothrece⟨s⟩ m*y*steri⟨i⟩s dius quidam amminister diis magnis.   Verbum esse Graecum arbitror, quod apud Callimachum in poematibus eius inveni.

35. Apud En⟨n⟩i⟨u⟩m¹ :

Subulo quondam marinas propter astabat p*lag*as.²

Subulo dictus, quod ita dicunt tibicines Tusci : quocirca radices eius in Etr⟨ur⟩ia, non Latio qu*a*erundae.³

36. Versibus quo⟨s⟩¹ olim Fauni² vatesque canebant.

Fauni dei Latinorum, ita ut et Faunus et Fauna sit ; hos versibus quos vocant Saturnios in silvestribus locis traditum est solitos fari ⟨futura,³ a⟩⁴ quo fando

§ 34.   ¹ *Mue., for* camilla.   ² *Turnebus, for* scamillus.
³ *Turnebus, for* quicum merum.   ⁴ *Turnebus, for* nectunc.
⁵ *For* casmillus.
   § 35.   ¹ *Laetus, for* enim. ·   ² *Mue., from Fest.* 309 a 5
M., *for* aquas.   ³ *Victorius, for* querunda e.
   § 36.   ¹ *Aldus, for* quo.   ² *Laetus deleted et after Fauni,
following Cicero, Div.* i. 50. 114, *Brut.* 18. 71, *Orator,* 51. 171.
³ *Added by Mue., from Serv. Dan. in Georg.* i. 11.   ⁴ *Added
by Aug.*

§ 34.   ᵃ Pacuvius, *Trag. Rom. Frag.* 232 Ribbeck³ ;
R.O.L. ii. 256-257 Warmington.   ᵇ Page 112 Funaioli.
ᶜ Probably certain belongings of the bride.   ᵈ Identified
with Hermes, the messenger of the gods, according to Macrobius, *Sat.* iii. 8. 6.   ᵉ More probably Etruscan than
Greek : there were Etruscans on Lemnos, not far from
Samothrace, which may explain the use of the similar word

34. In the *Medus* [a]:

> Long awaited, *camilla* of the gods, thou comest;
> guest, all hail!

A *camilla*, according to those who have interpreted [b] difficult words, is a handmaid assistant; one ought to add, in matters of a more secret nature: therefore at a marriage he is called a *camillus* who carries the box the contents of which [c] are unknown to most of the uninitiated persons who perform the service. From this, the name *Casmilus* is given, in the Samothracian mysteries, to a certain divine personage who attends upon the Great Gods.[d] The word, I think, is Greek,[e] because I have found it in the poems of Callimachus.[f]

35. In Ennius there is the verse [a]:

> Once a *subulo* was standing by the stretches of the sea.

Subulo is said, because that is the name which the Etruscans give to pipers; therefore the roots of the word are to be sought in Etruria, not in Latium.

36. With those verses which once the Fauns used to sing, and the poets.[a]

Fauni 'Fauns' are divinities of the Latins, of both sexes, so that there are both *Faunus* and *Fauna*; the story has come down that they, in the so-called Saturnian verses, were accustomed in well-wooded spots *fari* 'to speak' those events that were to come, from which speaking they were called *Fauni*.[b] As for

in the mysteries celebrated there. [f] *Frag.* 409 Schneider; Callimachus had occasion to mention the Samothracian rites.
§ 35. [a] *Sat.* 65 Vahlen[2]; *R.O.L.* i. 388–389 Warmington: perhaps referring to the story in Herodotus, i. 141.
§ 36. [a] Ennius, *Ann.* 214 Vahlen[2]; *R.O.L.* i. 82–83 Warmington; 'sing' in the sense of 'prophesy.' [b] Wrong etymologies, both for *Faunus* and for *vates*.

Faunos dictos. Antiqu*i*[5] poetas vates appellabant a versibus viendis, ut ⟨de⟩[6] poematis cum scribam ostendam.

37.   Corpore Tartarino prognata Paluda virago.

Tartarino dict*u*⟨m⟩[1] a Tartaro. Plato in IIII de fluminibus apud inferos quae sint in his unum Tartarum appellat : quare Tartari origo Graeca.   Paluda a paludamentis. Haec insignia atque ornamenta militaria : ideo ad bellum cum exit imperator ac lictores mutarunt vestem et signa incinuerunt, paludatus dicitur proficisci ; quae propter quod conspiciuntur qui ea habent ac fiunt palam, paludamenta dicta.

38.   Plautus :

Epeum fumificum, qui legioni nostrae habet
Coctum cibum.

Epeum fumificum cocum, ab Epeo illo qui dicitur ad Troiam fecisse Equum Troianum et Argivis cibum curasse.

39.   Apud N*a*evium :

Atque[1] prius pariet   lucusta[2] Lucam bovem.

Luca bos ele*ph*ans ; cur ita sit dicta, duobus modis

[5] *Canal and L. Sp., for* antiquos.   [6] *Added by L. Sp., cf.* vi. 52.
§ 37.   [1] *Laetus, for* dicta.
§ 39.   [1] *For* at quae.   [2] *For* lucustam.

---

e This applies both to words and to music.   *d* Page 213 Funaioli.
§ 37.   *a* Ennius, *Ann.* 521 Vahlen[2]; *R.O.L.* i. 96-97 Warmington; referring to *Discordia*, an incarnation of chaos. *b* *Phaedo*, 112-113 ; in Thrasyllus' numbering of Plato's dialogues, the *Phaedo* was the fourth in the first tetralogy. But in Plato's account, Tartarus is not a river of Hades, but the abyss beneath, into which all the rivers of Hades empty. *c* Of unknown etymology ; not from *palam*.

vates ' poets,' the old writers used to give this name to poets from *viere* ' to plait ' *c* verses, as I shall show when I write about poems.*d*

37.　　Born of a Tartarine body, the warrior maiden Paluda.*a*

Tartarinum ' Tartarine ' is derived from *Tartarus.* Plato in his *Fourth Dialogue,b* speaking of the rivers which are in the world of the dead, gives *Tartarus* as the name of one of them ; therefore the origin of *Tartarus* is Greek. *Paluda c* is from *paludamenta,* which are distinguishing garments and adornments in the army ; therefore when the general goes forth to war and the lictors have changed their garb and have sounded the signals, he is said to set forth *paludatus* ' wearing the *paludamentum.*' The reason why these garments are called *paludamenta* is that those who wear them are on account of them conspicuous and are made *palam* ' plainly ' visible.

38.　　Plautus has this *a* :

Epeus the maker of smoke, who for our army gets
The well-cooked food.

Epeus *fumificus* ' the smoke-maker ' was a cook, named from that Epeus who is said to have made the Trojan Horse at Troy and to have looked after the food of the Greeks.*b*

39.　　In Naevius is the verse *a* :

And sooner will a lobster give birth to a *Luca bos.*

Luca bos is an elephant ; why it is thus called, I have

§ 38.　*a Fab. inc. frag.* 1 Ritschl.　　*b* Epeus is not else-where said to have been a cook, though he is said to have furnished the Atridae with their water supply.
§ 39.　*a Frag. Poet. Lat.*, page 28 Morel ; *R.O.L.* ii. 72-73 Warmington.

inveni scriptum. Nam et in Cornelii Commentario
erat ab Lib*y*cis Lucas, et in V*ergilii*[3] ab Lucanis
Lucas ; ab eo quod nostri, cum maximam quadripedem quam ipsi haberent vocarent bovem et in
Lucanis Pyrr*h*i bello primum vidissent apud hostis
ele*ph*antos, id est[4] item quadripedes cornutas (nam
quos dentes multi dicunt sunt cornua), Lucanam
bovem quod putabant, Lucam bovem appellasse⟨nt⟩.[5]

40. Si ab Libya dictae essent Lucae, fortasse an
pantherae quoque et leones non Africae bestiae
dicerentur, sed Lucae ; neque ursi potius Lucani
quam Luci. Quare ego[1] arbitror potius Lucas ab
luce, quod longe relucebant propter inauratos regios
clupeos, quibus eorum tum ornatae erant turres.

41. Apud Ennium :

> Orator sine pace redit regique refert rem.

Orator dictus ab oratione : qui enim verba[1] haberet
publice adversus eum quo leg*a*batur,[2] ab oratione
orator dictus ; cum res maior erat ⟨act⟩ion*i*,[3] lege-

---

[3] *For* uirgilius.   [4] *Aug. deleted* non *after* est.   [5] *G, H,*
Mue., for appellasse.
§ 40.   [1] *G, H, M, for* ergo.
§ 41.   [1] *Sciop. deleted* orationum *after* verba.   [2] *Scali-*
ger, for legebatur.   [3] *GS.* (maior erat *Turn.*), *for* maiore
ratione.

---

[b] *Cf.* v. 150.   [c] An otherwise unknown author ; page 106
Funaioli.   [d] Varro is wrong ; elephants' tusks are teeth.
[e] Apparently correct ; *Lucanus* was in Oscan *Lucans*, pronounced *Lucas* by the Romans, to which a feminine form
Luca was made.

found set forth by the authors in two ways. For in the *Commentary* of Cornelius [b] was the statement that *Lucas* is from *Libyci* ' the Libyans,' and in that of Vergilius,[c] that *Lucas* was from *Lucani* ' the Lucanians ' : from the fact that our compatriots used to call the largest quadruped that they themselves had, a *bos* ' cow '; and so, when among the Lucanians, in the war with Pyrrhus, they first saw elephants in the ranks of the enemy—that is, horned quadrupeds likewise (for what many call teeth are really horns [d]), they called the animal a *Luca bos*, because they thought it a *Lucana bos* ' Lucanian cow.' [e]

40. If the *Lucae boves* were really named from Libya, quite probably panthers also and lions would be called not African beasts, but *Lucae* ' Lucan '; and bears are no more Lucanian than Lucan, though they are called Lucanian. Therefore I rather think that *Lucas* is from *lux* ' light,' [a] because the elephants glistened afar on account of the gilded royal shields, with which their towers [b] at that time were adorned.

41. In Ennius there is this [a] :

> Back without peace comes th' *orátor*, hands back to
> his ruler the business.

Orator ' spokesman ' is said from *oratio* ' speech '; for he who was to present a verbal plea before the one to whom [b] he was sent as envoy, was called an *orator*, from *oratio*. When the business was of greater im-

---

§ 40. [a] See § 39, note *e*. [b] War-towers on the backs of the elephants, too high to be called merely howdahs.

§ 41. [a] *Ann.* 207 Vahlen²; *R.O.L.* i. 72-73 Warmington; referring to an embassy to another ruler, making demands the refusal of which will result in a declaration of war, *cf.* Livy, i. 22. [b] *Quo* ' whither ' is here used with a masculine antecedent.

bantur potissimum qui causam commodiss⟨im⟩e orare poterant. Itaque Ennius ait :

> Oratores doctiloqui.

42. Apud Ennium :

> Olli respondit suavis sonus Eg⟨e⟩riai.[1]

Olli valet dictum illi ab olla et ollo, quod alterum comitiis cum recitatur a praecone dicitur olla centuria, non illa ; alterum apparet in funeribus indictivis, quo dicitur

> Ollus leto[2] datus est,

quod Graecus dicit λήθη, id est oblivioni.

43. Apud Ennium :

> Mensas constituit idemque ancilia ⟨primus.[1]

Ancilia⟩[2] dicta ab ambecisu, quod ea arma ab utraque parte ut Thracum incisa.

44.   Libaque,[1] fictores, Argeos et tutulatos.

Liba, quod libandi causa fiunt. Fictores dicti a fingendis libis. Argei ab Argis ; Argei fiunt e scirpeis, simulacra hominum XXVII ; ea quotannis de

§ 42.   [1] *Victorius, for* egria i.   [2] *For* laeto.
§ 43.   [1] *Added by Scaliger.*   [2] *Added by B,* Laetus.
§ 44.   [1] *Victorius, for* incisa saliba quae (*which includes the end of* § 43).

---

[c] *Ann.* 582 Vahlen[2]; *R.O.L.* i. 438-439 Warmington.

§ 42.   [a] *Ann.* 119 Vahlen[2]; *R.O.L.* i. 42-43 Warmington; a conversation between Numa Pompilius and his adviser, the nymph Egeria.   [b] Fest. 254 a 34 M. inserts *Quiris* in this formula after *ollus.*   [c] Of uncertain etymology, but not from the Greek.

§ 43.   [a] *Ann.* 120 Vahlen[2]; *R.O.L.* i. 42-43 Warmington; enumerating the institutions of Numa Pompilius.   [b] Of the priests ; *cf.* Livy, i. 20.   [c] *Cf.* vi. 22.

§ 44.   [a] Ennius, *Ann.* 121 Vahlen[2]; *R.O.L.* i. 42-43

port, those were selected for the pleading who could plead the case most skilfully. Therefore Ennius says [c] :

> Spokesmen, learnedly speaking.

42. In Ennius is this [a] :

> *Olli* answered Egeria's voice, speaking softly and sweetly.

Olli ' to him ' is the same as *illi*, dative to feminine *olla* and to masculine *ollus*. The one of these is said by the herald when he announces at the elections " *Olla* ' that ' century," and not *illa*. The other is heard in the case of funerals of which announcement is made, wherein is said

> *Ollus* [b] ' that man ' has been given to *letum* [c] ' death,'

which the Greek calls λήθη, that is, oblivion.

43. In Ennius this verse is found [a] :

> Banquets [b] he first did establish, and likewise the
>   shields [c] that are holy

The *ancilia* ' shields ' were named from their *ambe-cisus* ' incision on both sides,' because these arms were incised at right and left like those of the Thracians.

44.   Cakes and their bakers, *Argei* and priests with
              conical topknots.[a]

Liba ' cakes,' so named because they are made *libare* ' to offer ' to the gods.[b]   *Fictores* ' bakers ' were so called from *fingere* ' to shape ' the *liba*.   *Argei* from the city Argos [c] : the *Argei* are made of rushes, human figures twenty-seven [d] in number ; these are each

Warmington ; continuing the list of Numa's institutions. [b] *Libare* is derived from *liba* !   [c] Etymology of *Argei* and of *tutulus* quite uncertain,   [d] On the number, see v, 45, note *a*.

VARRO

Ponte Sublicio a sacerdotibus publice deici[2] solent in
Tiberim. Tutulati dicti hi, qui in sacris in capitibus
habere solent ut metam ; id tutulus appellatus ab eo
quod matres familias crines convolutos ad verticem
capitis quos habent vit⟨ta⟩[3] velatos[4] dicebantur tutuli,
sive ab eo quod id tuendi causa capilli fiebat, sive ab
eo quod altissimum in urbe quod est, Arcs,[5] tutissimum vocatur.

45. Eundem Pompilium ait fecisse flamines, qui
cum omnes sunt a singulis deis cognominati, in quibusdam apparent ἔτυμα, ut cur sit Martialis et Quirinalis ; sunt in quibus flaminum cognominibus latent
origines, ut in his qui sunt versibus plerique :

> Volturnalem, Palatualem, Furinalem,
> Floralemque[1] Falacrem et Pomonalem fecit
> Hic idem,

quae o⟨b⟩scura sunt ; eorum origo Volturnus, diva
Palatua, Furrina, Flora, Falacer pater, Pomona.[2]

46. Apud Ennium :

> Iam cata signa ferae[1] sonitum dare voce parabant.

Cata acuta : hoc enim verbo dicunt Sabini : quare

> Catus Aelius Sextus

[2] *Rhol.*, *for* duci.   [3] *Mue.;* vittis *Popma; for* uti.
[4] *Laetus, for* velatas.   [5] *For* ares.
§ 45. [1] *Mue., for* floralem qui.   [2] *Turnebus, for* pomo-
rum nam.
§ 46. [1] *So F; but* fera (*agreeing with* voce) *Mue.*

[a] See § 44 note c.
§ 45. [a] Ennius, *Ann.* 122-124 Vahlen[2]; *R.O.L.* i. 44-45
Warmington.   [b] The protecting spirit of the Palatine.
§ 46. [a] *Ann.* 459 Vahlen[2]; *R.O.L.* i. 182-183 Warmington.   [b] Ennius, *Ann.* 331 Vahlen[2]; *R.O.L.* i. 120-121

year thrown into the Tiber from the Bridge-on-Piles,
by the priests, acting on behalf of the state. These
are called *tutulati* ' provided with *tutuli*,' since they at
the sacrifices are accustomed to have on their heads
something like a conical marker ; this is called a
tutulus from the fact [e] that the twisted locks of hair
which the matrons wear on the tops of their heads
wrapped with a woollen band, used to be called *tutuli*,
whether named from the fact that this was done for
the purpose of *tueri* ' protecting ' the hair, or because
that which is highest in the city, namely the Citadel,
was called *tutissimum* ' safest.'

45. He says [a] that this same Pompilius created
the flamens or special priests, every one of whom gets
a distinguishing name from one special god : in certain cases the sources are clear, for example, why one
is called Martial and another Quirinal ; but there are
others who have titles of quite hidden origin, as most
of those in these verses :

> The Volturnal, Palatual, the Furinal, and Floral,
> Falacrine and Pomonal this ruler likewise created ;

and these are obscure. Their origins are Volturnus,
the divine Palatua,[b] Furrina, Flora, Father Falacer,
Pomona.

46. In Ennius is this verse [a] :

> Now the beasts were about to give cry, their shrill-tonèd
>   signals.

In this, *cata* ' shrill-toned ' is *acuta* ' sharp or pointed,'
for the Sabines use the word in this meaning ; therefore

> Keen Aelius Sextus [b]

Warmington ; Sextus Aelius Paetus, consul 198, censor
194, a distinguished writer on Roman law.

VARRO

non, ut aiunt, sapiens, sed acutus, et quod est :

> Tunc c⟨o⟩epit memorare simul cata[2] dicta,

accipienda acuta dicta.

47. Apud Lucilium :

> Quid e*st* ?[1] Th*y*nno capto co*b*ium[2] excludunt foras,

et

> Occidunt, Lupe, saperd*ae* te[3] et iura siluri

et

> Sumere te atque amian.

Piscium nomina sunt eorumque in Graecia origo.

48. Apud Ennium :

> Quae cava corpore caeruleo ⟨c⟩ort*i*na receptat.[1]

Cava cortina dicta, quod est inter terram et caelum ad similitudinem cortinae Apollinis ; ea a corde, quod inde sortes primae existimatae.

49. Apud Ennium :

> Quin inde invitis sumpser*u*nt[1] perduellibus.

---

[2] *Bergk filled out the verse by reading* simul stulta et cata *; Vahlen, by proposing* simul lacrimans cata.
§ 47. [1] *L. Sp., for* quidem. [2] *Mue., for* corium.
[3] *Turnebus, for* lupes aper de te.
§ 48. [1] *Mue. (following Turnebus in* cava *and* cortina receptat, *and Scaliger in deleting* in *and* caelo *; he himself deleted* que *and transposed* corpore cava*), for* quaeque in corpore causa ceruleo caelo orta nare ceptat.
§ 49. [1] *M, Laetus, for* sumpserint.

---

[c] Page 115 Funaioli. [d] Ennius, *Ann.* 529 Vahlen[2]; *R.O.L.* i. 458-459 Warmington.
§ 47. [a] Respectively 938, 54, 1304 Marx. [b] Lucilius puns on *iura*, ' sauces ' and ' rights, justice,' and on *Lupe*, a man's name and also a kind of fish. [c] Respectively θύννος ' tunny,' called horse-mackerel and tuna in America ; κωβιός ' sand-goby,' a worthless fish ; σαπέρδης, perhaps ' salted perch,' the word coming from the region of Pontus ; σίλουρος
312

does not mean ' sage,' as they say,[c] but ' sharp '; and in the verse [d]

> Then he began to say at the same time words that
> were *cata*,

the *cata* words must be understood as sharp or pointed.

47. In Lucilius are the following [a] :

> What then ? A tunny caught, they throw the
> goby out.

And

> Sauces of salted perch and of catfish are killing
> you, Lupus.[b]

And

> That you take a . . . and a bonito.

These words are names of fishes ; they originated in Greece.[c]

48. In Ennius we find [a] :

> What the hollow caldron takes back in its sky-
> bluish belly.

Cava cortina ' hollow caldron ' is thus said because that which is between earth and sky is somewhat in the shape of Apollo's tripod-caldron [b] ; *cortina* is derived from *cor* ' heart,' because it is from this caldron that the first fortune-telling lots are believed to have been taken.

49. In Ennius we find [a] :

> Nay even, they carried them off from there despite
> the foes.

' sheatfish,' a large river-fish of the catfish type ; ἀμία, a variety of the tunny which ascends rivers.

§ 48. [a] *Ann.* 9 Vahlen[2]; *R.O.L.* i. 432-433 Warmington; meaning the inverted kettle-shaped space between the earth and the sky. [b] At Delphi.

§ 49. [a] *Trag. Rom. Frag.* 385 Ribbeck[3]; *R.O.L.* i. 366-367 Warmington.

Perduelles dicuntur hostes ; ut perfecit, sic per-
duell*is*,[2] ⟨a per⟩[3] et duellum : id postea bellum. Ab
eadem causa facta Duellona[4] Bellona.

50. Apud Plautum :

Neque Iugula,[1] neque Vesperugo, neque Vergiliae
occidunt.

Iugula signum, quod Accius appellat Oriona, cum ait :

Citius Orion patefit.

Huius signi caput dicitur ex tribus stellis, quas infra
duae clarae, quas appellant Umeros ; inter quas quod
videtur iugulum, Iugula dicta. Vesperugo stella
quae vespere oritur, a quo eam Opillus scribit Vesperum : itaque dicitur alterum :

Vesper adest,

quem Graeci dicunt di⟨vum⟩[2] ἑσπέριον.

51. Naevius :

Patrem suum supremum   optumum appellat.

[2] *L. Sp., for* perduellum.   [3] *Added by A. Sp.*   [4] *For*
duelliona.

§ 50.   [1] *This is certainly Varro's text (so F ; cf.* Iugula *in
the next line also) ; but Plautus has* Nec Iugulae, *which is
assured by the trochaic rhythm.*   [2] *Fay, for* di.

§ 50.   [a] *Amph.* 275. Varro quotes from memory, and
incorrectly ; *cf.* critical note.   [b] *Trag. Rom. Frag.* 693
Ribbeck[3] ; *R.O.L.* ii. 576-577 Warmington.   [c] Usually
called Orion's Belt.   [d] Properly not 'rising' in the
evening, but visible at that time.   [e] Page 93 Funaioli.
Aurelius Opillus, a freedman of Oscan origin, and teacher
at Rome, voluntarily accompanied Rutilius Rufus into
exile at Smyrna about 92 B.C.; the extant fragments of
his works bear on the interpretation of difficult words.
[f] Some think that Opillus is mentioned as using the word

The enemy are called *perduelles* ' foes ' ; as *perfecit* ' accomplished ' is formed from *per* ' through, thoroughly ' and *fecit* ' did,' so *perduellis* is formed from *per* and *duellum* ' war ' : this word afterward became *bellum*. From the same reason, *Duellona* ' Goddess of War ' became *Bellona*.

50. In Plautus is this [a] :

> Not the Collar-Bone nor Evening-Star nor Pleiads
> now do set.

Iugula ' Collar-Bone ' is a constellation, which Accius calls Orion when he says [b] :

> More quickly now Orion comes to sight.

The head of this constellation is said to consist of three stars, below which are two bright stars which they call the Shoulders [c] ; the space between them is the neck, as it were, and is called the *Iugula* ' Collar-Bone. *Vesperugo* ' Evening-Star ' is the star which rises *vespere* ' in the evening,' [d] from which Opillus [e] writes its name as Vesper [f] : therefore the word is said in a second meaning [g] :

> Vesper is here,[h]

he whom the Greeks call the Evening-time Deity.[i]

51. Naevius has the following [a] :

> She addresses her own father, the best and the supreme.

---

as a neuter, *Vesperum*, but this is not a necessary inference. [g] For the meaning of *alterum, cf.* v. 179.   [h] A phrase familiar in marriage hymns, as in Catullus, 62. 1: *Vesper* is not a mere star, but is personified as a deity.   [i] An explanation of *Vergiliae* is expected here, but is not in the extant text.

§ 51.   [a] *Frag. Poet. Lat.*, page 20 Morel ; *R.O.L.* ii. 52-53 Warmington ; Saturnian verse.

VARRO

Supremum ab superrumo dictum : itaque Duodecim Tabul*ae*[1] dicunt :

> Solis occasu diei suprema tempestas esto.

Libri Augurum pro tempestate tempestutem dicunt supremum augurii tempus.

    52. In Cornicula⟨ria⟩[1] :

> Qui regi latrocinatus decem annos Demetrio.

Latrones dicti ab latere, qui circum latera erant regi atque ad latera habebant ferrum, quos postea a stipatione stipatores[2] appellarunt, et qui conducebantur : ea enim merces Graece dicitur λάτρον.[3] Ab eo veteres poetae nonnunquam milites appellant latrones. ⟨At nunc viarum obsessores dicuntur latrones,⟩[4] quod item ut milites ⟨sunt⟩[5] cum ferro, aut quod latent ad insidias faciendas.

    53. Apud N*ae*vium :

> Risi egomet mecum cassabundum ire ebrium.

Cassabundum a cadendo.   Idem :

> D*i*abathra in pedibus[1] habebat, erat amictus ep*i*croco.

Utrumque vocabulum Graecum.

§ 51. [1] *Sciop., for* tabulis.
§ 52. [1] *Vertranius, for* cornicula *, cf.* v. 153.   [2] *For* stipateres.   [3] *Victorius, for* CATPON.   [4] *Added by Kent, from Festus,* 118. 16 *M. ; the lacuna was first noted by L. Sp.*   [5] *Added by GS., from Serv. Dan. in Aen.* xii. 7.
§ 53. [1] *Rhol., for* pecudibus.

---

[b] Page 119 Schoell ; *cf.* vi. 5. By Roman law, legal proceedings could not continue after sunset. [c] Page 16 Regell.
§ 52. [a] Plautus, *Corn.* frag. II Ritschl.   [b] Derivation from the Greek, and not from Latin *latus*, seems to be right. [c] As in Plautus, *Mil.* 76, *Poen.* 663, etc.
§ 53. [a] *Com. Rom. Frag.* 120 Ribbeck[3]; *R.O.L.* ii. 144-

Supremum is derived from *superrimum*, superlative of *superum* ' higher ' : therefore the *Twelve Tables* say [b] :

> Let the last (*suprema*) time of day be at sunset.

The *Books of the Augurs* [c] call the last time for augury a *tempestus* and not a *tempestas.*

52.   In *The Story of the Helmet-Horn* is the verse [a] :

> Who for ten years fought for wages (*latrocinatus*)
>   for the King Demetrius.

Those were called *latrones* ' mercenaries ' from *latus* ' side,' who were at the King's side and had a sword at their own side (afterwards they called them *stipatores* 'body-guards ' from *stipatio* ' close attendance ') and were hired for pay : for this pay is in Greek called λάτρον.[b]   From this, the old poets sometimes call regular soldiers *latrones.*[c]   But now the name *latrones* is given to the highwaymen who block the roads, because like regular soldiers they have swords, or else because they *latent* ' lie in hiding ' to ambush their victims.

53.   In Naevius [a] :

> I laughed inside to see a drunk go tottering.

Cassabundum ' tottering,' from *cadere* ' to fall.'   The same author has this :

> Slippers on his feet he wore, he was wrapped about
>   with a saffron robe.[b]

Both words (*diabathra* ' slippers ' and *epicrocum* ' saffron robe ') are Greek.

---

145 Warmington.   [b] *Trag. Rom. Frag.* 54 Ribbeck³; *R.O.L.* ii. 130-131 Warmington.   This and the preceding quotation were formerly attributed to the *Lycurgus*, a tragedy of Naevius ; while Bergk, *Philol.* xxxiii. 281-282, joined them (reading *moechum* for *mecum* and omitting *habebat*) as consecutive lines in an unidentified comedy.

VARRO

54. In Menaechmis :

Inter ancillas sedere iubeas, lanam carere.

Idem hoc est verbum in Cemetria Naevii. Carere
a carendo, quod eam tum purgant ac deducunt, ut
careat spurcitia ; ex quo carminari dicitur tum lana,
cum ex ea carunt[1] quod in ea haeret neque est lana,
quae in Romulo Naevius appellat asta ab Oscis.

55. In Persa :

Iam pol ille hic aderit, credo, congerro meus.

Congerro a gerra ; hoc[1] Graecum est et in Latina
cratis.[2]

56. In Menaechmis :

Idem istuc aliis ascriptivis fieri ad legionem solet.

Ascriptivi dicti, quod olim ascribebantur inermes
armatis militibus qui succederent, si quis eorum
deperisset.

57. In Trinummo :

Nam illum tibi[1]
⟨Ferentarium esse amicum inventum intellego⟩.[2]

Ferentarium a ferendo id ⟨quod non⟩[2] est inane ac

§ 54. [1] *Neukirch, for* carent.
§ 55. [1] *L. Sp. and Groth, for* hic.   [2] *For* gratis.
§ 57. [1] *Victorius, for* libi.   [2] *Added by L. Sp.*

---

§ 54. [a] Plautus, *Men.* 797.   [b] Doubtless a corrupted
name : for which *Commotria* was proposed by Turnebus,
Cosmetria by Mue., *Demetria* by GS.; *R.O.L.* ii. 597
Warmington.   [c] Properly *carrere* ; not connected with
carēre ' to lack.'   [d] *Trag. Rom. Frag., Praet.* I Ribbeck[3].   [e] Of uncertain meaning ; possibly ' nap, pile,'
from *ad-sta-* ' stand on.'

§ 55. [a] Plautus, *Persa*, 89.   [b] That is, ' companion,
playfellow' from 'fellow-trifler' ; see next note.   [c] Usually

318

54. In *The Menaechmi* [a] :

> Why, you'd bid me sit among the maids at work and
>> card the wool.

This same word *carere* ' to card ' is in the *Cemetria* [b] of
Naevius. *Cărĕre* [c] is from *cărēre* ' to lack,' because
then they cleanse the wool and spin it into thread,
that it may *carere* ' be free ' from dirt : from which the
wool is said *carminari* ' to be carded ' then when they
carunt ' card ' out of it that which sticks in it and is
not wool, those things which in the *Romulus* Naevius [d]
calls *asta*,[e] from the Oscans.

55. In *The Persian* [a] :

> Now sure he'll be here at once, I think, my jolly chum.

Congerro [b] ' chum,' from *gerra* [c] ' wickerwork ' ; this
is a Greek word,[d] the Latin equivalent of which is
cratis

56. In *The Menaechmi* [a] :

> The others enrolled as extras in the army are treated
>> just that way.

Ascriptivi ' enrolled as extras ' were so called because
in the past men who did not receive arms *ascribebantur*
' used to be enrolled as extras,' to take the place of the
regularly armed soldiers if any of them should be
killed.

57. In *The Three Shillings* [a] :

> For I clearly see
> In him a *ferentarius* friend has been found for you.

Ferentarius, from *ferre* ' to bring ' that which is not

plural *gerrae*; with derived meaning of ' trifles, non-
sense.'   [d] γέρρον ' wickerwork ' or anything made of
it, especially shields.

§ 56. [a] Plautus, *Men.* 183.
§ 57. [a] Plautus, *Trin.* 455-456.

sine fructu ; aut quod ferentarii equites hi dicti qui
ea modo habebant arma quae ferrentur, ut iaculum.
Huiuscemodi equites pictos vidi in *A*esculapii *a*ede
vetere et ferentarios ascriptos.

58. In Frivolaria :

> Ubi rora*rii*[1] estis ? En[2] sunt. Ubi sunt accensi ?
> Ecce ⟨sunt⟩.[3]

Rora*rii*[1] dicti ab rore qui bellum committebant, ideo
quod ante rorat quam plu*it*.[4] Accensos[5] ministra-
tores Cato esse scribit ; potest id ⟨ab censione, id
est⟩[6] ab arbitrio : nam ide⟨m⟩[7] ad arbitrium eius
cuius minister.

59. Pacuvius :

> Cum deum triportenta . . .[1]

60. In Mercatore :

> Non tibi[1] istuc magis dividiaest[2] quam mihi hodie fuit.

(Eadem ⟨vi⟩[3] hoc est in Corollaria N*a*evius ⟨usus⟩.[4])
Dividia ab dividendo dicta, quod divisio distractio est
doloris : itaque idem in Curculione ait :

> Sed quid tibi est ?—Lien ene*c*at,[5] renes dolent,
> Pulmones distrahuntur.

§ 58. [1] *Rhol., for* rorani.   [2] *F*[2], *for* an *F*[1].   [3] *Added
by Kent, to complete verse metrically.*   [4] *H*[2] *and p, for*
plusti.   [5] *For* acensos *F*[1], adcensos *F*[2].   [6] *Added by GS.*
[7] *Brakmann, for* inde.
  § 59. [1] *Lacuna marked by Scaliger.*
  § 60. [1] *L. Sp. deleted in* mercatore non tibi, *here repeated
in F.*   [2] *Aug., for* diuidia est, *from the text of Plautus.*
[3] *Added by GS.*   [4] *Added by L. Sp.*   [5] *b, for* liene negat.

────────────────────────────

[b] That is, not to be retained in the hand during use.
  § 58. [a] Plautus, *Friv. frag.* IV Ritschl.   [b] Page 81. 14
Jordan.   [c] For correct etymology, see vi. 89, note *a*.
  § 59. [a] *Trag. Rom. Frag.* 381 Ribbeck[3] ; *R.O.L.* ii. 304-
320

empty and profitless ; or because those were called *ferentarii* cavalrymen who had only weapons which *ferrentur* 'were to be thrown,'[b] such as a javelin. Cavalrymen of this kind I have seen in a painting in the old temple of Aesculapius, with the label "*ferentarii*."

58. In *The Story of the Trifles*[a] :

> Where are you, *rorarii*? Behold, they're here.
> Where are the *accensi*? See, they're here.

Rorarii 'skirmishers' were those who started the battle, named from the *ros* 'dew-drops,' because it *rorat* 'sprinkles' before it really rains. The *accensi*, Cato writes,[b] were attendants ; the word may be from *censio* 'opinion,' that is, from *arbitrium* 'decision,' for the *accensus*[c] is present to do the *arbitrium* of him whose attendant he is.

59. Pacuvius says[a] :

> When the gods' portents triply strong . . .

60. In *The Trader*[a] :

> That's no more a *dividia* to you than 'twas to me to-day.

(This word was used by Naevius in *The Story of the Garland*,[b] in the same meaning.) *Dividia* 'vexation' is said from *dividere* 'to divide,' because the *distractio* 'pulling asunder' caused by pain is a division ; therefore the same author says in the *Curculio*[c] :

> But what's the matter ?—Stitch in the side, an aching
> back,
> And my lungs are torn asunder.

305 Warmington; perhaps referring to portents of the infernal deities.
§ 60. [a] Plautus, *Merc.* 619.   [b] *Com. Rom. Frag.* IX Ribbeck[3].   [c] Plautus, *Curc.* 236-237 ; literally, ' my spleen kills me, my kidneys hurt me.'

VARRO

61.   In Pagone :

> Honos syncerasto peri⟨i⟩t,[1] pernis, gla⟨n⟩dio.[2]

Syncerastum est omne edulium[3] antiquo vocabulo Graeco.

62.   In Parasito Pigro :

> Domum ire c⟨o⟩epi tramite ⟨in⟩[1] dextra via.

Trames[2] a transverso dictus.

63.   In Fugitivis :

> Age ⟨e⟩rgo[1] specta, vide vibices[2] quantas.—Iam
> inspexi.   Quid est ?[3]

Vibices[2] alte[4] excitatum verberibus corpus.

64.   In Cistellaria :

> Non quasi nunc haec sunt hic limaces, lividae.

Limax ab limo, quod ibi vivit.

> Diobolares, sch⟨o⟩enicolae,[1] miraculae.

Diobolares a binis obolis.[2]   Sch⟨o⟩enicolae[3] ab sch⟨o⟩eno, nugatorio ung⟨u⟩ento.[4]   Miraculae a miris, id est monstris ; a quo Accius ait :

§ 61.   [1] *L. Sp., for* perit.   [2] *Pius, for* gladios.   [3] *Aug., for* medullium.

§ 62.   [1] *Added by Kent.*   [2] *Laetus, for* tramis.

§ 63.   [1] *L. Sp., for* agerge.   [2] *Aug., with B, for* vivices.
[3] quid B, Laetus, est *Scaliger, for* quidem esset.   [4] *L. Sp., for* alii.

§ 64.   [1] *Turnebus, for* scenicolae.   [2] B, *Victorius, for* sabini sobolis.   [3] *Turnebus, for* scenicolas F^2, -is F^1.
[4] *Aldus, for* nungento.

---

§ 61.   [a] Plautus, *Frag.* 101 Ritschl ; the play's name is otherwise unknown : Pius proposed *in Phagone*, Ladewig proposed *in Phaone* (*cf.* Ritschl, *Parerga*, 151, 205 ; *Rhein. Mus.* X. 447 = *Opusc.* ii. 731).   [b] That is, the speaker has lost his appetite.

61.   In the *Pagon* [a] :

> Respect for hash is gone,[b] for haunch of ham, for
> chops.

Syncerastum ' hash ' is all kinds of food mixed together, under an old Greek name.

62.   In *The Lazy Hanger-on* [a] :

> I started to go home by a side-way to the right.

Trames [b] ' side-way ' is said from *transversum* ' turned
across.'

63.   In *The Runaways* [a] :

> Then come and look, and see what welts.—I've looked
> now ; well, what next ?

Vibices ' welts,' the flesh of the body raised high by
lashes.

64.   In *The Story of the Trinket-Box* [a] :

> As if they aren't here now, the dark and dirty slugs.

Limax [b] ' slug ' from *limus* ' slimy mud,' because it
lives there.

> Diobolous women, rush-perfumed, quite wonder-foul.[c]

Diobolares ' diobolous,' from two obols [d] apiece.
Schoenicolae ' rush-perfumed,' from *schoenus* ' aromatic
rush,' an unpleasant perfumed ointment.   *Miraculae* [e]
' wonder-foul,' from *mira* ' wonderful things,' that is,
monstrosities ; from which Accius says [f] :

§ 62.   [a] Plautus, *Frag.* 108 Ritschl.   [b] Probably from
trans and *meare* ' to go.'
§ 63.   [a] Plautus, *Frag.* 90 Ritschl.
§ 64.   [a] Plautus, *Cist.* 405.   [b] Probably from Greek
λείμαξ ' slug,' though akin to *limus.*   [c] Plautus, *Cist.* 407.
[d] One third of a drachma, or franc of the pre-war standard ;
now somewhat over five pence British, or ten cents U.S.A.
[e] Used of ugly things by the early Romans, according to
Festus, 123. 5 M.   [f] *Frag. Poet. Rom.*, page 271 Baehrens ;
R.O.L. ii. 582-583 Warmington.

Personas distort*is*[5] oribus deformis miriones.

65.   Ibidem :

Scrati*ae*, s⟨c⟩rup⟨i⟩ped*ae*, s⟨t⟩rittabillae,[1] tantulae.[2]

Ab excreando scrati*ae*[3] sic⟨c⟩as significat.[4]   Scrup⟨i⟩-
ped*am*[5] Aurelius scribit a*b* scauripeda[6] ; Iuventius
comicus dicebat a vermiculo piloso, qui solet esse in
fronde cum multis pedibus ;   Valerius a pede ac
scrupea.   Ex eo Acci positum curios*e*[7] : itaque est
in Melanippo[8] :

Reicis abs te religionem ?   Scrupeam[9] imponas ⟨tibi⟩.[10]

Strittabillas a strettillando ; strittare ab eo qui sistit
*a*egre.

66.   In Astr*a*ba[1] :

Acsitios*ae*[2] annonam caram e vili concinnant viris.

Ideo in Sitellitergo idem ait :

Mulier es⟨t⟩[3] uxorcula :
Ut[4] ego novi, scio acsitio⟨s⟩a quam[5] si⟨e⟩*t*.[6]

[5] *Madvig, for* distortas.

§ 65.   [1] *Mue.* (stritabillae *Bentinus*), *for* scraties ruppae
ides rittabillae.   [2] *So F ; but Gellius,* iii. 3. 6, *and Nonius,*
169. 9 *M., have* sordidae.   [3] *A. Sp., with B, for* scraties.
[4] *L. Sp. ;* siccam significat *Turnebus ; for* sic assignificat.
[5] *A. Sp. ;* scrupipedas *Mue. ; for* scruppidam.   [6] *Bothe ;*
a scauro pede *Turnebus ; for* auscauripeda.   [7] *Ribbeck,*
for curiosa.   [8] *Warmington, for* melanippa.   [9] *For*
scruppeam.   [10] *Added by Mue., metri gratia.*

§ 66.   [1] *Aldus, for* astriba.   [2] *GS. ;* axitiosae *Aldus ;*
for ac sitiose.   [3] *Seyffert ;* mulier es *Turnebus ; for*
mulieres.   [4] *A. Sp., for* uxorculauit.   [5] axitiosa quam
GS. ; axitiosam *Aldus ; for* ac sitio aquam.   [6] *Kent,*
metri gratia ; sit *GS. ; for* sic.

---

§ 65.   [a] Plautus, *Nervolaria, Frag.* 100 Ritschl ; describing harlots.   The first three words are of very uncertain
meaning.   [b] Possibly ' lean with tuberculosis,' or ' worthy

324

Misshapen masks with twisted features, ugly wonders (*miriones*).

65. In the same writer [a]:

Just withered women, limping, tottering, worthless quite.

Scratiae [b] ' withered women,' from *excreare* ' to cough and spit,' indicates those that are *siccae* ' dried up.' *Scrupipeda* [c] ' limping,' Aurelius [d] writes, is from *scauripeda* ' having swollen ankles '; Juventius [e] the writer of comedies said that it was from a hairy caterpillar which is found on foliage and has many *pedes* ' feet '; Valerius [f] derived it from *pes* ' foot ' and *scrupea* ' difficulty.' From this Accius has set it down in an interesting way: thus there is in the *Melanippus* [g] the verse:

You throw your scruples off? A difficulty you'd take upon your back.

Strittabillae is from *strettillare*, itself from *strittare*, said of a person who with difficulty keeps on his feet.

66. In *The Riding-Saddle* [a]:

Wives united make their husbands' harvest dear instead of cheap.

So in *The Bucket-Cleaner* [b] the same writer says:

My darling wife a woman is:
As I have learned, I know how unionist she is.

of being spat upon.' [c] Most probably ' walking on sharp stones,' and therefore ' limping '; from *scrupus* ' sharp stone ' and *pes* ' foot.' [d] Page 91 Funaioli. [e] *Com. Rom. Frag.* V Ribbeck³. [f] *Frag. Poet. Lat.*, page 40 Morel. [g] *Trag. Rom. Frag.* 430-431 Ribbeck³; *R.O.L.* ii. 468-469 Warmington; ' your freedom from a light burden entails the carrying of a heavier one.'

§ 66. [a] Plautus, *Astraba*, *Frag.* II, verse 11 Ritschl. [b] Plautus, *Frag.* 116-117 Ritschl.

VARRO

Claudius scribit axitiosas demonstrari consupplica-
trices. Ab agendo axitiosas : ut ab una faciendo
factiosae, sic ab una agendo ⟨axitiosae, ut⟩[7] actiosae,
dictae.

67. In Cesistione :

Di⟨s⟩ stribula[1] ⟨a⟩ut[2] de lumbo obscena viscera.[3]

Stribula, ut Opil*l*us[4] scribit, circum coxendices[5] sunt
bovis[6] ; id Gr*a*ecum est ab eius loci versura.

68. In ⟨N⟩ervolaria[1] :

Scobina[2] ego illu*n*⟨c⟩[3] actutum adrasi ⟨s⟩en*em*.[4]

Scobinam a scobe : lima enim materia⟨e⟩[5] fabrilis est.

69. In P⟨o⟩enulo :

Vinceretis ce*r*vum curs*u*[1] vel gral⟨l⟩atorem[2] gradu.[3]

Gral⟨l⟩ator[2] a gradu[3] magno dictus.

70. In Truculento :

Sine virtute argutum civem mihi habeam pro praefica.

⟨Praefica⟩[1] dicta, ut Aurelius scribit, mulier ab luco
quae conduceretur quae ante domum mortui laudis

---

[7] *Added by Mue., whose* et *was changed to* ut *by GS.*

§ 67. [1] *Buecheler, for* distribula. [2] *Sciop., for* ut.
[3] *Mue., for* obscenabis cera, *with* o *above first* e *and* v *above
second* b, *F*[1]. [4] *GS.* (*cf.* vii. 50), *for* opilius. [5] *Aldus,
for* coxa indices. [6] *Sciop., for* uobis.

§ 68. [1] *Aldus, for* eruolaria. [2] *Sciop., for* scobinam.
[3] *A. Sp., metri gratia, for* illum. [4] *Lachmann, for* enim.
[5] *Canal, for* materia.

§ 69. [1] *Aldus, from Plautus, for* circumcurso. [2] -ll-,
from Festus, 97. 12 *M.* [3] *Aldus, from Plautus, for* gradum.

§ 70. [1] *Added by B, Aldus.*

---

[e] Page 97 Funaioli. [d] *Cf.* M. Leumann, *Glotta*, xi. 185-
188 ; E. Leumann, *Glotta*, xii. 148.

§ 67. [a] Plautus, *Frag.* 52 Ritschl. [b] Page 92 Funaioli.
[c] Of uncertain etymology ; Festus, 313 a 34 M., has *strebula*,
and calls it an Umbrian word. [d] Varro perhaps derived
it from Greek στρεβλός ' twisted.'

Claudius *c* writes that women who make joint entreaties are clearly shown to be *axitiosae* ' united, unionist.' *Axitiosae* *d* is from *agere* ' to act ' : as *factiosae* ' partisan women ' are named from *facere* ' doing ' something in unison, so *axitiosae* are named from *agere* ' acting ' together, as though *actiosae*.

67.   In the *Cesistio* *a* :

> For the gods the thigh-meats or the lewd parts from
>   the loins.

Stribula ' thigh-meats,' as Opillus *b* writes, are the fleshy parts of cattle around the hips ; the word *c* is Greek, derived from the fact that in this place there is a socket-joint.*d*

68.   In *The Story of the Prison Ropes* *a* :

> At once I with my rasp did scrape the old fellow clean.

Scobina ' rasp,' from *scobis* ' sawdust ' ; for a file belongs to a carpenter's equipment.

69.   In *The Little Man from Carthage* *a* :

> You'd outdo the stag in running or the stilt-walker
>   in stride.

Grallator ' stilt-walker ' is said from his great *gradus* ' stride.'

70.   In *The Rough Customer* *a* :

> Although without a deed of bravery I may have
> A clear-toned citizen as leader of my praise.

Praefica ' praise-leader,' as Aurelius *b* writes, is a name applied to a woman from the grove of Libitina,*c* who was to be hired to sing the praises of a dead man in

§ 68.   *a* Plautus, *Frag.* 94 Ritschl.
§ 69.   *a* Plautus, *Poen.* 530.
§ 70.   *a* Plautus, *Truc.* 495.   *b* Page   90   Funaioli.
c Where the wailing-women had their stand ; *cf.* Dionysius Halic. iv. 15.

eius cancret. Hoc factitatum Aristoteles scribit in libro qui ⟨in⟩scribitur[2] Νόμιμα βαρβαρικά,[3] quibus testimonium est, quod ⟨in⟩ Freto est[4] Naevii :

> Haec quidem hercle, opinor, praefica est : nam mortuum collaudat.

Claudius scribit :

> Quae praeficeretur ancillis, quemadmodum lamentarentur, praefica est dicta.

Utrumque ostendit a praefectione praeficam dictam.
71. Apud Ennium :

> Decem Coclites quas montibus summis
> Ripaeis fodere.[1]

Ab oculo cocles, ut ocles, dictus, qui unum haberet oculum : quocirca in Curculione est :

> De Coclitum prosapia ⟨te⟩[2] esse arbitror :
> Nam hi sunt unoculi.

IV. 72. Nunc de temporibus dicam. Quod est apud Cassium :

> Nocte intempesta nostram devenit domum,

intempesta nox dicta ab tempestate, tempestas ab

[2] *Aug., with B, for* scribitur. [3] *Turnebus, for* nomina barbarica. [4] *GS. ;* Freto inest *Canal ; for* fretum est.
§ 71. [1] *a, Turnebus, for* federe. [2] *Added by Aug., from Plautus.*

---

[d] *Frag.* 604, page 367 Rose. [e] *Com. Rom. Frag.* 129 Ribbeck[3]; *R.O.L.* ii. 142-143 Warmington. [f] Page 98 Funaioli.
§ 71. [a] *Sat.* 67-68 Vahlen[2]; *R.O.L.* i. 392-393 Warmington. The one-eyed Arimaspi of northern Scythia (where the Rhipaean or Rhiphaean mountains were located) were said to have taken much gold from their neighbours the *Grypes* (or Griffins) ; *cf.* Herodotus, iii. 116, iv. 13, iv. 27, who

front of his house. That this was regularly done, is stated by Aristotle in his book entitled *Customs of Foreign Nations* [d]; whereto there is the testimony which is in *The Strait* of Naevius [e]:

> Dear me, I think, the woman's a *praefica*: it's a dead man she is praising.

Claudius writes [f]:

> A woman who *praeficeretur* ' was to be put in charge ' of the maids as to how they should perform their lamentations, was called a *praefica*.

Both passages show that the *praefica* was named from *praefectio* ' appointment as leader.'

71. In Ennius we find [a]:

> Treasures which ten of the *Coclites* buried, High on the tops of Rhiphaean mountains.

Cocles ' one-eyed ' was derived from *oculus* ' eye,' as though *ocles*,[b] and denoted a person who had only one eye; therefore in the *Curculio* [c] there is this:

> I think that you are from the race of Coclites; For they are one-eyed.

IV. 72. Now I shall speak of terms denoting time. In the phrase of Cassius,[a]

> By dead of night he came unto our home,

intempesta nox ' dead of night ' is derived from *tempestas*, and *tempestas* from *tempus* ' time ': a *nox*

quotes (with incredulity) from a poem by Aristeas of Proconnesus. *Fodere = infodere.* [b] Varro means, from *co-ocles* ' with an eye '; but the word is derived from Greek κύκλωψ, through the Etruscan. [c] Plautus, *Curc.* 393-394.

§ 72. [a] Accius, *Com. Rom. Frag. Praet.* V, verse 41 Ribbeck[3]; *R.O.L.* ii. 562-563 Warmington; repeated from vi. 7, where see note *a* on authorship.

VARRO

tempore ; nox intempesta, quo tempore nihil[1]
agitur.

73.   Quid noctis videtur ?—In altisono
        Caeli clipeo temo superat
        Stellas sublime⟨n⟩[1] agens etiam
        Atque etiam noctis iter.

Hic multam noctem ostendere volt a temonis motu ;
sed temo unde et cur dicatur latet.   Arbitror antiquos
rusticos primum notasse quaedam in caelo signa, quae
praeter alia erant insignia atque ad aliquem usum,
⟨ut⟩[2] culturae tempus, designandum convenire
animadvertebantur.

74. Eius signa sunt, quod has septem stellas
Graeci ut *H*omerus voca⟨n⟩t ἅμαξαν[1] et propinquum
eius signum βοώτην, nostri eas septem stellas
⟨t⟩*r*⟨i⟩o*nes*[2] et temonem et prope eas axem : triones
enim et boves appellantur a bubulcis etiam nunc,
maxime cum arant terra*m*[3] ; e quis ut dicti

                Valentes glebarii,

qui facile proscindunt glebas, sic omnes qui terram
arabant a terra terriones, unde triones ut dicerentur
⟨E⟩ detrito.[4]

75. Temo dictus a tenendo : is enim continet

§ 72.   [1] *For* nichil.
§ 73.   [1] *Skutsch, after Buecheler, for* sublime.   [2] *Added
by Mue.*
§ 74.   [1] *For* ΑΜΑΣΑΝ.   [2] *L. Sp., for* boues.   [3] *For*
terras.   [4] *Aug., for* de tritu.

---

§ 73.   [a] Enni*u*s, *Trag. Rom. Frag.* 177-180 Ribbeck[3] ;
R.O.L. i. 300-301 Warmington ; freely adapted from Euripides, *Iphig. in Aul.* 6-8 ; anapaestic. *Cf.* v. 19, above.
[b] *Signa* in this and the following seems to vary in meaning
between ' signs = marks ' and ' signs = constellations.'
§ 74.   [a] *E.g., Od.* v. 272-273.   [b] Charles' Wain, or the
Great Dipper ; and other parts of the constellation Ursa
330

intempesta ' un-timely night ' is a time at which no activity goes on.

73. What time of the night doth it seem ?—In the shield
Of the sky, that soundeth aloft, lo the Pole
Of the Wain outstrippeth the stars as on high
More and more it driveth its journey of night.[a]

Here the author wishes to indicate that the night is advanced, from the motion of the *Temo* ' Wagon-Pole ' ; but the origin of *Temo* and the reason for its use, are hidden. My opinion is that in old times the farmers first noticed certain signs [b] in the sky which were more conspicuous than the rest, and which were observed as suitable to indicate some profitable use, such as the time for tilling the fields.

74. The marks of this one are, that the Greeks, for example Homer,[a] call these seven stars the Wagon [b] and the sign that is next to it the Ploughman, while our countrymen call these seven stars the *Triones* ' Plough-Oxen ' and the *Temo* ' Wagon-Pole ' and near them the *Axis* ' axle of the earth, north pole ' [c] : for indeed oxen are called *triones* by the ploughmen even now, especially when they are ploughing the land ; just as those of them which easily cleave the *glebae* ' clods of earth ' are called

Mighty *glebarii* ' clod-breakers,'

so all that ploughed the land were from *terra* ' land ' called *terriones,* so that from this they were called *triones,*[d] with loss of the E.

75. *Temo* is derived from *tenere* ' to hold ' [a] : for it

Major. [c] Or perhaps even the Pole-Star itself. [d] *Trio* is a derivative of *terere* ' to tread out (the grain from the stalks),' *cf.* perf. *trivi* and ptc. *tritus.*
§ 75. [a] Wrong etymology.

VARRO

iugum et plaustrum, appellatum a parte[1] totum, ut multa. Possunt triones dicti, VII quod ita sitae stellae, ut ternae trigona faciant.

76.   Aliquod lumen—iubarne ?—in caelo cerno.

Iubar dicitur stella Lucifer, quae in summo quod habet lumen diffusum, ut leo in capite iubam. Huius ortus significat circiter esse extremam noctem. Itaque ait Pacuius :

> Exorto iubare, noctis decurso itinere.

77.   Apud Plautum in Parasito Pigro :

> Inde hic bene potus[1] prim⟨ul⟩o[2] crepusculo.

Crepusculum ab Sabinis, et id dubium tempus noctis an diei sit. Itaque in Condalio est :

> Tam crepusculo, ferae[3] ut amant, lampades accendite.

Ideo ⟨d⟩ubiae res[4] creperae dictae.

78.   In Trinummo :

> Concubium sit noctis priusquam ⟨ad⟩[1] postremum perveneris.

Concubium a concubitu dormiendi causa dictum.

§ 75.   [1] B, Laetus, for aperte.
§ 77.   [1] Pius, for de nepotus.   [2] Scaliger, for primo.
[3] Buecheler, for fere.   [4] Laetus, for ubi heres.
§ 78.   [1] Added by Aug., from Plautus.

[b] Wrong etymology.
§ 76.   [a] Ennius, Trag. Rom. Frag. 336 Ribbeck[3] ; R.O.L. i. 226-227 Warmington ; cf. vi. 6 and vi. 81.   [b] Iubar and iuba are not etymologically connected.   [c] That is, shortly before sunrise, when it is visible in the eastern sky. [d] Trag. Rom. Frag. 347 Ribbeck[3] ; R.O.L. ii. 320-321 Warmington ; cf. vi. 6.

continet ' holds together ' the yoke and the cart, the whole being named from a part, as is true of many things. The name *triones* may perhaps have been given because the seven stars are so placed that the sets of three stars make triangles.[b]

76. I see some light in the sky—can it be dawn ? [a]

The morning-star is called *iubar*, because it has at the top a diffused light, just as a lion has on his head a *iuba* ' mane.' [b]   Its rising [c] indicates that it is about the end of the night. Therefore Pacuvius says [d] :

> When morning-star appears and night has run her course.

77. Plautus has this in *The Lazy Hanger-on* [a] :

> From there to here, right drunk, he came, at early dusk.

Crepusculum ' dusk ' is a word taken from the Sabines, and it is the time when there is doubt whether it belongs to the night or to the day.[b]   Therefore in *The Finger-Ring* there is this [c] :

> So at dusk, the time when wild beasts make their love, light up your lamps.

Therefore doubtful matters were called *creperae*.[b]

78. In *The Three Shillings* [a] :

> General resting time of night 'twould be, before you reached its end.

Concubium ' general rest ' is said from *concubitus* ' general lying-down ' for the purpose of sleeping.[b]

§ 77. [a] *Frag.* I, verse 107 Ritschl. [b] *Cf.* vi. 5 and notes. [c] Plautus, *Frag.* 60 Ritschl.

§ 78. [a] Plautus, *Trin.* 886 ; that is, " if I should try to tell you my name." [b] *Cf.* vi. 7 and note *c*.

VARRO

79. In Asinaria :

> Videbitur, factum volo : redito[1] conticinio.[2]

Putem a conticiscendo conticini*u*m[3] sive, ut Opil*l*us[2]
scribit, ab eo cum conticuerunt homines.

V. 80. Nunc de his rebus quae assignificant aliquod tempus, cum dicuntur aut fiunt, dicam.

Apud Accium :

> Reciproca tendens nervo equino concita
> Tela.

Reciproca est cum unde quid profectum redit eo ; ab
recipere reciprocare fictum, aut quod poscere procare[1]
dictum.

81. Apud Plautum :

> Ut[1] transversus,[2] non proversus cedit quasi cancer
> solet.

⟨Proversus⟩[3] dicitur ab eo qui in id quod est ⟨ante,
est⟩[4] versus, et ideo qui exit in vestibulum, quod est
ante domum, prodire et procedere ; quod cum le*n*o[5]
non faceret, sed secundum parietem transversus iret,

---

§ 79.   [1] *A. Sp. ;* redito huc *Vertranius, from Plautus ;* at
redito *Rhol. ; for* ad reditum.   [2] *Laetus, for* conticinno.
[3] *Laetus, for* conticinnam.   [4] *GS., for* o pilius *; cf.* vii. 50,
vii. 67.

§ 80.   [1] *B, Aldus, for* prorogare.

§ 81.   [1] *H, Bentinus, for* aut.   [2] *Aug., for* transuersum *;
the* MSS. *of Plautus have* non prorsus uerum ex transuerso
cedit . . .   [3] *Added by L. Sp.*   [4] *Added by Christ.*
[5] *Aldus, for* lemo.

---

§ 79.   [a] Plautus, *Asin.* 685 ; where the text is *redito huc.
Cf.* vi. 7.   [b] Page 88 Funaioli.

§ 80.   [a] That is, words of actions, whether or not they are
verbs.   [b] Philoctetes, *Trag. Rom. Frag.* 545-546 Ribbeck[3] ;
R.O.L. ii. 512-513 Warmington.   *Reciproca tela* is properly

79. In *The Story of the Ass* there is this verse [a] :

I'll see to it, I wish it done ; come back at *conticinium*.

I rather think that *conticinium* ' general silence ' is from *conticiscere* ' to become silent,' or else, as Opillus [b] writes, from that time when men *conticuerunt* ' have become silent.'

V. 80. Now I shall speak of those things which have an added meaning of occurrence at some special time, when they are said or done.[a]

In Accius [b] :

The elastic weapon bring into action, bending it
With horse-hair string.

Reciproca ' elastic ' is a condition which is present when a thing returns to the position from which it has started. *Reciprocare* ' to move to and fro ' is made [c] from *recipere* ' to take back,' or else because *procare* was said for *poscere* ' to demand.' [d]

81. In Plautus [a] :

How sidewise, as a crab is wont, he moves,
Not straight ahead.

Proversus ' straight ahead ' is said of a man who is turned toward that which is in front of him ; and therefore he who is going out into the vestibule, which is at the front of the house, is said *prodire* ' to go forth ' or *procedere* ' to proceed.' But since the brothel-keeper was not doing this, but was going sidewise along the wall, Plautus said " How sidewise

only the Homeric (*Iliad*, viii. 266, x. 459) παλίντονα τόξα ' backward-stretched bow,' and not as Varro interprets it. [c] Probably from *reque proque* ' backward and forward ' ; not as Varro interprets it.   [d] That is, ' demand return.'

§ 81.   [a] *Pseud.* 955 ;   said of the brothel-keeper as he enters.

dixit " ut transversus cedit quasi cancer, non proversus ut homo."

82. Apud Ennium :

Andromachae nomen qui indidit, recte[1] indidit.

Item :

Quapropter Parim pastores nunc Alexandrum vocant.

Imitari dum voluit[2] Euripiden[3] et ponere ἔτυμον, est lapsus ; nam Euripides quod Graeca posuit, ἔτυμα sunt aperta. Ille ait ideo nomen additum Andromachae, quod ἀνδρὶ μάχεται[4] : hoc Enniu⟨m⟩[5] quis potest intellegere in versu[6] significare

Andromachae nomen qui indidit, recte indidit,

aut Alexandrum ab eo appellatum in Graecia qui Paris fuisset, a quo Herculem quoque cognominatum ἀλεξίκακον, ab eo quod defensor esset hominum ?

83. Apud Accium :

Iamque Auroram rutilare procul
Cerno.

Aurora dicitur ante solis ortum, ab eo quod ab igni solis tum aureo aer aurescit. Quod addit rutilare, est ab eodem colore : aurei enim rutili, et inde eti⟨a⟩m[1] mulieres valde rufae rutilae dictae.

§ 82. [1] *Victorius deleted* ei *after* recte. [2] *Aldus, for* uolunt. [3] *For* euripeden. [4] *Aldus, for* andromachete. [5] *L. Sp., for* ennii. [6] *Turnebus, for* inuersum.
§ 83. [1] *Laetus, for* enim.

§ 82. [a] *Trag. Rom. Frag.* 65 Ribbeck[3] ; *R.O.L.* i. 252-253 Warmington; presumably from the *Andromacha*. [b] *Trag. Rom. Frag.* 38 Ribbeck[3] ; *R.O.L.* i. 240-241 Warmington. [c] But not obvious in the Latin version. [d] Greek ἀλέξειν and Latin *defendere* both mean ' to defend ' a person from a danger and ' to ward off ' a danger from a person.

he moves like a crab, not *proversus* ' turned straight ahead ' like a man."

82. In Ennius [a]:

Who gave Andromache her name, he gave aright.

Likewise [b]:

Therefore Paris now the shepherds as Alexander do address.

In wishing to imitate Euripides and set down the radical, he fell into an error ; for because Euripides wrote in Greek the radicals are obvious.[c] Euripides says that Andromache received her name because she ἀνδρὶ μάχεται ' fights her husband ' : who can understand that this is what Ennius means in the verse

Who gave Andromache her name, he gave aright ?

Or that he who had been Paris was in Greece called Alexander from the same source from which Hercules also was termed *Alexicacos* ' Averter of evils '— namely from the fact that he was a defender of men ? [d]

83. In Accius [a]:

And now afar off I see that the dawn
Is red.

Aurora ' dawn ' is said of the phenomenon before sunrise, from the fact that the air *aurescit* ' grows golden ' from the sun's fire, which at that time is golden. As for his addition of *rutilare* ' to be red,' [b] that is from the same colour ; for *rutuli* [c] is an expression for golden hair, and from that also women with extremely red hair are called *rutilae* ' Goldilocks.' [d]

§ 83. [a] *Trag. Rom. Frag.* 675 Ribbeck[3] ; *R.O.L.* ii. 566–567 Warmington ; anapaestic. [b] More precisely, ' golden-red.' [c] With *rutili* understand *capilli*. [d] A politer term !

84. Apud Terentium :

Scortatur,[1] potat, olet unguenta de meo.

Scortari est saepius meretriculam ducere, quae dicta a pelle : id enim non solum antiqui dicebant scortum, sed etiam nunc dicimus scortea ea quae e corio ac pellibus sunt facta ; in aliquot sacris ac sacellis scriptum habemus :

Ne quod scorteum adhibeatur,

ideo ne morticinum quid adsit. In Atellanis licet animadvertere rusticos dicere se adduxisse pro scorto pelliculam.

85. Apud Accium :

Multis nomen
Vestrum numenque[1] ciendo.

Numen dicunt esse imperium, dictum ab nutu, ⟨quod cuius nutu⟩[2] omnia sunt, eius imperium maximum esse videatur : itaque in Iove hoc et Homerus et A⟨c⟩cius[3] aliquotiens.

86. Apud Plautum :

⟨Ni⟩si[1] unum : epi*ty*rum[2] estur[3] insane bene.

Epi*ty*rum vocabulum est cibi, quo frequentius Sicilia

§ 84. [1] *So F ; but the codd. of Terence have* obsonat. *See A. Spengel, Bemerkungen* 268-270.
§ 85. [1] *For* numerique. [2] *Added by Lachmann.* [3] *Vahlen, for* alius.
§ 86. [1] *From Plautus, for* si. [2] *Aldus, for* epytira. [3] *B, Laetus, for* estuer.

§ 84. [a] *Adelphi* 117 ; see critical note. [b] With *meo* supply *sumptu.* [c] *Quia ut pelliculae subiguntur,* Festus, 331. 1 M. ; the *pelles* were kneaded in the process of making them into soft leather. [d] Page 7 Preibisch. [e] To prevent pollution of the sacred fire. [f] *Com. Rom. Frag., Atell. inc. nom.* ix., page 335 Ribbeck[3]. [g] Euphemism.

84. In Terence [a] :

He whores, he drinks, he's scented up at my expense.[b]

Scortari ' to whore ' is to consort quite frequently with a harlot, who gets her name *scortum* from *pellis* ' skin ' [c] : for not only did the ancients call a skin *scortum*, but even now we say *scortea* for things which are made of leather and skins. In some sacrifices and chapels we find the prescription [d] :

Let nothing *scorteum* ' made of hide ' be brought in,

with this intent, that nothing dead should be there.[e] In the Atellan farces [f] you may notice that the countrymen say that they have brought home a *pellicula* [g] rather than a *scortum*.

85. In Accius [a] :

By invoking your name
And your *numen* with many a prayer.

Numen ' divine will or sway,' they say, is *imperium* ' power,' and is derived from *nutus* ' nod,' because he at whose *nutus* ' nod ' everything is, seems to have the greatest *imperium* ' power ' ; therefore Homer [b] uses this word in application to Jupiter, and so does Accius a number of times.

86. In Plautus [a] :

There's one thing I except :
The olive-salad [b] there is eaten just like mad.

Epityrum ' olive-salad ' is the name of a food which was

§ 85. [a] *Trag. Rom. Frag.* 691-692 Ribbeck³ ; *R.O.L.* ii. 576-577 Warmington; anapaestic.   [b] *Iliad*, i. 528, etc.
§ 86. [a] *Miles Glor.* 24, where the text is *insanum bene*, as also *Most.* 761 (cod. A, in both passages).   [b] A preparation of olives garnished with cheese.

VARRO

quam Italia usa. Id vehementer cum vellet dicere
⟨edi⟩,[4] dixit insane, quod insani omnia faciunt vehementer.

87. Apud Pacuium :

> Flexanima ta⟨m⟩quam[1] lymphata ⟨aut Bacchi sacris
> Commota.

Lymphata⟩[2] dicta a lympha ; ⟨lympha⟩[3] a Nympha,
ut quod apud Graecos Θέτις, apud Ennium :

> Thelis[4] illi mater.

In Graecia commota mente quos νυμφολήπτους[5] appellant, ab eo lymphatos dixerunt nostri. Bac⟨c⟩hi,
⟨qui⟩[6] et Liber, cuius comites a ⟨Baccho⟩ Ba⟨c⟩chae,[7]
et vinum in *H*ispania bacca.

88. Origo in his omnibus Graeca, ut quod apud
Pacuium :

> Alcyonis ritu litus pervolgans feror.[1]

Haec enim avis nunc Graece dicitur ἀλκυών.[2] nostri

---

[4] *Added here by GS. ; after* id *by Mue.*
§ 87. [1] *Aug., for* flex animat aquam.   [2] *Added by
Turnebus, cf. Cicero, Div.* i. 80.   [3] *Added by L. Sp.*
[4] *Turnebus, for* thetis *; cf. Varr. R.R.* iii. 9. 19.   [5] *Aldus,
for* lympholemptus.   [6] *Added by GS., cf.* v. 53.   [7] a
Baccho Bacchae *L. Sp., for* abache *F* (a bacchae *H*).
§ 88. [1] *Victorius, for* furor.   [2] *Aldus, for* abcyon.

---

§ 87. *a Trag. Rom. Frag.* 422 Ribbeck[3]; *R.O.L.* ii. 300-
301 Warmington.   *b Trag. Rom. Frag.* 392 Ribbeck[3];
R.O.L. i. 306-307 Warmington.   *c Thelis* for *Thetis* is
cited by Varro, *De Re Rust.* iii. 9. 19.   *d* There is still a
belief among the Greeks that the Nymphs, now called
Nereids, can render men insane.   *e* Such a meaning for
bacca is nowhere else attested, and is very doubtful ; *bacca*
normally meant ' olive,' but occasionally denoted other small

340

commoner in Sicily than in Italy. When he wanted
to say that this was eaten impetuously, he said *insane*
' crazily,' because the crazy do everything impetuously.

87. In Pacuvius [a] :

Deeply affected, as though frenzied by the Nymphs
Or stirred by Bacchus' ceremonies.

Lymphata ' frenzied by the Nymphs ' is said from
lympha ' water, water-goddess,' and *lympha* is from
Nympha ' water-nymph,' as for example Thetis among
the Greeks, mentioned by Ennius [b] :

Thelis [c] was his mother.

Persons of disturbed (*commota*) mind, whom in Greece
they call νυμφόληπτοι ' seized by the Nymphs,' [d] our
fellow-countrymen from this called *lymphati*. *Bacchi*
' of Bacchus,' who is called also Liber ; his followers
were called *Bacchae* ' Bacchantes,' from Bacchus ;
and wine was in Spain called *bacca*.[e]

88. All these are of Greek origin, as is also that
which is in the verse of Pacuvius [a] :

I roam, in halcyon fashion [b] frequenting the shore.

For this bird is now called in Greek the *halcyon*, and by
our fellow-countrymen the *alcedo* ' kingfisher ' ; be-

---

fruits ; and was therefore applicable to the grape and to its
product wine.
§ 88.　[a] *Trag. Rom. Frag.* 393 Ribbeck[3] ; *R.O.L.* ii. 314–
315 Warmington.　　[b] Like Halcyone, watching for the ship
that might bring back her husband Ceyx. When his dead
body drifted ashore at her feet, the gods in pity changed
them into kingfishers, and imposed calm on the sea for two
weeks before the winter solstice, that they might hatch
their brood unharmed in a floating nest. This period of
calm weather in December is a reality in Greece.

alcedo ; haec hieme quod pullos dicitur tranquillo
mari facere, eos dies alcyon⟨i⟩a[3] appellant.   Quod est
in versu " alcyonis ritu," id est eius instituto, ut cum
haruspex praecipit, ut suo quique[4] ritu sacrificium
faciat, et nos dicimus XVviros Graeco ritu sacra, non
Romano facere.   Quod enim fit rite, id ratum ac
rectum est ; ab eo Accius

rite perfectis sacris

⟨recte⟩[5] volt accipi.
    89.   Apud Ennium :

Si voles advortere animum, comiter monstrabitur.

Comiter hilare ac lubenter, cuius origo Graeca κῶμος,
inde comis⟨s⟩atio Latine dicta et in Graecia, ut
quidam scribunt, κωμῳδία.[1]
    90.   Apud Atilium :

Cape, caede, Lyde,[1] come, condi.[2]

Cape, unde accipe ; sed hoc in proximo libro re-
tractandum.

---

[3] *GS., for* alciona ; *cf. Serv. in Georg.* i. 399.   [4] *Fay, for*
quisque ; *but understand as abl.*   [5] rite perfectis sacris
recte *Turnebus, for* recte perfectis sacris.
    § 89.   [1] *L. Sp. ;* comoedia *Aug. ; for* comodiam.
    § 90.   [1] *Aug., for* lide.   [2] *Kent, for* conde.

---

[c] *Cf.* Plautus, *Poen.* 355-356.   [d] In charge of the *Sibylline Books.*   [e] No etymological connexion.   [f] *Trag. Rom.
Frag.* 690 Ribbeck[3]; *R.O.L.* ii. 574-575 Warmington.
    § 89.   [a] *Trag. Rom. Frag.* 365 Ribbeck[3]; *R.O.L.* i. 374-
375 Warmington.   [b] Not of Greek origin, but adverb
to the native adjective *comis* ' affable.'   [c] Correct etymologies ; but apparently not all ancient authorities agreed
that κωμῳδία came from κῶμος. It is not a question of
(Latin) *comodia* or *comoedia*.

cause it is said to hatch its young in winter, at a time when the sea is calm,[c] they call these days the *Halcyonia* 'Halcyon Days.' As for the expression *alcyonis ritu* 'in halcyon fashion' in the verse, this means "according to the habit of that bird," as when the seer directs the making of each sacrifice in its own *ritus* 'fashion,' and we say that the Board of Fifteen [d] conduct the ceremonies in the Greek *ritus* 'fashion,' not in the Roman fashion. For what is done *rite* 'duly,' that is *ratum* 'valid' and *rectum* 'right'[e]; from this, Accius wishes [f]

When the ceremonies have been *rite* 'duly' performed

to be understood as *recte* 'rightly' performed.

89. In Ennius [a] :

If you'll give me your attention, 'twill be courteously explained.

Comiter [b] 'courteously' means cheerfully and willingly; it is derived from the Greek word κῶμος 'merry-making,' from which come the Latin *comissatio* [c] 'revel' and in Greek, as certain authorities write, κωμῳδία [c] 'comedy.'

90. In Atilius [a] :

Take it, Lydus, cut it, fix it, season it.

Cape [b] 'take,' the same word from which comes the compound *accipe* 'receive'; but this must be taken up again in the next book.[c]

§ 90. [a] *Com. Rom. Frag.*, page 38 Ribbeck[3]. A direction to the cook, to prepare some dish : *come* 'bring together' the main ingredients ; *condi* 'put in the seasoning,' more probably than the manuscript *conde* 'store away' in the pantry or storeroom. [b] This seems to indicate that the imperative *cape* was not in common use unless compounded with a prefix. [c] This promise is not fulfilled.

VARRO

91. Apud Pacuium :

Nulla res
Neque cicurare neque mederi potis est neque ⟨rem⟩[1]
reficere.

Cicurare[2] mansuefacere : quod enim a fero discretum,
id dicitur cicur, et ideo dictum

cicur ingenium optineo

mansuetum ; a quo Veturii quoque nobiles cognominati Cicurini. Natum[3] a cicco cicur videtur ;
ciccum dicebant membranam tenuem, quae est ut in
malo Punico discrimen ; a quo etiam Plautus dicit :

Quod volt de⟨me⟩nsum,[4] ciccum non interduo.

92. Apud Naevium :

Circumveniri video⟨r⟩[1] ferme iniuria.

Ferme dicitur quod nunc fere ; utrumque dictum a
ferendo, quod id quod fertur est in motu atque ad-
ventat.

93. Apud Plautum :

Euax, iurgio uxorem tandem abegi a[1] ianua.

§ 91. [1] *Added by A. Sp.* [2] *For* cicorare. [3] *Groth*
(Cicurini *Aug.*), *for* cicuri innatum. [4] *Canal, for* densum.
§ 92. [1] *Ribbeck, for* ciccum venire uideo.
§ 93. [1] *After* abegi ab *of Plautus, for* ab regia.

---

§ 91. [a] *Com. Rom. Frag.* 388-389 Ribbeck[3] ; *R.O.L.* ii.
312-313 Warmington ; the double negative is here intensify-
ing, as in Greek (*cf.* also Plautus, *Mil. Glor.* 1141 and *Persa*
535), instead of cancelling as is regular in Latin.   [b] For
this name, *cf. C.I.L.* 1[1]. page 630.   [c] Very improbable etymology.   [d] *Frag. inc. fab.* 2 Ritschl: literally, ' as for the
fact that he wants his rations, I do not set even a *ciccus* as
the value of the difference to me whether he gets them or
344

91. In Pacuvius [a] :

> There's no device
> Which can tame or cure the business or remake it new.

Cicurare ' to tame ' is the same as *mansuefacere* ' to make tame ' ; for what is distinct from the *ferum* ' wild ' is called *cicur* ' tame,' and therefore the saying

> A *cicur* nature I possess

means a tame or civilized nature ; from which the nobles of the Veturian clan had the added name Cicurinus.[b] *Cicur* seems to be derived from *ciccus* ; *ciccus* is the name which they gave to the thin membrane which is the division between the sections in, for example, a pomegranate [c] ; from which moreover Plautus says [d] :

> But that he wants his rations,[e] I don't care a whit.

92. In Naevius [a] :

> I see I'm nigh encircled by unrighteousness.

Ferme ' nigh ' is said for that which is now *fere* [b] ' approximately ' ; both are derived from *ferre* ' to bear,' because that which *fertur* ' is borne ' is in motion and approaches some goal.

93. In Plautus [a] :

> 'Ray ! by my wordy strife my wife at last I've driven
> from the door.

not.' *Cf.* Plautus, *Rudens*, 580.   [e] The slave's food, which was measured out to him.

§ 92.   [a] *Trag. Rom. Frag.* 56 Ribbeck[3]; *R.O.L.* ii. 150-151 Warmington.   [b] *Fere* was not derived from *ferre* ; its superlative *ferme* was little used in Varro's time, but became common again in Livy and Tacitus.

§ 93.   [a] *Men.* 127, which has : *Euax, iurgio hercle tandem uxorem*, etc.

VARRO

Euax verbum nihil[2] significat, sed effutitum naturaliter
est, ut apud Ennium :

> Hahae,[3]
> Ipse clipeus cecidit ;

apud Ennium :

> Eu,[4] mea puella, ⟨e⟩[5] spe quidem id success*it*[6] tibi ;

apud Pompilium :

> Heu, qua me causa, Fortuna, infeste premis[7] ?

Quod ait iurgio, id est litibus : itaque quibus res erat
in controversia, ea vocabatur lis : ideo in actionibus
videmus dici

> quam rem sive litem[8] dicere oportet.

Ex quo licet videre iurgare esse ab iure dictum, cum
quis iure litigaret ; ab quo obiurgat is qui id facit
iuste.

94.   Apud Luc*i*lium[1] :

> Atque aliquo⟨t⟩ sibi[2] ⟨si⟩[3] ab rebus clepsere foro qui.

Clepsere dixit, unde etiam alii clepere, id est corri-
pere, quorum origo a clam, ut sit dictum clapere, unde
clepere E ex A[4] commutato,[5] ut multa.   Potest vel a
Graeco dictum κλέπτειν clepere.

---

[2] *For* nichil.   [3] *A. Sp., for* hehae.   [4] *Ribbeck, for*
heu.   [5] *Added by Ribbeck.*   [6] *Mue., for* succenset.
[7] *For* promis.   [8] *Aldus, for* militem.
   § 94.   [1] *Vertranius, for* Lucretium.   [2] *Kent ;* aliquo
sibi *GS. ; for* aliquos ibi.   [3] *Added by Marx.*   [4] *L. Sp. ;*
ex E A *Aug. ; for* et ex ea.   [5] *Aug., for* commutatio.

---

[b] *Trag. Rom. Frag.* 333-334 Ribbeck[3]; *R.O.L.* i. 368-369
Warmington.   [c] *Trag. Rom. Frag.* 402 Ribbeck[3]; *R.O.L.*
i. 380-381 Warmington; *heu* of the manuscript is an
error for *eu*, since Varro would hardly devote two of his
four examples to the same interjection. [d] *Trag. Rom.*

Euax ' hurray ! ' is a word that in itself means nothing, but is a natural ejaculation, like that in Ennius [b] :

> Aha, his very shield did fall !

Also in Ennius [c] :

> Bravo, my child !   That's happened better than you hoped.

In Pompilius [d] :

> Alas !   O Fortune, why do you crush me hostilely ?

As for *iurgio* ' by wordy strife,' that is *litibus* ' by contentions ' : therefore men between whom a matter was in dispute, called this a *lis* ' suit ' ; therefore in legal actions we see it said :

> Matter or suit to which one must make a plea.

From this, you may see that *iurgare* [e] ' to contend in words ' is said from *ius* ' right,' when a person *litigaret* ' went to law ' *iure* ' with right ' ; from which he *obiurgat* ' rebukes,' who does this *iuste* ' with justice.'
94.   In Lucilius [a] :

> And if some of the things any stole for themselves from the forum.

He said *clepsere* ' stole,' from the same source whence others say *clepere*, that is ' to snatch away ' ; they come from *clam* [b] ' secretly,' giving *clapere* and then *clepere*, with change of A to E, as in many words.   But *clepere* can quite well be said from Greek κλέπτειν ' to steal.'

Frag., page 263 Ribbeck³.   [e] From the radicals in *ius* and *agere*, as *litigare* from those in *lis* and *agere*.
§ 94.   [a] 1118 Marx ;   *ab rebus*, partitive with *aliquot*, though *ab* is rarely so used.   For postponed indefinite *qui*, cf. Lucilius, 263 and 266 Marx.   [b] *Clepsere* and *clam* are both from the root in *celare* ' to conceal,' and akin to (not derived from) Greek κλέπτειν.

95. Apud Matium :

Corpora Graiorum m*aereba*t[1] mandier igni.

Dictum mandier a mandendo, unde manducari, a quo et[2] in Atellanis Do*ss*enum[3] vocant Manducum.

96. Apud Matium :

Obsc*ae*ni[1] interpres funestique om⟨i⟩nis[2] auctor.

Obsc*ae*num dictum ab sc*ae*na[3] ; eam, ut Graeci, et[1] Accius scribit scena⟨m⟩.[5] In pluribus verbis A ante E alii ponunt, alii non, ut quod partim dicunt ⟨scaeptrum, partim⟩[6] sceptrum, alii Plauti Faeneratricem, alii Feneratricem[7] ; sic faenisicia ac fenisicia,[7] ac rustici pappum Mesium,[8] non M*ae*sium,[9] a quo Lucilius scribit :

Cecilius ⟨pretor⟩[10] ne rusticus fiat.

§ 95. [1] *Mue.*, *for* merebar.   [2] a quo et *L. Sp.*, *for* et a quo.   [3] *For* ad obsenum.

§ 96. [1] *Vertranius*, *for* obsceni.   [2] *Aug.*, *for* omnis.   [3] *Vertranius, H, for* scena.   [4] *Norisius, for* aut.   [5] *Lachmann, for* scena.   [6] *Added by B.*   [7] fen- *Laetus, for* foen-.   [8] *Laetus, for* maesium.   [9] *L. Sp., for* moesium.   [10] praetor *added by Scaliger* (*whence* pretor *Mue*)., *from Diomedes,* i. 452. 18 *Keil.*

---

§ 95. [a] *Frag. Poet. Lat.*, page 48 Morel. Cn. Matius, fl. 95-80, translated the *Iliad* into Latin, and wrote also mimiambi.   [b] Translating *Iliad*, i. 56.   [c] Derivative of *dorsum* ' back.'   [d] Why the Humpback should be called Chewer, is not clear. Both were stock characters in the Atellan Farces ; Horace, *Epist.* ii. 1. 173, has *quantus sit Dossennus edacibus in parasitis* ' how great a Dossennus he is among the greedy hangers-on,' which suggest that Dossennus also was a large eater.

95. In Matius [a] :

> Grief he felt that the bodies of Greeks were chewed
> by the fire.[b]

Mandier ' to be chewed ' is said from *mandere* ' to
chew,' whence *manducari* ' to chew,' from which also
in the Atellan Farces they call *Dossennus* [c] ' Humpback ' by the name *Manducus* ' Chewer.' [d]

96. In Matius [a] :

> He the interpreter, sponsor of foul and funereal omen.

Obscaenum ' foul ' is said from *scaena* ' stage ' [b] ; this
word Accius writes *scena*, like the Greeks.[c] In a considerable number of words some set A before the E,
and others do not [d] ; so what some spell *scaeptrum* [e]
' sceptre,' others spell *sceptrum*, and some spell the
name of Plautus's play *Faeneratrix* ' The Woman
Money-lender,' others *Feneratrix*.[f] Similarly *faenisicia* [f] ' mown hay ' and *fenisicia* ; and the countrymen call the old man's character *Mesius*,[g] not *Mae-
sius*, from which peculiarity Lucilius is able to
write [h] :

> *Cecilius* let's not elect to be countrified *pretor*.

§ 96. [a] *Frag. Poet. Lat.*, page 48 Morel : apparently
translating *Iliad*, i. 62.   [b] Probably a correct etymology,
and the variation in the orthography of *scena* is the basis for
that in the adjective.   [c] Greek σκηνή.   [d] The country-
folk pronounced as E what the city Romans sounded as
AE ; Greek η in σκηνή and σκῆπτρον was perhaps represented by AE in the speech of city Romans trying to
avoid a country accent.   [e] From Greek σκῆπτρον.
[f] Originally with E, not AE.   [g] A stock character
in the farces ; *cf.* vii. 29.   [h] 1130 Marx ; ridiculing the
country pronunciation of the candidate, who sounded the
AE like E. *Rusticus* instead of *urbanus*.

Quare turpe ideo obs*caen*um,[11] quod nisi in scaena[12] palam dici non de*b*et.[13]

97. Potest vel ab eo quod pueris[1] turpicula res in collo quaedam suspenditur, ne quid obsit, bonae[2] sc*ae*vae causa sc*ae*vola appellata. Ea dicta ab scaeva, id est sinistra, quod quae sinistra sunt bona auspicia existimantur ; a quo dicitur comitia aliudve quid, si⟨cu⟩t[3] dixi, ⟨scaeva fieri⟩[4] av*i*,[5] sinistra quae nunc est. Id a Gr*ae*co est, quod hi sinistram vocant σκαιάν[6] ; quare, quod dixi, ⟨ob⟩sc*ae*num[7] omen est omen turpe ; quod unde id dicitur ⟨os⟩,[8] osmen, e quo S[9] extritum.

98. Apud Plautum :

> Quia ego antehac te amavi ⟨et mihi amicam esse
> crevi.[1]

Crevi⟩[2] valet constitui : itaque heres cum constituit se heredem esse, dicitur c*ern*ere,[3] et cum id fecit, crevisse.

[11] *Vertranius,* B, *for* obserroum.   [12] *Vertranius,* for scaenam.   [13] *For* dedet.

§ 97.   [1] *Aug.,* *with* B, *for* puerilis, *with* l *erased.*   [2] *Aug.,* *with* B, *for* ubonae.   [3] *GS.,* *for* sit.   [4] *Added by GS.*   [5] *Turnebus,* *for* aut.   [6] *Aldus,* *for* scean.   [7] *Aug.,* *for* sceuum.   [8] *Added by L. Sp.*   [9] *Mue.,* *for* quod.

§ 98.   [1] *Added by Aug., from Plautus.*   [2] *Added by L. Sp.*   [3] *Victorius,* *for* canere.

---

§ 97.   [a] An amulet in the shape of a *membrum virile*, as a charm against the evil eye.   [b] In taking the auspices by the flight of birds, the Roman faced south and the Greek faced north ; therefore, as the east (where the sun rose) was always the favourable part of the *templum* (*cf.* vii. 7), the Roman considered the left side favourable and the Greek

Wherefore anything shameful is called *obscaenum*, because it ought not to be said openly except on the *scaena* 'stage.'

97. Perhaps it is from this that a certain indecent object [a] that is hung on the necks of boys, to prevent harm from coming to them, is called a *scaevola*, on account of the fact that *scaeva* is 'good.' [b] It is named from *scaeva*, that is *sinistra* 'left,' because those things which are *sinistra* 'on the left side' are considered to be good auspices ; from which it is said that an assembly or anything else takes place, as I have said, with *scaeva avi* 'a bird on the left side,' which is now called *sinistra*. The word is from the Greek, [c] because they call the left side σκαιά ; wherefore, as I have said, [d] an *obscaenum omen* is a foul omen : *omen* itself, because that by which it is spoken is the *os* 'mouth,' is by origin *osmen*, [e] from which S has been worn away by use.

98. In Plautus [a] :

Since long ago I loved you and decided you're my
    friend.

Crevi [b] 'I decided' is the same as *constitui* 'I established' : therefore when an heir has established that he is the heir, he is said *cernere* 'to decide,' and when he has done this, he is said *crevisse* 'to have decided.'

considered the left unfavourable. Confusion with the Greek method resulted in a double meaning of *sinistra* in Latin. [c] *Scaeva* is cognate to the Greek word, not derived from it. [d] vii. 96 ; apparently as though *ob-scaevum*, opposite of *scaevum*, though in this Varro contradicts his view expressed in vii. 96.   [e] An older form *osmen* is correct, but not the connexion with *os*.

§ 98.   [a] *Cist.* 1, where the codd. have *cum ego* ; metre, bacchiac.   [b] Not perfect of *crescere* 'to grow,' but of *cernere*, whose literal meaning was 'to separate.'

VARRO

99.   Apud eundem quod es*t* :

> Mi[1] frequentem operam dedistis,

valet assiduam : itaque qui adest assiduus fere ⟨e⟩t
quom[2] oportet, is[3] frequens, ⟨cui infrequens⟩[4] opponi
solet.   Itaque illud quod eaedem mulierculae dicunt :

> ⟨Pol ist⟩o[5] quidem nos pretio ⟨facile[6]
> O⟩ptanti est[7] frequentare :
> Ita in prandio nos lepide ac nitide
> Accepisti,

apparet dicere : facile est curare ut ⟨adsidue⟩[8] adsimus, cum *tam*[9] bene nos accipias.

100.   Apud Ennium :

> Decretum est stare ⟨atque fodari⟩[1] corpora telis.

Hoc verbum Ennii dictum a fodiendo, a quo fossa.

101.   Apud Ennium :

> Vocibus concide, fac ⟨s⟩i mus⟨s⟩et[1] obrutum.

§ 99. [1] *Aug., for* quo desimi.   [2] *Ellis ;* fere quom
Canal ; for ferret quem.   [3] *Aug., with* B, *for* his.
[4] *Added by* L. *Sp.*   [5] *GS.* (pol istoc *Aug., from Plautus*),
for dicunto.   [6] *Added by Aug., from Plautus.*   [7] *Schoell*
(*after* A. *Sp., who proposed and rejected* optanti), *for* ptanti
F, *with* p *deleted by cross-lines.*   [8] *Added by GS.*   [9] *Aug.,*
for iam.

§ 100.   [1] *GS., after Fest.* 84. 7 *M. ;* est stare et fossari
Bergk ; est fossare B, *Vertranius ; for* est stare.

§ 101.   [1] L. *Sp. ;* fac is musset *Mue. ;* face musset *Turne-*
bus ; for facimus et.

---

§ 99   [a] Plautus, *Cist.* 6.   [b] *Frequens* usually means
' in numbers ' (that is, many at one place at the same time)

352

99. In the same author,[a] the word *frequentem* [b] 'frequent' in

> Frequent aid you gave me

means *assiduam* 'busily present': therefore he who is at hand *assiduus* 'constantly present' *fere et quom* 'generally and when' he ought to be, he is *frequens*, as the opposite of which *infrequens* [c] is wont to be used. Therefore that which these same girls say [d]:

> Dear me, at that price that you say it is easy
> For one who desires it to be frequently with us;
> So nicely and elegantly you received us
> At luncheon,

clearly means: it is easy to get us to be constantly present at your house, since you entertain us so well.

100. In Ennius [a]:

> Resolved are they to stand and be dug through their
> bodies with javelins.

This verb *fodare* 'to dig' which Ennius used, was made from *fodere* 'to dig,' from which comes *fossa* 'ditch.'

101. In Ennius [a]:

> With words destroy him, crush him if he make a sound.

and not 'frequent' (that is, one in the same place at many different times), which is why the word here needs explanation. Varro takes it as a shortening of the phrase *fere et quom=f'r'e'quom + s*, which needs no refutation. [c] Used especially of a soldier *qui abest afuitve a signis* 'who is or has been absent from his place in the ranks' (Festus, 112. 7 M.). [d] *Cist.* 8-11, with omissions; anapaestic and bacchiac verses alternately.

§ 100. [a] *Ann.* 571 Vahlen[2]; *R.O.L.* i. 190-191 Warmington.

§ 101. [a] *Trag. Rom. Frag.* 393 Ribbeck[3]; *R.O.L.* i. 378-379 Warmington.

VARRO

Mussare dictum, quod muti non amplius quam μῦ
dicunt ; a quo idem dicit id quod minimum est :

> Neque, ut aiunt, μῦ facere audent.

102.   Apud Pacuium :

> Di[1] monerint meliora atque amentiam averruncassint
> ⟨tuam.[2]

Ab⟩[3] avertendo averruncare, ut deus qui in eis rebus
praeest Averruncus.   Itaque ab eo precari solent, ut
pericula avertat.

103.   In Aulularia :

> Pipulo te[1] differam ante aedis,

id est convicio, declinatum a pi⟨p⟩atu[2] pullorum.
Multa ab animalium vocibus tralata in homines,
partim quae sunt aperta, partim obscura ; perspicua,
ut Ennii :

> Animus cum pectore latrat.

Plauti :

> Gannit odiosus omni totae familiae.

⟨Cae⟩cilii[3] :

> Tantum rem dibalare ut pro nilo habuerit.

§ 102.   [1] For dim.   [2] Added from Festus, 373. 4 M.
[3] Added by Turnebus.
§ 103.   [1] So F ; but pipulo te hic Nonius, 152. 5 M., pipulo
hic Plautus.   [2] Aldus, for piatu.   [3] Laetus, for cilii.

---

[b] Onomatopoeic, as Varro indicates.   [c] Ennius, Inc. 10
Vahlen[2] ; R.O.L. i. 438-439 Warmington.
§ 102.   [a] Trag. Rom. Frag. 112 Ribbeck[3] ; R.O.L. ii.
206-207 Warmington ; quoted by Festus, 373. 4 M., with
tuam, and by Nonius, 74. 22 M. (who assigns it to Lucilius,
Bk. XXVI.) with meam.   [b] Monerint is perf. subj. of
monere, a form known from other sources also.   [c] The
word combines averrere ' to sweep away ' with runcare
' to remove weeds.'   [d] Mentioned elsewhere only by
354

Mussare [b] ' to make a sound ' is said because the *muti* ' mute ' say nothing more than *mu* ; from which the same poet uses this for that which is least [c] :

> And, as they say, not even a *mu* dare they utter.

102. In Pacuvius [a] :

> May the gods advise [b] thee of better things to do, and thy madness sweep away !

Averruncare [c] ' to sweep away ' is from *avertere* ' to avert,' just as the god who presides over such matters is called Averruncus.[d] Therefore men are wont to pray of him that he avert dangers.

103. In *The Story of the Money-Jar* [a] :

> By my cheeping I'll bring you into disrepute before the house.

This *pipulus* ' cheeping ' is *convicium* ' reviling,' derived from the *pipatus* ' cheeping ' of chicks. Many terms are transferred from the cries of animals to men,[b] of which some are obvious and others are obscure. Among the clear terms are the following : Ennius's [c]

> For it his mind and his heart both are barking.

Plautus's [d]

> The odious fellow yelps at all his household, every one.

Caecilius's [e]

> To bleat the thing abroad, so that he thought it nought.

Gellius, v. 12. 14, as a god who may avert ills from men if his favour be won.
§ 103. [a] Plautus, *Aul.* 446. [b] The special words in this and the next section are properly used of animal cries and noises, but in these citations are applied to sounds made by human beings. [c] *Ann.* 584 Vahlen[2] ; *R.O.L.* i. 174-175 Warmington ; *cf. Odys.* xx. 13. [d] *Fab. inc., frag.* III Ritschl. [e] *Com. Rom. Frag.* 249 Ribbeck[3] ; *R.O.L.* i. 554-555 Warmington.

Lucilii :

> Haec, inquam, rudet ex rostris atque hei⟨u⟩litabit.[4]

Eiusdem :

> Quantum hinnitum atque equitatum.

104.   Minus aper*ta*, *ut*[1] Porcii ab lupo :

> Volitare ululantis.

En⟨n⟩ii[2] a vitulo :

> Tibicina maximo labore mugit.

Eiusdem a bove :

> Clamore[3] bovantes.

Eiusdem a leone :

> Pausam fecere[4] fremendi.

Eiusdem ab *hae*do[5] :

> Clamor ad caelum volvendus per *a*ethera vagit.

Sue*i* a[6] ⟨merula⟩[7] :

> Frendi*t* e fronde et fritinni⟨t⟩[8] suaviter.

---

[4] *From Nonius*, 21. 20, *for* hcilitabit.
   § 104.   [1] *L. Sp.;* aperta *Aug.; for* aperiant.   [2] *For*
enii.   [3] *Aldus, for* clamorem.   [4] *Rhol., for* facere.
[5] *Aug., for* edo.   [6] *Luc. Mueller, for* sucta.   [7] *Added by*
GS., after Heraeus.   [8] *Stowasser, for* frendice frunde et
fritinni *F ;* fronde *Kent.*

---

[f] 261 Marx ; said of a man seeking the support of the
voters, according to Nonius, 21. 18 M.   [g] 1275 Marx.
   § 104.   [a] *Cf.* page 46 Morel.   [b] *Inc.* 7 Vahlen[2]; *R.O.L.*
i. 438-439 Warmington.   [c] *Ann.* 585 Vahlen[2]; *R.O.L.*
i. 174-175 Warmington; *boare* from Greek βοᾶν 'to shout,'
with assimilation to *bov-em* ' ox.'   [d] *Ann.* 586 Vahlen[2];
R.O.L. i. 174-175 Warmington.   [e] *Ann.* 531 Vahlen[2];

Lucilius's [f]

> This, I say, he'll bray from the stand and lament
> to the public.

The same poet's [g]

> How much neighing and prancing like horses.

104. Less clear are the following, such as that of Porcius, an expression derived from wolves [a] :

> To flutter while howling.

That of Ennius, from calves [b] :

> The piper-girl doth bleat with great to-do.

That of the same poet, from oxen [c] :

> Bellowing with uproar.

That of the same poet, from lions [d] :

> A stop they made of the roaring.

That of the same poet, from young goats [e] :

> Shouting rolls to the sky and wails through the
> ether.

That of Sueius, from blackbirds [f] :

> From 'midst the leaves he [g] snaps his bill [h] and
> sweetly chirps.[i]

R.O.L. i. 156-157 Warmington ; perhaps *clamos* or *clamorque* should be read, or the word order changed, to give a long syllable in the second place.   [f] Sueius, page 54 Morel ; writer of idylls and on the habits and breeding of birds ; perhaps identical with the *eques* M. Sueius, aedile in 74, friend of Varro and Cicero and owner of a profitable bird-breeding establishment.   [g] Denoting a man, not a bird. [h] *Frendere*, often meaning 'to gnash the teeth,' here means 'to make a harsh note,' as certain birds do.   [i] *Cf. Corpus Gloss. Lat.* vi.-vii., on *fritamentum* (*vox merulae*) and *fritinniunt*.

VARRO

Macci[9] in Casina, a fringuilla :

> Quid fringuttis ?   Quid istuc tam cupide cupis ?

Suei[10] a volucribus[11] :

> Ita tradet aeque in re⟨m⟩ neque[12] in
> Iudicium Aesopi nec theatri trittiles.

105.   In Colace :

> Nexum . . .

⟨Nexum⟩[1] Manilius[2] scribit omne quod per libram et
aes geritur, in quo sint mancipia ; Mucius, quae per
aes et libram fiant ut obligentur, praeter quom[3]
mancipio detur. Hoc verius esse ipsum verbum
ostendit, de quo quaerit⟨ur⟩[4] : nam id aes[5] quod
obligatur per libram neque suum fit, inde nexum
dictum. Liber qui suas operas in servitutem pro
pecunia quam debebat ⟨nectebat⟩,[6] dum solveret,
nexus vocatur, ut ab aere obaeratus. Hoc C. Poetelio

---

[9] *GS., after* Mati *Mue., for* Maccius.   [10] *Baehrens, for*
sues.   [11] *Mue. ;* a volucri *L. Sp. ;   for* auoluerat.
[12] *Kent, for* tradedeque inreneque.
§ 105.   [1] *Added by* L. Sp., *who recognized the lacuna.*
[2] *Laetus, for* mamilius.   [3] *Huschke, for* quam.   [4] *Aug.,
for* querit.   [5] *Mommsen, for* est.   [6] debebat nectebat
Kent ; debeat dat *Aug. ;   for* debebat.

---

[j] Plautus, *Cas.* 267 ; the more common orthography is
fringilla and *friguttis.*   [k] *Frag. Poet. Lat.*, page 54
Morel ;   wrongly listed by Ribbeck[3] as Juventius, *Com.
Rom. Frag.* IV.   [l] *Trit*, the sound made by the crushing
or breaking of a hard grain or seed, as by the strong-beaked
birds. If the text is correctly restored, the passage refers
to a complaint against *trittiles*, that is, persons who made
similar noises and thereby ‘disturbed a theatrical performance ; the poet says that he will refer the complaint to a
regular law-court, and not to the prejudiced decision of the
358

That of Maccius in the *Casina*, from finches [j] :

> What do you twitter for ? What's that you wish so
>   eagerly ?

That of Sueius, from birds [k] :

> So he'll bring the snappers [l] fairly into court and not
> To the judgement of Aesopus [m] and the audience.

105. In *The Flatterer* [a] :

> A bound obligation . . .

Nexum ' bound obligation,' Manilius [b] writes, is everything which is transacted by cash and balance-scale,[c] including rights of ownership ; but Mucius [d] defines it as those things which are done by copper ingot and balance-scale in such a way that they rest under formal obligation, except when delivery of property is made under formal taking of possession. That the latter is the truer interpretation, is shown by the very word about which the inquiry is made : for that copper which is placed under obligation according to the balance-scale and does not again become independent (*nec suum*) of this obligation, is from that fact said to be *nexum* ' bound.' A free man who, for money which he owed, *nectebat* ' bound ' his labour in slavery until he should pay, is called a *nexus* ' bondslave,' just as a man is called *obaeratus* ' indebted,' from *aes* ' money-debt.' When Gaius Poetelius Libo Visulus [e] was

offended actor and of the annoyed fellow-spectators.
[m] Famous tragic actor of Cicero's time.

§ 105.   [a] Plautus, *Frag.* IV Ritschl ; but possibly from the *Colax* of Naevius.   [b] Page 6 Huschke.   [c] That is, by agreement to pay a sum of money, measured by weight.   [d] Page 18 Huschke.   [e] Consul in 346, 333 (?), 326 (Livy, viii. 23. 17), and dictator in 313 (Livy, ix. 28. 2), in which Varro sets the abolition of slavery for debt, though Livy, viii. 28, sets it in his third consulship.

VARRO

⟨Li⟩*bone Visolo*[7] dictatore sublatum ne fieret, et omnes qui Bonam Copiam iurarunt, ne essent nexi dissoluti.

106. In Ca⟨sina⟩ :

> Sine ame*t*,[1] sine quod lubet id facia*t*,[2]
> Quando tibi domi nihil[3] delicuum est.

Dictum ab eo, quod ⟨ad⟩ deliquandum non sunt, ut turbida quae sunt deliquantur, ut liquida fiant. Aurelius scribit delicuum es*se*[4] ab liquido ; Cla⟨u⟩dius ab eliquato. Si quis alterutrum sequi malet,[5] habebit auctorem.

Apud Atilium :

> Per laetitiam liquitur
> Animus.

Ab liquando liquitur fictum.

VI. 107. Multa apud poetas reliqua esse verba quorum origines possint dici, non dubito, ut apud Naevium in *A*esiona mucro[1] gladii " lingula " a lingua ; in Clastidio " vitulantes " a Vitula ; in Dolo

---

[7] Poetelio Libone Visolo *Lachmann ;* Poetelio Visolo *Aug. ; for* popillio vocare sillo.

§ 106. [1] In Casina *Laetus,* sine amet *Aldus (from Plautus), for* in casineam esses. [2] *Aug. (from Plautus), for* facias. [3] *Plautus has* nihil domi. [4] *For* est. [5] *Laetus, for* mallet.

§ 107. [1] Aesiona *Buecheler,* mucro *Groth, for* esionam uero.

---

f That is, swore that they were not regular slaves, but were held in slavery for debt only. *g* Mentioned also by Ovid, *Met.* ix. 88.

§ 106. *a* Plautus, *Cas.* 206-207 ; anapaestic. *b* Apparently meant by Plautus as ' lacking,' from *delinquere* ' to lack,' and so understood by Festus, 73. 10 M., who glosses it with *minus.* Varro has taken it as ' strainable, subject to straining (for purification),' and has connected it with *liquare* and *liquere* ' to strain, purify,' also ' to melt.' *c* Page

dictator, this method of dealing with debtors was done away with, and all who took oath *f* by the Good Goddess of Plenty *g* were freed from being bond-slaves.

106. In the *Casina* *a* :

> Let him go and make love, let him do what he will,
> As long as at home you have nothing amiss.

Nihil delicuum *b* ' nothing amiss ' is said from this, that things are not *ad deliquandum* ' in need of straining out ' the admixtures, as those which are turbid are strained, that they may become *liquida* ' clear.' Aurelius *c* writes that *delicuum* is from *liquidum* ' clear '; Claudius,*d* that it is from *eliquatum* ' strained.' Anyone who prefers to follow either of them will have an authority to back him up.

In Atilius *e* :

> With joy his mind is melted.

Liquitur ' is melted ' is formed from *liquare* ' to melt.'

VI. 107. I am quite aware *a* that there are many words still remaining in the poets, whose origins could be set forth ; as in Naevius,*b* in the *Hesione,*c* the tip of a sword is called *lingula*, from *lingua* ' tongue '; in the *Clastidium,*d* *vitulantes* ' singing songs

89 Funaioli. *d* Page 97 Funaioli. *e* Com. Rom. Frag., inc. fab. frag. II, page 37 Ribbeck³.

§ 107. *a* Cf. the beginning of § 109. *b* All the citations in § 107 and § 108 are from Naevius ; R.O.L. ii. 88-89, 92-93, 96-97, 104-105, 136-137, 597-598 Warmington. *c* Trag. Rom. Frag. 1 Ribbeck³ ; for the spelling of the title, cf. Buecheler, Rh. Mus. xxvii. 475. *d* Trag. Rom. Frag., Praet. I Ribbeck³ ; *vitulari* was glossed by Varro with παιανί-ζειν, according to Macrobius, Sat. iii. 2. 11. It is difficult to connect the two words with Latin *victus* and *victoria*, so that the resemblance may be fortuitous—unless *Vitula* be a dialectal word, with CT reduced to T.

"caperrata fronte " a caprae fronte ; in Demetrio
"persibus " a perite : itaque sub hoc glossema
'callide ' subscribunt ; in Lampadione " protinam "
a protinus, continuitatem significans ; in Nagidone
" clu⟨ci⟩da*t*us "² suavis, tametsi a magistris accepi-
mus mansuetum ; in Romulo " ⟨con⟩sponsus "³ contra
sponsum rogatus ; in Stigmatia " praebia " a prae-
bendo, ut sit tutus, quod si⟨n⟩t⁴ remedia in collo
pueris ; in Technico⁵ " confic*t*ant"⁶ a conficto convenire dictum ;

108. In Tarentilla " p⟨r⟩ae⟨l⟩u⟨c⟩idum "¹ a luce,
illustre ; in Tunicularia :

eꞇbol⟨ic⟩as² aulas quassant

quae eiciuntur, a Graeco verbo ἐκβολή³ dictum ; in
Bello Punico :

nec satis sardare⁴

² *Scaliger, for* caudacus.   ³ *Neukirch, with Popma, for*
sponsus.   ⁴ *Laetus, for* sit.   ⁵ *For* thechnico.   ⁶ *Turne-*
bus, for conficiant.
    § 108.   ¹ *Mue., for* pacui dum.   ² *Kent, for* exbolas,
metri gratia.   ³ *Aldus, for* exbole.   ⁴ *A. Sp. (from*
Festus, 323. 6 *M.*), *for* sarrare.

ᵉ Com. Rom. Frag. after 49 Ribbeck³ ; *caperrata* may be
related to *capra* only by popular etymology.   *ᶠ Com. Rom.*
Frag. after 49 Ribbeck³ ; *persibus* is seemingly an Oscan
perfect participle active, *cf.* Oscan *sipus,* from which perhaps
it is to be corrected to *persipus.*   ᵍ Page 113 Funaioli.
ʰ *Com. Rom. Frag.* after 60 Ribbeck³.   ⁱ *Com. Rom.*
Frag. after 60 Ribbeck³ ; *clucidatus* is a participle to a Latin
verb borrowed from Greek γλυκίζειν ' to sweeten.'   ʲ *Trag.*
Rom. Frag., Praet. II Ribbeck³ ; for *consponsus, cf.* vi. 70.
ᵏ *Com. Rom. Frag.* 71 Ribbeck³.   ˡ *Com. Rom. Frag.* after
93 Ribbeck³ ; *confictant,* derived from *confingere.*

of victory,' from *Vitula* 'Goddess of Joy and Victory'; in *The Artifice*,[e] *caperrata fronte* 'with wrinkled forehead,' from the forehead of a *capra* 'she-goat'; in the *Demetrius*,[f] *persibus* 'very knowing,' from *perite* 'learnedly': therefore under this rare word they write [g] *callide* 'shrewdly'; in the *Lampadio*,[h] *protinam* 'forthwith' from *protinus* (of the same meaning), indicating lack of interruption in time or place; in the *Nagido*,[i] *clucidatus* 'sweetened,' although we have been told by the teachers that it means 'tame'; in the *Romulus*,[j] *consponsus*, meaning a person who has been asked to make a counter-promise; in *The Branded Slave*,[k] *praebia* 'amulets,' from *praebere* 'providing' that he may be safe, because they are prophylactics to be hung on boys' necks; in *The Craftsman*,[l] *conficiant* 'they unite on a tale,' said from agreeing on a *confictum* 'fabrication.'

108. Also, in *The Girl of Tarentum*,[a] *praelucidum* 'very brilliant,' from *lux* 'light,' meaning 'shining'; in *The Story of the Shirt*,[b]

> They shake the jars that make the lots jump out,

ecbolicas 'causing to jump out,' because of the lots which are cast out, is said from the Greek word ἐκβολή ; and in *The Punic War* [c]

> Not even quite *sardare* 'to understand like a Sardinian,'

---

§ 108. [a] *Com. Rom. Frag.* after 93 Ribbeck³. [b] *Com. Rom. Frag.* 103 Ribbeck³; *R.O.L.* ii. 106-107 Warmington (with different interpretation). [c] *Frag. Poet. Rom.* 53-54 Baehrens; *R.O.L.* ii. 72-73 Warmington. According to Festus, 322 a 24 and 323. 6 M., *sardare* means *intellegere*, perhaps 'to understand like a Sardinian,' that is, very poorly, for the Sardinians had in antiquity a bad reputation in various lines. The verse of Naevius runs: *Quod bruti nec satis sardare queunt.*

ab serare dictum, id est aperire ; hinc etiam sera,*
qua remota fores panduntur.

VII. 109. Sed quod vereor ne plures sint futuri
qui de hoc genere me quod nimium multa scripserim[1]
reprehendant quam quod[2] reliquerim[3] quaedam
accusent, ideo potius iam reprimendum quam pro-
cudendum puto esse volumen : nemo reprensus qui e
segete ad spicilegium reliquit stipulam. Quare in-
stitutis sex libris, quemadmodum rebus Latina
nomina essent imposita ad usum nostrum : e quis tris[4]
scripsi Po.[5] Septumio qui mihi fuit quaestor, tris tibi,
quorum hic est tertius, priores de disciplina verborum
originis, posteriores de verborum originibus. In illis,
qui ante sunt, in primo volumine est quae dicantur,
cur ἐτυμολογική[6] neque ar⟨s⟩ sit[7] neque ea utilis sit,
in secundo quae sint, cur et ars ea sit et ⟨ut⟩ilis[8] sit,
in tertio quae forma etymologiae.[9]

110. In secundis tribus quos ad te misi item
generatim discretis, primum in quo sunt origines
verborum[1] locorum et earum rerum quae in locis
esse solent, secundum quibus vocabulis te⟨m⟩pora
sint notata et eae res quae in temporibus fiunt, tertius

<hr>

[5] *Ed. Veneta, for* serae.
§ 109. [1] *Laetus, for* rescripserint. [2] quam quod *Aldus,
for* quamquam. [3] *For* reliquerint. [4] *Laetus, for* tres.
[5] po *stands here in F, but with lines drawn through the letters.*
[6] *L. Sp., for* ethimologice. [7] ars sit *V, p, L. Sp., for* ansit.
[8] et utilis *Turnebus;* et illis utilis *V; for* et illis *F.* [9] *For*
ethimologiae.
§ 110. [1] *Crossed out by F[1], but required by the meaning.*

<hr>

[d] In such an etymology, Varro is operating on the basis that
things may be named from their opposites ; *cf.* Festus, 122.
16 M., *ludum dicimus, in quo minime luditur.*
§ 109. [a] A *liber* or ' book ' was calculated to fill a *volumen*

where *sardare* is said from *serare* ' to bolt,' [d] that is, *sardare* means ' to open '; from this also *sera* ' bolt,' on the removal of which the doors are opened.

VII. 109. But because I fear that there will be more who will blame me for writing too much of this sort than will accuse me of omitting certain items, I think that this roll must now rather be compressed than hammered out to greater length [a] : no one is blamed who in the cornfield has left the stems for the gleaning.[b] Therefore as I had arranged six books [c] on how Latin names were set upon things for our use [d] : of these I dedicated three to Publius Septumius who was my quaestor,[e] and three to you, of which this is the third—the first three on the doctrine of the origin of words, the second three [f] on the origins of words. Of those which precede, the first roll contains the arguments which are offered as to why Etymology is not a branch of learning and is not useful ; the second contains the arguments why it is a branch of learning and is useful ; the third states what the nature of etymology is.

110. In the second three which I sent to you, the subjects are likewise divided off : first, that in which the origins of words for places are set forth, and for those things which are wont to be in places ; second, with what words times are designated and those things which are done in times ; third, the present

or ' roll ' of convenient size for handling.   [b] That is, who has cut off the ears of standing grain and left the stalks. [c] Books II.-VII. ; *cf.* v. 1.   [d] This sentence is resumed at *Quocirca*, in the middle of § 110.   [e] Varro held office in the war against the pirates and Mithridates in 67–66, under Pompey, and again in Pompey's forces in Spain in 49 and at Pharsalus in 48 ; but it is unknown in which of these he had Septumius as quaestor.   [f] Books V.-VII.

hic, in quo a poetis item sumpta ut il*la*[2] quae dixi in duobus libris sol*u*ta[3] oratione. Quocirca quoniam omnis operis de Lingua Latina tris feci partis, primo quemadmodum vocabula imposita essent rebus, secundo quemadmodum ea in casus declinarentur, tertio quemadmodum coniungerentur, prima parte perpetrata, ut secundam ordiri possim, huic libro faciam finem.

[2] *Victorius, for* utilia.   [3] *Sciop., for* solita.

book, in which words are taken from the poets in the same way as those which I have mentioned in the other two books were taken from prose writings. Therefore,[a] since I have made three parts of the whole work *On the Latin Language*, first how names were set upon things, second how the words are declined in cases, third how they are combined into sentences—as the first part is now finished, I shall make an end to this book, that I may be able to commence the second part.

§ 110. [a] This resumes the sentence interrupted at the middle of § 109.